In the
Company
of Books

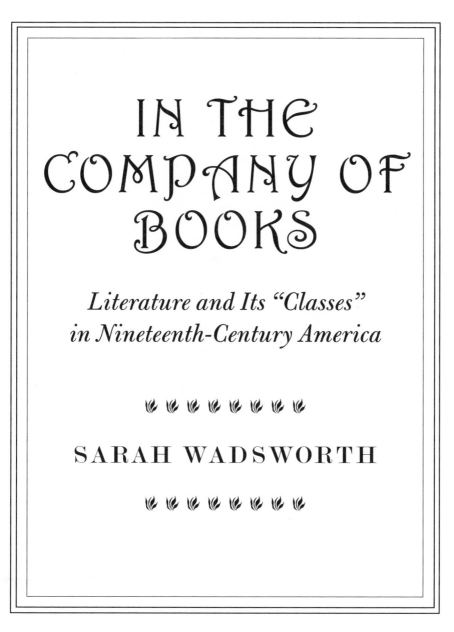

# IN THE COMPANY OF BOOKS

*Literature and Its "Classes"
in Nineteenth-Century America*

❦ ❦ ❦ ❦ ❦ ❦ ❦ ❦

## SARAH WADSWORTH

❦ ❦ ❦ ❦ ❦ ❦ ❦ ❦

University of Massachusetts Press
AMHERST & BOSTON

LC 2006003174
ISBN 1-55849-540-1 (library cloth ed.); 1-55849-541-X (paper)

Designed by Dean Bornstein
Set in Bulmer by BookComp, Inc.
Printed and bound by The Maple-Vail Book Manufacturing Group, Inc.

Library of Congress Cataloging-in-Publication Data

Wadsworth, Sarah, 1963–
    In the company of books : literature and its "classes" in nineteenth-century
America / Sarah Wadsworth.
        p. cm. — (Studies in print culture and the history of the book)
        Includes bibliographical references and index.
        ISBN 1-55849-540-1 (library cloth : alk. paper)—ISBN 1-55849-541-x (pbk. :
alk. paper)
    1. Publishers and publishing—United States—History—19th century.   2. Booksellers
and bookselling—United States—History—19th century.   3. Books and reading—
United States—History—19th century.   4. Children's literature—Publishing—United
States—History—19th century.   5. Children—Books and reading—United States—
History—19th century.   6. Authors and readers—United States—History—19th
century.   7. American literature—19th century—History and criticism.   8. Popular
culture--United States—History—19th century.   9. Market segmentation—United
States—History.
    I. Title. II. Series.
    Z473.W33   2006
    070.5097309034—dc22

                                                                        2006003174


British Library Cataloguing in Publication data are available

To Marc
Sabrina and Blaise

# Contents

# Illustrations

# Acknowledgments

This book benefited from the support and contributions of many colleagues, organizations, and institutions, and my gratitude to each of them far exceeds the confines of these acknowledgments. Donald Ross deserves special thanks for his invaluable guidance and criticism during my research. I am also deeply indebted to Edward M. Griffin, who responded to early versions of each chapter with utmost care and discernment, and to Michael Hancher, who helped me understand American book history within the larger context of Anglo-American print culture. I am also grateful to the following scholars for their careful readings and insightful comments on the manuscript at various stages: Rob Brault, Michael Cohen, Hazel Dicken-Garcia, Christine Krueger, Elisabeth Malm, Toni A. McNaron, Karen Hartmann Roggenkamp, Angela Sorby, Danielle Tisinger, Emily B. Todd, Karen Woods Weierman, and the anonymous reviewers for University of Massachusetts Press. In addition, Ken Carpenter, Frederick Newberry, Louisa Smith, Susan M. Griffin, and anonymous readers for the *Henry James Review* and *The Lion and the Unicorn* provided crucial feedback on portions of individual chapters. I would also like to thank Paul M. Wright for his dedication and continuing contribution to book history scholarship through his role as editor for the University of Massachusetts Press, and Carol Betsch, managing editor, and Patricia Sterling for their elegant editorial wizardry.

Portions of the research and writing of this book were funded by scholarships and grants. I would like to express my gratitude to the following institutions and organizations for their generous support: the University of Minnesota for a Thomas H. Shevlin Fellowship, a Doctoral Dissertation Fellowship, and a Supplemental Research Fellowship; the P.E.O. Sisterhood for a P.E.O. Scholar Award; the Houghton Library for a Houghton Mifflin Fellowship in Publishing History; and the American Association of University Women for a short-term American Fellowship. In addition, I am grateful to Marquette University for providing me with research assistants and the opportunity to pursue my research while teaching. I particularly thank my research assistants, Christina K. Phelps at Carleton College, and Erin Kogler, Heather Pavletic, Moon-ju Shin, and Matthew Van Zee at Marquette, for their painstaking assistance with manuscript preparation and permissions letters. I also warmly thank my colleagues Tim W. Machan at Marquette University, Susan Jaret-McKinstry at Carleton College, and John Watkins at the University of Minnesota for their sage advice on scholarly matters.

For their numerous small services that have accumulated to form larger ones, I would also like to thank Karen Nelson Hoyle and John Barneson of the Children's Literature Research Collections at the University of Minnesota; Becky Hoffman, of the Interlibrary Loan office at the University of Minnesota; Elizabeth Chenault, of the Rare Book Room at the University of North Carolina at Chapel Hill; Doris O'Keefe, of the American Antiquarian Society; Cornelia King, of the Free Library of Philadelphia; Mark A. Williams, of Rare Books and Special Collections at the Northern Illinois University Libraries; William M. Fowler Jr. and Peter Drummey of the Massachusetts Historical Society; James M. Smith of the Rare Books and Manuscripts Library at Ohio State University; and Stuart Walker of Boston Public Library. For permission to quote and to use illustrations, I am indebted to the Houghton Library, Harvard University; the Massachusetts Historical Society; the Rare Books and Manuscripts Library at Ohio State University; the Rare Books and Special Collections at the Northern Illinois University Libraries; the Rare Book Collection at the University of North Carolina at Chapel Hill; and the Children's Literature Research Collections at the University of Minnesota. The following materials are cited by permission of the Houghton Library, Harvard University: Thomas Niles letters, bMS Am 1130.81 (1–44); Henry James Jr. letters, bMS Am 1094 (1781), (1784), (1790), (1802), (1817); William P. Ticknor letters, James T. Fields letters, and cost book 1867–70, bMS Am 1083 (570), (572); and manuscript material by Frederick Law Olmsted, bMS 1083.1 (59) and bMS Am 1083.2 (70).

Earlier, abbreviated versions of several chapters appeared as articles in the following peer-reviewed publications: Chapter 1 as "Nathaniel Hawthorne, Samuel Goodrich, and the Transformation of the Juvenile Literature Market," *Nathaniel Hawthorne Review* 26.1 (Spring 2000): 1–24; Chapter 2 as "Louisa May Alcott, William T. Adams, and the Rise of Gender-Specific Series Books," *The Lion and the Unicorn: A Critical Journal of Children's Literature* 25.1 (January 2001): 17–46, published by the Johns Hopkins University Press; Chapter 5 as "Innocence Abroad: Henry James and the Re-Invention of the American Woman Abroad," *The Henry James Review* 22.2 (Spring 2001): 107–27, published by the

Johns Hopkins University Press; and Chapter 6 as "A Blue and Gold Mystique: Reading the Material Text in Louisa May Alcott's 'Pansies' and Ticknor & Fields's *Blue and Gold Series*," *Harvard Library Bulletin* 11.2 (Summer 2000): 55–80. Many thanks go to the publishers and editors of these journals for permission to reprint this material.

Finally, I reserve my profoundest gratitude for Marc R. Black, Sabrina B. Black, Blaise X. Black, Beverley A. Wadsworth, Robert and Roberta Black, and Tamra L. Maroushek for lightening, in countless ways, the many hours I have spent in the company of books.

In the
Company
of Books

# PROLOGUE

## Following the Reader

> The great public, in the first place, is made up of a vast number of little publics, very much as our Union is made up of States.
>
> —Henry James, "Mary Elizabeth Braddon" (1865)

IN THE FALL of 1865, Henry James Jr. finished reading the latest transatlantic sensation, Mary Elizabeth Braddon's *Aurora Floyd*, and sat down in the third-floor bedroom of his family's Beacon Hill home to sum up its dubious merits for the readers of the *Nation*. Although he was still years away from his first novel, James was already a shrewd analyst of literary trends. He studied the literary marketplace the way other men of his age and class studied the law, theology, medicine, trade: "Every book that he reviewed was a testing ground for his thought" (Novick 129). At twenty-three, James was already a professional *littérateur*, contributing pieces to nearly every issue of the weekly *Nation* and quarterly *North American Review*. ("The verb to contribute," James later reminisced, "took on at once to my ears a weird beauty of its own, and I applied it during that early time with my best frequency and zeal" [*Literary Criticism* 1: 179]). For the young James, the question of audience was one of professional survival, and he tackled the puzzle of Braddon's success with a determination borne of raw self-interest. The answer, deceptively simple, was also, as he must have understood, stubbornly recursive. In recognizing among the "great public" a "vast number of little publics," James was able to "class" Braddon's audience rather precisely, at least in theory: "It is that public which reads nothing but novels, and yet which reads neither George Eliot, George Sand, Thackeray, nor Hawthorne" (*Literary Criticism* 1: 744). In practical terms, however, his formulation left him no closer to claiming his own "little public," let alone the "great public" he yearned to captivate.

Like the novelist-in-training, the *Nation* in 1865 was in its nonage, and its staff also struggled with the sense that its words and ideas were pitched to an elusive audience existing quite apart from the cultural mainstream. In a letter to Charles Eliot Norton, *Nation* cofounder Frederick Law Olmsted wrote that he "regard[ed] The Nation as an experiment upon the ability of the public to recognize, appreciate and sustain a public journal which shall be free from certain qualities now common in the newspapers of the country and which it is evident are generally assumed by their proprietors to be necessary to their pecuniary success."[1] For Olmsted and other *Nation* supporters, the future of this upstart publication was of enormous consequence. Its success would call into question the low assessment of the reading public's taste, which was supposedly both indulged and stimulated by the popular press. Its failure would only confirm that the newspapers had been right all along about the American populace; in this sense, the failure of the *Nation* would be a failure of the *nation*, indeed.

The problem that Henry James faced as a high-toned writer with mass-market aspirations and that the *Nation* confronted as an organ of the intelligentsia in a market dominated by family papers and the penny press reflects a perpetual concern of authors, editors, and publishers—namely, how to get the right publications into the right hands. In 1865, however—and indeed, throughout the nineteenth century—the problem of matching readers and texts reverberated far beyond the confines of the publishing industry, radiating outward to affect all classes of readers as the nineteenth century defined them. As this book illustrates, specialized or audience-specific marketing strategies, reading practices, and authorial and editorial approaches profoundly affected American culture in the nineteenth century; the literary practices deployed to respond to the nation's myriad "little publics" had an impact that far exceeded the immediate and ostensible goal of selling books.

Although the notion that the general reading public comprises many disparate audiences did not originate with the *Nation*'s review of *Aurora Floyd*, James's formulation is noteworthy for its subtle linking of literary consumption, particularized readerships, and national identity. Perhaps James was inspired by the Union army's ultimate victory a few months earlier; or perhaps he was prompted by the title of the new journal, the *Nation*, which came into being just as the defeated Confederacy was being absorbed back into the United States. In either event, James's metaphoric comparison of the American reading public to the thirty-six states of the reunited Union aptly evokes the spirit of a national unity and political cohesion capable of transcending geographical boundaries and bridging cultural divides. Two years later, in the prospectus for its third year of publication, the *Nation* explicitly connected private reading practices and public life (both artistic and political); it confidently touted the magazine as "an aid to sound thinking and right living" and pressed readers "to subscribe to *The Nation*; not only for your own sake, but in the interest of American literature and the public welfare."[2]

As suggested by such rhetorical yoking of reading and public life, literature occupied a highly privileged position in nineteenth-century America, and a great deal of power accrued to its capacity to mold readers—both individually and in the aggregate—and to shape society locally, regionally, and nationally. Certainly, earlier generations of authors, critics, and readers had linked literacy and literature with the public welfare. Many, associating cultivation with inward virtue (Rubin 2), had worried about the impact of certain types of reading matter on specific groups of readers, as evidenced by the recurring debates over women's reading, novel reading, and reliance on foreign literature. From the 1830s onward, however, the substance and scope of these debates shifted in response to a complex array of factors, including the ascendancy of literature over other "civilizing" forces (especially religious institutions), voluminous expansion of the literary marketplace, and nationwide cultural and political tensions. Ralph Waldo Emerson, Herman Melville, Catharine Maria Sedgwick, and Harriet Beecher Stowe are just a few of the prominent literary figures who addressed the relationship between reading, writing, and national identity. Meanwhile, the newspapers and journals of the day gave voice to many less celebrated writers who shared the view that the nation's literature had the capacity to consolidate national identity, unite a diverse and scattered citizenry, and influence national politics (see, for example, Perry Miller, *The Raven and the Whale*).

Following the Civil War, Walt Whitman carried forward into the Gilded Age the conversation about literature as political adhesive and democratizing force. The visionary poet who had preached national unity from the pages of the first edition of *Leaves of Grass* (1855) voiced a new theory of literature and politics in *Democratic Vistas* (1871), initially published as a pair of essays in the *Galaxy*.[3] With some urgency, Whitman pleaded for the creation of "a new and greater literatus order," which he regarded as "the condition, not only of our future national and democratic development, but of our perpetuation." Like many earlier critics, he stressed the folly of "mould[ing] ourselves or our literature" on foreign models and insisted on the importance of developing a new literature "in terms consistent with the institution of these States." Expanding upon this familiar creed, Whitman enjoined readers to participate actively in the creation of the books they read—to "construct" these texts for themselves. Cautioning that modern civilization, with its "highly artificial and materialistic bases," is in danger of following "the road to a destiny, a status, equivalent, in its real world, to that of the fabled damned" (442–43), he contended that

> a new theory of literary composition for imaginative works of the very first class, and especially for highest poems, is the sole course open to these States. Books are to be call'd for, and supplied, on the assumption that the process of reading is not a half-sleep, but, in highest sense, an exercise, a gymnast's struggle; that the reader is to do something for himself, must be on the alert, must himself or herself construct indeed the poem, argument, history, metaphysical essay—the text furnishing the hints, the clue, the start or frame-work. Not the book needs so much to be the complete thing, but the reader of the book does. That were to make a nation of supple and athletic minds, well-train'd, intuitive, used to depend on themselves, and not on a few coteries of writers. (443–44)

Whitman's vision of empowered readers actively constructing the literary text reflects a new way of thinking about the relationship between books and readers. Working from the "hints" and "frame-work" supplied by the text, readers are to fill in the gaps and "complete" the text so that the *reader* becomes "the complete thing," the intellectually liberated, self-reliant citizen upon whom true democracy depends. The new American literature, in Whitman's formulation, functions as a necessary catalyst, sparking a reaction in which the literate individual is the agent, active reading the reagent, and an enlightened, spiritualized form of national cohesion the resulting compound.

Recently, literary and cultural historians have paid increasing attention to the connections between literary practices and various kinds of group identity (individual, communal, and national)—connections that many nineteenth-century readers took for granted. Benedict Anderson laid the groundwork for subsequent scholars to explore the role of print culture in solidifying national identity. The influence of print in colonial America has been the subject of fruitful studies focusing on national identity (Warner), social cohesion at the local and regional levels (Brown), and literary cultures informed by gender and class (Davidson). Gender critics have illuminated the impact of literacy on women's sense of identity and community from the early republic (Cott) through the antebellum period (Baym, Tompkins, Robbins) and beyond (Hunter, Radway, Inness). Other

scholars have investigated ways in which specific genres or venues identified, addressed, and divided particular audiences—periodicals (Klancher,
Lehuu), theater (Butsch), juvenile magazines (Kelly), children's books
(Clark, Segel, Vallone), dime novels (Denning), and the "popular" and the
"literary" (Brodhead, Levine). This book responds to and extends the discussion by examining the impact of segmentation and diversification in the
nineteenth-century literary marketplace on the construction of American
readerships.

The relationship among readers, books, individual autonomy, and collective identity that nineteenth-century authors proclaimed (and recent
scholars have explored) was no less pertinent to the "vast number of little
publics" than to the "great public" of the American nation. The expansion of the market for literature in nineteenth-century America brought
about a proliferation of publications that targeted specialized readerships
along with an increase, both in number and in size, of these diverse literary subcultures. In fact, by the time James articulated his conception of the
subdivided reading public, the American publishing industry was quite
attuned to the existence of many "little publics" and becoming increasingly
adept at assessing and responding to the demands of these discrete submarkets. Indeed, one of the most conspicuous developments in the nineteenth-century publishing industry was its ability to target specific classes
of readers with individual titles, series, or clusters of books tailored, packaged, and advertised to appeal to their particular interests. In the infancy
of the American book trade, when markets were still highly localized,
such specialization had been both impracticable and largely unnecessary
(see Boynton 139). Geographically scattered, colonial printers and booksellers typically catered to the wide-ranging needs of the relatively small
number of readers they served. By the end of the eighteenth century, however, some publishers in New England were selling their books nationally
(Amory 315). Over the next few decades the publishing business became
increasingly centralized in Boston, New York, and Philadelphia, even as
the markets it served became increasingly diffuse (Charvat, *Literary Publishing*). Faced with a large, national market and many competitors vying
for their business, publishers and retailers sought refuge from competition
in specialized branches of the trade. As Henry Walcott Boynton observed,
the "cut-throat conditions of the early nineteenth-century . . . forced many
publishers to specialize in fields where competition was not so general and
returns were more stable" (144). Some specialized in religious publishing

5

(E. P. Dutton), others in medical books (Blanchard & Lea), law (Little, Brown), scientific and technical books (John Wiley), or school texts. At the same time, many of the larger firms took advantage of the relative security of specialized readerships by extending their lists to encompass the more lucrative specialties. In large firms and small presses alike, the pattern was to establish an identity that clearly linked a coherent line of books to a recognizable body of readers and to market the books accordingly. Writing in 1900, Henry Holt advised, "Not a little experience . . . convinces us that the more books of the same general character and appealing to the same general class there are on one list, the better for each of them. . . . The closer any publisher associates with a given market, the better he is able to serve his clients" (qtd. in Sheehan 103).

Through the eighteenth century, fiction and poetry—overshadowed by devotional books, almanacs, schoolbooks, and other nonfiction genres such as legal, medical, and travel books—still constituted a small proportion of the overall book trade. The average press run for fiction in 1830 has been estimated at around one thousand copies. By the middle of the nineteenth century, however, sales of the top-selling novels could exceed one hundred thousand volumes (Baker 87). Fiction began to occupy a substantial place on the lists of general publishing houses, and belles lettres became an economically viable specialty.[4] By the 1870s, fiction appeared to dominate the market. Writing in 1878, in the midst of a financial panic that crippled the industry, one reviewer estimated:

> Fiction constitutes three-fourths of the people's reading. . . . The American novel is the only really popular book in this republic. Whether it be in yellow covers and sold for a half dime; whether it assume a long-drawn serial form, and appear weekly in a hebdomadal consecrated to sensational romance and wood-cuts; whether it appear in a more pretentious style, and reach the circulating libraries in gaudy binding, with several pages of flattering "press notices," the novel is the only universal book among the American readers. Hundreds of thousands never read anything else.

The reviewer proceeded to expand upon the economic advantage of publishing novels, even in a financially precarious market:

> The publishing business has felt severely the general depression of the period; novels have been considered the only safe goods to put on the market. . . . Novels are the only books on which printers have not lost. Their sale has scarcely been affected by the protracted panic. In all the trade-sales

6

and book-auctions of the last few years the counters were freighted with contributions to science, to art, to humanity; there were few or no novels among them. . . . American publishers of metropolitan experience have learned the public taste in romance so well that they make now few blunders in accepting manuscripts. Novels, if at all tolerable, are accepted, and with these the literary market is well stocked. ("The American Novel—with Samples" 325–26)

Like most other contemporary accounts of the American book trade, these statements must be appraised as impressionistic commentaries by interested, informed observers rather than objective, quantitatively precise analyses of the industry. Nevertheless, when numerous observers concur in their impressions, these firsthand accounts gain substance and cohere as legitimate and persuasive evidence. That publishers came to see belles lettres as an increasingly significant and diversified sector of the marketplace is further reflected in the Classified Index to the *Publisher's Trade List Annual* for 1876. In place of the previous year's Index to Specialties— an alphabetical listing that included cards, charts, games, albums, and other ancillary items—the *PTLA* for 1876 carried an index to the major categories of books published by American firms, including "Foreign Books and Books in Foreign Languages," "History, Biography, Travel, Etc.," "Illustrated Books," "Juveniles and Sunday-School Books" (further subdivided to distinguish publishers of "Sunday-School books" from those of "toy books"), "Novels" (breaking out those publishers specializing in Bulwer, Cooper, Dickens, George Eliot, Scott's Waverley novels, and Thackeray), and "Standard Authors" (with a separate listing for Shakespeare)—most of which could be considered (wholly or in part) "belles lettres." As the nineteenth century progressed, enterprising book publishers began to look for even more effective ways to segment the now reliable literary market into distinct and manageable submarkets.

Significantly, James, commenting on the state of the literary marketplace in the 1890s, not only observes the fracturing, or "breaking into pieces," of the market for fiction but also predicts that a heightened specialization in the types of novels produced will have a positive impact on the state of the art. Echoing and then expanding upon the geopolitical metaphor of his 1865 commentary, he points out that "the public we somewhat loosely talk of as for literature or for anything else is really as subdivided as a chessboard. . . . The comparison too much sharpens and equalizes; but there are certainly, as on a map of countries, divisions and boundaries; and if these

7

varieties become, to assist individual genius or save individual life, accentuated in American letters, we shall immediately to that tune be rewarded for our faith" (*Literary Criticism* 2: 653–54). James concedes that "the American world of to-day is a world of combinations and proportions different from those amid which Emerson and Mrs. Stowe could reach right and left far enough to fill it." He then suggests that the "novelist interested in the general outlook of his trade" may find the most attractive opportunities in the still-untapped possibilities of "the imagination in particular—the vision of the distinguishable poetry of things, whether expressed in such verse or (rarer phenomenon) in such prose as really does arrive at expression." Pointing to the examples of Owen Wister's tales of cowboy life and the fictional possibilities afforded by the American businessman (largely neglected by novelists), James envisions a more deliberately and subtly differentiated field for American fiction: "I cannot but think that the American novel has in a special, far-reaching direction to sail much closer to the wind" (*Literary Criticism* 2: 654–55). Comparing British and American fiction, William Dean Howells echoes James's directive in a 1901 article for the *North American Review*: "To put it paradoxically, our life is too large for our art to be broad. In despair at the immense variety of material offered it by American civilization, American fiction must specialize, and turning down superabundance of character it must burrow far down in a soul or two" ("A Possible Difference" 135).

My purpose here is not simply to argue that publishers successfully segmented the literary marketplace in nineteenth-century America (much less to date the origins of this intricate and complex development, which unquestionably reach back to the colonies). Rather, I call attention to a fact of the nineteenth-century literary marketplace, widely assumed yet seldom examined, in order to analyze its implications for readers, writers, and literature itself.[5] In this endeavor, I contend that the deeper significance of this process of market segmentation and of the solidification of belles lettres as a bona fide area of specialization is that the editorial and marketing tactics employed, in concert with the narrative strategies of authors and the reading practices of the general public, inescapably transformed the landscape of the cultural field. I hope to demonstrate how the segmentation of the literary marketplace fundamentally altered the relationships among authors, texts, readers, and publishers by fashioning communities of readers ("imagined communities," in Anderson's terms), fostering new

8

areas of literary production, and ushering in new configurations of audience and genre.

The chapters that follow track various segments of the literary marketplace that emerged or solidified in nineteenth-century America, each market segment mapping (for the purposes of illustration) to a corresponding genre or subgenre. Individually, these case studies analyze the process whereby authors and publishers carved up the field of literary production into a multitude of distinct niches or submarkets, differentiated their products, and targeted specific groups of potential readers in order to guide their book-buying decisions. It was a process that grew out of changing perceptions of specific demographic subsets of the population, which, for marketing purposes, were grouped and identified as discrete classes of readers. Taken together, the case studies demonstrate how market segmentation effectively led to new roles for the book in American culture, the innovation of literary genres, and new relationships between books and readers.[6]

This book is concerned less with individual historical readers than with large groups of readers joined through shared literacy practices—that is, readerships. It builds on and complements studies of the reading practices of real readers, such as those focusing on library records (Augst, Pawley, Todd, Zboray), private diaries (Hunter, Sicherman, Zboray and Zboray), book clubs (Gere, McHenry), inscriptions and marginalia (Davidson), and interviews with readers (Radway); but its emphasis is on larger groups than such analyses can reasonably encompass and on entire readerships as projections or "constructions." In his essay "The Writer's Audience Is Always a Fiction," Walter J. Ong points out that, as a noun, "'readership' . . . is an abstraction in a way that 'audience' is not." Since a writer cannot possibly envision each of the readers constituting his actual or potential audience, "he has to make his readers up, fictionalize them." Having "[cast] them in a made-up role," the writer then "[calls] on them to play the role assigned"—to "fictionalize" themselves and "to conform themselves to the projections of the writers they read, or at least . . . to operate in terms of these projections." Of course, as Ong acknowledges, a highly original writer "can do more than project the earlier audience, he can alter it," and when that happens, readers must "adjust" to the innovation. Recognizing the discrepancy between actual readerships (virtually impossible to recover and reconstruct) and imagined readerships, Ong concludes that a "history of the ways audiences have been called on to fictionalize themselves would be a correlative to the history of literary genres and literary works, indeed of culture itself" (409–11, 421).

This book contributes to such an enterprise by exploring the ways in which nineteenth-century authors and publishers imagined the readerships of particular texts, or clusters of texts. It is simultaneously an exploration of an increasingly segmented print culture through the lens of nineteenth-century American literature and an analysis of nineteenth-century American literature from the perspective of this subdivided cultural field. My sources chiefly comprise literary professionals—authors, editors, publishers, critics—and the kinds of *un*common readers who recorded their observations on reading, writing, and the marketing of books in letters, journals, memoirs, and trade publications. These literary insiders (or elites) conceived of the literary marketplace as structured in a particular way. They constructed the reading public as an array of discrete readerships, or classes of readers (a designation keyed to reading interests and often implicitly influenced by demographic factors). Individual readers were, of course, free to accept or reject such efforts to define, segment, and target these discrete submarkets, but enough readers evidently went along with the program to account for the cohesion of various classes and the mapping-out of new divisions and boundaries in the literary field. At the same time, however, the resistance of individual authors and readers, along with the impossibility of neatly parceling out the literary marketplace in chessboard fashion, created space for some of the more interesting and innovative developments in nineteenth-century American literature.

I contend that when publishers and authors segmented particular groups of readers into distinct categories and targeted them with specific types of books, they effectively created or fashioned each readership by summoning its members together into a composite or communal existence, thereby granting them a collective identity and group presence (with a certain amount of power accruing to it) both in the literary marketplace and, ultimately, in American culture and society, broadly defined. In other words, diverse types of readers were there all along, but when literary institutions formally recognized them ("imagined" them) as distinct entities, isolated them from other groups, and began to treat them in the aggregate for marketing purposes, they conferred upon these specific clusters of readers collective identities that exerted their own force in the literary marketplace and beyond. The discrete categories of books that I treat here—each one linked in some concrete way to a particular segment of the literary marketplace—were not so much products of those market segments as the reverse: the market segments were products, or functions, of the books that collectively addressed them. In a very real sense, then, books actually *made* culture[7]—not in the purely intellectual sense of propagating or disseminating "Culture" but in the sociological sense of describing, assembling, and giving shape to various constituents of the broad cross-section of society that constituted the market for books. Simply put, the book was not merely a conveyance or reflection of culture, or even a product of culture; rather, culture (literary culture) was a product, a construction, of the book.

Three fundamental critical assumptions have informed my approach and methodologies. First, it is at best unproductive and at worst counterproductive to condemn, deride, or disdain the material and economic conditions that gave rise to a text without investigating the causes and consequences—positive as well as negative—of those conditions. As Charles Johanningsmeier cautions, "Too often an amorphous agent called capitalist 'power' or 'the "inevitable" forces of urbanization, commercialization, and industrialization' are invoked as responsible for historical change or cultural production" (9). A similar haziness often attends discussions of the "commodification of literature," a problematic phrase that has become something of a cliché in contemporary criticism and theory. Used as a synonym for "commercialization of literature," it is imprecise and ambiguous; used to imply that intellectual properties have been reduced to fungible assets, it is both inaccurate and misleading. As an economic term, "commodity" evokes products that are perfectly substitutable, such as one bushel of a particular grade of corn or wheat for another. Literature, however, like other symbolic goods, is necessarily valued for its uniqueness. Notwithstanding hyperbolic complaints that publishers, as "dealers[s] in certain commodities," valued books as "so much pork, cotton and corn" (qtd. in Harper 153), literary texts can never be reduced to their physical constituents: one Hawthorne story is not interchangeable with one Melville story, even if printed and bound with identical materials. No substitute *can* exist for any individual literary text, imbued with and indeed defined by the unique essence of its authorial identity.

Second, along with others engaged in the history of the book, I consider the study of literary texts to be meaningfully enriched when the disembodied text that has descended to us over the course of many decades is reattached to as many of its original contexts as possible. Striving to unite textual analysis with historical and cultural inquiry, I have rallied evidence

11

from diverse literary and historical sources, enlisting authors' correspondence and biographical as well as bibliographical materials, trade publications, editorial correspondence, publishers' records, and the physical book itself to aid in the explication and contextualization of the literary texts that form the backbone of this study. I situate exceptional texts that traditionally have been regarded as canonical within the context of the popular, the mainstream, and the ephemeral, and I investigate relationships between the material book and the literary text. By reinserting the texts of canonical authors into the contexts of the books that conveyed them to nineteenth-century readers, the publishing economy that was responsible for disseminating them, the competing productions that informed their development as texts and influenced their consumption as books, and the readers who purchased and read them, I engage and interrogate the full cultural work of "the book" in nineteenth-century America, in its various tangible and intangible manifestations.[8]

Third, although I am interested in reading, writing, and publishing specifically in the United States, I recognize that all these activities occurred as well within a broader, transatlantic context. Along with Michael Winship and other scholars researching American literature and culture in the context of international economics, politics, and cultural exchange, I am cognizant of the facts that readers in nineteenth-century America read foreign texts and purchased foreign books along with American ones, that American authors were often mindful of a potential British audience (and vice versa), and that publishers on both sides of the Atlantic engaged in importing, exporting, and reprinting on a large scale. As Winship advises, literary historians who fail to recognize "the great extent to which books and texts have been shared across borders and oceans . . . run the risk of conceiving of print culture too narrowly, without recognizing its full transatlantic dimensions" ("Transatlantic Book Trade" 99). These dimensions reveal connections between European and American cultures, but they also bring to light disparities and even occasionally the reaction of one culture against the other. In the case of children's literature, for example, most specialists view British and American texts as belonging to a single "relatively homogeneous body of work" (Thacker and Webb 8); nevertheless, "the desire of American publishers to struggle against their dependence on British literary production influenced the growth of an exclusively child-oriented publishing industry" in the United States (Thacker and Webb 15). Although I focus on the American experience, therefore, the authors, readers, and publishers I discuss continually remind us of the large degree to which that experience is embedded in—and frequently strains against—a transatlantic literary culture.

The case studies that follow are arranged in approximate chronological order. The chapters overlap to some degree, however, or focus on multiple points in the chronology of American literary history. Part One addresses segmentation by age and gender by exploring the shifting perceptions and experience of childhood in conjunction with the ways in which literary professionals assessed and responded to the needs and desires of young people. Chapter 1, which addresses Hawthorne's writing for children, examines several conflicting and concurrent "reforms" of children's literature that emerged in the first half of the nineteenth century as various parties who had invested in the juvenile literature market attempted to redefine literature for children and, through books, to influence young readers. Chapter 2 traces the nearly parallel development of fiction for boys and fiction for girls in the latter half of the nineteenth century, taking note of the ways that Alcott's Little Women series simultaneously responds to and revises popular boys' series as well as earlier representations of young women in literature. Chapter 3 probes the tensions among the generic conventions of the "boy-book," the presumed expectations and requirements of juvenile readers, and Mark Twain's own ambivalence about that audience in *The Adventures of Tom Sawyer*, *Adventures of Huckleberry Finn*, and the numerous sequels that he projected, drafted, and, in two cases, published. Each of these chapters investigates the use of author series (sets of books united by authorial identity and, often, shared sets of characters) as a means of consolidating and exploiting a writer's literary reputation in order to attract and retain readers. All three chapters show authors striving to offer new forms of literary expression to young people—imaginative fantasy stories, realistic stories for girls, humorous and irreverent stories for boys—as well as new ways of imagining childhood and adolescence.

In Part Two, I examine intersections of gender and social class in the segmented marketplace of the Gilded Age. Focusing on the final decades of the nineteenth century, Chapter 4 illustrates how traditional book buyers and the established trade persistently identified cheap books with readers of low economic and cultural caste and initiated a round of "culture wars" that ultimately changed the nature of American literary culture by opening up the literature to a broader audience and a wider range of new styles and genres. One of these new genres becomes the centerpiece of Chapter

5, which shows a young James oscillating between two sets of poles: the popular versus the elite; the feminine versus the masculine. The chapter reveals a Protean young writer who loosely modeled his work on women's novels that he regarded as frivolous, even while emulating the European Realists whose work he held in highest regard. Chapter 6 concludes the section on class and symbolic power by analyzing the relationship between the female reader and the physical book through a close reading of Louisa May Alcott's short story "Pansies," a tale which proposes that the young lady who wished to be well turned out mentally, as well as sartorially, should attend carefully to her selection of both physical book and literary text.[9] Together, these chapters illustrate the role of publishers' series (books by multiple authors united by publisher's imprint, packaging, and, often, genre or subject matter) in bridging the gap between well-defined clusters of books and the aggregates of readers who composed their target audiences. The book concludes with an epilogue that examines the role of race and ethnicity in the segmentation of the literary marketplace, factors that were beginning to have a perceptible impact on the increasingly variegated landscape of the literary field.

*In the Company of Books* revises conventional narratives of literary history by revealing that a vital, even transformative, feature of American culture in the nineteenth century was the awareness that the literary marketplace consisted not of a single, unified, relatively homogeneous reading public ("the great public") but rather of many disparate, overlapping reading communities differentiated by interests, class, and level of education as well as by gender and stage of life.[10] Bringing together textual analysis, the history and sociology of reading and of texts, and analysis of the popular and material culture of the book allows us to grasp more fully the meaning not only of the text in nineteenth-century America but of its consumption and embodiment in the form of the book.

# PART ONE

# From "Girls and Boys" to Tomboys and Bad Boys

There is a distinct class of books which has grown up quite within the memory of men now living. It is involved with industrial and commercial interests; it invites the attention of authors, and the infrequent criticism of reviewers; it has its own subdivisions like the larger literature; it boasts of cyclopëdias and commentaries; it includes histories, travels, poems, works in science, theological treatises. It is a distinct principality of the Kingdom of Letters.

—Horace Scudder, *Childhood in Literature and Art* (1894)

Like James's comparison of the many "little publics" that make up the "great public" to the states of the American Union, Horace Scudder's metaphor of children's literature as "a distinct principality of the Kingdom of Letters" (178) reflects a keen awareness of the opposing forces of fragmentation and cohesion, of differentiation and incorporation within a larger body, which attended the segmentation of the literary marketplace in nineteenth-century America. As the trope suggests, children's literature is a subset or province of "the larger literature," reflecting and responding to the same cultural and economic forces at work in society as a whole. But it is also something of a sovereign territory—an "enclave," as one recent critic has termed it (MacLeod, *American Childhood* 125)—a body of texts walled off from the general literature and guided by a set of codes and standards that operate more subtly and with freer play outside that carefully guarded realm. Traditionally, children's literature has been both shielded from and systematically purged of disruptive elements that society considers inappropriate or unwholesome for youth in much the way that society, in its attempt to protect children, strives to shelter them from other harmful influences. As a result, the mass of children's literature is at once more conservative than literature for adults in its treatment of controversial issues[1] and yet highly responsive to those currents of thinking and behavior that the culture deems worthwhile and improving.[2]

The proliferation of new books for young people that accelerated in the mid-nineteenth century, together with the efflorescence of both literary writing and fine illustration in books for children, helps account for Scudder's perception that this "distinct class of books" had only recently "grown up." As editor of the *Riverside Magazine for Young People* and later the *Atlantic Monthly* (1890–98), Scudder was well positioned to observe such trends, and, to his credit, recent scholarship tends to corroborate his assertion. Dubbed by twentieth-century critics the "Golden Age of Children's Literature," the Victorian period witnessed tremendous growth in the production of children's books and periodicals in both Britain and the United States, improvement in the quality of these texts, the introduction of the term "Juveniles" as a label for this category of books,[3] and new efforts to appeal directly to the reading preferences of children rather than to the tastes and mores of their elders.

The movement toward a formal separation of adult and juvenile readerships can be linked to the expansion of the middle class, increasing literacy among young people, improved and extended schooling, the shift from mixed-age classrooms to grade levels structured by age, increasing time for leisure activities, rising levels of spending money among children as well as adults, and, not least, the popularization of a Romantic sensibility that fundamentally reconceived of the nature and status of childhood and the significance of childhood as a uniquely privileged stage of life. In Scudder's perspective, this altered perception of childhood was characterized by a new appreciation of the child as an individual in his or her own right: that is, "by a recognition of personality in childhood as distinct from relationship." He explains, "The child as one of the family had always been recognized, and the child also in its more elemental nature; it was the child as possessed of consciousness, as isolated, as disclosing a nature capable of independent action, thought, and feeling, that now came forward into the world's view, and was added to the stock of the world's literature, philosophy, and art" (234–35).[4] And even as the idea of the child altered (and, by extension, the child in literature), so too did the popular construction of the "child-as-audience" (Thacker and Webb 10). As Glenda Riley explains, the "prevailing view of children became less one of a miniature adult to be rescued from original sin and more one of a pliable and innocent being whose upbringing demanded specialized equipment, toys, and books" (48). Young readers thus became the recipients of a new literature, conceived specifically for and about them and featuring a new breed of child protagonists. Further, as Americans came to observe (or observe differently) a distinct stage of life between childhood and adulthood, new branches of juvenile literature sprang up to accommodate the newly valued audience of adolescent readers. The social construction of childhood (and, John Demos has shown, of the life course more broadly) changed dramatically over the course of the nineteenth century, and the literature associated with it was reinvented accordingly.

Of course, the roots of writing for children extend back to folktales and fairy tales, nursery rhymes, jingles, and other oral compositions (many of them not devised specifically for children), but once the publishing industry took note of the potential market for specialized publications, it played a vital role in the development of juvenile literature. And, as Scudder's remark suggests, nineteenth-century observers were fully aware of the relationships among collective identity, formal recognition, and power: "There have been, it is true, nursery tales in all ages: ditties, and songs, and lullabies; unwritten stories, which mothers in England told when they themselves could have read nothing; but there came a time when children were distinctly recognized as the occasion of formal literature, when authors and publishers began to heed a new public" (172).[5] This moment ushered in the dedicated publishing of children's books, which (in the English-speaking world) famously began in 1744 with John Newbery, of St. Paul's Churchyard, London. In Revolutionary America, enterprising publishers such as Hugh Gaine and Isaiah Thomas seized with alacrity on this new branch of publishing and followed Newbery's example (often to the point of unauthorized reprinting) in publishing books written for children as well as versions for children of adult books.[6] The trend developed further throughout the nineteenth century with the result that the reading practices of children and adults continued to diverge substantially.

Anne Scott MacLeod's observation that "the production of juvenile literature by American authors, which was only a trickle in the 1820s, had become a steady stream by the 1830s and a positive torrent by the 1850s" (*A Moral Tale* 20–21) is substantiated by an 1856 editorial in the *American Publishers' Circular and Literary Gazette*: "It is no longer a question to be debated with preliminary dubitation, whether such and such a book shall be published, when it is intended only for the use of the little people at best; for the consumption of purely Juvenile publications is growing so rapidly and with such a healthy rate of increase, that the printed page brings in to the publisher a handsome return for the time, labor, and means which he has invested in its production" ("Educational Books" 317). Twenty-five years later, Brander Matthews, writer, critic, and professor of literature at Columbia University, quantified the trend with statistics. Using the figures provided annually in *Publishers' Weekly*, Matthews tabulated 278 new juvenile titles in 1882 and 458 in 1886, an increase of 65 percent. The only area that experienced higher growth was law, at 80 percent; overall growth across all categories was 35 percent (Matthews 581). At the close of the nineteenth century, in his essay "The Future of the Novel," Henry James affirmed with undisguised condescension, "Nothing is so striking in a survey of this field, and nothing to be so much borne in mind, as that the larger part of the great multitude that sustains the teller and the publisher of tales is constituted by boys and girls. . . . The literature, as it may be called for convenience, of children is an industry that occupies by itself a very considerable quarter of the scene" (*Literary Criticism* 1: 101).

James was not alone in his concern about the swelling juvenile market. In an 1898 article titled "Books That Separate Children from Their Parents," an anonymous reviewer in the *New York Times Saturday Review of Books and Art* lamented that children's books "widen the gulf between children and parents" (qtd. in Payne 26). Similarly, Scudder, who argued that the best books for children were the classics, the "noble literature" prized by adults, cautioned: "The separation of a class of books for the use of the young specifically is not now to be avoided, but in the thoughtlessness with which it has been accepted as the only literature for the young a great wrong has been inflicted. The lean cattle have devoured the fat" (241). Such reservations were not misplaced. According to MacLeod, although a shared body of books enjoyed by adults and children alike still existed at the turn of the twentieth century, by 1910 "the era of shared reading [reading the same books as well as reading together in the family circle] was coming to an end," and by 1920 "the common aesthetic of the late nineteenth century was gone" as "adults and children read different authors, different books" (*American Childhood* 124–25). Reading aloud was arguably the most common form of entertainment in Victorian homes (Hunter 62), but as individual silent reading displaced shared social reading, literary interests could become more individualized and reading matter more particularized.

Eventually, as publishers became more accustomed to thinking of children as a specialized (and surprisingly lucrative) market, the effort to create juvenile books and match them with the appropriate subsets of readers fell to the hands of specialized editorial and marketing staff rather than to authors.[7] MacLeod explains: "As specialists trained their attention on books for children, they redefined the literature in accord with the requirements of its readers as they saw them. Reading, like teaching, became more and more specifically geared to age and grade. Adult books were dropped not because they were deemed morally unsuitable for children . . . but because they were too long or too complex for this or that child reader" (*American Childhood* 124). Similarly, Leslie Howsam observes of the British market, "It was publishers, much more than authors, who during the eighteenth century created and fostered the genre of children's literature" (12). Before long, authors and publishers were no longer merely heeding their new public, as Scudder had suggested; instead, they were defining its boundaries, interpreting its abilities and preferences, and shaping its culture (see figure 1).

The mediating role of the publisher is particularly crucial to children's literature because the target audience and the buyers are not coterminous entities. Indeed, as Beverly Lyon Clark notes, the fact that "its authors and critics are almost never members of the presumed audience" creates "a gap that makes children's literature theoretically unique" (*Girls, Boys, Books, Toys* 2). The question of who the actual buyers were—adults or children— is an important one. The author of the 1865 article "Books for Our Children" declared, "Our children are generally supplied with pocket-money to an extent unknown in the good old times; and the books that circulate among them at holiday seasons, and are sometimes found in school and Sunday libraries, often have a richness and beauty that were never seen fifty years ago on the parlor tables or shelves of parents" (726). In referring to children's pocket-money as well as to gift (Christmas) books and library books, the author indicates that children and adults were both consumers in the juvenile book market. Yet the implied relationship between the books' "richness and beauty" and the increased spending power of children hints at the growing influence of children's own tastes and preferences on the production and marketing of their books.

The three chapters of Part One analyze the ways in which particular nineteenth-century children's books defined and shaped their readerships, and vice versa. One important strategy that both authors and publishers used to attract young readers and hold their attention over a sustained period of time was to group similar books in low-priced, high-profile series. Many authors (including Hawthorne, Alcott, and Mark Twain) made it a point to follow a successful juvenile book with a sequel. In the case of the most popular books, one sequel inevitably led to another. Although authors' series were nothing new, their frequency and extent after mid-century—particularly in the area of juvenile and what we would now call "young adult" books—was unprecedented. James Fenimore Cooper's five

DEC. 1, 1863.

# ELEGANT PRESENTATION BOOK.

## Flowers from my Garden. Drawn and Co-

*lored from Nature. By L. C. Munson. With* 18 *Colored Illustrations, and Poetical Letter-Press.* 1 *vol. 4to. Cloth, bevelled boards.* $10.00. *Turkey Morocco,* $15.00.

Only 250 Copies have been Published.

## NEW JUVENILES.

LITTLE THREADS. By the Author of the Susy Books. 16mo. 75 cents.

ONE HOUR A WEEK. By the Author of Jesus on Earth. 16mo. 85 cents.

PRECIOUS STONES FROM BIBLE MOUNTAINS. By F. N. ZABRISKIE. 18mo. 60 cents.

GENERAL FRANKIE. A Story for Little Folks. 16mo. 75 cents.

FREDERICK MORTIMER. 18mo. 40 cents.

THE RIGHT WAY. And how Agnes Turner walked in it. 30 cents.

LOST AND FOUND. 35 cents.

COLUMBUS AND HIS TIMES. By Mrs. BRADFORD. *New Edition.* 75 cents.

Attractive and Salable Juveniles, Fixed up in Sets.

## LIBRARIES FOR YOUNG PEOPLE.

THE PEARL LIBRARY, for Girls in their Teens. Price, $2.50.
A Little Leaven and What it Wrought.
Watson's Woods: or, Margaret's Experiment.
Margaret at Home; or, The Leaven still working.

OUR COUSIN'S LIBRARY FOR GIRLS, from Ten to Fourteen Years of Age. $1.75.
Mary Burns. Under the Pear Tree.
Meggie of the Pines. Coming to the Light.

THE GLENWOOD LIBRARY, for Girls from 14 to 16 Years of Age. Price, $3.50.
The Flower of the Family. The Canterbury Bells.
Watson's Woods. Rest and Unrest.

COUSIN KATE'S LIBRARY. For Boys and Girls from 14 to 16 Years of Age, Price, $2.50.
Horace and May. Sydney Stuart.
Hope Campbell. Lily Gordon.

THE SUNNY-BROOK LIBRARY. For Boys and Girls from 6 to 9 Years of Age. Price, $3.25.
Peterchen and Gretchen. Translated by the Author of "Susy's Six Birthdays."
Our Summer at Sunny Brook.
Henry and Bessie.

THE SCHOOL-GIRL'S LIBRARY. For Girls from 14 to 16 Years of Age. 3 vols. Price, $1.80.
A Little Leaven and What it Wrought.
The Orphan Nieces. Heart and Hand.

OUR COUSIN'S LIBRARY. For Boys from 12 to 14 Years of Age. 4 vols. Price $1.75.
Upward and Onward. Charles Hubert.
Little Ben. The Two Heaps.

AUNT FRIENDLY'S LIBRARY. For Boys and Girls from 9 to 12 Years of Age. 6 vols. Price, $1.80.
Hatty and Marcus. Kate Darley.
Bound Out. The Orange Seed.
The Little Musicians. Poor Little Joe.

THE CLOVER-GLEN LIBRARY. For Boys and Girls from 9 to 12 Years of Age. 6 vols. Price, $1.80.
The Gleaners. Painstaking.
Clover Glen. Gentle Gracie.
Black Judy. Grafted Trees.

LITTLE SUSY'S LIBRARY. For Children from 4 to 7 Years. 3 vols. Price $1.80.
Little Susy's Six Birthdays. Little Susy's Teachers.
Little Susy's Servants.

## DEVOTIONAL BOOKS, ETC.

The following are printed on fine paper, and done up in extra binding; suitable for presents:—

THE CHANGED CROSS. A volume of religious Poems. 12mo. Cloth, antique. 50 cents.

SPIRITUAL SONGS AND DEVOTIONAL HYMNS. 24mo. Cloth, antique, 50 cents.

HYMNS FROM THE LAND OF LUTHER. 24mo. Cloth, antique. 60 cents.

THE EARNEST COMMUNICANT. 24mo. Cloth, antique. 50 cents.

GO AND TELL JESUS, and WAIT ON THE LORD. 24mo. Cloth, antique. 50 cents.

NONE LIKE CHRIST, and MY TIME'S IN HIS HAND. 24mo. Cloth, antique. 50 cents.

PEARLS OF THOUGHT. Selected from old authors. 18mo. Cloth, antique. 75 cents.

POEMS BY REV. R. C. TRENCH. 12mo. Bevelled boards, antique. $1.25.

SONGS OF THE WOODLAND, THE GARDEN, AND THE SEA. Small 4to. With seven beautiful Colored Illustrations. Cloth, gilt, bevelled boards. $1.

RAYS OF LIGHT FOR DARK HOURS. 16mo., antique, bevelled. 75 cents.

Published by

**ANSON D. F. RANDOLPH,**
683 Broadway, New York.

FIGURE 1. Authors and publishers often drew fine distinctions among juvenile audiences based on narrowly defined age groups, as in this 1863 advertisement in the *American Literary Gazette*. Courtesy, University of Minnesota Libraries.

Leatherstocking Tales dwindle in magnitude beside such prodigious series as Martha Finley's Elsie Dinsmore books, which grew to twenty-eight titles in the course of forty-two years, and Jacob Abbott's Rollo series, comprising twenty-six titles. Sometimes publishers corralled loosely related books by a single author into a series in order to give them a clearer identity and stronger presence in the marketplace, and in the hope that the success of one title would help sell the others. But when a series really took off, it was as much owing to the readers' response as to the efforts of author and publisher, for it was the persistent demand for new titles with recurring characters and varied plots that justified the authors' expenditure of time and the publishers' investment of money.

These chapters trace the development of juvenile publishing from a sector of the industry addressing a vaguely defined audience of "youth" to one increasingly segmented by gender, age, and class, and from a market dominated by didactic and pedagogical texts to one that produced imaginative and realistic fiction for young people, as well as the prototypes of the children's series books that are still very much a cornerstone of the juvenile fiction market.[8] In charting this development, I argue that a key factor was the creation of multiple children's markets in response to the recognition of multiple juvenile audiences, defined largely by gender and age but to some extent by social class as well. (As Clark observes, "Age is not just a simple term of difference but is always complicated by race, class, gender" [*Kiddie Lit* xiv].) These markets and the genres associated with them were organized, in the nineteenth-century mind, hierarchically. An 1856 editorial in the *American Publishers' Circular and Literary Gazette* explained:

> Babes need to be fed upon the pure milk, and afterwards upon strong meat. At first, there is a class of picture affairs, the tone of which is not, by the way, always as chaste as might be expected in these civilized days,—and after this, when the boy wearies of pap and can take nourishment more gross and substantial, there is the series of Boy's Own Books, and for the budding Misses the Girl's Own Book, and the Parley Tales, and Balloon Voyages,[9] and Dickens' Little Nell, and Paul, and Dora, and Florence, and hosts of fairy creations that kindle the juvenile ideas, implant virtuous lessons, and serve to create a relish for those other books that tell of men and strange nations, and of customs, boundaries, physical peculiarities, and then of the sciences of every-day life and the arts that minister to daily comfort. ("Educational Books" 317)

The examples of Hawthorne, Alcott, and Mark Twain collectively illustrate that this hierarchy of markets and genres did not spontaneously "evolve" but rather was organized and cultivated assiduously by both successful children's authors and their publishers to address the perceived needs and manifest desires of the nation's young consumers.

# WONDER BOOKS

> . . . all sorts of tomfoolery—
> —Nathaniel Hawthorne (1851)

IN DECEMBER 1834 an anonymous tale titled "Little Annie's Ramble" appeared in the *Youth's Keepsake: A Christmas and New Year's Gift for Young People* (dated 1835), an annual gift book edited by Park Benjamin.[1] Seemingly sentimental and innocuous, the sketch describes various scenes in a New England town as perceived through the innocent eyes of childhood. Readers follow five-year-old Annie and her adult companion as they meander through town, peering into shop windows and gazing at the animals they encounter along the street and in a traveling menagerie. Absorbed by the enchanting sights of toys, sweets, and pictures, as well as by the domestic and wild animals, the child and the man lose track of time, along with the fact that they have strayed from Annie's home without apprising her parents. By and by the voice of the town crier recalls them to mundane reality and alerts them that Annie has been declared missing. When the sketch was republished in the first edition of *Twice-told Tales* two years after its appearance in *Youth's Keepsake*, the authorship of "Little Annie's Ramble" was for the first time publicly acknowledged by Nathaniel Hawthorne.

Although reviews of the 1837 edition of *Twice-told Tales* often singled out "Little Annie's Ramble" for praise, more recent critics have been decidedly unenthusiastic about Hawthorne's first published attempt to write specifically for a juvenile audience.[2] Certainly it lacks the complexity, subtlety, and moral ambiguity that fascinated Hawthorne's readers throughout the twentieth century; nevertheless, the tale is not without interest to readers today as an index to its author's artistic aspirations and development as a writer of juvenile literature.

During the course of her ramble through town, Annie proceeds (with a certain implicit logic) from a confectioner's window to a bookseller's display. The narrator observes: "Here are pleasures, as some people would say, of a more exalted kind, in the window of a bookseller. Is Annie a literary lady? Yes; she is deeply read in Peter Parley's tomes, and has an increasing love for fairy tales, though seldom met with now-a-days, and she will subscribe, next year, to the Juvenile Miscellany" (*Twice-told Tales* 124).[3] Into this brief passage, Hawthorne telescopes a number of significant allusions that foreshadow important developments in his own career. In fact, he contributed sketches to several juvenile periodicals and miscellanies and within two years would be employed as a ghostwriter for the popular children's author known as Peter Parley. Moreover, his journals and correspondence reveal an ongoing and increasing interest in fantasy and fairy tales for children. In this context, the narrator's observations regarding Annie's literary preferences take on heightened significance.

The juxtaposition of Peter Parley's ubiquitous "tomes" and the more esoteric "fairy tales" reflects a tension in Hawthorne's own juvenile writing between the relatively prosaic Parley-type historical sketches he produced in the 1840s and the highly fanciful mythological tales he published a decade later in *A Wonder Book for Girls and Boys* (1851, dated 1852) and *Tanglewood Tales, for Girls and Boys; Being a Second Wonder Book* (1853). An exploration of Hawthorne's career as a writer of children's books illuminates these two disparate modes of juvenile writing: as distinct facets of Hawthorne's craft, they mirror the broad development of children's literature in the United States.[4] Moreover, such an exploration substantiates the assertion that although the early material was a calculated attempt to tap into the sizable juvenile nonfiction market aggressively mined by didactic writers such as Samuel Griswold Goodrich (1793–1860), aka Peter Parley, and Jacob Abbott (1803–79), Hawthorne's later success in the field of adult fiction freed him from the necessity of writing in a conventional juvenile format that had already become formulaic.[5] Finally, an analysis of Hawthorne's writing for children in the context of contemporary juvenile publishing reveals that his studied transition from conventional works of pedagogy to innovative retellings of classical myths closely parallels a radical concurrent transformation of the juvenile literature market: American children, sated with histories, geographies, and other nonfiction texts designed "for the instruction and amusement of youth," were acquiring (along with Little Annie) an increasing taste for literary morsels expressly concocted for their satisfaction and delight.

"Little Annie's Ramble" marks the beginning of Hawthorne's career as a writer of juvenile literature, a career that spanned more than twenty years (see Schorer). Two other early sketches also made their debuts in juvenile magazines: "Little Daffydowndilly," an allegory about a child who learns not to despise hard work, appeared in the *Boys' and Girls' Magazine* in August 1843; "A Good Man's Miracle," an "apocryphal" account of the founding of the Sunday School movement, graced the pages of the *Child's Friend*, a publication of the American Sunday School Union (see Klaus) the following February. These latter tales, which, Roy Harvey Pearce observes, reveal further "concessions to the taste of the popular audience and the publishers who catered to it" (288), appeared between the publication of the second edition of *Twice-told Tales* (1842) and *Mosses from an Old Manse* (1846), at a time when Hawthorne was searching for his niche in the literary marketplace and contributing pieces to a variety of publications, from audience-specific periodicals such as *Godey's Lady's Book* and divers children's publications to general-interest magazines such as the *Knickerbocker* and *New-England Magazine*.[6]

By far the single largest market for Hawthorne's sketches in the years between the publication of *Fanshawe* (1828) and the first edition of *Twice-told Tales* (1837), however, was the *Token* (1827–42), a popular gift book published annually for the Christmas and New Year's trade. The *Token* was launched by Samuel Goodrich, of Peter Parley fame, who published it for two years, went on to edit thirteen of the fifteen volumes, and contributed prolifically to its pages (Roselle 102). Goodrich conceived of the *Token* as an American version of the English *Forget Me Not*, which began publication in 1823. It was to be distinct from other American gift books, such as the *Atlantic Souvenir* (with which it merged in 1833), in its effort to showcase and promote American authors, American illustrators, and American themes.[7] As publisher and editor of this ambitious nativist literary project, Goodrich needed to be on the lookout for American literary and artistic talent. It was in his capacity as acquisitions editor that he became acquainted with Hawthorne and proceeded to recruit him to contribute to the *Token*. In fact, Goodrich was one of Hawthorne's earliest admirers. In 1829, after the publisher of *Fanshawe* apparently tipped him off as to the authorship of the anonymous romance, Goodrich wrote to Hawthorne to express interest in him as a possible contributor (*Recollections* 2: 270–71). By way of reply to Goodrich's overtures, Hawthorne sent him several manuscripts in 1830, including some pieces that he wrote specifically for the *Token*. In doing so, he joined the ranks of such popular authors as Henry Wadsworth Longfellow, Nathaniel Parker Willis, Lydia Maria Child, Lydia

Sigourney, Catharine Maria Sedgwick, and Oliver Wendell Holmes, who also contributed to the *Token*. Over the next eight years, Goodrich published some twenty-seven of Hawthorne's sketches and tales, typically paying him between 75 cents and a dollar per page (Gross 236–38; Wayne Allen Jones, "Hawthorne-Goodrich Relationship"). Many of these pieces were later collected in *Twice-told Tales*, which Hawthorne, erroneously believing himself to be newly indebted to Goodrich, considered dedicating to the editor of the *Token*.[8]

Demand for the Parley books and his children's textbooks was so steady that Goodrich employed a succession of freelance writers to produce new volumes according to plans that he developed himself (Roselle 63).[9] Despite his feeling that Goodrich had exploited him in the past,[10] Hawthorne agreed to compile, with his sister Elizabeth, one such volume: *Peter Parley's Universal History on the Basis of Geography* (MacDonald 195; Roselle 77–78). Evidently, Hawthorne accepted the assignment (at least in part) because he regarded the work as relatively easy. In explaining the project to Elizabeth, he observed, "It need not be superiour [*sic*], in profundity and polish, to the middling Magazine articles," and regarding compensation, he wrote, "Our pay, as Historians of the Universe, will be 100 dollars the whole of which you may have. It is a poor compensation; yet better than the Token; because the kind of writing is so much less difficult." (*Letters* 15: 245, 247).

Apparently pleased with the two manuscript folios he received on 23 September 1836, Goodrich wrote to Hawthorne on 13 December with a follow-up offer: "If you are disposed to write a volume of six hundred small 12mo pages on the manner, customs, and civilities of all countries,—for $300,—I could probably arrange it with you. I should want a mere compilation from books that I would furnish. It might be commenced immediately. Let me know your views. It would go in old Parley's name" (Pearce 289). No record survives of Hawthorne's presumably negative reply to this invitation to masquerade a second time as the fictitious—yet enterprising—Peter Parley.

If Hawthorne found the task of ghostwriting for this imaginary author unremunerative, he must have been aware that "old Parley" was doing quite well by his creator. Indeed, Goodrich, "with his literary enterprises and assistants" (qtd. in Boynton 191), who had occupied space in William D. Ticknor's Old Corner Bookstore from October 1826, gradually expanded his quarters to fill the entire second floor of this Boston landmark. In his

*Recollections of a Lifetime; or, Men and Things I Have Seen* (1857), Goodrich estimated that seven million of his books had been sold to date and were currently selling at an annual rate of 300,000 (2: 543).[11] Goodrich also calculated that he was "the author and editor of about one hundred and seventy volumes—one hundred and sixteen bearing the name of Peter Parley" (*Recollections* 2: 543). (That statistic casts light on Charles Kingsley's caricature of Peter Parley as "Cousin Cramchild" in *The Water Babies*.) His first geography book, *Peter Parley's Method of Telling about Geography to Children* (1829), sold two million copies worldwide (Roselle 71),[12] and even the *Universal History*, the volume over which Nathaniel and Elizabeth Hawthorne diligently labored, reportedly sold more than a million copies (Roselle 77; Schorer 209). Moreover, the Hawthornes' "Parley" was adapted for use in schools, and the revised text, issued concurrently with the original version under the title *Peter Parley's Common School History*, went through six editions in four months and was adopted by "many of the best schools in the United States" (Roselle 79). The success of these volumes, if known to Hawthorne, must have been galling, considering that they appeared at a time when he, having been paid so little for writing them, was diligently but unsuccessfully attempting to earn a living by his pen. Perhaps even more exasperating, Goodrich published his first Peter Parley book, *Peter Parley's Tales about America*, in 1827—one year before Hawthorne published *Fanshawe*—and while only a small portion of the thousand copies of *Fanshawe* sold, the first Peter Parley quickly became a hit, allowing its author to achieve international fame and great wealth over the course of the same ten-year period that Hawthorne grudgingly spent supplying material to the *Token* at the disappointing rate of (at best) a dollar per page.[13]

Goodrich's successes in the field of juvenile literature were by no means limited to the Peter Parley books. In the 1820s he entered the textbook market, generating plans for school books, hiring the writers, and publishing the resulting texts. By 1830 he was writing his own textbooks, which included geographies, histories, books of natural history, arithmetic texts, and a line of Goodrich Readers, which were widely used in New England. As Daniel Roselle notes, "From 1830 to 1850 Goodrich was as active in writing children's textbooks as he was in setting down the Peter Parley tales or in editing the writings of contributors to his magazines" (63–64).

Perhaps it was Goodrich's success in the children's textbook market that encouraged Hawthorne to entertain plans to write pedagogical works of a similar nature. In a letter to Longfellow dated 21 March 1838, he complained of being "terribly harassed with magazine scribbling," adding that he had received "overtures from two different quarters, to perpetrate childrens' histories and other such iniquities" (*Letters* 15: 266). One of these "quarters" was Horace Mann (his future brother-in-law), to whom he had been recommended by Elizabeth Peabody (his future sister-in-law) (W. Jones, "Sometimes Things Just Don't Work Out" 16). Mann, as secretary of the newly established Massachusetts Board of Education, was planning to publish a series of standard texts for school libraries (Mellow 153). As Hawthorne explained in a subsequent letter to Longfellow: "Really I do mean to turn my attention to writing for children, either on my own hook, or for the series of works projected by the Board of Education—to which I have been requested to contribute. It appears to me that there is a very fair chance of profit" (*Letters* 15: 288).[14] The other quarter was the Boston firm of Marsh, Capen & Lyon (publisher of *Fanshawe*), which, in January 1840, announced as forthcoming "*New-England Historical Sketches*, by N. Hawthorne. Author of 'Twice Told Tales,' &c." Although the projected volume was never published, "it seems likely that it is closely related to, perhaps indeed part of, the *Grandfather's Chair* series," which appeared a short time later (Pearce 291–92).

By 1840, when Hawthorne published the three volumes of that series—*Grandfather's Chair*, *Famous Old People*, and *Liberty Tree*—the market for histories and inspirational biographies for children had already been well established by Goodrich, Lydia Maria Child, the American Tract Society, Francis L. Hawks (aka Francis Lister), and others.[15] Considered alongside these earlier productions, Hawthorne's histories clearly manifest a superior execution and a more sophisticated narrative style and structure. Indeed, the noteworthy innovation of *The Whole History of Grandfather's Chair* (as the three volumes came to be known), in which Hawthorne organizes the tales around appearances of the old man's chair at various junctures in New England history, has been generally admired by critics (Laffrado 40; Baym, *Shape of Hawthorne's Career* 90).[16] Nevertheless, the resemblance between Goodrich's Peter Parley books and Hawthorne's juvenile nonfiction is more than superficial, as Andrew Preston Peabody observed when, in 1852, he described *Grandfather's Chair* as written "in the Peter Parley style" (A. Peabody 228).[17] Both series consist of a sequence of framed narratives in which the narrator is an elderly gentleman addressing a fictional audience of young boys and girls.[18] Although rendered less artistically than the Grandfather's Chair series, *Biographical Stories for Children* (1842), which Hawthorne wrote shortly after his departure from the Transcendentalist community of Brook Farm (Mellow 192), likewise employs a narrative frame as a middle-aged man, Mr. Temple, tells the stories to his invalid son and other members of his family circle. In addition, both *The Whole History of Grandfather's Chair* and Hawthorne's *Biographical Stories for Children* follow the pattern of Peter Parley in relating, in a conversational style, factual material dressed in overtly moralistic trappings. This narrative technique is especially conspicuous in *Biographical Stories*, in which, for example, the sketch of Samuel Johnson (issued separately, slightly abridged, as a Sunday School pamphlet in 1842) highlights Johnson's remorse and penance for disobeying his father. This shift toward a more didactic posture suggests the possibility that Hawthorne, after dispensing with the fanciful chair device of the earlier series, deliberately cultivated a more "Parley-like" expository mode in the later collection.

If, by adapting Goodrich's narrative techniques, Hawthorne was hoping to achieve a success to rival that of Peter Parley, he must have been sorely disappointed. His correspondence suggests that he regarded these early juvenile stories as a kind of hackwork that might bring its author money, if not literary fame. On 4 June 1837 he had written to Longfellow: "I see little prospect but that I must scribble for a living. But this troubles me much less than you would suppose. I can turn my pen to all sorts of drudgery, such as children's books &c, and by and bye, I shall get some editorship that will answer my purpose" (*Letters* 15: 252). Five years later, it was abundantly clear that these early efforts had missed their market. In fact, Elizabeth Peabody, who originally published the individual volumes of the Grandfather's Chair series, evidently had a fair amount of trouble disposing of remainders and finding another publisher to take over the series (Pearce 295 n). It wasn't until Ticknor and Fields reissued the sketches collectively as *True Stories from History and Biography* (1850) in the wake of *The Scarlet Letter* that the project finally began to pay.[19]

Hawthorne's disillusionment with what he had once regarded as a potentially lucrative line of literary labor reverberates through a letter he wrote to bookseller and publisher Samuel Colman.[20] It is dated 27 September 1843, shortly after "Little Daffydowndilly" appeared in Colman's *Boys' and Girls' Magazine*:

> I am afraid that I cannot find time to write a regular series of articles for the "Boys [*sic*] & Girls' Magazine." It would give me pleasure to comply

with your request; but it could not be done without interrupting other pursuits, and at a greater sacrifice than the real value of my articles. If I saw a probability of deriving a reasonable profit from juvenile literature, I would willingly devote myself to it for a time, as being both easier and more agreeable (by way of variety) than literature for grown people. But my experience hitherto has not made me very sanguine on this point. In fact, the business has long been overdone. Mr [Jacob] Abbot [*sic*] and other writers have reaped the harvest; and the gleanings seem to be scarcely worth picking up. (*Letters* 16: 1)[21]

Given the imminent explosion of children's literature in the United States, it may be surprising that in 1843 Hawthorne considered the field already thoroughly saturated. Nevertheless, Jacob Abbott and Samuel Goodrich (whose popular success Hawthorne must also have had in mind) were, assuredly, overwhelming forces in the juvenile literature market. Like Goodrich, Abbott was spectacularly prolific. He wrote an estimated two hundred books, averaging four per year. His first popular hit, *The Young Christian*, remained in print continuously from 1832 to 1891, but his most successful production by far was the Rollo series, consisting of twenty-six volumes of travel, geography, and science, plus fifteen Rollo Story Books and volumes of poetry (Gay, "Jacob Abbott" 6). In addition, Abbott wrote numerous volumes of history for youth, as well as moral tales for the very young.

With such popular authors as Abbott and Goodrich generating a steady stream of juvenile nonfiction, it is perhaps not surprising that Hawthorne should soon abandon the project of writing schoolbooks and juvenile histories in the Parley tradition—albeit wistfully and with evident reluctance, for he retained a vestigial interest in authoring children's textbooks, even as his thoughts began to turn toward new modes of juvenile writing. In a letter to Evert A. Duyckinck (15 April 1846), he confessed, "I have had in my head, this long time, the idea of some stories to be taken out of the cold moonshine of classical mythology, and modernized, or perhaps gothicized, so that they may be felt by children of these days" (*Letters* 16: 153). Three years later, still uncertain as to which direction to pursue, he professed in a letter to Horace Mann (8 August 1849) to be thinking of "writing a school-book—or, at any rate, a book for the young" (*Letters* 16: 293). The critical distinction Hawthorne observes syntactically between "a schoolbook" and "a book for the young," emblematic of the growing division between instruction and entertainment in the juvenile literature market, foreshadows the turn his own career was about to take. Encouraged by publisher James T. Fields's suggestion that "a Book of Stories for children for next season would do wonderfully well" (qtd. in J. D. Crowley, "Historical Commentary" 388), Hawthorne finally resumed writing for children in the spring of 1851. Now, with *The Scarlet Letter* and *The House of the Seven Gables* behind him, Hawthorne broke with the Peter Parley school of juvenile literature and struck off in an entirely new direction.

In his *Recollections*, Goodrich writes of a "desire [he] had long entertained of making a reform—or at least an improvement—in books for youth" (2: 167). Hawthorne, too, cherished hopes of reforming children's literature, writing to Longfellow on 21 March 1838 of his interest in collaborating on a children's book that "may make a great hit, and entirely revolutionize the whole system of juvenile literature" (*Letters* 15: 266).[22] Earlier that month, on 3 March, Elizabeth Peabody had explained in a letter to Horace Mann that, although Hawthorne had "not thriven with the booksellers," he had always "had in his mind one great moral enterprise . . . —to make an attempt at creating a new literature for the young—as he has a deep dislike to the character of the shoals of books poured out from the press" (199–200; see also W. Jones, "Hawthorne-Goodrich"). Goodrich's "reform" had involved substituting such salubrious fare as histories, geographies, and the like for fairy tales, Mother Goose rhymes, and other "tales of horror," which he felt were "commonly put into the hands of youth, as if for the express purpose of reconciling them to vice and crime" (*Recollections* 1: 166).[23] In contrast, Hawthorne aspired with his version of a "new literature for the young" to reinvest children's reading with precisely the kind of imagination and fancy that Goodrich considered to be potentially detrimental. The project he had envisioned for himself and Longfellow—a collection of fairy tales tentatively called "The Boys' Wonder-Horn," after the German folk collection *Des Knabens Wunderhorn* (1805–8)—never came to fruition (evidently not for lack of enthusiasm on Hawthorne's part).[24] Nevertheless, Hawthorne achieved his own "revolution" in children's literature with the classical myths, "gothicized" and "Yankeeized," of *A Wonder Book* and *Tanglewood Tales*, a project he described to Fields (7 April 1851) in distinctly un-Goodrichian terms: "It shall not be exclusively Fairy tales, but intermixed with stories of real life, and classic myths, modernized and made funny, and all sorts of tomfoolery—The Child's Budget of Miscellaneous Nonsense" (*Letters* 16: 417).

This revolt against Goodrich and Peter Parley must be seen not only in the context of Hawthorne's personal antipathy toward Goodrich and his earlier efforts with factual children's stories. Rather, it must be considered in connection with the decline of Puritanism in America, the growing influence of Romanticism, and the attendant shifts in the cultural construction of childhood. Social historian Bernard Wishy neatly captures the essence of this shift in coining the terms "The Child Redeemable" and "The Child Redeemer." The Child Redeemable, reflecting the perception of childhood that prevailed from about 1830 to 1860, emphasizes "the flexible character of the child"—that is, the child's capacity for moral progress, if not perfection—through Christian nurture (17). Gradually supplanting this image, The Child Redeemer is capable of redeeming "adult failures" by virtue of "superior energy, purity, or magic." And, as Wishy explains, "from this point on (circa 1870) the sentimental notion that somehow it is better to be a child than an adult, that the best standards of life are those of naive and innocent children becomes an increasingly powerful theme in American culture" (85). The contrast between The Child Redeemer and The Child Redeemable provides a useful framework for understanding both the antithetical reforms cherished by Hawthorne and Goodrich and the striking disparity between Hawthorne's early children's histories and his classical tales of the 1850s.

The very subject matter of *A Wonder Book* is revolutionary in the context of nineteenth-century American children's literature. Fantasy remained rare in the juvenile literature of the United States long after it had begun to flourish in Britain, where it was nourished by the earlier influence of Romanticism, with its backlash against the drab moralistic children's stories of the later eighteenth century. Although there was a steady increase after 1830 of children's literature in which imagination and fantasy overshadowed overt moralizing (Wishy 53), many literary historians place Hawthorne at the beginning of the tradition of the American literary fairy tale.[25] As Hawthorne intimates in his letter to Fields, however, it is the "intermixing" of fairy tales, myth, and "stories of real life" that is most remarkable about *A Wonder Book*. Earlier, in *Grandfather's Chair*, he had instilled a trace of the fantastic into otherwise factual chapters of New England history, as the chair itself descended through time, witnessing, in almost human fashion, the scenes and events Grandfather describes. Indeed, in the final sequence, "Grandfather's Dream," Hawthorne brings the chair to life and endows it with the power of speech—although Grandfather scrupulously separates fact from fable, "warning the children that they must not mistake this story for a true one" (*The Stories* 205).[26] In *A Wonder Book* and *Tanglewood*

*Tales*, the categories of fantasy and reality become blurred, as Hawthorne catapults the myths of ancient Greece into contemporary New England and invests them with a beguiling blend of romance and detail drawn from real life. His strategy, as he explains in the preface to *A Wonder Book*, is "to clothe [the fables] with . . . [the] garniture of manners and sentiment, and to imbue [them] with . . . [the] morality" of the present age (*Wonder Book and Tanglewood Tales* [hereafter *WB and TT*] 3).

In the preface to *The House of the Seven Gables* (published less than two months before he began *A Wonder Book*), Hawthorne had cautioned the writer of romance "to mingle the Marvellous rather as a slight, delicate, and evanescent flavor, than as any portion of the actual substance of the dish offered to the Public," adding, "He can hardly be said, however, to commit a literary crime, even if he disregard this caution" (*House* 1). In *A Wonder Book* and *Tanglewood Tales*, the proportions shift as Hawthorne begins with material that is essentially "Marvellous" and proceeds to stitch it securely into a real-world context which, in consequence, takes on a fantastic quality of its own. Thus, in the preamble to "The Golden Touch," Hawthorne accounts for the inspiration of Eustace Bright, a student at Williams College, in narrating the story of King Midas: "It had come into his mind, as he lay looking upward into the depths of a tree, and observing how the touch of Autumn had transmuted every one of its green leaves into what resembled the purest gold. And this change, which we have all of us witnessed, is as wonderful as anything that Eustace told about, in the story of Midas" (*WB and TT* 39).

Similarly, Eustace presents the outlines of each myth in a factual manner but freely acknowledges embellishing them with creations of his own imagination. In introducing "The Golden Touch," for example, he begins, "Once upon a time, there lived a very rich man, and a king besides, whose name was Midas; and he had a little daughter, whom nobody but myself ever heard of, and whose name I either never knew, or have entirely forgotten. So, because I love odd names for little girls, I choose to call her Marygold" (*WB and TT* 40). Even Eustace's auditors, the little children whom he regales with the romanticized myths, take on a fantastic quality, as Hawthorne endows them with names that "might better suit a group of fairies than a company of earthly children" (*WB and TT* 6).

The characterization of both the spritelike children who make up Eustace's fictional audience and the children within the stories further illustrates the extent to which Hawthorne had transcended the constraints of his earlier biographical and historical vein and embraced the Romantic conception of childhood. Within the contexts of their narrative frames, both *Grandfather's Chair* and *Biographical Stories for Children* are addressed to stereotyped sets of children (Laurence, Charley, Clara, and Alice in the former; Edward, George, and Emily in the latter), and both collections contain stories that reinforce traditional gender roles or critique those who deviate from them. The life of Queen Christina, for example, is said to be "chiefly profitable as showing the evil effects of a wrong education, which caused this daughter of a King to be both useless and unhappy" (*True Stories* 275). Accordingly, Hawthorne describes the basis of this "wrongful education":

> [King Gustavus] determined to educate her exactly as if she had been a boy, and to teach her all the knowledge needful to the ruler of a kingdom, and the commander of an army.
>
> But Gustavus should have remembered that Providence had created her to be a woman, and that it was not for him to make a man of her. (*True Stories* 277)

The tale concludes with a blatant moral aimed squarely at "The Child Redeemable": "Happy are the little girls of America, who are brought up quietly and tenderly, at the domestic hearth, and thus become gentle and delicate women! May none of them ever lose the loveliness of their sex, by receiving such an education as that of Queen Christina!" (*True Stories* 283).[27]

In the mythological tales, in contrast, Hawthorne not only dispenses with such overt didacticism but portrays childish whimsy and naughtiness as natural and even preferable to a more mannered and artificial state. Indeed, in "The Paradise of Children," his version of the Pandora's box story, his description of an untroubled prelapsarian world in which "the children never quarrelled among themselves; neither had they any crying-fits; nor, since time first began, had a single one of these little mortals ever gone apart into a corner, and sulked!" (*WB and TT* 66), strains uneasily against his depiction of impish Pandora, who spends her time quarreling with Epimetheus and brooding over the forbidden contents of the sealed box. Moreover, in *A Wonder Book* and, to a lesser degree, *Tanglewood Tales* (which lacks the elaborate frame of the earlier volume), Hawthorne abandons the customary audience of conventional boys and girls in favor of a playful, rambunctious, occasionally querulous assortment of youngsters

36

called by the whimsically Shakespearean, pastoral, gender-ambiguous names of Primrose, Periwinkle, Sweet Fern, Dandelion, Blue Eye, Clover, Huckleberry, Cowslip, Squash Blossom, Milkweed, Plantain, and Buttercup.[28] Both the avoidance of stereotypical boy and girl characters and the positive portrayal of childhood mischievousness are unusual in Anglo-American juvenile literature of the mid-nineteenth century. They represent not only an important artistic innovation on Hawthorne's part (one that recalls the characterization of Pearl in *The Scarlet Letter*) but also a concurrent development in the course of juvenile literature in the United States and Britain, as fictionalized children became less angelic, less idealized, and less constrained by traditional social roles even as they embodied a kind of redemptive innocence and hinted of "a natural connection between children and higher truths" (Thacker and Webb 16).

The influence of his wife Sophia and her sisters, Mary Peabody Mann (author of *The Moral Culture of Infancy* and wife of Horace Mann) and Elizabeth Peabody (Bronson Alcott's partner in founding the innovative Temple School for children in 1834), was undoubtedly significant in Hawthorne's changing response to children in his writing. All three of the Peabody sisters had connections to what T. Walter Herbert called "the network of educational reformers and theorists of child rearing who relied on the premise that infants are not infected by original sin but bring a primal innocence into the world to be preserved and cultivated" (156). But Hawthorne's newfound success both in depicting and in appealing to children in his books of myth also derived from a heightened sensitivity toward children and their literary preferences, born, inevitably, of his role as a parent. His journals from the late 1840s and early 1850s charmingly record his interactions with Una, Julian, little "Rosebud," and their ill-fated pet "Bunny" (see his *American Notebooks* 398–556), and as he was writing *A Wonder Book*, Hawthorne reportedly read what he had written each day to his children "by way of a test" (qtd. in Schorer 16). In the Hawthorne Family Notebook, a collaborative journal, Sophia recorded Julian's reaction to her reading of "The Chimaera": "Was ever any thing so divine as that story? Julian was powerfully affected. He had not heard it for a long time & he was thrilled & stirred by every sentence . . . The color mounted up to his curls & his eyes softened & were suffused . . . As for me, I could scarcely read, I was so moved" (qtd. in Herbert 16). The emotional current channeled through the act of storytelling apparently flowed in both directions: according to Horace Scudder, "The presence of an audience of children had a singular power over him"

(277). This sense of reciprocity finds expression in the dialogic structure of *A Wonder Book*, which reenacts the storytelling process.

As narrator, Eustace Bright is ideally positioned between childhood and adulthood. Although he is of college age and presumably full grown, his affinities clearly lie with the children who surround him rather than the adults who occasionally intrude. He differentiates between these two audiences with a self-consciousness that becomes evident midway through *A Wonder Book*, when Primrose informs him that Mr. and Mrs. Pringle wish to hear one of his stories. Although rather pleased "at the opportunity of proving to Mr. Pringle what an excellent faculty he had in modernizing the myths of ancient times," Eustace is aware that what pleases the children may find less favor with their elders. After Mr. Pringle turns to him "in a way that made him feel how uncombed and unbrushed he was, and how uncombed and unbrushed, likewise, were his mind and thoughts," Eustace informs him, "You are not exactly the auditor I should have chosen, Sir, . . . for fantasies of this nature" and, before beginning "The Three Golden Apples," asks that the Pringles "be kind enough to remember, that I am addressing myself to the imagination and sympathies of the children, not to your own" (*WB and TT* 88–89). His remarks reflect the clear separation Hawthorne observed between literary fare for children and for adults (despite a mixed audience), his determination to cater directly to the preferences of the young, and a Romantic sense of loss in the implicit gulf between "the imagination and sympathies of children" and the remote, unreceptive adult mind.

Eustace's reference to "the admirable nonsense that I put into these stories, out of my own head, and which makes the great charm of the matter for children" (*WB and TT* 88) unmistakably announces the author's new approach. By the time he wrote *A Wonder Book*, Hawthorne, as the father of three young children, had acquired considerable firsthand experience with youngsters and was well qualified to speak with authority about their literary tastes, as evidenced by his knowing assertion that "it is a truth, as regards children, that a story seems often to deepen its mark in their interest, not merely by two or three, but by numberless repetitions" (*WB and TT* 8). Earlier, in the preface to *Grandfather's Chair*, he had confessed a degree of uncertainty about his "ponderous tome": "The author's great doubt is, whether he has succeeded in writing a book which will be readable by the class for whom he intends it. To make a lively and entertaining narrative for children, with such unmalleable material as is presented by the sombre, stern, and rigid characteristics of the Puritans and their descendants, is quite as difficult an attempt, as to manufacture delicate playthings out of the granite rocks on which New England is founded" (*True Stories* 5–6).[29]

A decade later, Hawthorne expressed a similar awareness that, in restyling classical myths, he was again working with recalcitrant literary material. But the diffidence of the earlier work gave way to a newfound aplomb in a letter to Fields: "I shall aim at substituting a tone in some degree Gothic or romantic, or any such tone as may best please myself, instead of the classic coldness, which is as repellant [*sic*] as the touch of marble" (*Letters* 16: 436). This confidence in his ability to assess and accommodate the tastes of his juvenile audience, underscored by his assertion that "the book, if it comes out of my mind as I see it now, ought to have pretty wide success amongst young people" (*Letters* 16: 437), resounds in the opening of *A Wonder Book*, where Hawthorne, in marked counterpoint to the preface of *Grandfather's Chair*, announces that "the author has long been of opinion, that many of the classical myths were capable of being rendered into very capital reading for children" (*WB and TT* 3).[30]

His assurance that he had succeeded at last in capturing a receptive juvenile readership was not misplaced. Henry James later proclaimed Hawthorne's Greek myths "among the most charming literary services that have been rendered to children in an age (and especially in a country) in which the exactions of the infant mind have exerted much too palpable an influence upon literature" (*Literary Criticism* 1: 417). Following publication of *A Wonder Book*, Hawthorne received many complimentary letters from children (Pearce 309), and both that collection and its sequel were well reviewed by the press.[31] An anonymous writer in *Graham's Magazine* effectively summed up Hawthorne's achievement when he contrasted these most recent juvenile productions with the kind of routine, unimaginative writing for children that was so prevalent at midcentury (and, indeed, of the kind that Hawthorne himself had "perpetrated" a decade earlier): "It is almost needless to say that all these stories [*Tanglewood Tales*] evince the felicity and transforming power of genius, and are to be rigidly distinguished from ordinary books for children. They have nothing of the book-making, hack-writing, soul-lacking character of job work, but are true products of imagination—of the literary artist as discriminated from the literary artisan" (qtd. in J. D. Crowley, *Hawthorne* 284).[32]

Of the writing of these mythological tales, which occurred in a brief span between early June and mid-July 1851 (Mellow 369), Hawthorne confessed, "It has been really a task fit for hot weather, and one of the most agreeable, of a literary kind, which he [the author] ever undertook" (*WB and TT* 4). That he found artistic satisfaction in them is evident in a statement he made to Washington Irving (16 July 1852), another literary artist whose retellings of Old World tales were avidly read by children: "I sent you 'The Wonder Book,' because, being meant for children, it seemed to reach a higher point, in its own way, than anything that I had written for grown people" (*Letters* 16: 570). The apparent paradox of reaching a "higher point" through writing for children is resolved in the preface to *A Wonder Book* with the Romantic writer's confidence in the spiritual purity of children: "The Author has not always thought it necessary to write downward, in order to meet the comprehension of children. He has generally suffered the theme to soar, whenever such was its tendency, and when he himself was bouyant enough to follow without an effort. Children possess an unestimated sensibility to whatever is deep or high, in imagination or feeling, so long as it is simple, likewise. It is only the artificial and the complex that bewilders them" (*WB and TT* 4).

As far back as 1838, Hawthorne had written to Longfellow with respect to their proposed collaboration on children's stories, "Seriously, I think that a very pleasant and peculiar kind of reputation may be acquired in this way—we will twine for ourselves a wreath of tender shoots and dewy buds, instead of such withered and dusty leaves as other people crown themselves with" (*Letters* 15: 266–67). Four years later, he reasoned in the preface to *Biographical Stories* that "in point of the reputation to be aimed at, juvenile literature is as well worth cultivating as any other. The writer, if he succeed in pleasing his little readers, may hope to be remembered by them till their own old age—a far longer period of literary existence than is generally attained, by those who seek immortality from the judgments of full grown men" (*True Stories* 214). To Horace Mann, Elizabeth Peabody conveyed Hawthorne's avowal "that were he embarked in this undertaking he should feel as if he had a right to live—he desired no higher vocation— he considered it the highest" (200). Fifteen years later, after Hawthorne had finally succeeded in this "undertaking," he declared in a letter to R. H. Stoddard (dated 16 March 1853) that the six myths of *Tanglewood Tales* are "fully equal, in their way, to Mother Goose," adding, "I never did anything else so well as these old baby-stories" (*Letters* 16: 649).[33] (Although critics have generally admired *Tanglewood Tales* less than its predecessor, there is sufficient evidence both within the tales and in their reception history to justify Hawthorne's unprecedented expressions of satisfaction.) In terms of aesthetic quality and the value ascribed by author, readers, and critics, the span between *Biographical Stories* and *A Wonder Book* epitomizes Hawthorne's growth, as a writer for children, from "book-making, hack-writing, soul-lacking" producer of literary "job work" to the rare kind of "literary artist" who "evince[s] the felicity and transforming power of genius."

The gradual shift from pedagogy and didacticism to entertainment and amusement in children's literature, and from juvenile history and geography to fantasy and other forms of highly wrought imaginative fiction, had a number of causes, including the growing influence of Romanticism; the secularization of Anglo-American culture, which helped broaden the horizons of children's literature beyond moral tales and Sunday School reading; and the increasing purchasing power that enabled children to vote with their pocket money—within the parameters of parental means and approval (see Avery, *Behold the Child*; and MacLeod, *Moral Tale*). In addition, given the thickening competition among publishers of juvenile literature, the marketing of children's books became increasingly aggressive in vying for the attention of young readers (see, for example, Kilgour, *Lee and Shepard*). Even Goodrich, writing in 1856, may have had in mind the new breed of literature conceived and marketed to appeal directly to the young when he urged his readers to "go to such a juvenile bookstore as that of C. S. Francis, in Broadway, New York, and behold the teeming shelves— comprising almost every topic within the range of human knowledge, treated in a manner to please the young mind, by the use of every attraction of style and every art of embellishment—and let him remember that nineteen twentieths of these works have come into existence within the last thirty years" (*Recollections* 1: 174).[34] One can imagine Goodrich and his contemporaries gazing in wonder upon the "teeming shelves" of the children's bookstore in much the manner of Little Annie gazing with astonished eyes upon the riches of the confectioner's shop. For readers today, it is enough to marvel that in 1856 the publishing trade had developed to the point that there *were* such specialized outlets as "juvenile bookstores."[35]

In any event, that by midcentury American children were eager for fanciful works such as *A Wonder Book* and *Tanglewood Tales* is indicated in a letter from Ticknor and Fields to their English agent, Thomas Delf, on 19 December 1849; Fields wrote, "We wish we had an £100 of Cundalls

Juveniles & as much more of other kinds—the rage is for 'Eng Juveniles'— & very few to be had" (qtd. in Pearce 295 n). In the 1840s the London firm of Joseph Cundall (1841–52), which specialized in high-quality, illustrated children's books, was publishing fairy tales, legends, nursery rhymes, ballads, folktales, and other kinds of imaginative story books in yet another attempt to "reform" juvenile publishing.[36] Series editor Henry Cole ("Felix Summerly") explained in the prospectus to Cundall's *Home Treasury*:

> The character of most Children's Books published during the last quarter of a century is fairly typified in the name of Peter Parley, which the writers of some hundreds of them have assumed. The books themselves have been addressed after a narrow fashion almost entirely to the cultivation of the understanding of children. The many tales sung or said from time immemorial, which appealed to the other, and certainly not less important elements of a little child's mind, its fancy, imagination, sympathies, affections, are almost all gone out of memory, and are scarcely to be obtained. The difficulty of procuring them is very great. Of our national nursery songs, some of them as old as our language, only a very common and inferior edition for children can be procured. Little Red Riding Hood and other fairy tales hallowed to children's use, are now turned into ribaldry as satires for men. As for the creation of a new fairy tale or touching ballad, such a thing is unheard of. That the influence of all this is hurtful to children the conductor of the proposed series firmly believes. He has practical experience of it every day in his own family, and he doubts not that there are many others who entertain the same opinions as himself. He purposes at least to give some evidence of his belief, and to produce a series of Works for children, the character of which may be briefly described as anti-Peter Parleyism. (Qtd. in McLean, *Joseph Cundall* 4)[37]

The scintillating volumes of Cundall's Juveniles, embodying just the kind of "tomfoolery" Hawthorne intimated to Fields with respect to *A Wonder Book*, could hardly have failed to attract the multitudes of American children who had become, like Little Annie, "deeply read in Peter Parley's tomes."[38] Indeed, as Marjorie N. Allen observes, "The English fantasy imports created a market in America for books that directly appealed to children and opened the door for American authors who preferred storytelling to moralizing" (7). (To be sure, one such author put a volume of Joseph Cundall's *Robin Hood and His Merry Foresters* into the hands of that most imaginative of fictional child readers, Tom Sawyer [Gribben,

*Mark Twain's Library* 1: 166].) Hawthorne's timely abandonment of the "book-making, hack-writing, soul-lacking" job of writing Parley-type historical tales in favor of the fantastic narratives he blithely characterized as "The Child's Budget of Miscellaneous Nonsense" thus happily coincided with the recognition—and the indulgence—of the growing literary appetite of American children who shared an "increasing love for fairy tales" with the diminutive heroine of "Little Annie's Ramble."

## Chapter Two

# STORIES OF THEIR LIVES

Few gentlemen, who have occasion to visit news-offices, can have failed to notice the periodical literature for boys, which has been growing up during the last few years. The increase in the number of these papers and magazines, and the appearance, from time to time, of new ones, which, to judge by the pictures, are always worse than the old, seem to indicate that they find a wide market.

—William G. Sumner, "What Our Boys Are Reading" (1878)

Girls, like boys, in recent years have been remarkably favoured in the matter of their reading. They cannot complain, with any justice, that they are ignored in the piles of juvenile literature laid annually upon the booksellers' shelves. Boys boast of a literature of their "very own," as they would call it. So do girls. . . . [T]hat so-called 'girls' books' continue to be published in shoals annually is sufficient proof that there is a market for them.

—Edward G. Salmon, "What Girls Read" (1886)

WRITING IN 1878 and 1886 respectively, William G. Sumner (681) and Edward G. Salmon (515) pointed to an increasingly conspicuous trend in British and American juvenile literature: the development of distinct genres written expressly for boys or expressly for girls. To today's reader, raised on Nancy Drew or the Hardy Boys, Trixie Belden or Chip Hilton, the Baby-Sitters' Club or Encyclopedia Brown, such a division may seem a natural and obvious one. As Salmon suggested, however, the shift from a more or less homogeneous body of literature for "boys and girls" to a body of juvenile fiction bifurcated by gender was considered an innovation in the latter half of the nineteenth century.[1] In the United States, the transformation began gradually in the 1830s, 1840s, and 1850s with popular authors such as Jacob Abbott, William T. Adams ("Oliver Optic"), and Rebecca Sophia Clarke ("Sophie May"); gained momentum in the 1860s, 1870s, and 1880s with the contributions of Louisa May Alcott, Horatio Alger, and Mark Twain; and accelerated rapidly toward the close of the nineteenth century as a result of publishers' unflagging efforts in the fields of gender-specific periodicals, dime novels, and, especially, series books.

Although many critics have noted that "adolescent or preadolescent boys and girls historically were not encouraged to share reading material" (Vallone 122), few distinguish between books written for both genders but appropriated primarily by one or the other (such as *Robinson Crusoe*, the prototype of many a later "boy-book") and books written with a single-sex target audience in mind. An exception is Gillian Avery, who observes, "From the mid-century onwards, as juvenile publishing became an industry, what had been unisex developed into two sharply differentiated categories. Writing for boys, and writing for girls, became professions in themselves" (190). Not coincidentally, as Avery suggests, the segmentation of the juvenile fiction market closely parallels the development of children's literature as a specialized branch of publishing.[2]

This chapter documents the impact of market segmentation on juvenile fiction and popular culture through an examination of the careers of William T. Adams and Louisa May Alcott. Perhaps more than any other writers in nineteenth-century America, these two exemplify how "writing for boys, and writing for girls, became professions in themselves." As early practitioners of gendered juvenile series, Alcott and Adams together illustrate the separation of boys' and girls' reading in the United States in the middle to late nineteenth century. A side-by-side study of the authors and their juvenile series shows that Alcott was both responding to and writing against Oliver Optic's books. At the same time, Alcott's books for girls reveal that she simultaneously resisted and revised traditional models of femininity while mediating her readers' desire for conventional female plots. As a result, she brought about an important development in the history of juvenile literature: in shaping a new kind of fiction aimed specifically at adolescent girls, she ushered in realistic female characters and plots that are as distinct from previous models of femininity and womanhood in fiction as they are from the characters and plots of the boys' books against which they were inevitably defined.[3] As one nineteenth-century reviewer put it, "Miss Alcott has plainly left her mark on the literature of the period, and almost created a special style of fiction for the young" (qtd. in Alton 517).

Ultimately, the impact of these authors extended beyond the books they wrote to the audiences who read them. In this respect, it is significant that Sheryl A. Englund refers to *Little Women* as a "genre-defining 'girl's book'" (201), and Cary Ryan pronounces it "a book that redefines what it means to be born a girl" (Alcott, *Louisa May Alcott* 36), for I argue that Alcott's books for girls—like Adams's books for boys—are both genre-defining and audience-defining and that the two functions are, in fact, interdependent.[4] Furthermore, I contend that in recognizing the changing roles of boys and girls in American society and their still-crystallizing presence in the maturing literary marketplace, Adams, Alcott, and their publishers effectively mobilized these segments of the juvenile fiction market. Just as Adams helped to define not only boys' series but also the audience for boys' books, so Alcott, as the most important American author to write fiction specifically for girls at this time, was instrumental in defining, shaping, reinforcing, and revising the qualities, interests, and aspirations of the readership that constituted that market.[5] *Little Women*, Englund remarks, "has been and remains an important text, particularly for women readers: a text that has unquestionably informed nineteenth- and twentieth-century constructions of white, middle-class femininity" (216).

In the second volume of *Little Women*, Louisa May Alcott describes Jo March's efforts (see figure 2) to produce a type of story that would be both salable and respectable. After her friend (and future husband) Professor Bhaer persuades her that sensational stories are morally corrupting to young readers, Jo abandons this lucrative genre and attempts a tale in the bland, instructive style of the British writers Mary Sherwood, Maria Edgeworth, and Hannah More.[6] The result, Alcott writes, "might have been more properly called an essay or a sermon, so intensely moral was it." After failing to find a purchaser for "this didactic gem," Jo turns her hand to

> a child's story, which she could easily have disposed of if she had not been mercenary enough to demand filthy lucre for it. The only person who offered enough to make it worth while to try juvenile literature was a worthy gentleman who felt it his mission to convert all the world to his particular belief. But much as she liked to write for children, Jo could not consent to depict all her naughty boys as being eaten by bears or tossed by mad bulls, because they did not go to a particular Sabbath-school, nor all the good infants, who did go, as rewarded by every kind of bliss, from gilded ginger-bread to escorts of angels, when they departed this life with psalms or sermons on their lisping tongues. So nothing came of these trials; and Jo corked up her inkstand. (366)

Unlike her semiautobiographical protagonist, Alcott refused to cork up her own inkstand but instead went on to write numerous stories for children, beginning with fairy tales in the mid-1850s and continuing largely in the

FIGURE 2. A Roberts Brothers ad for the Little Women series showing "Jo in a Vortex" of "scribbling." The illustration is by Hammat Billings. Author's collection.

fantasy mode pioneered by Hawthorne until about 1868.[7] Finally, in the spring of that year, she hit upon a combination of style and subject matter that succeeded in earning her the stacks of "filthy lucre" she dreamed of, in addition to literary fame and respectability as the author of *Little Women*.

Following the publication of her first book, *Flower Fables* (1854), Alcott wrote to her sister Abigail May Alcott, "I hope to pass in time from fairies and fables to men and realities" (*Selected Letters* 11). The statement is revealing, as it indicates a course through children's literature that runs counter to that pursued by her Concord neighbor Nathaniel Hawthorne: it reflects Alcott's greater commitment to literary realism; it suggests a primary interest in writing for adults; and, finally, it signals a writer with little predisposition to write solely for the young.

Ironically, Louisa May Alcott did not want to write girls' books. In fact, she was rather strongly opposed to the suggestion, offered by Thomas Niles of the publisher Roberts Brothers, that she write a novel for girls. Her distaste for the project, which she recorded in a journal entry of September 1867, is amusing in retrospect:

> Niles, partner of Roberts, asked me to write a girls book. Said I'd try.
> Fuller asked me to be the Editor of "Merry's Museum." Said I'd try.
> Began at once on both new jobs, but didn't like either. (*Journals* 158)

As it happened, the task of editing *Merry's Museum*, another of Samuel Griswold Goodrich's legacies, proved to be a drain on Alcott's time and energy.[8] Consequently, her progress on the projected "girls book" was hindered as much by the demands of reading manuscripts and writing her monthly story and editorial as by her evident resistance to the project Niles proposed.

While Alcott continued to produce fairy tales, writing for *Merry's Museum* an eight-part serial with the Hawthornesque title *Will's Wonder Book*, as well as several other fantasy stories for *Youth's Companion, St. Nicholas*, and *Harper's Young People*, Niles renewed his interest in her "girls book."[9] In May 1868 his prompting elicited another tepid response from Alcott: "Father saw Mr. Niles about a fairy book. Mr. N. wants a *girls' story*, and I begin 'Little Women.' Marmee, Anna, and May all approve my plan. So I plod away, though I don't enjoy this sort of thing. Never liked girls or knew many, except my sisters; but our queer plays and experiences may prove interesting, though I doubt it" (*Journals* 165–66). The following month she again voiced her lack of enthusiasm, noting in her journal that she had "sent twelve chapters of 'L. W.' to Mr. N. He thought it *dull*; so do I. But work away and mean to try the experiment; for lively, simple books are very much needed for girls, and perhaps I can supply the need" (*Journals* 166).

Alcott's pessimism is particularly striking in light of the high praise Thomas Niles conveyed to her in a letter of 16 June 1868: "I have read the 12 chapters & am pleased—I ought to be more emphatic & say delighted,—so *please* to consider 'judgement' as favorable."[10] Alcott's mingled diffidence and indifference seem to have arisen in part from her facility with fairy tales and inexperience with the genre of girls' books and in part from her preference for boys over girls, both in literature and in life. To Alfred Whitman (one of the models for the fictional Laurie) she had confided: "There was always something very brave & beautiful to me in the sight of a boy when he first 'wakes up' & seeing the worth of life takes it up with a stout heart & resolves to carry it nobly to the end through all disappointments & seeming defeats. I was born with a boys nature & always had more sympathy for & interest in them than in girls, & have fought my fight for nearly fifteen [years] with a boys spirit under my 'bib & tucker' & a boys wrath when I got 'floored'" (*Selected Letters* 51–52).

Her friend and biographer Ednah Cheney attested, "Miss Alcott's fancy had always been for depicting the life of boys rather than girls" (155), and Whitman affirmed that "the sweetest and most attractive side of her nature" was "her real love for boys, which sprang from the boy nature that was hers in so marked a degree": "She always said she ought to have been a boy, and that she could not be was one of the many crosses she had to bear" (5–6).[11] In *Little Women*, Alcott has Jo, her alter ego, declare that she likes "boys' games and work and manners" and cannot get over her "disappointment in not being a boy" (5). Of her own childhood she wrote, "No boy could be my friend till I had beaten him in a race, and no girl if she refused to climb trees, leap fences, and be a tomboy"; at the age of thirteen, she had even recorded in her journal, "I am old for my age, and don't care much for girl's things. People think I'm wild and queer" (*Louisa May Alcott* 1, 34). Given this predilection, then, it is likely that had Niles not repeatedly pressed her to write a girls' book, Alcott might never have attempted the novel that soon debuted as *Little Women; or Meg, Jo, Beth, and Amy. The Story of Their Lives. A Girls' Book*.[12]

Thomas Niles's persistence in the face of Alcott's continuing reluctance is perhaps surprising until we consider both the unprecedented success then being enjoyed by authors of "realistic" juvenile fiction and the talent of this up-and-coming editor for assessing the literary market of the day.[13] As Englund notes, "The market was ripe for Alcott in 1868; the demand for secular juvenile books, especially novels for adolescent girls, and the extreme genre specialization of authors were new, even within the span of a few years in Alcott's own career" (202). Alcott's biography reveals that a powerful incentive to Niles (and, by extension, to Alcott) was provided by the example of popular writer Oliver Optic in the arena of boys' books. Niles's obituary in *Publishers' Weekly* (9 June 1894) reported that "the success of Oliver Optic's books suggested to Mr. Niles the thought of similar books for girls, and having been much pleased by 'Hospital Sketches,' by Louisa M. Alcott, published in 1867 by Ticknor and Fields [*sic*], he sent for Miss Alcott and engaged her for this work" ("T. Niles" 859–60). More recently, Gene Gleason has related that Niles asked Alcott to "'do something like Oliver Optic,' but for girls" (648). Madeleine Stern reconstructs the scenario in her biography of Alcott: "From his office at number 143 Washington Street he [Niles] had seen vast quantities of books by 'Oliver Optic' leaving the rooms of Lee and Shepard at number 149. There must be a similar market for a full-length novel that would be as popular among girls as 'Oliver Optic's' narratives were among boys" (168).[14]

Who was this paragon of juvenile authorship who reportedly inspired both Thomas Niles and Louisa May Alcott to experiment with realistic fiction aimed specifically at adolescent girls? With approximately 126 titles to his credit, Oliver Optic was a pen name of the staggeringly prolific Reverend William Taylor Adams (1822–97), whose most popular books sold at a rate of more than 100,000 a year (Gay, "William Taylor Adams" 16). The indefatigable Adams also wrote approximately 1,000 short stories, used at least eight different pseudonyms, and was editor at various times of *Student and Schoolmate, Our Little Ones,* and *Oliver Optic's Magazine (Our Boys and Girls)* (Gleason 647–48). By the time of his death an estimated two million copies of his books had been sold, making the former principal and Sunday School teacher one of the best-paid writers of his time as well as (according to at least one source) the most widely read (D. Jones xvi).[15] A glimpse into the career of the illustrious Oliver Optic provides insight into the role of the Little Women series in the nineteenth-century literary marketplace.

Just as Niles prompted Alcott to write a book for girls, so Adams's publisher had provided the initial impetus for the young minister to write a book for boys. Adams, whose first two books, *Hatchie the Guardian Slave*

(1852) and *In Doors and Out* (1854), were for adults, revealed a lack of confidence in the undertaking that mirrors Alcott's. According to Raymond L. Kilgour, "when he was asked to try a book for boys he declined, saying he couldn't do such a thing. Being finally persuaded, he wrote *The Boat Club* (1855), which was so popular that he could no longer resist, and followed it with five more" (*Lee and Shepard* 30). A story about two rival groups of boys and their boating adventures on a New England lake, *The Boat Club; or, The Bunkers of Rippleton. A Tale for Boys* (dated 1854), was originally published by Brown, Bazin and Co. In 1855, however, Phillips, Sampson picked it up, and the book was later republished by William Lee, who spurred Adams on to produce sequel after sequel. Lee, as a partner in the newly established firm of Lee & Shepard, capitalized on the popularity of the six-volume Oliver Optic's Library for Young People, which he helped to create, and managed to keep Adams in his stable of authors for the next forty years.

By the mid-1860s, William Lee and Charles Shepard, whose firm was to become the largest publisher of children's books in the United States from the 1860s to the late 1880s, had arrived at some important realizations concerning the juvenile fiction market.[16] First, they had discovered during the Civil War that children's books sold well even in difficult economic times. Second, they found that long-term sales were largely responsible for the success of their juvenile productions. Many of their children's books proved to be steady sellers for several generations (perhaps in part because parents and older siblings influence the reading tastes of children); in accordance with the laws of supply and demand, then, these "evergreens" appeared season after season, often updated with new bindings and enhanced, from time to time, with new illustrations (Kilgour, *Lee and Shepard*).

Lee and Shepard also evinced a rare gift for marketing. In 1884 fellow publisher J. C. Derby marveled that "they seem to know intuitively the salable qualities of a book" (519). As Kilgour explains, their strategy "was to get a wide variety of books, for children of all ages, and to advertise them to the limit" (*Lee and Shepard* 35). In addition to aggressive advertising, which "was almost modern in its abundance, its ceaseless reiteration, its frequent cleverness and equally frequent blatancy" (Kilgour, *Lee and Shepard* 137), the firm pioneered the marketing tactic of issuing as sets books that had initially been sold separately. The practice of cobbling together half a dozen loosely related books by a single author was supplemented in time by series consisting of various authors[17] as well as single-author series that were more unified in character and narrative (for example, Oliver Optic's Lake Shore Series, Young America Abroad series, and others). Sometimes the firm divided an author's juvenile books by gender and then marketed them to single-sex audiences (as shown in figure 3). More often, however, individual authors became strongly associated with either the boys' market or the girls' market: for example, Sophie May, Amanda M. Douglas, and Virginia F. Townsend wrote for girls; Elijah Kellogg, J. T. Trowbridge, and James De Mille joined Oliver Optic in writing for boys. This practice culminated in authors' series such as Kellogg's Elm Island Series and De Mille's Young Dodge Club Series and in two gender-specific publisher's series launched in the early 1870s: the American Boys' Series and the complementary American Girls' Series.

Lee & Shepard had more authors writing for boys than for girls, however, and the firm's series for boys were achieving a degree of commercial success that none of their girls' series managed to approach. In general, their boys' collections had stronger series identities and ran to many more volumes. Recognizing that the girls' market remained underdeveloped and encouraged by success with the boys' market, Lee & Shepard decided to enlist its most popular boys' author in a bold attempt to kick-start the lagging trade in girls' books. Oliver Optic's Library for Young People and the subsequent Riverdale Story Books, which William Lee had acquired from Phillips, Sampson, had been so successful with their attractive new bindings and illustrations by Hammat Billings that "Adams was summoned to the publishers' office and asked to prepare a new series for girls—which might also be read by boys!" (Kilgour, *Lee and Shepard* 35).[18]

Adams agreed to give it a try. The preface to *Little by Little* (1860), the last of the Boat Club series, anticipates the shift of audience—and illustrates differences in the literary tastes that boys and girls were presumed to possess—as Adams explains to his readers (with a significant allusion to an earlier, female Adams—i.e., Abigail, who famously entreated her husband to "Remember the Ladies"): "Paul Duncan, the hero of this volume, is a nautical young gentleman, and most of the events of the story occur upon the water; but the author hopes his young lady friends will not make faces at him on this account. The boys insisted upon having a sea story, and being the 'lords of creation,' of course they must be indulged; but the writer most solemnly promises to remember the girls next time" (6). The promised volume for girls was *Rich and Humble; or, The Mission of Bertha Grant* (1863)—the first volume of the Woodville Stories—in which Adams confirms his intent with a repetition of his favorite epithet for the masculine sex: "Agreeably to the promise made in the preface of 'Little by Little,' the author presents the following story to his young lady friends, though he confidently expects it will prove as acceptable to the embryo 'lords of creation' as to those for whom it was more especially written" (5).

What is perhaps most interesting about *Rich and Humble* (aside from the rags-to-riches plot line for which Adams's protégé Horatio Alger would become even more famous) is the explicit claim it makes to targeting a female audience. This claim is borne out in the novel itself, which revolves around a virtuous girl's journey from luxury to penury and back. Adams had been writing boys' books for more than a decade by this time, however, and he was clearly reluctant to abandon his primary audience. As earlier entries in the field of children's literature suggested and the Boat Club series undeniably proved, books for boys already constituted a viable sector of the juvenile fiction market, whereas girls' books were as yet something of an unknown quantity. Despite claiming to address a female readership, therefore, *Rich and Humble* is designated "A Story for Young People" in the series subtitled A Library for Boys and Girls. Moreover, in his preface to the volume, Adams addresses male and female readers in turn, directing the attention of the two groups of readers to different aspects of the text:

> The girls will find that Bertha Grant is not only a very good girl, but that her life is animated by a lofty purpose, which all may have, though they fail to achieve the visible triumphs that rewarded the exertions of the heroine of "Rich and Humble."
>
> The boys will find that Richard Grant was not always a good boy because his life was not animated by a lofty purpose; but the author hopes, in another volume, to present him in a higher moral aspect, and more worthy the imitation of those who, like him, have wandered from the true path. (5)

Aware that his readers would be most interested in characters of their own sex, Adams was careful to include in the novel enough male characters (including a rafting ragamuffin who bears a surface resemblance to Huckleberry Finn) and enough sport and rowdiness to satisfy Oliver Optic's established audience of boys. (In fact, Lee & Shepard later reissued the novel as volume 33 of their American Boys' Series.) *Rich and Humble* was not an immediate success; still, the long-term sales of this domestic novel eventually outpaced many of Adams's boys' books (Kilgour, *Lee and*

## MRS. LESLIE'S JUVENILE SERIES,

### FOR GIRLS.

Put up in a neat box. Price $3.60 a set, or 90 cts. a vol. Comprising

**LITTLE AGNES.**

**This little book is an entertaining and instructive story of a girl whose patience, industry, and fidelity raised her to eminence, honor, and happiness.**

**TRYING TO BE USEFUL.**

**A narrative showing the happy results of worthy resolution and endeavor.**

**I'LL TRY.**

**An exhibition of the successful reward of perseverance in the acquisition of fortune and fame.**

**ART AND ARTLESSNESS.**

**In this admirable volume the virtues which adorn female loveliness appear in bold and enviable contrast with the arts of coquetry and deception.**

---

The above elegant series have been recently issued, and are written in an attractive style, and calculated to interest the young. A sound moral tone pervades each volume, and in point of interest and instruction they are unsurpassed by any series published. Each volume contains, on an average, 260 pages, 16mo, is elegantly illustrated, bound in muslin, and entirely distinct from the rest.

---

LEE & SHEPARD, PUBLISHERS, BOSTON.

FIGURE 3. Lee & Shepard ads from *Rich and Humble* by Oliver Optic, promoting Madeline Leslie's books for boys and books for girls. Courtesy, University of Minnesota Libraries.

*Shepard* 39–40), providing persuasive evidence that a ready market for girls' series books awaited those prepared to meet the demands of a female readership. Nevertheless, Adams seems not to have repeated the experiment of focusing on a primarily female audience.[19]

Of course, fiction for boys was preceded by practical advice books for boys;[20] so, too, girls had their own handbooks, conduct books, and lesson books such as Lydia Maria Child's *The Little Girl's Own Book* (1831); *The American Girl's Book* (1831), edited by Eliza Leslie; Mrs. A.J. Graves's *The Young Lady's Book of Good Examples* (1848); and Lydia Sigourney's *Letters to Young Ladies* (1833) and *The Girls' Reading-Book* (1838). In addition, the "courtesy novels" of the late eighteenth and early nineteenth centuries offered female readers a distinct hybridized form. Linda C. Hunt, writing of the British scene, explains: "As the novel developed, the courtesy book could not compete with the novels from the circulating library which were so much more entertaining, and so the courtesy book writers attempted to liven their teachings by fictional devices borrowed from the novel; at the same time some of the novelists attempted to justify and dignify the new genre by including the moral and utilitarian material of the courtesy books" (18). In spite of these early beginnings, however, realistic fiction written specifically for the amusement of young girls was still uncommon a full decade after the appearance of Oliver Optic's books for boys. Although Lee & Shepard exhibited customary foresight in staking out a corner of the girls' market, most publishers apparently did not yet consider it necessary or sufficiently profitable to publish books designed exclusively for this particular subset of readers.

One reason for the recognition of boys as a separate audience well before girls was that the boys' market was seen as including girls, whereas the girls' market was commonly thought to exclude boys. In fact, it was a common perception that boys *required* a separate body of literature. A Hurst & Co. advertisement from the early twentieth century asserted that "Oliver Optic has the faculty of writing books full of dash and energy, such as healthy boys want and *need*, yet free from any objectionable dime-novel sensationalism" (qtd. in Adams, *Try Again*, n.p.; emphasis added). In 1879 Thomas Wentworth Higginson similarly emphasized boys' needs when he defended Adams's books by declaring: "If . . . nothing takes hold of a neglected Irish boy, for instance, like Oliver Optic's stories, then I would give him Oliver Optic in copious draughts, and give it at public expense; he will be all the less likely to supply himself with *The Police Gazette* at his own cost" (qtd. in Kilgour, *Lee and Shepard* 196). In contrast, girls could enjoy domestic tales as well as adventure stories directed at a male audience. The popular British author Charlotte M. Yonge, whose family story *The Daisy Chain; or, Aspirations* (1856) influenced *Little Women* (P. Hunt, *Children's Literature* 191; see also Crisler 35), accordingly explained her decision to include a category of "boys' books" without a complementary listing of "girls' books" in her compendium *What Books to Give and What to Lend* (1887): "The mild tales that girls will read simply to pass away the time are ineffective with [boys]," but the works in this catalogue "are not merely suited to lads, for though girls will often greatly prefer a book about the other sex, boys almost universally disdain books about girls" (29–30).[21]

Yonge's view is corroborated by the American Robert M. Lovett, who, in his 1926 article "A Boy's Reading Fifty Years Ago," confessed that although reading girls' books was a habit he "fell into . . . in a period of starvation," it was one of which he had been "ashamed" (335).[22] Some boys and men undoubtedly read girls' fiction surreptitiously (Stoneley 9), but girls seemed to feel no compunction to disguise a liking for boys' books (see Hunter 80). Nevertheless, Frances Willard—reformer, icon of the Woman's Christian Temperance Union, and one of the most famous women in nineteenth-century America—recalled of her childhood reading: "I . . . got hold of a story book, 'The Prairie Bird,' another called 'Wild Western Scenes,' and a third, 'The Green-Mountain Boys,' and secretly devoured all three without leave or license. They . . . produced on my imagination the same effect that they would upon a boy's. Above all things in earth or sky I wanted to be, and meant to be, a mighty hunter." Willard goes on to say that her father had no objections to her reading of *Robinson Crusoe* and *Swiss Family Robinson* "because they were not 'miserable love stories,' as he said—for at these he drew the line firmly and would not allow them in the house" (50–51).

Alcott was well aware of the double standard, for in *Little Women* she has Jo read boys' books (a significant but little noticed counterpoint to her oft-noted reading of *The Wide, Wide World* in the backyard apple tree), and even delicate Beth finds occasion to feel "glad that she had read one of the boys' books in which Jo delighted" (152). Even well into the twentieth century, a commentator on "trends in children's books" announced that "librarians report an appetite for so-called boys' books by girls, but no corresponding eagerness by boys" (Evans 337). Given these attitudes toward boys' and girls' reading, it is not difficult to see why entertaining novels conceived specifically for boys emerged earlier than comparable books designed for girls.

The belated discovery of girls as a separate audience, in spite of increased gender stereotyping after 1850 and "sex-typing" within households (Demos 103, 107), was also influenced by a persistent misapprehension of what girls wanted to—or should—read. Although Oliver Optic was not without critics (especially late in his career), his tales of outdoor adventure for boys received widespread praise. Long after the fading of the notion that boys must be spoon-fed didactic and moral tales of the type Alcott satirizes in *Little Women*, stories for girls continued to consist largely of sugarcoated lessons in piety and femininity. Many seemed to agree with Charlotte Yonge's assessment that "if the boy is not to betake himself to 'Jack Sheppard' literature [sensational crime fiction], he must be beguiled by wholesome adventure," whereas "if the girl is not to study the 'penny dreadful,' her notions must be refined by the tale of high romance or pure pathos" (6). One result of this double standard was that authors, publishers, and parents continued to encourage girls to keep to a carefully restricted diet consisting largely of pious and sentimental narratives (such as Martha Finley's *Elsie Dinsmore* novels, while permitting boys to feast their fancies on fast-paced stories of travel and adventure. Another result, however, was that girls eagerly appropriated their brothers' books because, as Salmon averred, "they [could] get in boys' books what they [could not] get in the majority of their own—stirring plot and lively movement" (524). In her authoritative study of early American girlhood, Jane Hunter cites "a small survey of girls in the West aged fourteen to eighteen" in which a "solid majority" reported that they "preferred adventure stories to 'anything about girls'" (80).

The discrepancy between boys' and girls' literary fare reflects the divergent paths boys and girls traced in the nineteenth century "through the separate-sphere economies of the domestic and commercial" (Vallone 122). As Anne Scott MacLeod points out, "Realistic children's literature nearly always bends toward socializing the young, imparting values, and distinguishing desirable behavior from the deplorable" (*American Childhood* 54). Boys' and girls' novels of the nineteenth century accomplished these tasks through plot as well as characterization: "Where the boys' books increasingly revolved around a young man's encounter with the outside world—in the army, in the West, in the city—and around active, extroverted adventure, girls' novels focused on character and relationships, as, of course, girls' lives did as they approached womanhood" (MacLeod, *American Childhood* 14).[23] Salmon's 1886 article "What Girls Read" explicitly prescribed the manner in which juvenile literature should prepare British children for their future roles as grown men and women: "Boys' literature of a sound kind ought to build up men. Girls' literature ought to help to build up women. If in choosing the books that boys shall read it is necessary to remember that we are choosing mental food for the future chiefs of a great race, it is equally important not to forget in choosing books for girls that we are choosing mental food for the future wives and mothers of that race" (526). Literature for American children had its own cultural work to perform in preparing boys and girls for adulthood, and for girls this meant teaching them that a woman's most valuable contribution was the use of her feminine influence for virtuous ends within the context of the domestic sphere.

Alcott's entry into the largely untried arena of realistic fiction for girls marked an important advance in the social function of girls' reading. Responding positively to the ongoing debate over women's role in society and to a "cultural revolution" in the way middle-class adolescent females thought about themselves (Hunter 2), *Little Women* and its sequels acknowledge girls as more than future wives and mothers: they advocate education and career opportunities for women and celebrate the individuality of spirited, intelligent, independent young women. In *Little Women*, which was enthusiastically hailed as "a capital story for girls" ("New Publications" 857), two of the three sisters who reach adulthood pursue careers other than or in addition to that of homemaker: Jo as a writer and Amy as an artist.[24]

In subsequent volumes of the series, concern with female education, training, and professionalization is even more pronounced.[25] In *An Old-Fashioned Girl* (1870), for example, Polly—whom Alcott described as "not . . . a perfect model, but . . . a possible improvement upon the Girl of the Period" (v)—supports herself as a young single woman in Boston by teaching music to children. In *Eight Cousins* (1875), Alcott shows the positive effects of a progressive education on a young girl—an education that includes arithmetic and physiology in addition to culinary and needle arts. She pursues this theme further in *Rose in Bloom* (1876), in which the heroine defers thoughts of courtship and marriage, resolving, "I won't have anything to do with love till I prove that I am something beside a house-keeper and baby-tender!" (10). Finally, in *Jo's Boys* (1886), Alcott conceives of Laurence College as a coeducational institution where the girls are encouraged to be career-minded, like Nan, a student of medicine. Even when working within the traditional boundaries of female roles, Alcott used her children's stories as a platform from which to lobby for improvements in girls' education. Of *Eight Cousins*, for example, she argued: "Young girls in America do not get a good education in various respects, even though much is taught to them. They know nothing of health care, or of housekeeping, and are presented into society too early. My story is intended to encourage a better plan of child-rearing, and my heroine shows that such a plan is feasible" (*Selected Letters* 194). As a girl, Louisa May Alcott may have been "the opposite of everything her family—and nineteenth-century New England—required a young woman to be," as the editor of her youthful diary, Cary Ryan, put it (*Louisa May Alcott* 1). Nevertheless, as the spectacular popularity of the Little Women series attests, her female protagonists represented precisely what the next generation of young women desired of their heroines in fiction.

Ironically, Oliver Optic, the quintessential boys' author of the mid-nineteenth century, may have inspired Alcott not only with the marketplace success of his books for boys but also with his creation of determined female characters who offered readers more than a lesson in docility and daintiness, matrimony and motherhood. *Rich and Humble*, in which he professed to address a female audience, was actually preceded, in 1858, by *Poor and Proud; or, The Fortunes of Katy Redburn*, a story about an eleven-year-old girl who raises herself and her mother, an invalid, from poverty through her own industry and discovers in the end that she is an heiress.[26]

*Poor and Proud* is hardly a revolutionary story, but its protagonist does have a kind of perseverance and independence that was still rare among female characters in juvenile literature; in his preface, Adams characterizes her as "a smart girl" (v).[27] Yet even as the spirited Katy is a substantial improvement over the earlier stock of nineteenth-century juvenile heroines, Alcott far surpassed Adams in her creation of the March sisters, and especially in her delineation of Jo. Jo March—boyish, impetuous, high-spirited, and quick-tempered—represents a new kind of heroine in juvenile fiction, one who would resonate strongly with generations of female readers to come.[28]

Although Alcott attributed the success of *Little Women* to its realistic portrayal of girls' lives, "not a bit sensational, but simple and true" (*Journals* 166), Jo, the central character, has typically been regarded as an exceptional rather than a typical example of nineteenth-century girlhood. Certainly, she flouts the characteristics ascribed by convention to nineteenth-century heroines: "Round shoulders had Jo, big hands and feet, a fly-away look to her clothes, and the uncomfortable appearance of a girl who was rapidly shooting up into a woman, and didn't like it" (*Little Women* 6). Picking up on this unfeminine description, a reviewer for the *Spectator* noted that "the writer's strength is principally given to the portraiture of Jo, *alias* Josephine, a boy, we may call her, who by some misadventure finds himself or herself in the shape of a girl" (*Little Women*, Norton Critical Edition 549). As MacLeod has recently argued, however, tomboyism, followed by its forced abandonment in the middle to late teens, was far more widespread among American girls of the nineteenth century than convention has led us to suppose. Drawing on diaries, letters, and memoirs as well as fictional accounts, MacLeod argues that girls of the later nineteenth century often enjoyed the same kinds of rough-and-tumble activities as their brothers until such time (typically between thirteen and fifteen) as society demanded that they become young ladies. Alluding to Carol Ryrie Brink's award-winning novel *Caddie Woodlawn* (1935), MacLeod writes:

> Far from being unique, what I think of as the *Caddie Woodlawn* Syndrome seems to have been common in America during that period. In a surprising number of memoirs is an account of just such an experience of childhood freedom followed by just the same closing of the doors as the girl neared puberty. If autobiography can be accepted as any kind of sample of common practice, then it would seem that in a good many households the sharp differentiation between appropriate behavior and activity for prepubescent boys and girls was not as firmly applied as we often suppose. Many American women could and did look back to their childhood years as a period of physical and psychic freedom unmatched by anything in their later life. ("*Caddie Woodlawn* Syndrome" 99–100)

MacLeod's research helps account for the popularity of *Little Women*, and especially of the beloved Jo. [29] Not only does Jo's character exhibit many of the traits of MacLeod's tomboys—independence, courage, an adventurous spirit, and a love of the outdoors—but the problem with which Jo contends throughout *Little Women* was evidently a pervasive and enduring one for American girls: the problem of how to bridge the gap between the "unmatched" liberty of girlhood and the potentially stifling constraints of womanhood.[30]

This overarching concern in Alcott's girls' books accorded well with the momentum of the juvenile book market, which demanded of every popular children's novel a sequel. In writing *Little Women*, Alcott quickly established a narrative pattern that she repeatedly reverted to in the eight volumes that ultimately formed the Little Women series. According to this pattern, Alcott would first introduce as her heroine a young girl on the brink of adolescence. After presenting, as a series of episodes, the ins and outs, ups and downs, of American girl-life, she would then reintroduce her heroine as a young woman in a continuation or sequel set several years later, contingent on the popularity of the initial part. Thus Jo's declaration in the first chapter of *Little Women*, "I hate to think I've got to grow up, and be Miss March, and wear long gowns, and look prim as a China-aster!" (5), presents a conflict that naturally carries over to *Little Women, Part Two* (1869), set three years later, when Jo has reached the age of nineteen.[31] Similarly, *An Old-Fashioned Girl* (1870) originally consisted of only seven chapters (published serially in *Merry's Museum*, July–December 1869), which take place during Polly Milton's fifteenth year. As Alcott states in her preface, however, "the demand for a sequel, in beseeching little letters that made refusal impossible, rendered it necessary to carry my heroine boldly forward some six or seven years into the future" (n.p.), a feat she accomplished in twelve additional chapters. In *Little Men: Life at Plumfield with Jo's Boys* (1871), in which Jo's character has matured and stabilized, the action shifts to a younger generation of boys and girls. Its sequel, *Jo's Boys and How They Turned Out* (1886), which begins ten years after the conclusion of *Little Men*, adheres to the pattern, following not only the progress of the boys—Dan, Nat, Demi, and their friends—but also of the girls, most notably "Naughty Nan," who has grown into "Dr. Nan." By the time she introduced her readers to thirteen-and-a-half-year-old Rose Campbell in *Eight Cousins; or, The Aunt-Hill* (1875), the pattern was so entrenched that Alcott was able to announce in her preface her intention to follow it with a second volume, "which shall attempt to show the Rose in Bloom" (n.p.). According to its preface, *Rose in Bloom* (1876), in which Alcott reintroduced her heroine (along with her friend Phebe and her seven boy cousins) two years advanced in age, "was simply written in fulfillment of a promise; hoping to afford some amusement, and perhaps here and there a helpful hint, to other roses getting ready to bloom" (n.p.).[32]

Of course, not all of Alcott's girl heroines can properly be termed tomboys; nevertheless, in each case, their stories serve to illustrate the wisdom of an observation put into the mouth of Uncle Alec in *Rose in Bloom*: "To me there is something almost pathetic in the sight of a young girl standing on the threshold of the world, so innocent and hopeful, so ignorant of all that lies before her, and usually so ill prepared to meet the ups and downs of life. We do our duty better by the boys; but the poor little women are seldom provided with any armor worth having; and, sooner or later, they are sure to need it, for every one must fight her own battle, and only the brave and strong can win" (8). The fact that each of these narratives elides the period, ranging from two to six years in length, during which the girl develops into a young woman underscores the unusually difficult and perhaps forced nature of the transition between childhood and womanhood in nineteenth-century America.[33] Yet despite these absences of several years, Alcott's heroines do not return from the hiatus ready-made, like butterflies emerging from their chrysalises. Instead, Alcott continues to explore the process of becoming, rather than being, an adult.[34] Her silence regarding the pivotal years of adolescence suggests that, for her, the crucial task was not to chart every step of the journey, or artificially compress a girl's "coming of age" into a single dramatic moment; it was rather to reassure her readers as to what lay on the other side of the daunting divide between girlhood and womanhood, to help resolve the tomboy's bind of reforming or remaining a child, and to illustrate that marriage was only one of many alternatives.[35] This must have been a reassuring message to the "multitude" of young female readers Henry James credited with sustaining the literary marketplace in "The Future of the Novel": "Nothing is so striking in a survey of this field, and nothing to be so much borne in mind, as that the larger part of the great multitude that sustains the teller and the publisher of tales is constituted by boys and girls; by girls in especial, if we apply the term to the later stages of life of the innumerable women who, under modern arrangements, increasingly fail to marry—fail, apparently, even, largely, to desire to. It is not too much to say of many of these that they live in a great measure by the immediate aid of the novel" (*Literary Criticism* 1: 100–101).

The practice of spinning off sequels and series was a marketing innovation that flourished in the late nineteenth and early twentieth centuries—an indication that authors and publishers were becoming quite adept at catering to the demands of the marketplace. William T. Adams and his publisher, Lee & Shepard, were masters of the technique. According to Kilgour, "Oliver Optic, for better or for worse, was certainly the great initiator of this method of mass production of books for children" (*Lee and Shepard* 270), a strategy that became standard practice in the years following the Civil War. Kilgour explains: "It was the appearance of similar series on every publisher's lists that provoked the comment from *The Independent*, two years later: 'The fashion of publishing books in sets, which has been growing for some time, seems now to be at its hight [*sic*]. Every other book is issued in some library or other; and since publishers follow, rather than create public taste, we infer that buyers prefer to purchase books of whose general nature they can tell something by the title of the series to which they belong'" (*Lee and Shepard* 167–68).[36] Of course, publishers do more than merely *follow* public taste, and to Lee & Shepard belongs much of the responsibility for creating, or encouraging, the trend for authors to write and publishers to package juvenile books in series and sets.

If Thomas Niles had indeed persuaded Alcott to emulate Oliver Optic and write books directed specifically at a single-sex juvenile audience, it is likely that he also had Adams's success with series in mind when he urged the author of *Little Women* to follow up with subsequent volumes of the "March Family Chronicles." Indeed, Niles had conceived of *Little Women* as a multivolume endeavor from the time he reviewed Alcott's first submission of twelve chapters and recognized that one book in a series could "be ever so great an aid to the sale of the others." In his letter of 16 June 1868, he had urged, "And now while we are about business, wont you be kind enough to set your price in this story, in an outright sum, the succeeding volumes, if this one prospers, to be furnished at the same." A month later, convinced that "it will 'hit', which means . . . it will sell well," Niles advised Alcott that "[a] chapter could well be added, in which allusions might be made to something in the future."[37]

To her uncle, Alcott (affecting the dialect of the Pickwickian Sam Weller) complained in a letter of February 1869, "I [d]ont like sequels, & dont think No 2 will be as popular as No 1, but publishers are very *perwerse* & wont let authors have thier [*sic*] way so my little women must grow up & be married off in a very stupid style" (*Selected Letters* 121–22); nevertheless, she obliged her editor with the new material.[38] Still Niles persevered with further requests for additional stories that might piggyback on the success of *Little Women*. When the second part of *Little Women* was still in press, he was already urging Alcott "to furnish the 'New Story by Miss Alcott'" (which he evidently was already advertising in a circular) and "to start another for publication in October or November." At the same time, he sought creative ways to incorporate her *Hospital Sketches* (previously published by James Redpath) into the Little Women series, suggesting that this earlier book "might make a very Companionable Volume to 'Little Women,'" and advising, "I am clearly of opinion that all should be brought out together, looking ahead to a *uniform set* of volumes."[39] As a reviewer for the *Galaxy* observed, Alcott had "struck a vein that will bear working" (*Little Women*, Norton Critical Edition 552), and Niles had no intention of letting someone else hit the paydirt.

Alcott's next girls' book was *An Old-Fashioned Girl*, and no sooner was it published than Niles was once again persuading Alcott of the need to satisfy her existing audience by following up with *Little Men*. After citing impressive initial sales figures for *An Old-Fashioned Girl*, he informed her that "anxious enquires are being made for 'Little Men.'"[40] Nine months later he persisted:

> It is now a year since "Old Fash Girl" was published and it wont do to let the poker get cold before striking again.
>
> It is my impression that a new work by author of "Little Women" if published in *May* would find the people ripe for it, with a dearth of *any popular* books to *aid* it, and I feel quite certain that you could present nothing more acceptable to the little million of admirers of "Jo" than a history of her boys. "Little Men; or the History of Jo's Boys" how's that for a taking title—or simply "Jo's Boys" wouldn't be bad.[41]

When an additional two months had elapsed, Niles's impatience became evident: "I am daily, nay, hourly, expecting to hear from you with word as to 'Little Men.' I have printed and circulated the enclosed circular by thousands all over the U.S. & the country will be ripe for the book before we can get it out."[42]

After completing *Little Men* in the spring of 1871, Alcott turned her attention to short fiction, her novel *Work: A Story of Experience* (1873), and the four remaining novels in the Little Women series; but eventually she obliged her readers with *Jo's Boys*, once again at the prompting of her editor, who was convinced that the book would "make an additional *furore*" and was "needed to keep up the enthusiasm & renew the demand for 'Little Men' & 'Little Women.'" The enterprising Niles even devised a spin-off series—*Aunt Jo's Scrap-Bag* in six volumes (consisting mostly of short fiction), published from 1872 to 1882—and succeeded in bringing out a uniform eight-volume Little Women set ("about as pretty a set of books as you would wish to look at"), as well as a special illustrated edition of the series' flagship novel.[43]

Alcott readily acknowledged her indebtedness to Niles in establishing her as a famous writer of books for girls, even referring to *Little Women* as a book that was "very hastily written to order" (*Selected Letters* 118). Her debt to Oliver Optic and the Lee & Shepard mode of mass production and marketing remained largely unacknowledged, however, both by Alcott and by her publisher. In fact, Alcott evidently came to regard Adams and his endless series books with contempt. In *An Old-Fashioned Girl* she presents a caricature of contemporary boys' books, depicting Tom Shaw "absorbed in one of those delightful books in which boys are cast away on desert islands, where every known fruit, vegetable and flower is in its prime all the year round; or, lost in boundless forests, where the young heroes have thrilling adventures, kill impossible beasts, and, when the author's invention gives out, suddenly find their way home, laden with tiger skins, tame buffaloes and other pleasing trophies of their prowess" (77). More pointedly, in *Eight Cousins* she attacks sensational stories as "*optical* delusions" and complains about the use of slang in popular boys' books—a rhetorical sally that provoked a cutting riposte from Adams.[44] As the parallel and intertwining careers of Louisa May Alcott and Oliver Optic reveal, however, both authors succeeded in the rapidly expanding literary marketplace by staking out newly demarcated segments of the juvenile fiction market defined principally by gender and age.[45] Both authors effectively responded to the literary tastes and interests of their target audiences, and both paid heed to the aspirations of their readers, as well as to the expectations society placed upon them. Their books were created and shaped by the markets they addressed, and, in turn, they shaped, defined, and fostered a sense of community among these respective groups of readers.[46]

In *Woman's Fiction: A Guide to Novels by and about Women, 1820–1870*, Nina Baym comments on the nearly simultaneous publication of Martha Finley's *Elsie Dinsmore* in 1867 and *Little Women* the following year, both books inaugurating series that would become spectacularly successful. According to Baym: "These two publishing events marked . . . the decline of woman's fiction . . . because they represent the transformation of woman's fiction into girl's fiction. The story of feminine heroism now becomes a didactic instrument for little girls" (296). Far from signaling the demise of women's fiction, however, the incidents Baym points to were actually part of a much larger progression encompassing both the rise to dominance of female readers in the nineteenth-century literary marketplace and the ascendancy of girls in the expanding market for juvenile books, in conjunction with the gradual supplanting of "True Woman" by "New Woman" as the current model of femininity. Rather than representing an attenuation

66

or diminishing of women's fiction, the publication of *Little Women* and its sequels heralded a watershed in U.S. social history: girls had at last come into their own as a discrete, viable, cohesive component of the American literary enterprise.

⚘ ⚘ ⚘

The developments in juvenile publishing ushered in by Oliver Optic and his publisher, and successfully exploited by Louisa May Alcott and her publisher, engendered conflicting reactions among critics and literary historians. As Kilgour argues, the immense success of Lee & Shepard's authors "gave unparalleled impetus to the widespread publishing of children's books; it was not only Louisa Alcott and Roberts Brothers who were urged on by L&S's burst of energy; authors and publishers all over the eastern United States responded to the challenge, to the great benefit of American children" (*Lee and Shepard* 280).[47] On the other hand, the anonymous author of an article published in the *Atlantic Monthly* in 1865 reported that "English critics of our juvenile literature say that much of it seems written for the market and counting-room rather than for the nursery and playground" ("Books for Our Children" 726).[48] Although the writer does not identify books or authors by name, it is quite likely, given the date of the article, that the objectionable books were those of the ubiquitous Oliver Optic and his imitators. The popularity of the juvenile series books of the latter half of the nineteenth century also paved the way for a subsequent generation of series books that were unambiguously condemned by the so-called "custodians of culture." According to Kilgour: "The credit, or the blame, if one prefers, for the series idea may rest squarely upon L&S: although their series were conceived as definite sets of from four to six books, in general, and were often unified in theme, they certainly, by their great success, suggested all the 'Rover Boys' and 'Tom Swifts' that were to follow, to the despair of librarians and the apparent delight of hordes of youngsters" (*Lee and Shepard* 168).[49] Whether for good or ill, however, the practices of segmenting the juvenile fiction market by gender and age, publishing juvenile books in readily identifiable series, and responding to the demands of young readers for realistic, entertaining reading matter proved to be much more than passing trends in the American literary marketplace.[50]

Writing in 1984 of nineteenth-century juvenile periodicals, R. Gordon Kelly observes that by the turn of the twentieth century "the working assumption of common youthful interests increasingly gave way to the assumption that interests, after the ages of nine or ten, were inescapably linked to biology; there was not one audience of 'youth' but two: boys and girls" (*Children's Periodicals* xxv–xxvi).[51] Although Kelly's observation applies equally to the audiences for juvenile books, there was at least a fleeting perception at the turn of the century that whereas the division between adults' and children's reading was permanent, the gulf between boys' and girls' reading was beginning to narrow.[52] In *Children's Books and Reading* (1907), Montrose J. Moses reminisced, "There was a time when girls' literature and boys' literature were more clearly differentiated, one from the other" (164–65). Moses unhesitatingly attributed the apparent conflation of boys' and girls' books to the increasing participation of girls in recreational activities traditionally reserved for boys, remarking that "their near approach has been due to a common interest in outdoor exercises" (164–65). In a similar spirit, Everett T. Tomlinson, writing for the *Atlantic Monthly* in 1900, elaborated on what he regarded as a merging of boys' and girls' interests:

> It may be well to note one change which has already become apparent, and that is the disappearance of the distinction between books for boys and those for girls. A few years ago this difference was marked, and books for girls were almost as numerous as those for boys. To-day the latter far outnumber the former, and there is every prospect that the distinction will almost, if not completely, disappear. And the explanation is not difficult to find.
>
> To-day, while few boys can be found who will read books written especially for girls, the converse is markedly true, and the sisters read their brothers' books almost with the avidity of the boys themselves. And the cause is plain. The days when girls remained indoors and worked samplers and guarded their complexions have ceased to be. Over the golf links and on the tennis courts the boys and girls contend together. At every college game girls are present, and follow the contestants with an interest and understanding as keen as that of their brothers. In schools and colleges for girls, crews and basket-ball teams are common to-day, while in the use of the bicycle the girls certainly are not far behind their companions and friends of the other sex. All this has had a marked effect upon the character of the books they read, as well as upon the lives they live, and as a natural consequence the literature which appeals to the one class is not without interest to the other. (698)

Although girls' books were never subsumed by boys' books, as these critics predicted, the comments of Moses and Tomlinson reflect their per-

ception of changing roles for girls in modern society, and the early twentieth century did see the appearance of such series as the Automobile Girls,
the Motor Girls, the Radio Girls, the Ranch Girls, the Flying Girls, and
the Moving Picture Girls, all of which reflected exciting new avenues for
young women, vocational as well as avocational, both in the world of imagination and in real life.[53] In reality the gap between boys' and girls' reading
continued to widen, however, becoming nearly as complete in the first half
of the twentieth century as that between adults' and children's books.[54]
And, although juvenile publishing expanded enormously from the 1850s
onwards, the evidence suggests that the reading habits of young people
in America became increasingly specialized throughout the twentieth century. As authors and publishers became more accustomed to thinking of
children as a distinct market and more systematic about anticipating and
influencing the wants of young readers, boys and girls were encouraged
and enabled to select from the growing array of books written and marketed specifically for their age and gender groups,[55] and, in some cases,
tailored to their social and cultural backgrounds.

# Chapter Three

## BOY'S LIFE

A boy's life is not all comedy; much of the tragic enters into it.
—Mark Twain, *Chapters from My Autobiography* (1907)

ALTHOUGH AMERICAN boys had a literature of their own from the 1850s on, not until 1876 did a text appear that would acquire the stature among books for boys that *Little Women* had gained among books for girls. Yet the success of *The Adventures of Tom Sawyer* was not immediate, and the inevitable sequels—of which there were several—were a long time coming. Like Louisa May Alcott, Samuel Clemens only reluctantly and with evident resistance embraced the audience with which he was to become most powerfully associated. Not only did he not intend to write a book for young people when he began *Tom Sawyer*, but even after completing the manuscript, he failed to recognize it as a boys' book. Moreover, although readers of the manuscript draft managed to persuade him that he had written a boys' book, Clemens remained ambivalent about writing for a juvenile audience, bucking the trend toward specialized markets and bridling against the demands of the genre. In fact, the Tom and Huck stories were plagued by problems arising in part from this ambivalence: the infamous controversies over *Adventures of Huckleberry Finn* (1884), the critical failure of *Tom Sawyer Abroad* (1894), the commercial disappointment of *Tom Sawyer, Detective* (1896), and Clemens's chronic inability to complete other sequels—including "Huck Finn and Tom Sawyer among the Indians" (1884), "Tom Sawyer's Conspiracy" (1897), and "Tom Sawyer's Gang Plans a Naval Battle" (c. 1900). I argue that Clemens's difficulties with the Tom and Huck narratives can be linked to continuing tensions among the author's material and style, the expectations and demands of a juvenile audience, the expectations and demands of the guardians of that audience, and the established conventions of the genre. Although, in time, Clemens became known as the boys' author par excellence—and Huck and Tom the quintessential "good bad boys" of fiction[1]—an analysis of his career as boys'-book author reveals recurring, persistent discontinuities and disjunctions among audience, genre, and text as he attempted, over a period of more than twenty years, to exploit and perpetuate the popularity of Tom and Huck in the ever expanding juvenile fiction market.

In many respects, Clemens was highly sensitive to the demands of the literary marketplace, attuned to both the nature of his audience and the literary fare it favored. Deeply invested in the business of publishing, as well as the craft of writing, he founded his own publishing company to produce and sell his books as well as those of other authors. It behooved him doubly, therefore, to know something about his readers and to be able to anticipate their tastes. But Clemens did not begin by publishing his own work. Rather, he resorted to professional self-publication only after falling prey to the machinations of an unscrupulous publisher.

Unlike *Little Women*, the product of one of the most fruitful author-editor relationships in American history, *The Adventures of Tom Sawyer* came into being despite an author-publisher alliance marred by deception, distrust, and disillusionment. As shown earlier, the relationship between Thomas Niles and Louisa May Alcott, like that between Lee & Shepard and Oliver Optic, was a business partnership in which the two parties worked together to assess and meet the demands of the literary marketplace. In contrast, Clemens frequently found himself working at cross-purposes with Elisha Bliss, proprietor of the American Publishing Company. Without question, Bliss was ruthless in his business dealings: according to Hamlin Hill, "He was coldly calculating, he was happy to cheat both authors and customers with a repertory of the worst tricks of salesmanship, and he apparently juggled books with the skill of a master accountant" (18). Clemens's own description of Bliss, even though tempered by the passage of years, is positively rancorous: he was, Clemens recalled, "a tall, lean, skinny, yellow, toothless bald-headed, rat-eyed professional liar and scoundrel. . . . He was a most repulsive creature" (*Mark Twain's Letters to His Publishers* 1).[2] Even many years after Bliss's death, the most charitable remark Clemens could bring himself to make about his erstwhile publisher was that, were it possible, he would send Bliss a fan—as a means of relief from the diabolical heat of his otherworldly destination! (*Autobiography* 227). Given this undisguised loathing, it is surprising to some that Clemens stuck with Bliss as long as he did. The fact that Clemens was unaware for quite some time of Bliss's dishonesty helps account for their continuing alliance. More important, however, Clemens was convinced that subscription publishing afforded the best sales channel for his books—he declared to William Dean

Howells that "anything but subscription publishing is printing for private circulation" (qtd. in Kaplan 62)—and the American Publishing Company was the undisputed leader in that mode of distribution.

Although subscription publishing was nearly phased out by the early years of the twentieth century (the American Publishing Company discontinued door-to-door soliciting in 1904), throughout the eighteenth and nineteenth centuries it provided a highly effective means of getting books to readers. In fact, "all of the large [Gilded Age] houses dealt in subscription books, and considered them the most profitable part of their business" (Sheehan 194). The subscription method solved several problems that confronted publishers in an age when the majority of the population lived in rural areas, far from bookstores, and when limited means of transportation prevented the efficient distribution of books. Rather than relying on customers to seek out their books, subscription publishers brought their books—or at least prospectuses and samples—directly to the doors of prospective buyers. Publishers' agents traveled the various regions in which potential markets were believed to exist, canvassing the local populations in advance of publication and fulfilling the orders once the complete books had been printed and bound.[3]

This method of selling and distributing books had several advantages. First, because the publisher brought the product directly to the consumer rather than waiting for the consumer to come to the product, sales of individual books could be much higher than in the trade. The *New York Times* of 21 January 1870 remarked, "It is one of the mysteries of the publishers' craft which only they can explain, that subscription books have a larger sale than those which see the light in an ordinary way" (qtd. in "New Subscription Books for 1870" 113). Clemens concurred with the assessment that subscription books had larger sales, boasting in a letter of 18 September 1887 to his nephew (and then publisher) Charles L. Webster, "We can sell 3 copies of *any* book where the trade can sell 1" (*MTLP* 233)—an estimate considerably lower than that touted in the promotional materials for *The Adventures of Tom Sawyer*, which claimed that "through our Agents we sell ten times more of our books than do the trade publishers."[4] Second, because the selling occurred prior to binding and even prior to the bulk of the printing, the publisher could calculate with some degree of accuracy how many copies to produce, thus saving on manufacturing costs as well as on inventory and storage. Third, subscription books often had a larger profit margin than trade books, owing to the high prices consumers were willing to pay for thick, lavishly illustrated, and gaudily bound volumes: the darlings of the subscription market. Such books were expensive to produce, but the increased costs to the publisher were more than compensated for by the higher cost to the purchaser. As Clemens explained, "We always charge about a third more for a book than the trade can venture to ask for it" (*MTLP* 233). (In the Publisher's Circular for *Adventures of Huckleberry Finn*, Clemens's publisher emphasizes accessibility over cost, informing agents that the book's "reasonable price . . . brings it within the reach of all classes" ["Confidential Terms to Agents" 307].) Finally, rather than supplying retailers with discounted books, the publisher saved money by selling through traveling agents, both male and female, who sold the books on commission. Given these facts, it is hardly surprising that Clemens was convinced that selling by subscription would best serve his interests both as author and as businessman. To him, "a book in the trade is a book thrown away, as far as money-profit goes" (*MTLP* 337).

Of course, subscription publishing catered to an entirely different demographic group from traditional publishing, and therein, according to many, lay its disadvantages. Whereas bookstores were concentrated in the cities, serving a predominantly urban, primarily eastern clientele, subscription agents roamed the towns, villages, and countryside, selling books to farm families and small-town dwellers throughout the South, Midwest, and West. Subscription customers represented a broader population, in terms of both geography and demographics, than the bookstore clientele.[5] According to an early reviewer of *The Gilded Age*, "The subscription business, more than the 'regular,' must suit a widely-dispersed average of customers" (qtd. in Hill 10). As far as many traditional authors, publishers, and book retailers were concerned, this "widely-dispersed average" represented a less desirable group. As a result, explains Hamlin Hill, "the 'regular trade' author consoled himself on the comparatively insignificant sales with the thought that he was at least circulating 'among the better class of readers' while the subscription author sacrificed prestige to popular appeal and profit" (10).

Clemens was well aware that subscription customers constituted a popular (if not "mass") market. In 1889 he wrote to Andrew Lang: "I have never tried in even one single instance, to help cultivate the cultivated classes. I was not equipped for it, either by native gifts or training. And I never had any ambition in that direction, but always hunted for bigger game—the masses" (*Mark Twain's Letters* 2: 527).[6] Publishing professionals perceived bookstore customers as well educated and well heeled; subscription purchasers constituted a class apart. In a letter of November 1896 regarding *Following the Equator*, Clemens (running with the big-game metaphor) commented upon this class of consumers and their spending habits: "Harper publishes very high-class books and they go to people who are accustomed to read. That class are surfeited with travel-books. But there is a vast class that isn't—the factory hands and farmers. *They* never go to a bookstore; they have to be hunted down by the canvasser. When a subscription book of mine sells 60,000, I always think I know whither 50,000 of them went. They went to people who don't visit bookstores" (*MTLP* 7).

Not surprisingly, the literary tastes of these two groups differed markedly. This meant that books that performed poorly in one distribution system might prosper in the other. Thus, for example, when sales of the illustrated edition of *Little Women* foundered in bookstores, Thomas Niles informed its author: "We have withdrawn it entirely from the booksellers & are trying to make a success of it by subscription."[7] Hill notes that "with specialized methods of manufacture, sales, and distribution, and with a specialized audience, the subscription author produced an extremely specialized kind of book" (10). In an 1870 article on subscription books, the *American Bookseller's Guide* observed that "the book of adventures, of wild sports, and pioneer life is dear to the people, and it is found on paper-covered shelves in company with clock and candlestick where literature in any other form seldom enters" ("New Subscription Books for 1870" 113).

In chapter 17 of *Adventures of Huckleberry Finn*, Mark Twain offers some insight into the characteristics of, and audience for, subscription books by giving us a glimpse through Huck's eyes of an assortment of these productions in their native habitat. Having recently arrived at the Grangerford home, Huck favors the reader with a description of the family's parlor, from the "big brass dog-irons" and gaudy knick-knacks to the chipped plaster-of-Paris fruit and "wild-turkey-wing fans" (136–37):

> There was some books too, piled up perfectly exact, on each corner of the table. One was a big family Bible, full of pictures. One was "Pilgrim's Progress," about a man that left his family it didn't say why. I read considerable in it now and then. The statements was interesting, but tough. Another was "Friendship's Offering," full of beautiful stuff and poetry; but I didn't read the poetry. Another was Henry Clay's Speeches, and another was Dr. Gunn's Family Medicine, which told you all about what to do if a body was sick or dead. There was a Hymn Book, and a lot of other books.

And there was nice split-bottom chairs, and perfectly sound, too—not bagged down in the middle and busted, like an old basket. (137)

The Grangerfords' preference for devotional and inspirational texts is in keeping with the perceived literary tastes of contemporary purchasers of subscription books. The American Publishing Company, which departed from its recognized forte when it brought out *Tom Sawyer* in 1876, had been known chiefly as a purveyor of religious books (with titles such as *Scripture Reading Lessons for Family Worship*, *Bible Lands Illustrated*, and *Illustrated History of the Bible*), although the firm also published such subscription staples as books of travel and exploration (*Sights and Sensations of Europe*, *Arctic Explorations*, *Overland through Asia*, *My Winter on the Nile*, *Among the Mummies and Moslems*), military histories (*Fac-simile of Gen'l Washington's Account with the United States*, *Personal History of U. S. Grant*, *Pictorial Field Book of the Civil War*), and sensational autobiographies (*Back from the Mouth of Hell; or, The Rescue from Drunkenness*, *Lament of a Mormon Wife*, *Narrative of My Captivity among the Sioux Indians*).

As the foregoing list suggests, nonfiction was the bread and butter of subscription book publishers; novels were quite rare and tended to be reprints of European classics.[8] The subscription audience appreciated weighty tomes and valued densely illustrated texts with decorative bindings. Indeed, Clemens often bulked up his own books to meet the expectations of subscribers—whether by adding material or printing on thick paper[9]—and he devoted a great deal of attention to commissioning illustrations. George Ade recalled in a retrospective appreciation, "Mark Twain and the Old Time Subscription Book," in *Review of Reviews* for June 1910, "Each [book] was meant for the center table, and it had to be so thick and heavy and emblazoned with gold that it could keep company with the bulky and high-priced Bible" (qtd. in Anderson 337). The irony that the less cultured buyers of the subscription market would favor such imposing and costly books was not lost on contemporary observers. Reviewing *The Innocents Abroad*, Bret Harte commented, "The book has that intrinsic worth of bigness and durability which commends itself to the rural economist, who likes to get a material return for his money" (qtd. in Cook, "Making His Mark," 170). More recently, Richard S. Lowry has accounted for the apparent incongruity between the target audience and the high-priced formats by explaining that "in *Tom Sawyer*, Twain does not write for the working masses, but for the middling masses. His is not a dime novel for the simple reason that it cost too much to buy; it aimed at satisfying precisely those buyers who valued at least the image of 'mature' reading, used books as signs of their own cultural distinction, and, most important, wanted those books written by known authors" (100). The American Publishing Company succinctly summed up the key critical criteria of its target market when it promoted its products, in a note "To the Public," as of exceptional "*weight, size,* and *popularity*"[10]—qualities that clearly emphasize physical format and social acceptability over intellectual content and literary aesthetics.

Naturally, the assumption of the trade was that the showy wares of the subscription book agent were of questionable literary merit. Hamlin Hill's assessment that "by and large, the subscription book was patently subliterary" (10) echoes many nineteenth-century appraisals. Inevitably, this complaint reflected upon the customers themselves. According to the *American Bookseller's Guide*, subscription books were "for the most part verbose compilations and revamped antiquities, which the publishers look to the energy and ingenuity of agents and the fascination of colored prints and wood-cuts to sell to those whose education and pursuits render them indifferent judges of their value" ("New Subscription Books for 1870" 113). Guilty by association, the authors of these books were also devalued in the eyes of the trade. In an article of August 1874, T. S. R. Crocker, editor of the *Literary World*, maintained that subscription books "cannot possibly circulate among the better class of readers, owing to the general and not unfounded prejudice against them as a class. Consequently an author of established reputation, who resorts to the subscription plan for the sake of making money, descends to a constituency of a lower grade and inevitably loses caste" (qtd. in Hill 7).

Clemens's preference for the subscription method and his involvement in publishing, as an entrepreneur who served on the board of directors of the American Publishing Company before establishing his own subscription publishing house, made him more aware of his audience than were many authors. In fact, he conceived of his readers less as patrons of the arts than as consumers. His willingness to pad his manuscripts and his various forays into humorous travel writing are only two of many examples that demonstrate his responsiveness to his target audience. But Clemens's eagerness to satisfy readers did not always translate into an intuitive sense

of how his own writing fit into the shifting structure of the literary marketplace. He relied to some extent, therefore, upon the direction of such
literary advisers and friends as William Dean Howells. Indeed, it was Howells who helped him to clarify the audience of his first noncollaborative
novel, *The Adventures of Tom Sawyer*, which Clemens composed over a
protracted period between the summer of 1872 and July 1875 (*Letters* 5:
261; 6: xxxiv).[11]

The prominent literary editors of the Gilded Age—men who had their
fingers firmly on the literary pulse—evinced a decided fondness for nostalgic, autobiographical narratives of boy-life. William Dean Howells and
Thomas Bailey Aldrich, successive editors of the *Atlantic Monthly*, penned
their own contributions to the genre, as did Charles Dudley Warner, who
edited *Harper's Magazine* and coauthored *The Gilded Age* with Clemens.
Howells initially urged Clemens to write *Tom Sawyer* and was eager to consider the work for serial publication in the *Atlantic Monthly*. On 3 July 1875,
he wrote to Clemens: "You must be thinking well of the notion of giving us
that story. I really feel very much interested in your making that your chief
work; you wont have such another chance; don't waste it on a *boy*, and don't
hurry the writing for the sake of making a book" (*Mark Twain—Howells
Letters* 1: 90).[12] Howells, significantly, recommends that Clemens direct the
story toward an adult, rather than a juvenile, audience—"don't waste it on a
*boy*"—and that he define himself as a novelist working in the grand manner
favored by such highbrow novelists as Howells himself and Henry James:
allowing the novel to develop thoughtfully over the course of many months
in serialized installments, and refining the piece for an *Atlantic* readership.
Clemens's reply, two days later, emphatically hastens to assure Howells that
he has picked up on the editorial signals: "It is *not* a boy's book, at all. It will
only be read by adults. It is only written for adults. . . . I would dearly like to
see it in the Atlantic" (*MTHL* 1: 91; *Letters* 6: 503).[13]

After reading the manuscript, however, Howells became convinced of
just the opposite. On 21 November 1875, he reported:

> I finished reading Tom Sawyer a week ago, sitting up till one A.M., to get
> to the end, simply because it was impossible to leave off. It's altogether the
> best boy's story I ever read. It will be an immense success. But I think you
> ought to treat it explicitly *as* a boy's story. Grown-ups will enjoy it just as
> much if you do; and if you should put it forth as a study of boy character
> from the grown-up point of view, you'd give the wrong key to it. . . . The

adventures are enchanting. I wish *I* had been on that island. The treasure-hunting, the loss in the cave—it's all exciting and splendid. I shouldn't think of publishing this story serially. Give me a hint when it's to be out, and I'll start the sheep to jumping in the right places. (Clemens, *MTHL* 1: 110–11; *Letters* 6: 595)

Despite its high praise for the manuscript, Howells's communication is, in essence, a coded rejection in which he informs the author that the manuscript is not suitable for the *Atlantic Monthly* after all. Instead, he tactfully guides Clemens toward a different approach and a different audience—the juvenile market—while assuring his friend that he will do what he can to promote the book.

Although Clemens initially resisted the idea of making *Tom Sawyer* a boy's book, he, too, soon became persuaded that children were the true audience for the novel. Olivia Clemens agreed with Howells that it should be a "boy-book" (*MTHL* 1: 118), and perhaps it was his wife's opinion that inspired Clemens to refashion the manuscript: he replied to Howells two days later, "Mrs. Clemens decides with you that the book should issue as a book for boys, pure & simple—& so do I. It is surely the correct idea" (*MTHL* 1: 112; *Letters* 6: 595). Having decided to pitch the book to a juvenile audience, Clemens then revised the manuscript, expunging profanity and mitigating its off-color humor. The book issued from the American Publishing Company in early December 1876, without a prior periodical appearance.

Thus, unlike Alcott—who, with Thomas Niles, conceived of *Little Women* from the outset as a book for a gendered juvenile audience—Clemens originally envisioned *Tom Sawyer* as a book for adults of both sexes. Whereas Alcott and Niles first identified the audience they wished to reach (adolescent girls) and then came up with a text to suit that audience, Clemens worked the other way around, starting with a text (*Tom Sawyer* or, even earlier, the untitled c. 1868 fragment that Albert Bigelow Paine christened his "Boy's Manuscript" [rpt. in *Huck Finn and Tom Sawyer among the Indians*]) and then attempting to discern its audience. This process necessitated an additional round of revisions—evidently only partly successful—as he struggled to reconcile text and target audience. Not surprisingly, confusion as to *who* constituted the audience for *Tom Sawyer* persisted. Shortly after he agreed that aiming the book at boys was "surely the correct idea," Clemens qualified his conception of the novel's intended readership. Expanding the audience to include both genders, he announced in a letter to Howells dated 18 January 1876 that "the book is to be for boys & girls.... [It] is now professedly and confessedly a boy's & girl's book" (*MTHL* 1: 122).

In the preface, Clemens again enlarged his conception of the book's audience: "Although my book is intended mainly for the entertainment of boys and girls, I hope it will not be shunned by men and women on that account" (ix).[14] To his English publisher, Moncure Conway, Clemens further departed from the notion that targeting boys was the "correct idea." His primary objective in marketing *Tom Sawyer* as a children's story was to sell books, and when, in 1876, Conway cautioned, "I don't think it would be doing justice to call it a boy's book and think it better be left [to] people to form their own conclusions" (qtd. in Norton 35), Clemens betrayed his eagerness to cast a wider net (9 April 1876): "You can leave out the preface; or alter it so that it will not profess to be a book for youth; or write a new preface and put your own name or initials to it.—Fix it any way you want to, if as you say, it will be best not to put it forth as a book for youth" (*MTLP* 97). In the end, Conway, echoing Clemens's own ambivalence, reversed his position in the London *Examiner* (17 June 1876), declaring, "The book will no doubt be a great favourite with boys, for whom it must in good part have been intended" (qtd. in Scharnhorst 25).

Still, one of the distinctive features of children's literature of the Victorian period was a tendency to address both adults and children and to appeal to the adult reader's desire to reawaken a "childlike" sense of belief, wonder, or innocence. This new approach to "The Child Redeemer" of the Romantic period gave rise to classic narratives written for a "dual audience" and manifesting a narrative "doubleness" by speaking simultaneously to adults and children (Thacker and Webb 41–55).[15] Understood in this context, *Tom Sawyer* is in some ways typical of an age in which adult readers sought to recover a childlike vision through the fictional construct of the "redemptive child." Yet the distinctive character of *Tom Sawyer* as a "boy-book" further complicates the relationship of subject matter to audience. In 1956, Edwin H. Cady characterized the boy-book as "distinct from the 'story for boys,' though ordinarily sold to editors and librarians as such, in that it contains a depth level at which an imaginative exploration of the nature and predicament of the man-child is carried out" (qtd. in Jacobson 4).

Clemens touched indirectly on this theoretical distinction between the "story for boys" and the "boy-book" in the preface to *Tom Sawyer*, in which he affirmed, "Part of my plan has been to try to pleasantly remind adults of what they once were themselves, and of how they felt and thought and talked, and what queer enterprises they sometimes engaged in" (ix). He originally envisioned having Tom Sawyer "drift into manhood" (*Letters* 6: 497)—and, indeed, in the book's conclusion he speculates that "some day it may seem worth while to take up the story of the younger [characters] again and see what sort of men and women they turned out to be" (275). Clemens soon abandoned this strategy, however, confiding to Howells that "if I went on, now, & took him into manhood, he would just be like all the one-horse men in literature & the reader would conceive a hearty contempt for him" (*Letters* 6: 503). The decision was fitting, of course, for the boy-book genre, as defined by Cady, rather than answering the forward-looking questions "how will I grow up?" and "who will I become?"—as Alcott does in the Little Women series—responds to the retrospective questions "who was I?" and "what was I like?"[16]

*The Adventures of Tom Sawyer*, however, belongs simultaneously to the "bad boy" tradition, characterized by Alan Gribben as "a movement that began by rebelling against the implausible portrayals of behavior in the pages of its listless predecessors and that (some would say) proceeded to the point of glorifying with nostalgic reverence the escapades of young village hooligans" (152).[17] Even after the tide of didactic children's literature had begun to ebb, most nineteenth-century writers of children's books retained an overtly moralistic outlook that found expression in their fiction. Even Oliver Optic, whose adventure stories were surely an improvement over the drab cautionary tales of the earlier nineteenth century, and who was censured by some (such as Alcott) on the grounds that his books contained too much entertainment and slang and too little instruction and improvement, goes out of his way to preach to his readers about acceptable behavior for boys. (He was a minister, after all.) Thus, in an early chapter of *The Dorcas Club; or, Our Girls Afloat* (1874), Adams provides a two-page rationalization of the plot, which involves a good boy rebelling against a bad guardian: "Truly it is an awful responsibility which one assumes in telling the story of a boy, who under any possible circumstances, rebels against his guardian; and before we do so, we must solemnly appeal to all our boy-readers not to confound their own situation to that of the hero" (36). Similarly, in *The Boat Club* (1856), he editorializes: "Perhaps my young friends cannot fully appreciate the amount of satisfaction which a parent derives from the good character of the child. Though the worthy shipmaster had a beautiful estate and plenty of money, if his son had been a liar, a thief, a profane swearer,—in short, if Frank had been a bad boy,—he could not have been happy" (10). Yet by Adams's standards—and by the standards of the nineteenth-century reading public—a "bad boy" is precisely what Tom Sawyer and his sidekick, Huck Finn, were.[18]

Of course, Tom was not the first "bad boy" to appear in American literature. "Ragged Dick," the wisecracking eponymous hero of Alger's novel (published in 1868, the same year as *Little Women*, by A. K. Loring, publisher of Alcott's *Moods*) is no "model boy" (Alger 6). He smokes, gambles, and drinks, although Alger steadily plots his path away from these vices. In *Eight Cousins* (published two years before *Tom Sawyer*), Alcott portrayed two of the younger boys, Will and Geordie, reading of just such a character as Ragged Dick as they while away a rainy afternoon "deep in the adventures of the scapegraces and ragamuffins whose histories are now the fashion" (154). Most notably, however, *Tom Sawyer* was preceded by Thomas Bailey Aldrich's *The Story of a Bad Boy* (1869), arguably the first full-length narrative to celebrate a "bad boy" as protagonist rather than antagonist (Wolf 47).[19] The quality that made both Tom Bailey and Tom Sawyer so distinctive to contemporary readers was their genuine boyishness; perhaps more than any other aspect of these texts, reviewers and critics responded favorably to their successful portrayal of "real" boys.[20] Certainly, earlier boys in fiction had gotten into scrapes: Alcott's Tom Shaw, for example, in *An Old-Fashioned Girl*, not only plays practical jokes on the girls but gambles and carelessly gets himself into debt. Nevertheless, a reviewer of *An Old-Fashioned Girl* complained that "the hero must preach a woman's notion of manliness—must be, violently, the nondescript known to woman as The Boy" (qtd. in Zehr 337). In contrast, readers unanimously recognized Aldrich's and Clemens's creations as bona fide boys' boys, decidedly reprehensible yet somehow still lovable. Literary critic Brander Matthews wrote of Huckleberry Finn: "Old maids of either sex will wholly fail to understand him or like him, or to see his significance and his value. Like Tom Sawyer, Huck Finn is a genuine boy; he is neither a girl in boy's clothes like many of the modern heroes of juvenile fiction, nor is he a 'little man,' a full-grown man cut down; he is a boy, just a boy only a boy. And his ways and modes of thought are boyish" (qtd. in Anderson 123). Indeed, so genuine a boy is Huck that when he disguises himself as Sarah Mary

Williams (thereby becoming a boy in girls' clothes) his masculine mannerisms quickly blow his cover.

In contrast to Alcott, who evokes scenes of human goodness and
domestic harmony occasionally disrupted by privation, illness, and youthful errors, Clemens and Aldrich trivialize human suffering and sorrow in
order to celebrate the more capricious, mischievous side of human nature
through the misdeeds of their bad-boy protagonists. Both Tom Sawyer and
Tom Bailey engage in pranks, seek out daring adventures, and, on occasion, fight, thieve, and dissemble. Contemporary readers, however, found
Mark Twain's Tom more difficult to reconcile with an audience of children than Aldrich's Tom. Although both novels arose from grown men's
reminiscences of boyhood, *Tom Sawyer* lacks the sense of an adult looking over the shoulder of his boyish self, expressing remorse for childish
misdeeds and, from time to time, dispensing fatherly wisdom. As a result,
although most critics agreed that Tom Sawyer and Huck Finn were realistic specimens of American boyhood, they disagreed sharply as to whether
such authentic scapegraces were suitable companions in fiction for flesh-
and-blood boys. One early reviewer stressed that the novel was "in the last
degree unsafe to put . . . into the hands of imitative youth" (qtd. in Scharnhorst 62), and Alcott tartly advised that "if Mr. Clemens cannot think of
something better to tell our pure-minded lads and lasses he had best stop
writing for them"—to which Clemens responded, "That will sell 25,000
for sure" (qtd. in Hart 150).

Further, although most reviewers assumed the book to be written for
young people, its unsuitability as children's entertainment led some to
question the candor of Clemens's assertion in the preface to *Tom Sawyer*
that "the book is intended mainly for the entertainment of boys and girls."
Alluding to this statement, an anonymous reviewer for the *Athenaeum* cautioned that "questions of intention are always difficult to decide. The book
will amuse grown-up people in the way that humorous books written for
children have amused before, but (perhaps fortunately) *it does not seem to
us calculated to carry out the intention here expressed*" (qtd. in Anderson
65; emphasis added). Similarly, a review in the *New York Times* contrasted
the "ugly realism" of contemporary children's literature with "good old
Peter Parley, who in this country first broke loose from conventional tram-
mels, and made American children truly happy." The reviewer went on to
admonish readers against allowing children to associate with those who

are "lawless or dare-devils," even in fiction: "A sprinkling of salt in mental food is both natural and wholesome; any cravings for the contents of the castors, the cayenne and mustard by children, should not be gratified. With less, then, of Injun Joe and 'revenge,' and 'slitting women's ears,' and the shadow of the gallows, which throws an unnecessarily sinister tinge over the story, (*if the book really is intended for boys and girls*) we should have liked *Tom Sawyer* better" (qtd. in Anderson 72; emphasis added).

Readers were not the only ones to wonder whether the book was better suited to adults or children; Clemens's own publisher seems to have had his doubts. Elisha Bliss envisioned an adult audience for *Tom Sawyer* and marketed the book accordingly, contrary to the author's express wishes. In spite of Clemens's repeated urgings "to issue in the autumn and make a Boy's Holiday Book of it" (16 April 1876; *MTLP* 98) and to "let Tom lay still till autumn . . . & make a holiday book of him to beguile the young people withal" (qtd. in Hill 118), Bliss failed to promote the novel as a boys' book, a children's book, or even a holiday book. According to Hill, "There was in Twain's mind a strong suspicion that Bliss was not marketing his books as they should be sold" (124), and *Tom Sawyer* is a case in point: Bliss

> made a significant sales pitch to adult readers, and not to children at all. If Livy, Twain, and Howells believed that *Tom Sawyer* was a children's book, Bliss did not: "In announcing this volume," he explained, "the publishers have no hesitation in declaring it to be one of the most original, unique, piquant and entertaining of all Mark Twain's works. The genius requisite to render the written adventures of a boy overwhelmingly fascinating to grown up readers, is possessed by but few, and challenges the deepest admiration. That Mr. Clemens has this, is evident from the burst of enthusiastic praise with which the publication of 'Tom Sawyer' in England, has been received." (Hill 118–19)

Moreover, the sample that the agents used to sell the book in advance of publication "combined the comic, sensational, and the morbid in a skillful but hardly juvenile blend" (Hill 119).

Hill characterizes the initial sales of *Tom Sawyer* as a "dismally disappointing financial failure" (99).[21] Although there are a number of explanations for its poor performance in the subscription market—low page count, fictional content, the fact that the American market was flooded with unauthorized reprints from Canada—Bliss's refusal to promote it as a children's book surely contributed to its lackluster sales. So disgusted was Clemens with Bliss's handling of *Tom Sawyer* that he decided to terminate his relationship with the American Publishing Company and seek a new publisher (Hill 120). His next book, the ambiguously subtitled *The Prince and the Pauper: A Tale for Young People of All Ages* (1882), was handled by James Osgood (who published *Life on the Mississippi* the following year) under an unusual contract whereby Clemens paid the production costs and Osgood received a 7.5 percent royalty for handling the sales. The following year, Clemens permanently terminated his relationship with the American Publishing Company when Bliss refused to offer him more than half the profits on his next book, a projected sequel to *Tom Sawyer*. Clemens promptly proceeded to establish his own publishing outfit; he engaged his nephew to run it; and in February 1885 the fledgling company of Charles L. Webster began distributing *Adventures of Huckleberry Finn, Tom Sawyer's Comrade*.

Although sales of *Tom Sawyer* remained tepid for several years, once it was out of Bliss's hands, the book did become popular among juvenile readers: "New printings of *Tom Sawyer*, marketed as a book for boys, were issued every two or three years during the 1880s and 1890s" (Scharnhorst 4). On 15 October 1883, Clemens was able to write to Howells of an upturn—and of the novel's long-awaited sequel: "Tom Sawyer has been steadily climbing for years—& now at last, as per enclosed statement, has achieved second place in the list of my old books. I think that this promises pretty well for Huck Finn. Although I mean to publish Huck in a volume by itself, I think I will also jam it & Sawyer into a volume *together* at the same time, since Huck is in some sense a continuation of the former story" (*MTHL* 1: 445–46). The following February, an advertisement in the *Dial* announced that "Mark Twain's next book will bear the title of 'Huckleberry Finn, A Sequel to Tom Sawyer'" (qtd. in Fiedler 277). Clemens had redefined his audience, *Tom* had found his market, and as a result the way was prepared for *Huck*. Once again, however, Clemens misjudged both his novel and the market.

Unlike *Little Women, Part Two, Little Men,* and most of the other sequels Alcott produced to satisfy her impatient readers, *Adventures of Huckleberry Finn* was a long time in the making. As early as 9 August 1876, when *Tom Sawyer*, then a new release, was still struggling in the subscription market, Clemens had informed Howells, "I began another boys' book. . . . It is Huck Finn's Autobiography" (*MTHL* 1:144). Eight years would pass, however, before the publication of *Adventures of Huckleberry Finn (Tom Saw-yer's Comrade)*, and, as Leslie Fiedler notes, Clemens spent seven of those years "bogged down and unable to write a line" (277), having reached an impasse at the end of chapter 15 with Huck and Jim approaching Cairo, Illinois.

Clemens's seven-year delay in completing the novel derives in part from the same confusion as to audience and genre that afflicted *Tom Sawyer*. In *Huckleberry Finn*, which made its debut as a series of advance chapters published in the *Century Magazine*, the subject matter is far more serious than that of its predecessor.[22] As a result, "for many critics the line between children's books and adults' books falls quite firmly between *Tom Sawyer* and . . . *Huckleberry Finn*" (P. Hunt, *Children's Literature* [2001] 232–33)—a book which, according to T. S. Eliot, "creates its own category" (348). Aside from the thrilling murder subplot involving Injun Joe and Muff Potter, Tom's weightiest concerns in *Tom Sawyer* involve courting Becky Thatcher and thwarting Aunt Polly in her attempts to get him to whitewash the fence and imbibe the dreaded Pain-Killer. In contrast, *Huckleberry Finn* takes on the enduring conflicts of American civilization—complex problems concerning race, liberty, and the value of human life—as Huck and Jim drift down the Mississippi River toward an elusive (and, for Jim, apparently receding) freedom. Although adult fiction of the period often used child characters to critique or challenge the corrupt adult world (Thacker and Webb 42), these problems were hardly the conventional material of children's literature, and many nineteenth-century readers seem to have heaved a sigh of relief when Tom and Huck landed, at last, on the Phelps Farm and, simultaneously, on more familiar and frivolous fictional terrain.

In *The Adventures of Tom Sawyer*, Tom is the undisputed ringleader of the town's mischievous posse of ragtag boys. An avid reader of adventure novels, Tom always knows how things should be done—that is, how they would be done by the heroes of these sensational yarns. When Tom, Huck, and their friends run off to Jackson's Island, for example, Tom—calling himself "the Black Avenger of the Spanish Main" after Ned Buntline's popular adventure story[23]—confidently takes charge, instructing "Huck Finn the Red-Handed" and "Joe Harper the Terror of the Seas" in the art of carrying out a first-class adventure:

> Tom tumbled his ham over the bluff and let himself down after it, tearing both skin and clothes to some extent in the effort. There was an easy, comfortable

85

path along the shore under the bluff, but it lacked the advantages of difficulty and danger so valued by a pirate. . . .

The Black Avenger of the Spanish Main said it would never do to start without some fire. That was a wise thought; matches were hardly known there in that day. They saw a fire smouldering upon a great raft a hundred yards above, and they went stealthily thither and helped themselves to a chunk. They made an imposing adventure of it, saying "Hist!" every now and then, and suddenly halting with finger on lip; moving with hands on imaginary dagger-hilts; and giving orders in dismal whispers that if "the foe" stirred, to "let him have it to the hilt," because "dead men tell no tales." They knew well enough that the raftsmen were all down at the village laying in stores or having a spree, but still that was no excuse for their conducting this thing in an unpiratical way. (115–16)

Although Huck is independent of Tom for the majority of *Adventures of Huckleberry Finn*, the final chapters of the novel mark a return to this earlier pattern. After Huck points out that they can free Jim, who has been chained to a bed, simply by raising the bedstead and slipping off the chain, Tom replies:

"Why, hain't you ever read any books at all?—Baron Trenck, nor Casanova, nor Benvenuto Chelleeny, nor Henri IV., nor none of them heroes? Whoever heard of getting a prisoner loose in such an old-maidy way as that? No; the way all the best authorities does, is to saw the bed-leg in two, and leave it just so, and swallow the sawdust, so it can't be found, and put some dirt and grease around the sawed place so the very keenest seneskal can't see no sign of it's being sawed, and thinks the bed-leg is perfectly sound. Then, the night you're ready, fetch the leg a kick, down she goes; slip off your chain, and there you are. Nothing to do but hitch your rope-ladder to the battlements, shin down it, break your leg in the moat—because a rope-ladder is nineteen foot too short, you know—and there's your horses and your trusty vassles, and they scoop you up and fling you across a saddle and away you go, to your native Langudoc, or Navarre, or wherever it is. . . . I wish there was a moat to this cabin. If we get time, the night of the escape, we'll dig one." (301)

Contemporary readers welcomed the return of Tom Sawyer at the end of *Huckleberry Finn*.[24] The jarring disparity between the first thirty-one chapters and the final twelve proved particularly troublesome to twentieth-century readers, however, prompting many to regard the novel as a botched masterpiece.[25] Undoubtedly, in reintroducing Tom and returning, in the Phelps Farm section, to the comical shenanigans that worked so well in *The Adventures of Tom Sawyer*, Clemens reveals a lingering uncertainty as to his market and an ongoing struggle to reconcile his recalcitrant subject matter with the "intended" audience of "boys and girls."[26]

Nevertheless, Clemens's confidence in Tom and in the expanding juvenile fiction market that had made him a popular icon was such that he revived him, along with his boon companion Huck, not just once but at least four more times. Clemens first resurrected Tom and Huck in good faith, in spite of poor initial returns on *The Adventures of Tom Sawyer*. In later sequels, however, he revived them owing to the initial novel's long-term success and the enduring popularity of its sequel. Although in the closing lines of his "autobiography," Huck demurs, "If I'd a knowed what a trouble it was to make a book I wouldn't a tackled it and aint't agoing to no more" (366), Clemens did not let those objections stand in his way: almost immediately after finishing *Huckleberry Finn*, he went to work on another adventure narrated by Huck. In a letter of 6 July 1884 he instructed his nephew, Charles Webster, to send him a book of frontier adventures by "Lieut. Col. Dodge, USA" and other books about the West, explaining, "I want several other *personal narratives* of life & adventure and yonder on the Plains & in the Mountains, if you can run across them.—especially life *among the Indians*. Send what you can find. I mean to take Huck Finn out there" (*Mark Twain, Business Man* 265).[27]

The resulting incomplete manuscript is an attempt to dramatize the consequences of Huck's determination, stated at the end of *Huckleberry Finn*, to "light out for the Territory ahead of the rest" (366). An attempt both to satirize and to tap into the popularity of dime-novel Westerns, "Huck Finn and Tom Sawyer among the Indians" is replete with abductions, scalpings, and other stock atrocities perpetrated by Indians on the warpath. In fact, so bloody was the subject matter that Clemens once again fell into difficulties as he attempted to adapt his disturbing material and realistic style to a juvenile audience. Ultimately, the effort failed: although in the first chapter Tom dismisses Jim's fear of "Injuns" with characteristic aplomb, the third chapter finds Huck witness to the brutal massacre of an emigrant family bound for Oregon in a covered wagon. Huck narrates the ambush of the unfortunate Mills family:

> The Injuns was up, and sidling around, the rest was chatting, same as before, and Peggy [the Mills's seventeen-year-old daughter] was gathering

up the plates and things. I heard a trampling like a lot of horses, and when it got pretty near, I see that other Injun coming on a pony, and driving the other ponies and all our mules and horses ahead of him, and he let off a long wild whoop, and the minute he done that, the Injun that had a gun, the one that Peggy fixed, shot her father through the head with it and scalped him, another one tomahawked her mother and scalped her, and then these two grabbed Jim and tied his hands together, and the other two grabbed Peggy, who was screaming and crying, and all of them rushed off with her and Jim and Flaxy [the Mills's seven-year-old daughter], and as fast as I run, and as far as I run, I could still hear her, till I was a long, long ways off. (47–48)

In *The Adventures of Tom Sawyer*, Tom, Huck, and Joe Harper pretended to be warring tribes and "killed and scalped each other by the thousands," an activity that was "gory" and "consequently . . . extremely satisfactory" (143). Later, Tom and Huck witnessed firsthand the horrors of violent death in Injun Joe's murder of the young doctor; and in *Adventures of Huckleberry Finn*, Huck witnessed the Shepardson-Grangerford feud, Colonel Sherburne's murder of Boggs, and the death of his own "Pap." These murders, however, were always on the periphery of Huck's own life, isolated incidents in the course of a highly episodic journey. In contrast, not only is the large-scale carnage of "Huck Finn and Tom Sawyer among the Indians" appallingly, horrifically gruesome, but it lies at the very center of the plot. In the passage cited above, Huck cannot outrun the terror he has witnessed, and one senses that the author, in plotting the novel's course, felt a similar inability to escape it. Not even Mark Twain could extract so much as a shred of humor from Huck's recapitulation of the tragedy to Peggy's sweetheart, Brace Johnson, although clearly he tries:

> "The one with the gun, that didn't have no war paint, he shot Mr. Mills, and scalped him; and he bloodied his hands, then, and made blood stripes across his face with his fingers, like war paint, and then begun to howl war-whoops like the Injuns does in the circus. And poor old Mrs. Mills, she was down on her knees, begging so pitiful when the tomahawk—"
>
> "I shall never never see her again—never never any more—my poor little darling, so young and sweet and beautiful—but thank God, she's dead!"
>
> He warn't listening to me.
>
> "Dead?" I says; "If you mean Peggy, she's not dead." (52)

Unlike Huck, Brace is not too naive to imagine a "fate worse than death" for the abducted maiden, and the specter of rape haunts the remaining six chapters Clemens penned before finally abandoning the project, apparently despairing of the possibility of reconciling text, topic, audience, and genre.

A decade passed before Clemens wrote to his publisher of another Tom Sawyer book, inspired by Jules Verne's popular *Five Weeks in a Balloon* (1863) and *Around the World in Eighty Days* (1872). The new sequel was tentatively titled "New Adventures of Huckleberry Finn."[28] On 10 August 1892, Clemens wrote: "I have started Huck Finn and Tom Sawyer (still 15 years old) and their friend the freed slave Jim around the world in a stray *balloon*, with Huck as narrator. . . . I have written 12,000 words of this narrative, and find that the humor flows as easily as the adventures and surprises—so I shall go along and make a book of from 50,000 to 100,000 words" (*MTLP* 314). In fact, so freely did the words flow—"It is easy work, and I enjoy it," he wrote (*MTLP* 315)—that Clemens conceived of an entire series based on the travels of Tom and Huck, perhaps equally inspired by such popular juvenile travel series as Abbott's Rollo books, Oliver Optic's Young America Abroad series, and Goodrich's Robert Merry books (which included *Balloon Travels of Robert Merry and His Young Friends* [1855]). Clemens was in dire financial difficulties at the time, and the purely commercial appeal of the series formula was not lost on him. As he explained to Fred J. Hall, manager of Charles L. Webster & Co., in a postscript to his letter of 10 August, "I have written 26,000 words of it—and can add a million if required, by adding 'Africa,' 'England,' 'Germany,' etc to the title page of each successive volume of the series" (*MTLP* 315). A few weeks later, when the manuscript was completed, he wrote:

> What I have to offer Harpers now, (for their *Young People's Magazine*—not the Bazaar or the Weekly or the Monthly—don't forget that) is—
> Tom Sawyer Abroad
>
> ---
>
> Part I—In the Great Sahara<br>By Huck Finn
>
> ---
>
> Edited by Mark Twain
> This part I contains about 40,000 words, and is finished.
> If the first numbers should prove popular, I could go on and furnish additional parts without delay, if desired. (*MTLP* 318)

Clemens's reference to the whole gamut of Harper's magazines— *Harper's Bazaar*, *Harper's Weekly*, and *Harper's New Monthly Magazine*, as well as *Young People's Magazine*—reflects the fact that Mark Twain's role in the literary marketplace was by no means fixed and that the editor needed direction, therefore, in positioning his work. It also shows that Clemens was trying to locate the right venue for the text among the general and specialized publications of the house of Harper. With this new "Tom and Huck" book, he apparently had no desire to make another debut in an adult magazine such as the *Atlantic* or the *Century*. Once again, however, Clemens resisted the artistic and demographic limitations of the juvenile market and, perhaps, also resisted the drop in status that went along with writing for children: "I conceive that the right way to write a story for boys is to write so that it will not only interest boys but will strongly interest any man *who has ever been a boy*. That immensely *enlarges the audience. . . .* It is a story for boys, of course, and I think will interest any boy between 8 years and 80" (*MTLP* 314).

Despite his initial intention to publish in Harper's *Young People's Magazine*, though, Clemens proceeded to submit the completed manuscript to general-interest periodicals for adults as well as specialized ones for children, insisting, "Now this story doesn't need to be restricted to a child's magazine—it is proper enough for any magazine, I should think, or for a syndicate. I don't swear it, but I think so" (*MTLP* 314). As with *Tom Sawyer*, Clemens's friends and family had better intuition about the novel's audience than its author did. As Clemens wrote to his publisher, "My family (tough people to please), like it first-rate, but they say it is for boys and girls. They won't allow it to go into a grown-folks' magazine. Don't forget *that* detail" (*MTLP* 318–19). In fact, of all the Tom Sawyer texts, *Tom Sawyer Abroad* is the most juvenile, with its fanciful flying machine, complete with mad scientist, so it is fitting that the novel finally found a home in a children's magazine. But *St. Nicholas*, where the novel appeared, was a very prestigious, highly literary juvenile magazine—"the youthful sibling of *The Century*" (*House of Appleton-Century* 35)—and editor Mary Mapes Dodge evidently felt obliged to expurgate Clemens's text, cleansing it of offensive language, a morbid death scene, a passing reference to drunkenness, and other elements she considered inappropriate for the magazine's readers (see Inge).

Perhaps offended by this treatment from the author of *Hans Brinker; or, The Silver Skates*, Clemens never did furnish additional volumes of *Tom Sawyer Abroad*. Instead, he produced *Tom Sawyer, Detective* (1896), a short novel that attempted to capitalize on the contemporary popularity of the Sherlock Holmes mysteries.[29] Clemens dashed off the novella quickly, pausing during the writing of *Joan of Arc* to complete the manuscript. His own publishing company, Charles L. Webster, having gone bankrupt just after the publication of *Tom Sawyer Abroad*, this latest sequel initially appeared as a serial in the family-oriented *Harper's New Monthly Magazine* for July and August 1896 and was published by Harper in an omnibus volume, *Tom Sawyer Abroad; Tom Sawyer, Detective, and Other Stories Etc., Etc.*, that November. Set on the Phelps Farm in the spring following the events narrated in *Huckleberry Finn, Tom Sawyer, Detective* begins with Huck afflicted by an aggravated bout of spring fever. Itching for adventure, Tom and Huck decide to journey down the river to Arkansas. Mark Twain the humorist is in top form as the two boys question a waiter aboard the steamship about the mysterious occupant of the stateroom next to their own. Huck comments: "It was always nuts for Tom Sawyer—a mystery was. If you'd lay out a mystery and a pie before me and him, you wouldn't have to say take your choice; it was a thing that would regulate itself. Because in my nature I have always run to pie, whilst in his nature he has always run to mystery" (122). Having imparted this pithy insight, Huck proceeds to relate the ensuing dialogue:

> Tom says to the waiter:
>   "What's the man's name?"
>   "Phillips."
>   "Where'd he come aboard?"
>   "I think he got aboard at Elexandria, up on the Iowa line."
>   "What do you reckon he's a-playing?"
>   "I hain't any notion—I never thought of it."
>   I say's to myself, here's another one that runs to pie. (122)

The plot soon gets in the way of the story, however, and Huck quickly subsides into the facile and familiar role of observer, chronicler, and admirer of Tom Sawyer. And, although such a formulaic treatment might have worked for an audience of children, the irony, the dialect, and even the protracted courtroom drama conspire to unfit it for the juvenile market. From 1897 until at least 1899 and possibly as late as 1902, Clemens worked on a second detective story, "Tom Sawyer's Conspiracy," which revolves around Tom's plan to disguise himself as a slave and revives the fraudsters of *Huckleberry Finn* (the King and the Duke of Bilgewater), but he abandoned the project within a few pages of completion (see Clemens, *Huck Finn and Tom Sawyer among the Indians* 290 and *Mark Twain's Hannibal, Huck and*

*Tom* 152–242). He also noted in his journal for 1891 and 1902 his idea for a story in which Huck and Tom meet fifty years later (*MTHL* 2: 748) and projected "Tom Sawyer's Gang Plans a Naval Battle" (c. 1900), but these, too, remained fragmentary.[30]

Inevitably, some contemporary critics viewed the Tom Sawyer books and their readers in a negative light. The Concord (Mass.) Public Library described *Adventures of Huckleberry Finn* as "suitable only for the slums," and the *Springfield Republican* averred that Huck's exploits "are no better in tone than the dime novels which flood the blood-and-thunder reading population" (qtd. in Vogelback 265, 270). Ultimately, however, Tom and Huck weathered the storm—at least insofar as the two major novels are concerned. Even as early as 1877, critics of Mark Twain's boy-books recognized that the reception of a book changes over time, in concert with broader social changes. An anonymous early review of *Tom Sawyer* in the *New York Times* for 13 January 1877 stated: "If, thirty years ago, *Tom Sawyer* had been placed in a careful father's hands to read, the probabilities would have been that he would have hesitated before giving the book to his boy—not that Mr. Clemens's book is exceptional in character, or differs in the least, save in its cleverness, from a host of similar books on like topics which are universally read by children today. It is the judgment of the bookgivers which has undoubtedly undergone a change, while youthful minds, being free from warp, twist, or dogma, have remained ever the same (qtd. in F. Anderson 69–70).

In targeting a juvenile audience, Clemens courted criticisms that his writing was unsuitable for young people, willfully overreaching the recognized boundaries of juvenile fiction. Nevertheless, Clemens did succeed in finding his niche among the "middling masses," a segment previously neglected by serious literary artists. According to George Ade, Mark Twain accomplished the "miracle of making the subscription book something to be read and not merely looked at" and "converted the Front Room from a Mausoleum into a Temple of Mirth" (qtd. in Anderson 339). In 1910, Ade recalled:

> Just when front-room literature seemed at its lowest ebb, so far as the American boy was concerned, along came Mark Twain. His books looked, at a distance, like the other distended, diluted, and altogether tasteless volumes that had been used for several decades to balance the ends of the center table. The publisher knew his public, so he gave a pound of book

for every fifty cents, and crowded in plenty of wood-cuts and stamped the outside with golden bouquets and put in a steel engraving of the author, with a tissue paper veil over it, and 'sicked' his multitude of broken-down clergymen, maiden ladies, grass widows, and college students on to the great American public.

Can you see the boy, a Sunday prisoner, approach the new book with a dull sense of foreboding, expecting a dose of Tupper's *Proverbial Philosophy*? Can you see him a few minutes later when he finds himself linked arm-in-arm with Mulberry Sellers or Buck Fanshaw or the convulsing idiot who wanted to know if Christopher Columbus was sure-enough dead? No wonder he curled up on the hair-cloth sofa and hugged the thing to his bosom and lost all interest in Sunday-school. *Innocents Abroad* was the most enthralling book ever printed until *Roughing It* appeared. Then along came *The Gilded Age*, *Life on the Mississippi*, and *Tom Sawyer*, one cap sheaf after another. While waiting for a new one we read the old ones all over again. (Qtd. in F. Anderson 338–39)

If, as R. Gordon Kelly argues, Oliver Optic appeared "at the beginnings of the kind of diversification in publication for children which occurs from the late 1840s on" and which "represents people from quite different positions within American society than . . . 'the gentry'" ("Social Factors" 46), a generation later Samuel Clemens brought that diversification to new heights as he spun out yarn after yarn in an attempt to unite the "good bad boys" of fiction with the good bad boys—both young and old—who would become his most avid readers.

# PART TWO

The Masses and the Classes

"Many people would think that what a bookseller—or indeed his clerk—
knows about literature *as* literature, in contradistinction to its character as
merchandise, would hardly be of much assistance to a person—that is, to an
adult of course—in the selection of food for the mind."
                    —Laura Hawkins, in Mark Twain and Charles Dudley Warner,
                                                        *The Gilded Age* (1873)


In 1873, three years before the publication of *The Adventures of Tom Sawyer* and a decade before *Huckleberry Finn*, Mark Twain coauthored his first
novel, *The Gilded Age: A Tale of To-day*, with fellow "boy-book" author and
later *Harper's New Monthly Magazine* editor Charles Dudley Warner. The
novel, whose title famously summed up the Zeitgeist of the 1870s, exposes
the rampant materialism and political corruption of the period as it traces
the rise and fall of the Hawkins family. The narrative is prodigious, encompassing sixty-three chapters (576 pages in the original edition) and a host
of characters and subplots. Amid this imposing bulk and expansive scope,
Clemens devoted an entire chapter to a tangential digression on bookselling, in which the refined, highly literate character Laura Hawkins swiftly
rebukes a brash bookstore clerk (figure 4) who persistently plies her with
*The Pirate's Doom; or, The Last of the Buccaneers, Gonderil the Vampire;
or, The Dance of Death*, and other disreputable "paper-covered" volumes.
Although the chapter does not materially advance the novel's plot, the
scene contributes eloquently to the authors' evocation of the spirit of the
age: an age characterized as much by the proliferation of print (especially
novels), the feminization of culture, and the cheapening of books (and,
many would argue, of literature) as by the rise of corporate capitalism and
political machines for which it is more generally known.[1]
    Having managed to locate Taine's *Notes on England* without assistance
from the inept clerk (who confuses Hippolyte Taine with eccentric presidential hopeful George Francis Train) and having abandoned hope of
securing a copy of Oliver Wendell Holmes's *The Autocrat of the Breakfast
Table* (which the clerk presumes to be a cookbook), Laura browses the
shelves, "finding a delight in the inspection of the Hawthornes, the Longfellows, the Tennysons, and other favorites of her idle hours" (330). As she
lingers over a copy of Howells's *Venetian Life*, however, the slick young
attendant interrupts her perusal of familiar passages to tout a paperbound

LAURA'S VISIT TO THE BOOK STORE

FIGURE 4. "The Bookstore Annoyance," the ignorant shop clerk in *The Gilded Age*. Courtesy, University of Minnesota Libraries.

novel "by the author of 'The Hooligans of Hackensack'" and "The Jokist's Own Treasury; or, The Phunny Phellow's Bosom Phriend." In response, Laura reproachfully compares him to the "peanut boy" of the railway, who "always measures you with his eye, and hands you out a book of murders if you are fond of theology; or [Baptist evangelist Henry Allen] Tupper or a dictionary or [temperance crusader] T[imothy] S[hay] Arthur if you are fond of poetry; or he hands you a volume of distressing jokes or a copy of the American Miscellany if you particularly dislike that sort of literary fatty degeneration of the heart—just for the world like a pleasant-spoken well-meaning gentleman in any bookstore" (333).

The clash between Laura's "highbrow" literary tastes and the clerk's decidedly "lowbrow" penchant for sensation novels and joke books points up an absorbing preoccupation in late nineteenth-century America: a near obsession with the cultural status of books, reading, and various types of readers. In the mid-1870s a crowd of upstart publishers flooded the market with inordinately cheap texts, most of them unauthorized reprints of popular British novels, marketed to a newly accessible mass audience of readers who seemed to value entertainment over improvement and cheapness over durability (i.e., the gilded over the golden). As a result, many people no longer perceived the world of books as the exclusive province of the educated, the privileged, and the intellectually refined. It had expanded to embrace, in its entirety, the literate—a category nearly as diverse and as various as the nation itself.[2]

In the eyes of some, the expansion of publishing networks into nonelite markets was tantamount to the democratization of literature. For others, it signaled a degradation of literature and the end of "polite" publishing. Although people disagreed about the implications and effects of cheap books for the masses it was nonetheless clear that the literary marketplace, like other arenas of the cultural field, had become stratified to a heightened degree.[3] Moreover, this stratification, represented in part by the rise of a mass market alongside the traditional "literary" market, necessitated new ways of classifying books, readers, and genres, as authors and publishers attempted to respond to the tastes of the new (or newly recognized) readerships. In 1853 a reviewer for the *Knickerbocker* had complained: "There is too much generalization [in the classification of books]. . . . Take the head of novels, for example; we have but two recognized divisions,—namely, the novel, properly so called, and the historical romance. Yet there are a multitude of fictions which require something more definite to express their peculiar qualities; and each of the two species includes almost an infinite of varieties" (qtd. in Baym, *Novels, Readers, and Reviewers* 197). The situation this reviewer describes had changed perceptibly by the end of the century, with publishers, readers, booksellers, and critics devising and continually revising new taxonomies to describe clusters of texts. Advertisements and trade periodicals from the late nineteenth century reveal a heightened awareness on the part of the literary community that belles lettres, an amorphous rubric that encompassed poetry, essays, history, some kinds of fiction, autobiography, travel narratives, and a host of other genres, could usefully be divided into a plethora of categories that better reflected and made sense of the diversity of the nation's literary production.[4]

Significantly, when publishers began to classify books into distinct market niches, they did not derive rubrics and marketing strategies solely from the attributes of the texts per se, as the *Knickerbocker* proposes, or even from the identities of the authors, but rather from the "classes" of readers the books ostensibly addressed. Just as the literary community in the 1850s and 1860s began to perceive fiction for boys and girls, young children and adolescents, as distinct entities securely tied to identifiable subcultures, so, by the end of the century, publishers, retailers, and other members of the trade increasingly differentiated various kinds of books according to the presumed class or status of the target audience, as well as according to "readerly interests" (Brodhead 5). As more and more types of readers entered the marketplace, literary professionals began to discriminate among readers of various backgrounds and social positions and to identify the books each class was thought to favor. In his study of Mark Twain, Richard Lowry observes:

> By the end of Twain's career ... editors and writers succeeded in establishing a relatively organized market for reading that linked different modes of writing with differing segments of the public. The result was a market shaped more or less as a hierarchical pyramid, with an elite form of literature occupying both the top of the structure and the smallest proportion of the market, and the penny press and dime novels serving as the base. In between lay a vast array of fiction, journalism, essays, textbooks, advice books, general interest magazines, and trade journals. (21)

As a result of this hierarchical structuring, "by the end of the [nineteenth] century ... there were various literary audiences" which, as Susan Coultrap-McQuin explains, the critics "rank[ed] ... in importance or quality" (187).[5]

Of course, these various readerships, or classes of readers, corresponded to social class only in an approximate way, and in a manner that was complicated by numerous other factors. In *Market Segmentation*, Donald E. Frank, William F. Massy, and Yoram Wind explain:

> It has long been known that markets and the customers who comprise them are heterogeneous. Early marketers tended to cater to particular groups of consumers, usually those located in relatively compact geographical areas. This was natural, given the problems of transporting goods and conducting business over wide areas. The large and obvious differentials between the social classes also contributed to this early marketing practice. People with high incomes had very different consumption patterns from those who were not well off—and there were relatively few people in the intermediate or middle-class category. Differences in education and cultural orientation, as well as in residence (urban or rural, "provinces" or "metropolitan center"), also led to clear differences in life style and hence in use opportunities and consumption habits. It was not difficult to exploit these differences for marketing purposes. (4)

In the late nineteenth century, however, definitions of class were shifting. Regional differences, contrasts between urban and rural, income level, and even the traditional dividing line between manual and nonmanual labor were becoming less reliable as keys to assessing lifestyle and consumption habits. Replacing these various social indicators, gentility became the new standard for determining social status, and refinement, or "taste," its unmistakable hallmark. Richard Bushman contends: "The division between rude and refined only roughly corresponded to wealth, education, family, work, or any other measure of social class. Genteel culture became an independent variable, cutting across society, and leading, I argue, to the confusion about class that has long been characteristic of American society. Gentility offered the hope that anyone, however poor or however undignified their work, could become middle-class by disciplining themselves and adopting outward forms of genteel living" (xv–xvi). Cultivating good taste in literature, as in other cultural forms, had important social ramifications in this new social order. As Richard Brodhead observes, "The correlation of newly severed literary worlds with newly sharpened class divisions, and the resultant conversion of literary taste into a prime sign of class difference . . . is a decisive feature of American cultural organization in the Gilded Age" (104–5). But for many literary elites, the emphasis on the "outward forms" of refinement (mere "display") at the expense of true gentility posed a serious threat to American culture and the organization of society.

Many nineteenth-century publishers exploited perceived (or presumed) social differences by devising specialized marketing practices to reach specific markets: instead of narrowing their lists to include only titles on a particular subject or only books aimed at a particular market segment, they followed the British practice of issuing several versions of the same text, or series of texts, in a range of different formats.[6] By printing books, especially novels, in both cloth and paper editions, for example, they could target audiences of varying means using different price points. As an 1864 article in the *Round Table* maintained, "It is well known to booksellers that new styles of the same work not only much increase its circulation, but oftentimes seem to open a new demand in other quarters" ("Literary Notes" 140).[7] Of course, this kind of specialization also occurred when different publishers issued competing editions of the same text directed at different audiences (if no single publisher claimed exclusive rights) or simply endeavored to make the work of a single author attractive to multiple audiences. Authors often encouraged this kind of diversification. A popular author such as Henry Wadsworth Longfellow, for example, was capable of exerting considerable influence over the marketing of his works. As William Charvat explains:

> At the very moment when the *New World* [a "crude, wretchedly printed" newspaper that carried "The Wreck of the Hesperus"] was selling on the New York newsstands for twelve and one-half cents, Longfellow's first collection, *Voices of the Night*, containing a scant two dozen lyrics, elegantly printed on fine paper, with wide margins, was being bought in Boston bookstores for seventy-five cents. These and succeeding small volumes throughout the forties were also re-issued in expensive large-paper editions, copies of which the author presented to ladies and gentlemen of Boston and Cambridge society. But in the same period he permitted a Boston mass-audience publisher of cheap fiction to issue a miserable little edition in pamphlet form, on poor paper, for twelve and a half cents. In the same year, a Philadelphia house brought out his collected poems, sumptuously illustrated, at from $3.50 to $7.00 a copy for the carriage trade. And six months later, Harper of New York issued a double-column, paper-covered pamphlet edition at fifty cents. For almost five years, these two editions, at fifty cents and seven dollars, were the only available "complete poems" of Longfellow." (*Literary Publishing* 71–72)

Although Charvat concludes from this information that "for five years he [Longfellow] tried to find out where he belonged between these two economic—and presumably cultural—extremes" (72), it seems more likely that he was striving, through variable pricing and multiple formats, to reach as many readers as possible and that he recognized the efficacy of segmenting the market by quality and price point.

Publishers also formed series using books by different authors, often conceiving of the series before acquiring any titles to put in it.[8] Sometimes, a publisher's series revolved around a certain topic or theme, with the target audience suggested by the subject matter: for example, Roberts Brothers' Famous Women series and Putnam's English Men of Letters, International Science, Heroes of the Nation, and Stories of the Nation (see Sheehan 129–30), as well as the juvenile series discussed in Part One. In many cases, however, publishers grouped books into series that had no clearly identifiable topic or theme or overtly indicated audience but, rather, through cover design, pricing, physical quality, and other peritextual characteristics, were calculated to appeal to particular socioeconomic groups. As Margaret Ezell explains with respect to the British market, "Principal among the advantages of purchasing books in series was the identification of different types of audiences with different financial situations and different cultural needs" (12).

The chapters in Part Two directly address the intersections of readership, class, gender, and genre in this increasingly stratified society and segmented marketplace. One way that literary institutions responded to the disparities between high and low culture was by self-consciously roping off the "literary" from the "popular," the latter category often constructed as "feminine" and labeled "sensational" (fiction) or "sentimental" (poetry, as well as prose). To an extent, these institutions were participating in what Anne M. Boylan identifies as "the larger social labor of defining class by defining gender" (88; see also Lawes 5). Chapter 4 focuses on popular reprint series targeting the mass audience for cheap fiction that emerged after the Civil War. This audience (with which the bookstore clerk in *The Gilded Age* is unmistakably identified) commanded very little cultural capital, according to the standards of the day. Chapter 5 explores the tension between the two poles—highbrow and lowbrow, literary and popular—as it investigates Henry James's appropriation and adaptation of a popular motif of the 1860s and 1870s: the figure of the American woman abroad. With reference to *The Europeans* (1878), a reviewer for *Scribner's Monthly* located James's audience somewhere between "the main bulk of novel-readers" and "the fastidious few who demand to be stirred by an author," finally situating his readership "in a highly respectable and well-read class, which may be termed the 'upper middle cultured'" (qtd. in Hayes 60). Chapter 6 examines the high end of the cultural spectrum, where Ticknor and Fields staked out a position of eminence and prestige by promoting highly literary, culturally sanctioned texts—among them, "the Hawthornes, the Longfellows, the Tennysons"—that is, the texts that establish Laura Hawkins's intellectual and social caliber in *The Gilded Age*. Together with the chapters in Part One, these case studies illustrate a full range of segmentation strategies, including the "mass market" strategy exemplified by the Seaside Library and other highly inclusive series that aimed to succeed "with one offering for all customers"; the "product differentiated" strategy, with which many established publishers, including Ticknor and Fields, "offer[ed] two or more products, each with different features to the same target market"; and "target marketing" (embraced by Lee & Shepard, among others), which "selects and develops offerings tailored to the wants and needs of specific target market segments" (Sandhusen 218). At the same time, this section examines the role of the physical book in canon formation, a process that is linked to both the cheap pocket edition and the *édition de luxe*.

Of course, individual authors had other ways of responding to the parceling up of the literary marketplace into an array of discrete submarkets. One response was to use genre, in much the way that publishers used series, as a way of tapping into the literary tastes of targeted groups. As authors and publishers became attuned to new readerships, they sometimes fashioned innovative subgenres with which to address them and respond to their needs. With reference to this practice, Marcia Jacobson characterizes the second half of the nineteenth century as "a period that embraced one new genre after another and elevated each to best-selling heights" (4). Indeed, one literary critic, writing in 1874, exhorted, "If we do not evolve some new forms adapted to our new [i.e., American] environment it will show pretty conclusively that there is small health in us" (qtd. in Hayes 63), a statement that lends support to recent theories that view genre as "a form of social action, a typified textual response to a typified social situation" (Winsor 155).[9] Howells may have been thinking of "genre" in precisely this way when he wrote that "our life is too large for our art to be broad. In despair at the immense scope and variety of the material offered it by

American civilization, *American fiction must specialize*, and . . . burrow far down in a soul or two" ("A Possible Difference" 135; rpt. *Heroines of Fiction* 264; emphasis added). James, too, cited the multifarious opportunities for specialization presented by the "fast-arriving billion" of the American literary marketplace, with its "[vast] implied habitat and the complexity of the implied history. . . . Life so colossal," he wrote, "must break into expression at points of proportionate frequency" (*Literary Criticism* 1: 653).

As shown in Chapter 2, Alcott defined a new genre around the dilemma involved in growing up female in nineteenth-century America. Similarly, American women of the 1860s and 1870s were the recipients of a new subgenre (explicated in Chapter 5) which responded to an unfamiliar social situation characterized, in part, by increased mobility and expanding opportunities for travel.[10] Ultimately, market segmentation opened up the field of literary expression to a wider range of authors and narrative types—an expression both of American democracy and of bourgeois assertiveness.[11] In the process, American literature was able to resist the homogenizing tendency of the mass market. As James predicted in 1898, the accentuation of the various "divisions and boundaries" in the American literary marketplace helped to cultivate "individual publics [that are] positively more sifted and evolved than anywhere else, shoals of fish rising to more delicate bait" (*Literary Criticism* 1: 654).

As a unit, then, Part Two demonstrates how the various constituents of the literary community participated in the social action of genres and the cultural work of publishers' series as they grappled with the issues of gender, genre, class, and "cultural capital" that redefined the American literary marketplace after the Civil War. No one really knew what was going on in this complex market; the idea of an identifiable universal formula for literary value was becoming lost in the shuffle. No longer could readers and reviewers assume a consensus with assertions such as "the formation of a correct taste is the first thing to be aimed at" ("Books and Girls" 211) or "the supposed aim of the maker of fiction [is] 'that morality of effect shall result from truth of representation'" ("The American Novel—with Samples").

Pondering the rapid expansion of the market for "stories" at the close of the nineteenth century, James reflected: "The sort of taste that used to be called 'good' has nothing to do with the matter: we are so demonstrably in presence of millions for whom taste is but an obscure, confused, immediate instinct. In the flare of railway bookstalls, in the shop-fronts of most booksellers, especially the provincial, in the advertisements of the weekly newspapers, and in fifty places besides, this testimony to the preference triumphs, yielding a good-natured corner at most to a bunch of treatises on athletics or sport, or a patch of theology old and new" (*Literary Criticism* 1: 101). A culture—indeed, individual readers—who could valorize James's soft-spoken, richly symbolic characters alongside Mark Twain's strident shop clerks and shysters clearly had no "taste" left to speak of.

## Chapter Four

# SEASIDE AND FIRESIDE

All civilization comes through literature now, especially in our country. A Greek got his civilization by talking and looking, and in some measure a Parisian may still do it. But we, who live remote from history and monuments, we must read or we must barbarize. Once we were softened, if not polished, by religion; but I suspect that the pulpit counts for much less now in civilizing.
                —William Dean Howells, *The Rise of Silas Lapham* (1885)

I N THE NINTH chapter of *The Rise of Silas Lapham*, a novel about a self-made millionaire who seeks acceptance among Boston's "old-money" elite, William Dean Howells throws two of his characters together in an understated scene in which books form the principal item of discussion. Seated in a bow window of Lapham's half-completed Beacon Street mansion, the millionaire's pretty young daughter Irene timidly informs Tom Corey, the scion of an eminent Boston family, that she has been reading *Middlemarch*. After Tom mentions that it has been several years since he read that novel, Irene, "with a little sense of injury in her tone," replies, "I didn't know it was so old. It's just got into the Seaside Library" (109). Returning home, young Corey meets his father, Bromfield Corey, who proceeds to impart his theory of the civilizing role of literature along with the memorable edict "We must read or we must barbarize." To readers today, the exchange between Tom and Irene amounts to little more than idle small talk, the allusion to the Seaside Library obscured by time, overshadowed by the allusion to George Eliot's *Middlemarch* and easily dismissed as inconsequential (apart from the vague foreshadowing of romantic developments yet to come). Far from trivial, however, Howells's carefully framed reference to the Seaside Library, and to reading more broadly, carried manifold layers of meaning for nineteenth-century readers and inscribed the scene with a crucial subtext. By explicitly locating Irene's frame of reference within the literary field, and by emphasizing, through Bromfield Corey, the "civilizing" status of literature, Howells evokes, with characteristic subtlety and economy, the formidable barriers of class and culture that intervene between the "elite" and the common reader.

Allusions to books and reading permeate *The Rise of Silas Lapham*. Indeed, Irene Lapham's reading of the Seaside Library edition of *Middlemarch* forms a thematic counterpoint to her sister Penelope's reading of *Tears, Idle Tears*, "the novel that was making such a sensation" (196) in Boston society.[1] Unlike *Middlemarch*, which in the Seaside Library is merely the right text in the wrong packaging, *Tears, Idle Tears* is, Howells indicates, the wrong text altogether. At the dinner party in chapter 14, Nanny Corey quips that the book ought to have been called *Slop, Silly Slop*, and Miss Kingsbury gushes that "it's perfectly heartbreaking," with a "hero and heroine . . . who keep dying for each other all the way through, and making the most wildly satisfactory and unnecessary sacrifices for each other" (196). When Mr. Sewell, the minister, muses, in turn, "I don't think there ever was a time when [novels] formed the whole intellectual experience of more people. They do greater mischief than ever," Howells alerts us to the potential danger of such "ruinous" (196) sentimentality. Later, when Penelope, an unwitting rival of her sister for Tom Corey, reads *Tears, Idle Tears* and finds her own predicament unmistakably reflected back at her in its hackneyed plot, she initially recognizes that the heroine's self-sacrifice is "silly" and "wicked" but then begins to be seduced by the novel's "pseudoheroism" (216). Eventually, Penelope comes to her senses and rejects the "psychical suicide" (197) valorized by the novel, but in the process Howells has carefully constructed a self-reflexive model of reading response in which the actual reader of *Silas Lapham* "reads" Penelope who, in turn, "reads" (and finds herself mirrored in) the heroine of *Tears, Idle Tears*. The actual reader, then, watches Penelope very nearly make an enormous mistake as a result of her sentimental identification with a fictional character. Howells is showing that literature provides a pattern for behavior, and when he has Mr. Sewell say that "the novelists might be the greatest possible help to us if they painted life as it is, and human feelings in their true proportions and relation. . ." (197), he is making a powerful case for the value of realistic fiction over sentimental fiction. Moreover, by allowing Penelope to recognize the folly of *Tears, Idle Tears*, he effectively rewrites the plot of this sentimental potboiler, thereby providing his own readers with a better pattern of behavior than poor Penelope had, and a more efficacious plot line to follow in resolving their own romantic dilemmas.[2]

If the role of *Tears, Idle Tears* in *The Rise of Silas Lapham* thus participates in Howells's theme of the civilizing role of literature and the moral responsibility of fiction, what is to be made of the appearance of the Seaside Library, and more specifically, what are we to make of Irene's reading of the Seaside *Middlemarch*? Clearly, Howells is not faulting the text, but in yoking an exemplary realistic novel such as *Middlemarch* to an inferior form of publication, he is suggesting that the materiality of the text impinges on literary value in potentially damaging ways. In this chapter, focusing on the Seaside Library and other cheap paperbound series, I probe the cultural meaning of the material text in the late nineteenth century. By examining the merchandising and distribution of these popular "libraries," I demonstrate how publishers of cheap books adopted key marketing strategies of the periodical publishers and how, as a result, these library publishers helped modernize the book industry and establish a national audience for literature.[3] At the same time, however, the publishers and consumers of cheap reprint series incurred the disapprobation of both of the "regular" trade and the literary establishment, who sought to distance their standard trade editions (timeless and literary) from the new cheap editions—often of the same texts—which, they argued, were as disposable, profitless, and perishable as the notions and comestibles they shared shelf space with.

⚜ ⚜ ⚜

In the fall of 1884, a writer for the *Critic* related an incident in which New York publisher D. Appleton & Company, acting on a tip from its London agent, ran its presses day and night to bring out a "neat, paper covered" edition of *The House on the Marsh*, by Florence Warden (Mrs. Florence Alice [Price] James), the latest novelistic success in Britain. Although Appleton's editor had carefully reviewed the lists of works recently released in cheap paperback series, he failed to discover that some fourteen months earlier George Munro had issued the same novel in his eminently popular Seaside Library. Naturally, the editor was "much chagrined," but "to his great surprise the book 'took hold'" and became "a great success, selling beyond the most sanguine expectations of the publishers." The moral of the story, according to the *Critic*, was that "the American novel-reading public is divided into two distinct classes—those who read the Seaside Library, and those who do not" ("The Lounger" 198).

The anecdote is significant in that it extends the contrast between the types of books published by "respectable" publishers, such as Appleton, and publishers of cheap paperbacks, such as Munro, to suggest that even the same text issued by two different houses, packaged in two different formats and distributed through two different sales channels, would appeal, inevitably, to two distinct audiences. Whereas traditional publishers distributed their books through conventional channels—the retail book trade and the subscription networks—publishers of cheap paperbacks often turned to wholesale distributors, or "jobbers," who positioned the books in the marketplace so as to reach a separate target audience: that is, the "class" of readers "who read the Seaside Library." Thus, even though in Howells's novel Tom Corey and Irene Lapham have both read *Middlemarch* (issued as No. 31 in the Seaside Library's Pocket Edition), they read it in entirely different formats. Moreover, the novel seems to have been unavailable to Irene (from a cultural standpoint, if not a financial one) prior to its Seaside appearance.

The Seaside Library was not the only cheap series of novels in nineteenth-century America, nor was George Munro the first publisher to issue novels in a cheap, newspaperlike format. Forty years earlier, during the heyday of the penny press, New York journalist Park Benjamin had launched a series of reprinted English novels called "extras." Undoubtedly, Benjamin was onto something new when he began to market novels like newspapers, using cheap paper, crowded type in multiple columns, and paper covers, but his more important innovation was in packaging these literary "extras" to resemble periodicals in *function* and disseminating them through the sales and distribution channels (or, in the jargon of the nineteenth century, the "distribution machinery") that was already circulating magazines and newspapers with unprecedented speed and efficiency.[4]

Even this innovation of 1842 had precursors, however. As early as 1839, a few publishers in New York had discovered a very pragmatic reason for marketing novels as if they were newspapers: cheap postal rates. Long before railroads and waterways provided the infrastructure necessary for a national distribution system, and at a time when booksellers were still largely confined to cities and large towns, the United States Post Office afforded an inexpensive, efficient way to circulate newsprint throughout the population.[5] Books were another matter, however, because separate postal rates applied to periodicals and bound volumes. In fact, the rate for books was sufficiently high as to render the use of the Post Office for the distribution of most books uneconomical.[6] Eventually, the price differential between texts classified as periodicals and those classified as books led several enterprising publishers to package their novels as periodicals in order to subvert the postal regulations and turn them to their own advantage. The resulting thinly disguised books, known as story-papers, generally contained novels (serialized or complete) laid out in tight columns on large folio pages, with a few random news items mixed in to satisfy the Post Office's requirement (apparently unenforced) that newspapers convey "public information." Story-papers such as *Brother Jonathan* and the *New World* flourished until 1843, when the Post Office reclassified them as books and effectively put them out of business. Although short-lived, the story-papers taught later publishers an important lesson: there existed a large market for very cheap books, particularly inexpensively bound novels issued complete rather than in parts. More important, the story-papers helped develop that market and establish a national infrastructure of newsstands and periodical dealers capable of supplying it (Noel 141).

The new postal regulations may have temporarily stanched the flow of cheap novels, but there was no reason not to continue the experiment once the regulations were relaxed or an alternative means of large-scale distribution could be devised. Not surprisingly, in the years following the Civil War a company specializing in the national distribution of newspapers and periodicals helped solve the problem by making available to book publishers the same channels that successfully conveyed newspapers and magazines to an increasingly literate and leisured mass audience.

In 1864 several of the country's largest wholesale newspaper distributors had joined forces to create the American News Company (ANC), a conglomerate dedicated to the "quick, efficient, and regularly timed distribution of periodicals" (Tebbel 2: 393).[7] In addition to supplying newspapers and magazines (the ANC was the exclusive distributor of the *Waverly Magazine*, *New York Weekly*, *Family Story Paper*, *Fireside Companion*, and *New York Ledger* [*Covering a Continent* 15]), the company carried stationery, notions, and popular books (only high-volume books were good candidates for ANC distribution), together with "every description of musical merchandise," selling to both book dealers and merchants outside the regular book trade.[8] The firm even published popular reprints—such as the edition of Mary Elizabeth Braddon's *Aurora Floyd* that James reviewed for the *Nation* in 1865 (see my prologue). Enormously successful from the start (the company earned $2,000,000 during its first year in business [Tebbel 2: 393]), the American News Company opened, on average, one new branch office annually for nearly twenty years. By 1888 it had set up branches to receive periodicals and supply vendors all across New England, the Great Lakes states, and the West, with facilities extending as far as San Francisco, New Orleans, and Montreal.[9] This constellation of nationally dispersed branch offices, which eventually numbered 400 (Nance 1: 10), allowed publishers to place their time-sensitive products in a nationwide network of newsstands, railway kiosks (the first extensive chain of retail outlets in the United States [*Covering a Continent* 48]), drygoods stores, "bazaars" (that is, bookstalls in department stores), hotel bookstalls, discount outlets referred to as "cheap johns," pushcart vendors, and newsboys who sold the books on street corners and aboard trains.[10] At the same time, it supplied retailers with a customized mix of newspapers, magazines, and cheap books, individually tailored to suit the needs of the local market, thereby eliminating the need to contract separately with dozens of publishers, agents, and subagents.

The American News Company organized consolidated deliveries of newspapers and magazines by arranging for their transportation by boat or train, plus a substantial volume of material traveling through the post.[11] Predictably, a newspaper publisher was the first to exploit these periodical channels for the widespread distribution of a successful series comprising complete novels: in 1873 the *New York Tribune* began publishing Tribune Novels, a series of quarto or octavo supplements, priced at 10 cents for single numbers or 20 cents for double numbers and issued sporadically over the succeeding decade.[12] The novels, by such popular authors as Margaret Oliphant, Thomas Hardy, Walter Besant, R. D. Blackmore, and Bret Harte, had made earlier, serialized appearances in the pages of the *Tribune*. Achieving both an economy of capital through the reuse of printing plates (Shove 3) and an economy of scale through the large print runs justified by wide circulation in the newsstands, the *Tribune* thereby set the pattern for the next generation of cheap fiction series.

The success of the Tribune Novels inspired a spate of cheap libraries, beginning with the Lakeside Library of Chicago-based Donnelley, Loyd & Co., in 1875.[13] The Lakeside Library, which contained reprints of popular foreign novels in quarto format, was in turn mimicked two years later by several other entries in the field, most notably Beadle & Adams's Fireside Library (possibly the first such series to appear in New York [Shove 57]), George Munro's Seaside Library, and the Riverside Library published by Norman Munro (brother of George).[14] George Munro, who rolled out the Seaside Library in May 1877,[15] had worked for the American News Company, for D. Appleton, and as a reader for the dime-novel publishers Beadle & Adams (Hertel 15) before establishing his own company in 1867 (see figure 5).[16] With new numbers issued at a rate of up to eight per week

The only Unabridged Library Edition Published.

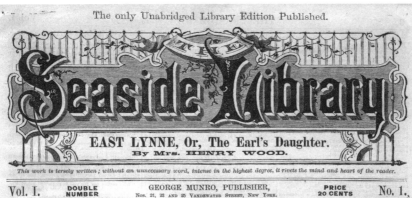

# Seaside Library

## EAST LYNNE, Or, The Earl's Daughter.
### By Mrs. HENRY WOOD.

*This work is tersely written; without an unnecessary word, intense in the highest degree, it rivets the mind and heart of the reader.*

| Vol. I. | DOUBLE NUMBER | GEORGE MUNRO, PUBLISHER, Nos. 21, 23 AND 25 VANDEWATER STREET, NEW YORK. | PRICE 20 CENTS | No. 1. |

## EAST LYNNE;
### OR,
## THE EARL'S DAUGHTER.

### CHAPTER I.
#### THE LADY ISABEL.

In an easy-chair of the spacious and handsome library of his town-house, sat William, Earl of Mount Severn. His hair was gray, the smoothness of its expansive brow was defaced by premature wrinkles, and his once attractive face bore the pale, unmistakable look of dissipation. One of his feet was cased in folds of linen, as it rested on a soft velvet ottoman, speaking of gout as plainly as any foot ever spoke yet. It would seem to look at the man as he sat there—that he had grown old before his time. And so he had. His years were barely nine-and-forty, yet in all, save years, he was an aged man.

A noted character had been the Earl of Mount Severn. Not that he had been a renowned politician, or a great general, or an eminent statesman, or even an active member in the Upper House; not for any of these had the earl's name been in the mouths of men. But for the most reckless among the spendthrifts among spendthrifts, for the gamester above all gamesters, and for a gay man outstripping the gay—by these characteristics did the world know Lord Mount Severn. It was said his faults were those of his head; that a better heart or a more generous spirit never beat in human form; and there was much truth in this. It had been well for him had he lived and died plain William Vane. Up to his five-and-twentieth year, he had been industrious and steady, had kept his terms in the Temple, and studied late and early. The sober application of William Vane had been a by-word with the embryo barristers around; Judge Vane, they ironically called him; and they strove ineffectually to allure him away to idleness and pleasure. But young Vane was ambitious, and he knew that on his own talents and exertions must depend his own rising in the world. He was of excellent family, but poor, counting a relative in the old Earl of Mount Severn. The possibility of his succeeding to the earldom never occurred to him, for three healthy lives, two of them young, stood between him and the title. Yet these have died off, one of apoplexy, one of fever, the third boating at Oxford; and the young Temple student, William Vane, suddenly found himself Earl of Mount Severn, and the lawful possessor of sixty thousand a year.

His first idea was, that he should never be able to spend the money; that such a sum, year by year, could not be spent. It was a wonder his head was not turned by adulation at the onset, for he was courted, flattered, and caressed by all classes, from a royal duke downward. He became the most attractive man of his day, the lion in society; for, independent of his newly-acquired wealth and title, he was of distinguished ap-

pearance and fascinating manners. But, unfortunately, the prudence which had sustained William Vane, the poor law student, in his solitary Temple chambers, entirely forsook William Vane, the young Earl of Mount Severn, and he commenced his career on a scale of speed so great, that all staid people said he was going to ruin and the deuce headlong.

But, a peer of the realm, and one whose rent-roll is sixty thousand per annum, does not go to ruin in a day. There sat the earl, in his library now, in his nine-and-fortieth year, and ruin had not come yet—that is, it had not overwhelmed him. But the embarrassments which had clung to him, and been the destruction of his tranquillity, the bane of his existence, who shall describe them? The public knew them pretty well, his private friends knew better, but himself best; but

Perhaps the earl himself was thinking so, as he sat there before an enormous mass of papers which strewed the library table. His thoughts were back in the past. That was a foolish match of his, that Greta Green match for love, foolish so far as prudence went; but the countess had been an affectionate wife to him, had borne with his follies and his neglect, had been an admirable mother to their only child. One child alone had been theirs, and in her thirteenth year the countess had died. If they had but been blessed with a son—the earl groaned over the long-continued disappointment still—he might then have seen a way out of his difficulties. The boy, as soon as he was of age, would have joined with him in cutting off the entail, and—

"My lord," said a servant, entering the room and interrupting the earl's castles in the air, "a gentleman is asking to see you."

"Who?" cried the earl, sharply, not perceiving the card the man was bringing. No unknown person, although wearing the externals of a foreign ambassador, was ever admitted unceremoniously to the presence of Lord Mount Severn. Years of duns had taught the servants caution.

"His card is here, my lord. It is Mr. Carlyle, of West Lynne."

"Mr. Carlyle, of West Lynne," groaned the earl, whose foot just then had an awful twinge, "what does he want? Show him up."

The servant did as he was bid, and introduced Mr. Carlyle. Look at the visitor well, reader, for he will play his part in this history. He was a very tall man, of seven-and-twenty, of remarkably noble presence. He was somewhat given to stooping his head when he spoke to any one shorter than himself; it was a peculiar habit, almost to be called a bowing habit, and his father had possessed it before him. When told of it he would laugh, and say he was unconscious of doing it. His features were good, his complexion was pale and clear, his hair dark, and his full eyelids drooped over his deep gray eyes. Altogether, it was a countenance that both men and women liked to look upon—the index of an honorable, sincere nature—not that it would have been called a handsome face, so much as a pleasing and distinguished one. Though but the son of a country lawyer, and destined to be a lawyer himself, he had received the training of a gentleman, had been educated at Rugby and taken his degree at Oxford. He advanced at once to the earl, in the straightforward way of a man of business—of a man who has come on business.

"Mr. Carlyle," said the latter, holding out his hand—he was always deemed the most affable peer of the age—"I am happy to see you. You perceive I cannot rise, at least without great pain and inconvenience. My enemy, the gout, has possession of me again. Take a seat. Are you staying in town?"

"I have just arrived from West Lynne. The chief object of my journey was to see your lordship."

"What can I do for you?" asked the earl, uneasily; for a suspicion now crossed his mind that Mr. Carlyle might be acting for some one of his many troublesome creditors.

Mr. Carlyle drew his chair nearer to the earl, and spoke in a low tone;

LADY ISABEL BOWED HER HEAD IN ACQUIESCENCE.

none, save himself knew, or could ever know, the worrying torment that was his portion, well-nigh driving him to distraction. Years ago, by dint of looking things steadily in the face, and by economizing, he might have retrieved his position; but he had done what most people will do in such cases—put off the evil day sine die, and go on increasing his enormous list of debts. The hour of exposure and ruin was now advancing fast.

FIGURE 5. Volume 1, number 1 of the Seaside Library, Quarto Edition, featuring *East Lynne* by Mrs. Henry Wood. Courtesy, Hess Collection, University of Minnesota Libraries.

(Shove 7), eventually accruing to approximately 4,000 numbered titles (Hertel 262), the Seaside Library attained success on an order of magnitude previously unknown—dwarfing, by comparison, even the 1,300-title Railway Library of George Routledge, the "leading figure" of the cheap reprint libraries in Britain, where the phenomenon had begun decades earlier (Altick, *English Common Reader* 299). At a time when new cloth-bound novels were typically issued in editions of 2,000, editions of these paperbound books generally consisted of 25,000 to 30,000 copies (Hertel 85). As John Tebbel records: "In its first two years, 'Seaside' distributed (through the American News Co.'s facilities and news dealers, for the most part) 5,500,000 copies, with many individual titles selling more than 50,000 and the average sale estimated at 10,000. By . . . 1890 it is estimated that nearly 30,000,000 volumes must have been sold" (2: 489).[17] *Publishers' Weekly*, which was hard pressed to keep up with the rapidly multiplying series, listed fourteen new libraries in September 1877, noting that they were "for sale generally by news companies" (qtd. in Shove 7).[18] Thereafter, the increase in the number of competing libraries was rapid, with twenty-six in 1886, a total of 49 in 1890, 78 in 1892, and 94 in the peak year of 1893 (Hertel 21, 65). By 1879, however, the Seaside dominated the market for cheap reprints, "having absorbed or forced out of business most of the competing series" (Shove 10).[19]

The American News Company never achieved the monopoly in the distribution of books that it had with newspapers and magazines (Sheehan 161). Nevertheless, with thirty-two branches and access to 19,000 news-dealers around the country (Hertel 19), its role as the primary distributor of cheap libraries was crucial.[20] Without the timely and efficient access to national markets provided by the American News Company, it is unlikely that popular libraries such as Seaside would have been able to reach a sufficiently large market to justify the large editions of low-priced books which, through the force of sheer numbers, exerted a powerful influence on the book trade and, more generally, on American popular culture.[21]

Although jobbers like the ANC provided the key to the critical issue of large-scale, low-cost distribution, the solution they offered came at a price: censure from more traditional book trade professionals and from conservative pundits and consumers who worried about the moral impact of cheap books on the publishing industry, on the literary culture of the day, and on the less discriminating members of the reading public (people of low educational and cultural capital, like the Laphams). The disapproval shown the cheap libraries, simultaneously arising from and masking a variety of socioeconomic concerns, underlies the debate that emerged over the distribution and sales of these popular book series.

⚜ ⚜ ⚜

In *Sensational Designs: The Cultural Work of American Fiction, 1790–1860*, Jane Tompkins contends: "The conditions of dissemination interpret the work for its readers . . . in that they flow from and support widely-held—if unspoken—assumptions about the methods of distribution proper to a serious (or non-serious) work. The fact that an author makes his or her appearance in the context of a particular publishing practice rather than some other is a fact about the kind of claim he or she is making on an audience's attention and is *crucial* to the success of the claim" (23–24). Although the local context of Tompkins's statement is an explication of the modes of dissemination of works by Nathaniel Hawthorne and Susan Warner (published, respectively, by the literary publisher Ticknor and Fields and by the religious publisher Robert Carter), her argument raises compelling questions about individual books distributed, with or without authorial consent, under two or more widely opposed sets of conditions. By implication, a single text produced and propagated within the contexts of radically different publishing practices would make competing—and contradictory—claims on an audience's attention. The controversy over cheap libraries, which surfaced in an 1884 debate in the correspondence columns of *Publishers' Weekly*, provides fertile ground upon which to explore the implications of Tompkins's assertion. Indeed, the cheap reprint libraries ushered in an array of economic changes that threatened to undermine the business of "regular" publishers and booksellers and, as a result, provoked a negative rhetoric originating within the professional discourse of the trade and filtering into the language of popular journalism, literary criticism, and even (as *Silas Lapham* reveals) literature itself. By emphasizing timelessness as a gauge of literary merit, literary nationalism as an expression of cultural autonomy, and relationships among the content of a text, the form of a book, and attitudes toward readers and reading as measures of value, this rhetoric promoted interpretive practices that effectively devalued the cheap libraries and the myriad texts they conveyed to the public.

Not coincidentally, the debate in *Publishers' Weekly* (coinciding with a parallel debate about the desirability of cheap literature in England) occurred at a time when all quarters of the book industry were feeling the impact of the cheap libraries on the literary marketplace. As an 1883 article in the *Hour* declared, "The increase in the number of books published in the United States . . . is the most significant fact in the history of printed literature" ("Cheap Books" [*Hour*] 498). The *Boston Globe* concurred that "this question of cheap literature is one of the most important of the time" ("Cheap Books" [*Globe*] 522). The same year, a writer for *Biographer* asserted, "The imprint containing the words 'George Munro' is the most familiar in the United States," further noting that editions of titles in the Seaside Library were never smaller than 10,000 copies and estimating the total number of volumes printed to be "many million books" (qtd. in Shove 61).[22] The year 1884 witnessed the appearance of 449 new Seaside volumes from the presses of George Munro, who had already begun to dominate the cheap book business, and an additional 266 volumes of his brother's Munro Library. In 1885, the year *The Rise of Silas Lapham* was published, the Seaside Library was reportedly "at the peak of production" (Shove 17, 42).[23] Such an enormous output was bound to have an effect on the book trade perceptible to individual booksellers, whether they profited from the series or not.[24]

Clearly, the *Publishers' Weekly* debate was sparked by a bookseller who had *not* personally profited from the popularity of the cheap libraries and who therefore felt the loss keenly. In 1884, under the heading "Starving the Book-Trade," the *PW* editors printed the following complaint of a correspondent identified only as "a leading bookseller of long experience . . . who therefore knows whereof he speaks":

> My point is this—the booksellers don't keep the "libraries." They can't—there is no profit in them, and they spoil on the shelves. Therefore, to all the people who frequent bookstores the "libraries" are non-existent. Personally I don't know what they contain. A few *Franklin Squares* I have but no others, and I sell very few of them, though they are near the door. The people who buy "libraries" are the people who take in the *New York Ledger*—utterly unknown to bookstores.
>
> Now for a concrete illustration. We sold a large quantity of "John Inglesant" at $1. There was a *Seaside* edition, but we never heard of it until a short time ago. We never had it. The gross return on a hundred copies of "John Inglesant" in cloth is $100. In the *Seaside* it would have been $20.
>
> Harpers, by putting their best books in the *Franklin Square Library*, are not doing themselves justice, and the trade is starved by the reduction of the volume of business.
>
> Libraries will never be handled by the booktrade. They are sold by people who keep newspapers, and sell apples and other promiscuous

eatables to be consumed on the spot. Something is wanted for booksellers to sell. (643)

This letter contains much of interest. To begin, its author points to a British novel, Joseph Henry Shorthouse's *John Inglesant* (1882), which, like Florence Warden's *The House on the Marsh* (1883), appeared simultaneously in cloth and cheap paper editions in the United States. This dual publication is not in itself surprising: the Seaside Library and other series like it were conceived as reprint libraries largely comprising pirated English and Continental novels.[25] Far from being exceptions to the rule, parallel editions such as those of *John Inglesant* and *The House on the Marsh* were simply the inevitable result of the rampant competition that flared up in the absence of international copyright regulation and the erosion of trade courtesy.[26] Indeed, the first titles of the Seaside Library included such popular British works as *East Lynne* by Mrs. Henry Wood; *John Halifax, Gentleman* by Dinah Maria Mulock (Craik); Charlotte Brontë's *Jane Eyre*; *The Last Days of Pompeii* by Edward Bulwer-Lytton; and George Eliot's *Adam Bede*—all of which had appeared in earlier British and American editions. Later, after they had already appropriated the most conspicuous European successes—along with the novels of James Fenimore Cooper and other popular American works no longer protected by copyright[27]—the libraries branched out by reprinting less distinguished popular novels and, eventually, near the end of their careers, expanded further to include new American works as well.

It is important to recognize that initially the detractors of the cheap series did not object to the titles themselves. After all, even though "sensation novels" were not unknown among the cheap editions (nor among high-priced ones, for that matter), the narratives contained in these reprint libraries were a far cry from the mass-produced, made-to-order dime novels of the period which were so strongly denounced by librarians, parents, teachers, and "respectable" booksellers. Indeed, the cheap reprint libraries carried many respectable, even canonical authors and titles. As Brodhead observes, however, "Literary features never by themselves establish the cultural placement of a work" (103). An array of economic factors influenced the cultural position of the cheap libraries: as the "leading bookseller of long experience" complained to *PW*, "There is no profit in them and they spoil on the shelves."

This pithy statement points up two distinct but related issues: first, booksellers, figuring on a profit of only 3 cents per copy (Tebbel 2: 483), considered the reprints too inexpensive to be worth their while. (Of course, a 3-cent profit on a 10-cent novel is a tidy 30 percent; nevertheless, the small unit price left many booksellers unimpressed.) In the following issue of *Publishers' Weekly*, two booksellers offered rebuttals drawing attention to the high-volume sales of the libraries and pointing out that, on the more expensive clothbound editions, retailers generally offered consumers a discount that cut into profits.[28] The cheap libraries, however, were by no means immune to the price-cutting practices of the "book butchers": as early as 1876 the Central Booksellers' Association had issued a resolution implicating the American News Company in the price-cutting epidemic: "Resolved: That a Committee be appointed to prepare a memorial to the American News Company, setting forth the evils that burden the trade from the sale of current books to the bazaars and fancy goods' dealers at rates which foster the system of underselling, and that the memorial be presented to the trade for signatures, and then transmitted to the American News Company" (qtd. in Sheehan 219). Nearly a decade later the *American Bookmaker* complained, "The introduction of great bazaars, like that of Macy or Ehrich's, in New York, or Wechsler & Abraham, in Brooklyn, is doing much to damage printers, binders, and booksellers" by routinely selling books "in cheap but attractive binding, paper and presswork cut down" at prices well below the publishers' list prices (qtd. in Shove 23).

An 1889 parody of contemporary trade practices advised the publisher to "put the price . . . at several times what you expect to get, so that when the books come to be sold the contrast between 'publishers' prices' and 'our prices' will prove a tempting bait to the unthinking public."[29] The article proceeds to explain the strategy of underselling as follows:

> The first thing to do is to sell to jobbers as much as they will buy and to send out travellers to the "regular" book trade throughout the country and stock up the retail stores to the greatest possible extent. This being done, the next point in the machinery is the supply of the dry-goods bazaar or of local "cheap john" agents at somewhat lower rates than you have been supplying the regular trade, so that the "butchers" may be induced to buy because of the opportunity to undercut the "regulars" to whom you have already sold. . . . The next thing to do is to start a peripatetic auctioneer, who can be sent into a town and undersell both the regular bookdealer to whom you have sold and the "cheap john" bazaar who has been undercutting him. In this way, a vast market can be made. ("How to Make Publishing 'Pay'" 930)

As a result of such tactics, many retailers regarded the cheap libraries with suspicion and resisted stocking them—with the exception of the Franklin

Square Library, whose Harper imprint "carried with it considerable pres-tige" (Shove 110)[30]—until the competition they created effectively forced them to do so.[31]

The second issue that the "leading bookseller" raises is that the books in these libraries were so cheaply made, with their poor paper and flimsy covers, that they lacked durability: mere ephemera, they were destined to "spoil on the shelf." In fact, many commentators likened the cheap books to the most ephemeral of commercial publications, the newspaper. A writer for the *Hour*, while acknowledging the inferior production of the libraries, actually granted them a favorable comparison on this basis: "The form in which most of them have been issued is not the most pleasing that could be devised, and the type is small, but form, paper, and typography are fully as good as those of that favorite American library known as the newspa-per" ("Cheap Books" [*Hour*] 498).[32] As with the story-papers of the 1840s, however, success in the marketplace depended on precisely those news-paperlike characteristics of cheapness and ephemerality which many regu-lar booksellers found disagreeable.

Forty years after the U.S. Post Office had stymied the story-paper pub-lishers, the publishers of cheap libraries took pains to give their publica-tions a more or less legitimate claim to the classification of "periodicals" that would permit them to circulate through the mail as such.[33] In the 1870s-90s they mimicked the more conventional periodicals in a variety of ways, including makeup, pricing, periodicity, timeliness, advertising con-tent, and sales methods, in addition to mode of distribution. New numbers of the more prolific of the libraries were issued practically daily, their lay-out and packaging playing up their ephemeral, time-sensitive nature.[34] In addition to their cheap paper and lack of durable covers, the earliest of the libraries were issued in a large format (tabloid-sized quartos, comparable in size and shape to the daily papers) and were laid out with cramped type in two or three columns per page, a design referred to as "cheap style."[35] At 10 cents for single numbers and 20 cents for double numbers, volumes in these libraries were only slightly more costly than newspapers. ("Penny papers" were 1 or 2 cents; the upmarket papers typically cost 6 cents.) Like newspapers, they were padded with paid advertisements (an additional source of revenue to their publishers)—full- and half-page display ads as well as classifieds—and, at least nominally, were available by subscrip-tion.[36] Newsdealers and petty merchants supplied by the American News Company sold them, and the circulation of the more popular titles reached an order of magnitude comparable to that of the midsized dailies. Finally, in order to convey a sense that each volume was part of an ongoing periodical series, Munro and his competitors dated and numbered each book and displayed the title of the library in an embellished masthead above the title of the individual volume (see figure 6), a practice producing the added—if serendipitous—result of increasing customers' awareness of the publishers' unique label by giving precedence to the "brand," or imprint (Seaside Library, Lakeside Library, etc.), over the individual "product," or text (e.g., *John Inglesant* or *The House on the Marsh*).[37] This attention to brand identity turned out to be a particularly useful strategy for the publishers of cheap reprints, as the titles they released were seldom their exclusive property. Whenever more publishers entered the field of cheap reprint libraries, it became increasingly necessary to promote the special features of each individual imprint in order to remain competitive. Thus, George Munro advertised that "The works in THE SEASIDE LIBRARY, Pocket Edition, are printed from larger type and on better paper than any other series published."[38] A Beadle & Adams ad (reproduced in Johannsen 304) touted the superlative moral quality of the firm's Waverley Library (1879–86):

> Each issue a complete novel by an author of established reputation—
> perfectly pure in tone, spirited and captivating in story,
> as the title 'Waverley' implies. Everything to please and nothing to avoid—
> *Wholesome, Vigorous and Fresh*

The far-reaching effects of this emphasis on brand over product in the modern mass market—resulting in a shift in the balance of relationships among manufacturer, retailer, and customer—were beyond the comprehension of the nineteenth-century book trade.[39] Perfectly transparent, however, was the fact that by passing off their publications as periodicals and disseminating them through the mail at the second-class rate, the publishers of the cheap libraries availed themselves of what many regarded as an unfair advantage.[40] The animosity that this practice engendered is evident in a series of editorials appearing after an 1885 congressional debate over the ambiguous postal definitions. A writer for the *Boston Daily Advertiser* pointed out that a purchaser could obtain one of these "periodical" books "with the rapidity and the surety of the mail, and the cheapness of the 'second-rate,' or newspaper postage," whereas the same book "might

FIGURE 6. The cover of *Middlemarch* (first half) in the Seaside Library, Pocket Edition (1883). Courtesy, Rare Books and Manuscripts Library of the Ohio State University Libraries.

be printed in the same form, on similar type, by another publisher, who does not carry on a 'periodical library,' and then the purchaser, in any part of the country, must pay for its transfer, if it come by mail, eight cents a pound, because it is not a 'periodical'" ("Periodicals vs. Books" 711). Three years later this double standard was still a sensitive topic, as the following 1888 letter from Philadelphia publisher T. B. Peterson attests:

> A newspaper or a magazine is properly a serial, but that a complete book can be so considered is absurd. The publishers of the cheap libraries put a subscription rate on their issues, but that anomaly, a subscriber to a cheap library, cannot be found, and as the publishers sell their individual issues exclusively through the news companies to the retail dealers, it is fair to presume that the subscription rate is merely a blind to preserve the low rate of postage, and that they do not desire to be burdened with a subscription list. The natural result of sending books through the mails under the pretext that they are serials, at one-eighth of what legitimate publishers have to pay for precisely the same books, which are issued without a date, a number, or a subscription rate, is to unduly favor a few persons and enable them to largely undersell all the legitimate publishing trade of the country. While it is clearly advisable in this enlightened age to place books at such low rates as to be within reach of all, it is as clearly inadvisable and unjust to discriminate in postal charges between publishers who issue books squarely as books and those who issue books under the flimsy pretext that they are serials, to the serious disadvantage of the former. (Peterson 422)[41]

Before long, the scope of the debate had extended to encompass the moral and aesthetic value of the texts disseminated in the cheap series. As an editorial in *Publishers' Weekly* astutely noted, "Whenever the postal question is argued, the literary and moral quality of the cheap libraries is almost sure to be lugged into the question," and it judiciously asserted that "there are decidedly two sides to the question": the same series giving the "best authors . . . to the public cheaply," *PW* pointed out, had also put before the public "a class of literature which they would not have other-wise read" ("The 'Cheap Libraries' Question" 634). Many others, however, were less equable, taking the view of the *New York Times* that "this nominal charge for carriage is given to a great deal of 'literature' of an unwholesome, not to say a vicious, character." Critics of the series typically ignored the "classics" reprinted in the cheap libraries while making a great deal of the "low character" of the potboilers ("Postage on Books" 635).

Economic factors undergird much of the criticism of the moral and literary merits of the cheap libraries. The 1884 debate in *Publishers' Weekly*, for example, explicitly linked the literary and moral quality of the libraries to the conditions of their dissemination and implicitly condemned them on that basis without reference to the texts themselves (the "leading bookseller" actually admitted of the libraries, "Personally I don't know what they contain"). In observing that the libraries "are sold by people who keep newspapers, and sell apples and other promiscuous eatables to be consumed on the spot," the *PW* correspondent suggested that like newspapers and foodstuffs, which are mingled in "promiscuous" fashion on the shelves of newsstands and "cheap johns" (small, inexpensive retail outlets), the libraries were to be consumed quickly, without forethought or afterthought. Similarly, although an 1887 *PW* article described a lower-priced but not "cheap" edition of Hardy's *Woodlanders* as "an intellectual feast" (qtd. in Tebbel 2: 486–87), Charles Dudley Warner, in his role of contributing editor to *Harper's New Monthly Magazine*, referred to the libraries as "cheap and chopped-up literary food" (807).

Some book trade observers actually applauded the new affordability and ready availability of this "intellectual food," and the *Boston Herald* informed readers that "cheap books are almost as necessary in these days as cheap bread" (qtd. in Shove 39–40). Others wondered what kind of an impact the cheap libraries would have on reading practices. The *American Bookmaker* extolled the informality and portability of the cheap libraries,— characteristics played up in such series titles as Seaside Library and Lakeside Library—in contrast to dime novel series such as the Dime and the Half-Dime, "the wordage calculated," as James Hart notes, "by the price":

O, they are here! Books for summer travelers, books for mountain and seaside resorts, books for loiterers and loungers at watering-places, books for those who "go a-fishing,["] handbooks for tourists, guide-books for excursionists, pocket-maps for tramp trips, &c., are now on the top wave of popular favor. . . . Being without covers, they have a cool and summery look, and from their flexibility may be readily stowed away in one's pocket or thrust into any unfilled corner of a traveling bag. They adapt themselves to any conceivable reading attitude, from the bolt upright to the recumbent position assumed on a sofa or lounge or in a steamer chair, hammock or bed, or stretched out on greensward or sandy beach. In fact, these libraries are the literary manna of this modern desert of push and struggle for material welfare. Their issues may almost be had for the trouble of stooping and gathering them up. ("Books in Summer Suits" 6)[42]

Still others contrasted the cheap editions with weightier tomes whose heft signaled that they were worth preserving. The same article that praised "books in summer suits" noted that, contrary to the implications of the series titles, "they are not intended to be stored in libraries" (6), and a later critic reminisced that "back in the seventies the summer book was . . . a book to read and then roll up for mailing to distant friends or throw into the waste-basket" (Halsey 79). Boston publisher Henry O. Houghton (who, along with James R. Osgood, influenced the characterization of Silas Lapham [Ballou 274]) agreed: "People who buy a cheap book will throw it away soon, and come and buy the better book we publish, and they will keep it. . . ." (qtd. in Comparato 128). Even Irene Lapham, informed as she is of the current offerings of the Seaside Library, recognizes that the Parkman, the Shakespeare, the Longfellow, and the Scott that are to "furnish" her family's home must be obtained "in the nicest bindings" (Howells, *Rise of Silas Lapham* 106). An 1895 article, "The Decadence of Cheap Books," remarked that "when the works of a well-known living or dead author are now republished they are likely to be in a dignified *definitive* edition, at a cost proportionate to the workmanship put into good composition, paper, and presswork" and added that Americans are "surely if slowly shedding the chrysalis of the 'cheap and nasty' book" (681). In a culture in which "display" had become a crucial component of class definition (Stoneley 33), the physical quality of the books in one's home carried significant social implications.

Those engaged in the debate over cheap series frequently assumed a correlation between the material characteristics of books and the aesthetic as well as moral quality of their contents. Durable books seemed to imply the existence of enduring literary quality. By the same token, an 1887 *Publishers' Weekly* article commended "books that can and will be preserved, and that will have more influence in cultivating a taste for good literature than a whole year's issue of the so-called 'cheap' literature" (qtd. in Tebbel 2: 486–87). Five years earlier, when the "decadence" of the cheap libraries had not yet been intimated, Postmaster General John Wanamaker contrasted "a book that is temporal and flimsy in its construction" with "one that is suitable for preservation" and inquired whether the discrimination of Congress should not "be in favor of the book which, being strongly made and therefore apparently more worthy of preservation, will last for the good of others than the purchaser rather than of the book which is thrown aside after it has served the purpose of its purchase?" (131). As all of these commentaries suggest, a book that was part of a cheap library was seen not as an investment—economic, moral, or intellectual—but merely as an incidental sale.

A few critics went so far as to charge that the informal aspect of the cheap libraries actually discouraged serious reading. Writing in 1893, James Russell Lowell speculated that the ease and affordability of printing "has supplanted a strenuous habit of thinking with a loose indolence of reading which relaxes the muscular fiber of the mind. . . . The costliness of books was a great refiner of literature" (qtd. in Rubin 18–19). Charles Dudley Warner also stressed the connection between the cost and physical makeup of a publication and the mental attention accorded it. Arguing that "it remains true that people value and profit only by that which it costs some effort to obtain," he declared: "Reading to any intellectual purpose requires patience and abstraction and continuity of thought. This habit of real reading is not acquired by the perusal of newspapers, nor by the swift dash which most people give to the cheap publications which are had for the picking up, and usually valued accordingly. It is an open question whether cheap literature is helping us any toward becoming a more thoughtful and reading people" (807). By extension, the unsubstantial format of the cheap series—not to mention such calculated titles as Holt's Leisure Moment Library (an inexpensive counterpart to his Leisure Hour Library)—was sometimes seen as a reflection on the texts themselves, which were therefore regarded as correspondingly weak or trivial: not timeless classics but rather ephemeral texts for the idle moment, which, like items in a newspaper, "spoil" (i.e., date) quickly and merit only passing notice.[43] Thus, in *Silas Lapham*, the time sensitivity and ephemerality of the Seaside Library are transferred to *Middlemarch*, which becomes passé in the context of the rapid-fire publishing economy of the cheap series, and, as a result, Eliot's text is declassed.

In addition to suggesting a short shelf life and virtually nonexistent afterlife (in an intellectual as well as a physical sense), the fact that the cheap series were sold alongside newspapers, produce, and housewares further underscored their commercial nature. Since newsstand jobbers such as the American News Company also dealt in stationery, notions, playing cards, games, globes, sheet music, and even musical instruments, the books they distributed frequently mingled, in what many regarded as an inappropriate or unseemly fashion, with housewares and dry goods. W. H. Rideing noted with blatant displeasure that the libraries could "be sold with flannel, laces, underwear and scented soap, for seven cents a copy" (56); and even the highly commercial Street & Smith, publishers of countless dime novels and story-papers, advertised in 1890 that their series "are not sold in dry-goods stores" (qtd. in Shove 145). Warner also hinted at a certain lack of decorum when he announced that "for the price of a box of strawberries or a banana you can buy the immortal works of the greatest genius of all time in fiction, poetry, philosophy, or science" (807). In Warner's estimation, even Great Works were trivialized by cheap packaging.

Advertisements, sales gimmicks, and merchandising techniques further degraded the literature by associating books with household goods.[44] Volumes in the Seaside Library not only promoted periodicals published by Munro (such as the *New York Fireside Companion* and *Fashion Bazaar*) but carried advertisements (figure 7) for such varied items as soap, pianos, and corsets (a telltale indication of the series' presumed female readership). Some publishers actually bundled their less successful novels with household products to provide consumers with an additional incentive to purchase. Raymond Shove relates: "Early in 1889 a soap manufacturer announced that he would give a copy of a celebrated novel, then recently issued, with every fifteen cent cake of soap! Another firm appropriately put on the market a machine to vend the mechanically produced paper volumes, so that by inserting a nickel in a slot and turning a crank a novel could be made to drop into one's hands. The *American Bookseller* noted that whole sets of books were being offered free with the purchase of a fifty cent bottle of patent medicine" (41–42). Indeed, department stores and manufacturers of household goods frequently gave away books as sales premiums. Late in 1883, when the American News Company returned over a million copies of the soon-to-be-discontinued quarto Seaside Library, Munro unloaded large numbers of them on soap companies (Comparato 125).[45]

Even the presumed audience of the cheap libraries suffered by the association with household goods and the irresistible comparison with newspapers suggested by their innovative mode of distribution. The obvious slur contained in the comment that "the people who buy 'libraries' are the people who take in the *New York Ledger*—utterly unknown to bookstores" identifies this audience with the readers of Robert Bonner's fiction-filled story-paper, famous for its sensation novels, sultry romances, sentimen-

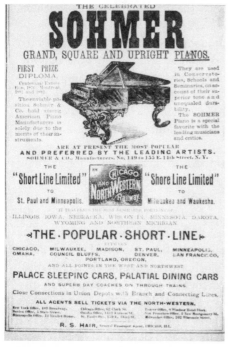

FIGURE 7. Advertisements from the Seaside Library no. 866 (1866), *Miss Harrington's Husband*, by Florence Marryat.

tal poetry, and moralistic essays.[46] Similarly, Howells implies that Irene Lapham is a stranger to bookstores, or at least to literature. In chapter 9 of *The Rise of Silas Lapham*, young Corey advises Irene which books to purchase for the Lapham family library. Although she professes to have "had ever so much about Shakespeare at school" (105), she makes several revealing blunders—"Is it Gibbon or Gibbons?" she asks (105)—even to the point of elevating the American poets over the British ones. She thinks she recalls hearing the name of Tennyson at school but gushes, "I think we ought to have *all* the American poets" (105). Moreover, although Silas Lapham stoutly maintains that the members of his family "do buy a good many books, first and last" (82), Howells hastens to add that he "probably had in mind the costly volumes which they presented to one another on birthdays and holidays" (82)—a clue that the Laphams are to be numbered among the bookstore-avoiding audience for subscription gift books. The exchange reflects the larger concern in the novel about the precariousness of social position in a booming Gilded Age economy that was "punctuated by a series of 'panics' and 'collapses'" and characterized as much by "loss of caste" as by "upward mobility" (Stoneley 14).

The majority of the commentators on the cheap-fiction phenomenon by and large fell into two camps: those who assumed that people of limited means would be glad to read such highbrow authors as Emerson and Carlyle if they could afford to; and those who believed that people without the means to purchase the full-priced, cloth-covered books had fundamentally different—and inferior—reading tastes. For those taking the former view, the issuance of the cheap libraries constituted a "literary revolution" that would "furnish the world with cheap literature and elevate American citizenship" ("Literary Revolution" 391); indeed, the "new pirate" was a "great public benefactor" who had embarked on a "noble undertaking" ("Old and New Pirates" 175). A writer for the *Hour*, for example, insisted that well-known British authors had found in America "a new set of readers"; "At such prices the poorest can afford to read. . . . Instead of subscribing to a public library . . . he can for the same amount of money per year buy outright twenty or thirty books" ("Cheap Books" [*Hour*] 498). Another optimist was R. Pearsal Smith, who wrote that the cheap libraries benefited "the lonely rancher in Dakota, the humble freedman at the south, and the poor student eager for a library of his own" (qtd. in Shove 38–39).

Houghton Dutton, a Boston dry goods vendor, echoed this sentiment: "The writer has traveled extensively in the United States, and seen George

Eliot, Carlyle, Scott, Victor Hugo, Emerson, Edwin Arnold, Homer, Goethe, Dante and Shakespeare read in the backwoods of Arkansas and in the mining camps of Colorado, in the popular 10 or 20 cent editions, by people who could never have afforded the books, and who probably would never have read them, had it not been for the price" (qtd. in Shove 39–40). Meanwhile, the *New York Evening Express* rhapsodized that in "an application of democracy to art," the libraries "are driving over the land like a snow-storm, finding their way into the rudest huts and the dingiest workshops; they are being read by working-people, shop-girls, and apprentice boys, giving entertainment and ideal enrichment to millions who else would not get such benefit" (qtd. in Schurman, "Those Famous American Periodicals" 45). This notion of "enrichment" or "improvement" had strong ties to the cultural meaning of books in the nineteenth century (Bushman 285; see also Rubin). As Jane Hunter points out, "Access to books did not define an American public, but increasingly it defined a class of those who hoped to rise in station" (59).

Among critics in the second camp, however, Brander Matthews considered the audience for the libraries "uneducated" (580), and Warner suggested not only that the cheap editions failed to improve the less fortunate but that the general readership actually suffered from the availability of the low-priced books: "we doubt if the class that were to be specially benefited by this reduction in price of intellectual food are much profited. . . . Who is it who buy the five, ten, and twenty cent editions? Generally those who could afford to buy, and did buy, books at a fair price, to the remuneration of author and publisher. And their serious reading habit has gone down with the price" (807). Similarly, in *The Rise of Silas Lapham*, Mrs. Corey expresses the opinion that the newly rich—people who can afford to buy "fair priced" (or, in any event, full-priced) books—actually prefer the cheap reprints. Of the Laphams, she sniffs: "I dare say they *never* buy a *new* book. I've met some of these moneyed people lately, and they lavish on every conceivable luxury, and then borrow books, and get them in the cheap paper editions" (97). Of course, Mrs. Corey's suspicions are borne out in the text. Although she is aware of its appearance in the Seaside Library, Irene Lapham obtains her copy of *Middlemarch* from a lending library.

Perhaps the most pervasive—and the most deceptive—of the criticisms leveled at the cheap libraries was the charge that the fiction they conveyed to the public was a corrupting influence on the masses. The fact that the libraries included highly literary titles such as *Middlemarch* was, apparently, beside the point: series of books implied patterns of reading, and in the overall design of the libraries the "literary" was eclipsed by the "sensational." Typically, this allegation was couched in overtly nationalistic terms, as the authors and texts deemed most objectionable largely emanated from England and France. W. H. Rideing, for example, declared that the pirated novel, "like a rank weed in a garden, is choking all fiction of native growth" (qtd. in Shove 31), and the *Boston Globe* reported that "the extent to which the Seaside and Franklin Square and other popular series are steeping our people in English thoughts . . . is considered with apprehension in many quarters" ("Cheap Books" [*Globe*] 522). Just as typically, however, complaints about the foreign origin of the texts occurred within the context of the debate over international copyright, with American authors, who often felt disadvantaged by the reprinting of European texts, overwhelmingly weighing in on the side of protective legislation.

Certainly, the vast majority of the texts in the cheap libraries were foreign reprints. Librarian of Congress A. R. Spofford estimated the ratio of foreign to American books in the cheap series to be nine to one, and in 1895 a contributor to *Publishers' Weekly* reported that "up to a few years ago 90 odd per cent of the fiction in the United States was English" (qtd. in Hertel 106). The clear majority of titles in the Seaside Library were British, with French texts constituting a distant second and American texts only a small minority.[47] The fact that many of the "representative" Seaside authors (those with numerous titles in the series)—Mary Elizabeth Braddon, Charlotte M. Braeme, Margaret Wolfe Hungerford ("The Duchess"), Louise de la Ramée ("Ouida"), Mrs. Henry Wood—were considered "sensational" tended to deflect attention from the fact that many novels held in esteem by the literary community (for example, those of Sir Walter Scott, Charles Dickens, Jules Verne, Alexandre Dumas, Margaret Oliphant, and George MacDonald, not to mention George Eliot) also appeared in the Seaside Library. (The lineup mirrors the lists of authors appearing in the British "yellow-backs"—"veritable rosters of Victorian bestsellerdom"—which boasted a correspondingly large number of texts by reprinted American authors, including Cooper, Irving, N. P. Willis, Longfellow, and Lowell [Altick, *English Common Reader* 299–300].) As a result, critics frequently admonished their readers against the libraries' foreign content. As Edmund Clarence Stedman solemnly advised (with reference to the issue of copyright), "In the literary market, just now, good home-made bread is quite as wholesome for Americans, as are French rolls or even English muffins" (Stedman and Gould 2: 407).

When the supply of noncopyrighted American works and European works subject to piracy eventually dried up, the regular publishers found a new cause for concern: with the cheap libraries including increasing numbers of new American works, the price competition these volumes created deterred many trade publishers from issuing the new texts in higher-priced cloth editions and brought about a disappointing decline in the number of new titles released. Propelled by the large investment in capital (steam presses and other mechanized equipment) that necessitated large print runs, as well as by the daily or weekly publication schedules that demanded an unending supply of new titles, the cheap libraries had glutted the market.[48] As a result, the trade was, in the language of the day, "demoralized."

The title "Starving the Book-Trade," under which *Publishers' Weekly* aired the complaint of the "leading bookseller of long experience," alludes to an interesting reversal in patterns of publication which occurred over the course of the libraries' brief history. Whereas the publishers of cheap series began by reprinting titles with established markets—titles that had often originally appeared in highly respected series such as Harper's Library of Select Novels (containing reprints of more than six hundred foreign books and perhaps half a dozen American ones [Boynton 185]) and Holt's Leisure Hour Library—by 1884 the highbrow publishers were raiding the lists of the cheap libraries for new titles. The Appleton edition of *The House on the Marsh* came about through an oversight, but a few months later D. Appleton & Company, apparently pleased with the sales of this book, announced its intention to publish *At the World's Mercy*, another novel by Florence Warden which had already appeared in the Seaside Library.[49] Thus, although the cheap libraries never escaped the negative rhetoric that spun around them, after only seven years the Seaside Library had developed from a series featuring only reprints with previously established markets to a series boasting an increasing number of original titles and first American editions of European texts. British works that appeared in America for the first time as volumes in the Seaside Library include Charles James Lever's *Kate O'Donoghue* (1877) and *Paul Gosslett's Confessions* (1881), as well as Mary Elizabeth Braddon's *The Mystery of Leighton Grange* (1878), *Asphodel* (1881), and *Married in Haste* (1883) (Dzwonkoski, "George Munro" 315).

The success of the Seaside and other cheap libraries proved to be short-lived, however. By 1887 the practice of underselling had turned on the library publishers, undermining their efforts to maintain prices and ultimately causing them to lose their grip on the literary marketplace.[50] Also in 1887 the pirate Munro himself became the victim of literary piracy at the hands of "some unscrupulous persons" who stole the Seaside Library name, attaching it to their own line of books (*PW* 32 [1887]: 39; Shove 63).[51] Then, in 1890, John W. Lovell, whose United States Book Company had been systematically acquiring the plates and publication rights of cheap series, bought out the original Seaside Library in what was to prove a failed attempt to curb price competition by establishing a kind of monopoly, or "book trust" (Shove 100–104). The final stroke to this over-extended business was dealt in 1891—seven years after *Publishers' Weekly* printed "Starving the Book-Trade"—when the United States finally legislated international copyright.[52] The decline and ultimate demise of the cheap series were still some years away, but by the early 1890s an excess of competition, overproduction, and diminishing sources for new titles had combined to seal the fate of the cheap libraries.[53]

⚜ ⚜ ⚜

Considering that the cheap series were widely regarded as ephemeral productions, it is paradoxical that John Tebbel describes the Seaside Library as George Munro's "lasting achievement" (2: 489). Nevertheless, although the individual volumes were short-lived, the collective series brought about permanent and far-reaching changes in the publishing industry. In addition to their innovative distribution methods—and the merchandising techniques that justified these methods—the marketing strategies of publishers such as George Munro successfully conflated the concept of the potential market with the concept of the nation itself (restricted as this concept was in terms of race and ethnicity). While specialized publishers attempted to segment the literary market by exploiting difference (gender, age, class, ethnicity), these early mass-market publishers emphasized commonality and sameness. (Clemens, whose personal library contained numerous volumes issued by Munro, Lovell, and other purveyors of cheap series [see Gribben, *Mark Twain's Library*], referred to cheap reprints as "the books the nation reads" [qtd. in Matthews 583].) Wholesalers supplied retailers around the country with the same books. Chain retail stores, which became increasingly important outlets for books, encouraged a standard inventory that tended toward uniformity. Meanwhile, advertising and sales gimmicks promoted an image of the book consistent with the kinds of mass-produced household goods that were already becoming staples of day-to-day life in all parts of the United States. Initially a means of enabling regional publishers to reach a broader audience, this effort to transcend cultural and physical boundaries rapidly became an end in itself as the concept of the nation grew up and merged with what business and the media came to recognize in the twentieth century as the mass market.

As a result of these cheap libraries, therefore, the book business became more commercialized and modernized: book production moved toward complete mechanization (Comparato 124); the industry fell increasingly under the control of large, impersonal corporations such as the American News Company[54] and the Lovell Combination; books were transformed from unbranded goods into branded merchandise distributed through chain retailers; and traditional book publishers finally succeeded in identifying and targeting the largest constituent of the literary marketplace: the mass reading public.[55] Most important, however, was the lasting contribution of these series to the development of a nationwide audience for fiction and, by extension, to the creation of a national identity that was informed by, and reflected in, the middle-class values of leisure and domesticity connoted by the winsome titles of cheap paperbound libraries such as the Lakeside, Riverside, Seaside, and Fireside.

# INNOCENCE ABROAD

O my country, may you not be judged by your travelling children!
—Ella W. Thompson, *Beaten Paths* (1874)

I N DECEMBER 1875, at the start of a publishing season that would witness keen interest in the already popular genres of travel writing, women's fiction, and internationally themed literature, the Chicago house of Jansen, McClurg & Company released a new novella by a young author who was just beginning to explore the relationships among nationality, setting, and character that would become career-long interests. Described by the *American Bookseller* as "an extremely lively story of an extremely lively American girl living in Rome," the narrative tells of a vivacious young woman who sparks first the affections and then the suspicions of a well-heeled American youth, who observes with puzzlement and dismay her unbecoming conduct toward an unsuitable Italian rival. Conscious that the *nouvelle*'s racy portrayal of the American girl abroad might vex its domestic audience, the *American Bookseller* cautioned that "most readers will call her [the eponymous protagonist] 'fast'" but went on to reassure the trade that the heroine's "desperate flirtations will interest a large class of novel readers" ("New Books" 52). Two years later, when Henry James's *Daisy Miller: A Study* sallied onto the scene, most readers and reviewers had likely forgotten *Mae Madden: A Story*[1] by Mary Murdoch Mason, the "extremely lively" tale that prefigured James's famous "invention" of the flighty American belle who runs afoul of the conventions and mores of her staid compatriots in Rome.[2]

The existence of a narrative that so closely parallels the setting, characterization, plot, and theme of *Daisy Miller* points up the fact that in writing *Daisy Miller*, James situated his work at the epicenter of a popular literary mode of the 1870s: the narrative of the American woman abroad. For more than a generation, female readers and writers had exerted a powerful influence in the literary marketplace.[3] Indeed, by 1850, the female audience had become the largest segment of the market for belles lettres (Baym, *Shape*

17–18), and by the early 1870s women were producing nearly three-fourths of all the novels published in the United States (Coultrap-McQuin 2). Consequently, authors and publishers alike became increasingly attuned to the tastes and reading preferences of women readers, so that what had been, in the 1850s and earlier, a distinctly demarcated niche emerged as the dominant fictional mode.[4] It was one that some male writers firmly embraced (Papashvily 50; Baym, *Shape* 13), with travel writing and polite fiction forming two of their most highly favored genres.[5]

The juxtaposition of *Mae Madden* and *Daisy Miller* illustrates how James, like Hawthorne and Howells, located his work at the intersection of those two highly fashionable spheres of literary activity, travel writing and women's fiction—effectively "colonizing" a fictional form pioneered by European women such as Madame de Staël and Anna Jameson and subsequently adapted and incorporated by generations of American women writers.[6] Indeed, fictional narratives of American women abroad constituted a subset of women's fiction that men could participate in more easily than the traditional domestic novel, since they moved women out of the domestic sphere and into the broader world. Keenly aware of "the competition of the 'lady-writers'" (*The Bostonians* 118), Henry James, as Alfred Habegger has shown, engaged throughout his career in "an appropriation, masterly and distorting, of American women's fiction" (4). I argue that the motif of the American woman abroad afforded James a point of entry into a distinct niche market comprising a predominantly female, middle-class readership. A close reading of *Mae Madden*, within the context of contemporary accounts of American women in Europe, illustrates how, and to what end, James artfully—and artistically—rewrote this earlier version of the naive and feckless American girl running amok in Rome.[7]

⁂ ⁂ ⁂

Critics and literary historians have long credited Henry James with the "invention" of the fictional motif of the American girl abroad. In 1903 Howells formally attributed to his friend this distinction when he asserted:

> Mr. James is not quite the inventor of the international novel, . . . but he is the inventor, beyond question, of the international American girl. He recognized and portrayed the innocently adventuring, unconsciously periculant American maiden, who hastened to efface herself almost as soon as she saw herself in that still flattering if a little mocking mirror, so that between two sojourns in Europe, a decade apart, she had time to fade from the vision of the friendly spectator. In 1860–1870, you saw her and heard

her everywhere on the European continent; in 1870–1880, you sought her in vain amidst the monuments of art, or on the misty mountain-tops, or at the tables d'hôte. (*Heroines of Fiction* 165–66)[8]

Howells's claim, bolstered by James's own identification of "the international young ladies" as his "appointed thematic doom" (*Daisy Miller and Other Stories* xlviii), has long gone unchallenged.[9] Nevertheless, a glimpse into the popular fiction of the decade preceding the appearance of *Daisy Miller* reveals a bevy of "international American girls" who share with Daisy the very qualities Howells singles out for comment. In fact, by the time *Mae Madden* appeared in 1876, the reading public was already intimately acquainted with her type. According to a review of Mason's novella in *Appleton's Journal*: "'Mae,' the heroine, has evidently cost the author some pains; but she only adds another item to the rapidly-accumulating evidence that the *ingénue*—the fresh, piquant, impulsive, unconventional child of Nature, impatient of restraint, ignorant of forms, charmingly doing wrong and as charmingly repenting of it—promises to become a literary nuisance of the first order ("Books and Authors" 90). As this reviewer implies, the character of the charming American ingénue was rather *too* familiar to contemporary readers. The American Girl Abroad, or International American Girl, was simply a variation on the theme, the same character in a different setting and already in danger of becoming shelf-worn and hackneyed before James breathed new life into a genre whose moment had already passed.[10]

Throughout the nineteenth century, travel writing enjoyed a large audience.[11] Apart from Harriet Beecher Stowe and Grace Greenwood, whose *Sunny Memories of Foreign Lands* and *Haps and Mishaps of a Tour Abroad* respectively appeared in 1854, the most popular American travel writers at midcentury were men—notably, Richard Henry Dana, Herman Melville (authors of travel-oriented novels), and Bayard Taylor (Bode 222). After the Civil War, however, the impact of female readers, and of female travelers, gathered momentum, with the result that women's travel narratives began to gain market share. By the early 1870s, narratives of American women travelers were decidedly in vogue. The house of Lee & Shepard, always highly attuned to popular reading tastes, showcased this popular genre when it touted its lineup for the summer of 1876.[12] A mere five months after the publication of *Mae Madden*, and a year and a half before *Daisy Miller*, the *American Bookseller* carried an advertisement from this enterprising firm (see figure 8) that included Mrs. S. R. Urbino's *An American Woman in Europe: The Journal of Two Years' Sojourn in France, Switzerland, Italy, and Germany* (1869), Adeline Trafton's *An American Girl Abroad* (1872), and Mrs. Ella W. Thompson's *Beaten Paths; or, A Woman's Vacation* (1874). Titles such as these provide ample support for Mary Suzanne Schriber's assertion that "nineteenth-century anxiety over gender took form in conduct books of travel, trunkloads of printed advice about how to dress, what to take abroad, and how to behave that swelled the discourses of femininity in America even as they swelled the pocketbooks of publishers" (*Telling Travels* xviii).

These "conduct books of travel" accomplished a great deal more in the way of cultural work than merely instructing women how to dress, what to pack, and how to behave. American women in the nineteenth century often enjoyed a freedom when traveling abroad that was unknown to them at home. The narratives that women such as Urbino, Trafton, and Thompson wrote about their journeys prepared other, similarly privileged women for the newfound freedom they would experience as travelers and, at the same time, allowed less advantaged women to witness this liberty vicariously as armchair travelers.[13] Indeed, the inviting premise that travel could liberate women informs these nonfiction accounts of American women travelers as well as many fictional (or fictionalized) narratives.

Ella W. Thompson's autobiographical travelogue, *Beaten Paths*, is instructive in that it provides a template of the recurring themes and motifs that characterize narratives of American women travelers in the 1860s and 1870s. Beginning with the epigraph "Stone walls do not a prison make, / Nor iron bars a cage," Thompson's first chapter clearly proclaims the familiar premise, heralding the theme of freedom abroad contrasted with restriction at home. After reassuring her readers that she is not what was known as a "strong-minded" woman (declaring, "I want to say, to begin with, that the writer of this book is one of 'the few, the immortal few,' left of her sex in America, who would rather have an India shawl any day than the suffrage"), Thompson proceeds to enumerate the kinds of restrictions American women experienced on their native soil:

> in dark moments, when both [shawl and suffrage] have seemed equally unattainable, it has occurred to her [the writer] that most women's lives are passed, so to speak, in long, narrow galleries, built about with customs and conventionalities more impervious than stone. Sometimes they contract to

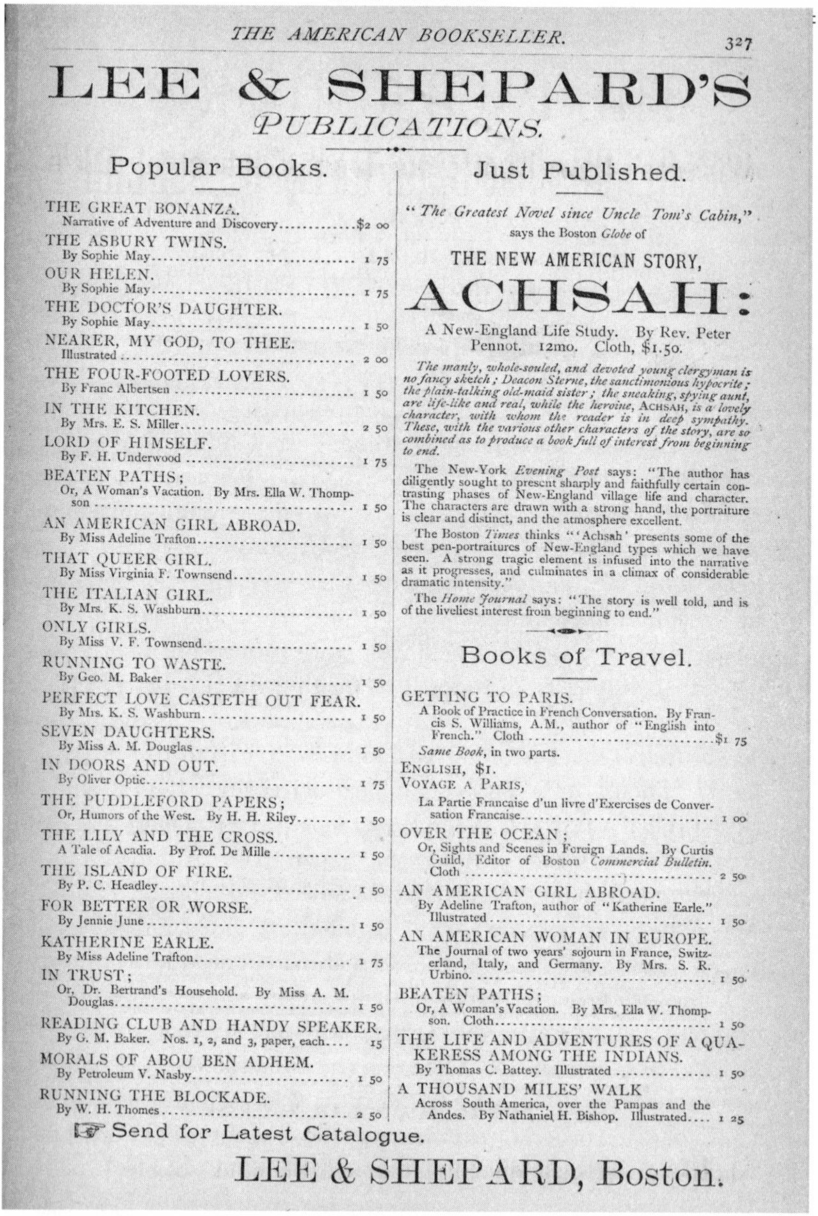

THE AMERICAN BOOKSELLER. 327

# LEE & SHEPARD'S PUBLICATIONS.

## Popular Books.

THE GREAT BONANZA.
Narrative of Adventure and Discovery ............ $2 00
THE ASBURY TWINS.
By Sophie May ............ 1 75
OUR HELEN.
By Sophie May ............ 1 75
THE DOCTOR'S DAUGHTER.
By Sophie May ............ 1 50
NEARER, MY GOD, TO THEE.
Illustrated ............ 2 00
THE FOUR-FOOTED LOVERS.
By Franc Albertsen ............ 1 50
IN THE KITCHEN.
By Mrs. E. S. Miller ............ 2 50
LORD OF HIMSELF.
By F. H. Underwood ............ 1 75
BEATEN PATHS;
Or, A Woman's Vacation. By Mrs. Ella W. Thompson ............ 1 50
AN AMERICAN GIRL ABROAD.
By Miss Adeline Trafton ............ 1 50
THAT QUEER GIRL.
By Miss Virginia F. Townsend ............ 1 50
THE ITALIAN GIRL.
By Mrs. K. S. Washburn ............ 1 50
ONLY GIRLS.
By Miss V. F. Townsend ............ 1 50
RUNNING TO WASTE.
By Geo. M. Baker ............ 1 50
PERFECT LOVE CASTETH OUT FEAR.
By Mrs. K. S. Washburn ............ 1 50
SEVEN DAUGHTERS.
By Miss A. M. Douglas ............ 1 50
IN DOORS AND OUT.
By Oliver Optic ............ 1 75
THE PUDDLEFORD PAPERS;
Or, Humors of the West. By H. H. Riley ............ 1 50
THE LILY AND THE CROSS.
A Tale of Acadia. By Prof. De Mille ............ 1 50
THE ISLAND OF FIRE.
By P. C. Headley ............ 1 50
FOR BETTER OR WORSE.
By Jennie June ............ 1 50
KATHERINE EARLE.
By Miss Adeline Trafton ............ 1 75
IN TRUST;
Or, Dr. Bertrand's Household. By Miss A. M. Douglas ............ 1 50
READING CLUB AND HANDY SPEAKER.
By G. M. Baker. Nos. 1, 2, and 3, paper, each .... 15
MORALS OF ABOU BEN ADHEM.
By Petroleum V. Nasby ............ 1 50
RUNNING THE BLOCKADE.
By W. H. Thomes ............ 2 50

## Just Published.

*"The Greatest Novel since Uncle Tom's Cabin,"* says the Boston *Globe* of

THE NEW AMERICAN STORY,

# ACHSAH:

A New-England Life Study. By Rev. Peter Pennot. 12mo. Cloth, $1.50.

*The manly, whole-souled, and devoted young clergyman is no fancy sketch; Deacon Sterne, the sanctimonious hypocrite; the plain-talking old-maid sister; the sneaking, spying aunt, are life-like and real, while the heroine,* ACHSAH, *is a lovely character, with whom the reader is in deep sympathy. These, with the various other characters of the story, are so combined as to produce a book full of interest from beginning to end.*

The New-York *Evening Post* says: "The author has diligently sought to present sharply and faithfully certain contrasting phases of New-England village life and character. The characters are drawn with a strong hand, the portraiture is clear and distinct, and the atmosphere excellent.

The Boston *Times* thinks "'Achsah' presents some of the best pen-portraitures of New-England types which we have seen. A strong tragic element is infused into the narrative as it progresses, and culminates in a climax of considerable dramatic intensity."

The *Home Journal* says: "The story is well told, and is of the liveliest interest from beginning to end."

## Books of Travel.

GETTING TO PARIS.
A Book of Practice in French Conversation. By Francis S. Williams, A.M., author of "English into French." Cloth ............ $1 75
*Same Book*, in two parts.
ENGLISH, $1.
VOYAGE A PARIS,
La Partie Francaise d'un livre d'Exercises de Conversation Francaise ............ 1 00
OVER THE OCEAN;
Or, Sights and Scenes in Foreign Lands. By Curtis Guild, Editor of Boston *Commercial Bulletin*. Cloth ............ 2 50
AN AMERICAN GIRL ABROAD.
By Adeline Trafton, author of "Katherine Earle." Illustrated ............ 1 50
AN AMERICAN WOMAN IN EUROPE.
The Journal of two years' sojourn in France, Switzerland, Italy, and Germany. By Mrs. S. R. Urbino ............ 1 50
BEATEN PATHS;
Or, A Woman's Vacation. By Mrs. Ella W. Thompson. Cloth ............ 1 50
THE LIFE AND ADVENTURES OF A QUAKERESS AMONG THE INDIANS.
By Thomas C. Battey. Illustrated ............ 1 50
A THOUSAND MILES' WALK
Across South America, over the Pampas and the Andes. By Nathaniel H. Bishop. Illustrated .... 1 25

☞ Send for Latest Catalogue.

LEE & SHEPARD, Boston.

FIGURE 8. A Lee & Shepard ad from *American Bookseller's Guide*, May 1876. The popularity of travel books and of books for female readers is evident in their list for the summer season. Several of these titles were also sold together as part of the firm's six-volume Girlhood Series. Courtesy, University of Minnesota Libraries.

a hot little kitchen, and the owner might as well be a Vestal Virgin, and done with it, her whole life being spent in keeping up the fire; again, like Maude Muller's, these walls "stretch away into stately halls."[14] They may be more or less hung with pictures or padded with books, but they are walls all the same. Plenty of doors lead out of these galleries, but only those marked "Church," "Visits," and "Shopping," move easily on their hinges. (9)

Travel, as Thompson discovers, offers the antidote to a life hemmed in by "customs and conventionalities":

Most of us, and especially those who have been nourished on the east winds of Boston, cast longing eyes at the door marked with the magical word "Europe," and it has opened freely enough when the husband said the "Open, sesame;" it is only of late years that women have made the amazing discovery that they can say it themselves with like success, but it is well to keep the hinges well oiled, and the rubbish cleared away from the threshold. When my turn came, I felt as if I had been taken into a high mountain and been promised all the kingdoms of the earth, and had at once accepted the offer. (10)

For Thompson and her traveling companions, "six other anxious, but no longer aimless women" (10), the unprecedented and heady sense of freedom that attends them as female travelers derives, in part, from the absence of men. "We meant to have no reproaches, nor men either" (10), she briskly announces. As the narrative proceeds (and with it, the grand tour), Thompson finds no cause to regret her decision. Instead, she informs her readers that "to go to Europe with a husband or father, who will take all the trouble and share all the pleasure, is somewhat like being carried about in an old-fashioned sedan chair on men's shoulders" (64). She exhorts: "Trust me, O beloved reader, the best of men and the dearest of husbands are all Turks in their hearts! They would hide their wives behind veils and lattices if they could, while *they* make 'the grand tour'" (64).

Of course, many American women who traveled to Europe were unmarried, and, indeed, a critical difference between Thompson, as traveler, and the fictional travelers of Mason and James is the marital status of the dramatis personae (Daisy's and Mae's trips are underwritten by fathers rather than by husbands). The role of the American ingénue and the plot of a romance on foreign soil, whether with a European or a fellow American, are unavailable to Thompson as central elements of her narrative. Nevertheless, like other nonfiction accounts of American women abroad, *Beaten Paths* alludes to the character of the unattached American ingénue and sketches the bare outlines of the romantic story line that many fictional accounts would incorporate. As observer, rather than as protagonist, Thompson supplies the crucial details of character and plot that enliven *Mae Madden* and *Daisy Miller*, beginning by establishing the pervasiveness of American women abroad. On several occasions, she enthusiastically lauds her own all-female entourage, declaring, "We felt that what seven women could not do was not worth doing" (10), and "To go [to Europe] with a party of lone women is to discover a new world. It involves self-sacrifice, sudden smothering of old prejudices, hard labor and harder patience; but so does everything else that is worth having" (64). Still, Thompson is clearly unprepared for the frequency with which she encounters similar parties of American women traipsing around Europe with no men to escort and chaperone them. With bemused satisfaction, she quotes a fellow traveler: "Nothing surprises me more than the perpetual appearance of American ladies travelling alone in all places of interest. From the heights of old Londonderry to the vaults of St. Peter's, they crop up everywhere, a rule unto themselves, self-possessed and regnant. If they have a vulnerable spot, it is not in their heels, for no rough road turns them back" (63).

Like many a novelist in the international vein, Thompson observes with vested interest the qualities that distinguish American girls from their European counterparts and comments at length on the unique characteristics that make them objects of fascination to foreign men:

> It may be only patriotism which leads every American to rejoice in the superior beauty of his countrywomen abroad. Foreigners think so too, if a prolonged and exhaustive scrutiny be any proof. Staring among foreign gentlemen is cultivated as a fine art. They look at a pretty American girl as Adam must have looked at Eve, when he woke from his long sleep and met her eyes for the first time. The gaze is at first curious, as of one who had never seen a woman before, and melts at last into an intense satisfaction. A young girl who has endured a season in a foreign hotel, going to table d'hôte every day, is safe to run any gantlet of eyes that will ever be bent on her at home. The old maxim, that "it takes two to make a stare," does not hold good in Europe. (173)

A paragraph later, she praises her countrywomen with evident pride: "There is no class on foreign soil that corresponds to American girls. At home they have their own way, and it makes even the plain ones piquant and stylish, full of gay talk and laughter. There is no other recipe so certain to develop a woman's beauty" (173).

In addition to noting the prevalence of American women abroad and the interest and admiration they attract, Thompson sets the stage for the inevitable *imbroglio* by hinting at the dangers lying in wait for the naive and vulnerable American girl:

—foreign "wolves": "Travelling is comparatively easy where people speak some sort of English (if not the best), but for women taking their lives in their hands, the wolf is waiting at every foreign corner. It is true you can always disarm him with a piece of money—if your money holds out, there is no fear of wolves or anything else in Europe" (105).

—Old World codes of behavior: "Madame X. [in Paris] was shocked and horrified by an American girl sitting on a sofa with a young man whom she had known from childhood, and who brought news of her family" (240).

—the malicious gossip of other women: "A lonely girl cannot be happy without being thought improper, at least in the eyes of female Heidelbergers; and I suppose men here, as at home, must think as their wives do. Women have a silent legislation in the realm of propriety none the less binding that it is not found in statute-books" (151).

—the devastating effects of social isolation: Heidelberg "is a place full of sorrows for a girl, who has no friends to receive and make a background for her. She may come from America, full of hope and courage, with her heart set solely on a good musical education, but the weight of German opinion will slowly and surely bear down her good cheer. She has to breathe air thick with suspicion, and in every German girl's eyes, she reads the pharisaic rejoicing that they are not as she is" (151).

—and the atmospheric hazards of European travel, particularly the notorious night air of the Roman summer.

Although Thompson is silent on the point, many other practitioners of the genre alluded to yet another peril to rival that of the foreign wolf or fortune hunter: the danger of "title-loving Americans" (Alcott, *Shawl-Straps* 13) losing their heads over impressively aristocratic titles, uniforms, and other trappings of Old World nobility. After observing that "counts, dukes, princes, &c., are as common in Baden-Baden as captain and squire in our good New England States" (29), Mrs. S. R. Urbino, whose *An American Woman in Europe* appeared in 1869, goes on to berate her compatriots for their sycophancy. According to a gentleman she meets, "One could always recognize them [Americans] in an instant by the extravagance of their dress, and their aping the manners of the nobility, into whose society they tried to force themselves" (31).

Ultimately, these dangers are little more than harmless detours on Thompson's *Beaten Paths*, for any complications that arise from them take place behind the scenes. Still, these elements—the "piquant" and "gay" American girl, the foreign "wolf," the clash between Old and New World social conventions, the web of gossip set to ensnare the carefree and careless young lady, and the lurking specter of disease—combine to trace the archetypal plot of the American woman abroad: a plot carried to very different ends in the parallel careers of *Mae Madden* and *Daisy Miller*.

☙ ☙ ☙

In the preface to *Shawl-Straps* (1872)—a series of sketches in which the author of *Little Women* recounts her recent travels and travails in Europe,[15]—Louisa May Alcott writes: "There is a sort of fate about writing books of travel which it is impossible to escape. It is vain to declare that no inducement will bribe one to do it, that there is nothing new to tell, and that nobody wants to read the worn-out story: sooner or later the deed is done, and not till the book is safely shelved does peace descend upon the victim of this mysterious doom" (v). Alcott's concern that "there is nothing new to tell" was evidently a common one well before the 1870s, when the popularity of American women's travel writing was at its peak.[16] *Beaten Paths*, published two years before *Shawl-Straps*, includes the following lines from *Faust* on its title page, further attesting to the prevalence of this anxiety among American travel writers:

> But, then, alas! they've read an awful deal.
> How shall we plan that all be fresh and new,
> Important matter, yet attractive too?

Thompson's solution to the problem was simply to use her engaging style and confiding voice to capture the unique experiences of the travelers at the expense of the oft-recounted facts and figures. Alcott adopted a similar strategy, explaining that "the only way in which this affliction may be lightened to a long-suffering public is to make the work as cheerful and as short as possible. With this hope the undersigned bore has abstained from giving the dimensions of any church, the population of any city, or description of famous places, as far as in her lay; but confined herself to the personal haps and mishaps, adventures and experiences, of her wanderers" (v). But the author of *Little Women* does more than that: she spices up the narrative by fictionalizing her "three lone women . . . on a wild-goose chase after health and pleasure" (3–4). As a result, Alcott rewards her readers with a novel glimpse into the real-life adventures of American women abroad.[17]

Like *Shawl-Straps*, both *Mae Madden* and *Daisy Miller* render women's travel writing in a semi-autobiographical, semi-fictional form.[18] In contrast to Alcott's sketches, however, these narratives of young American women abroad are more novel than travelogue, more drama than description. If the story of *Daisy Miller* is so familiar that a synopsis is unnecessary, that of Mason's novella, which drifted into obscurity shortly after publication, bears retelling. Prefaced by a poem of Joaquin Miller's, this enjoyable romp is quickly summarized.[19] At the time of its release, *Publishers' Weekly* offered the following précis:

> "Mae Madden," by Mary Murdoch Mason, with an introductory poem by Joaquin Miller. (Jansen, McClurg & Co.)[20] Joaquin Miller's poem, "A Dream of Italy," is a short allegory, introducing "Mae Madden," the fantastic heroine of the story—a young American girl who with some friends goes abroad and spends a winter in Rome. Her escapades and love quarrels are quite amusing, and the descriptions of the carnival really clever. 16 mo, cloth, red edges, $1.25. ("Books Received" 936)

To this, one might add that among nineteen-year-old Mae's traveling companions are her two brothers, studious Albert and fun-loving Eric; Albert's sweetheart, Edith; Edith's mother, the pious Mrs. Jerrold, "a Puritan of the Puritans," who "had breathed in the shorter catechism and the doctrine of election with the mountain air and sea-salt of her childhood" (Mason 79); and Eric's college buddy Norman Mann, cousin of the Jerrolds. Norman is very much taken with the winsome young Mae, whose romantic interest in him appears to be in no way vitiated by her admiration for a dazzling Piedmontese officer named Bero, who has a habit of turning up unexpectedly at awkward moments. As a result, misunderstandings occur, overheard confidences are misconstrued, notes are intercepted, and Mae and Norman continually rebound between conflict and reconciliation. Up to this point, the story is remarkably similar to *Daisy Miller*. At its denouement, however, Mae sharply departs from her famous sister, absconding to the Bay of Naples to pursue her dream of a sunny Italian Heaven, with both Mr. Mann and Signor Bero in hot pursuit. By the end of the novella the love triangle has resolved itself, and the couples are paired off appropriately: Mae is engaged to Norman, the dashing Bero is betrothed to a mysterious Italian beauty named Lillia, and Edith and Albert are newlyweds.

On the surface, Mason's tale unambiguously fulfills the traditional conventions of the "American girl abroad" narrative (as represented by such accounts as Thompson's *Beaten Paths* and Alcott's *Shawl-Straps*) as surely as it satisfies—and as surely as *Daisy Miller* flouts—the generic expectations of romantic comedy. Like Daisy, Mae travels to Europe without a traditional male guardian, in the company of other young people (male as well as female) and an older woman for a chaperon (the mother of her friend).[21] In addition, Mae, like Daisy, is pretty and vivacious, and she clearly has the power to captivate the men with whom she comes in contact.[22] Presented from the female point of view, however, *Mae Madden* contains no passage to rival James's initial description of his heroine (or, at least, of her attire): "She was dressed in white muslin, with a hundred frills and flounces, and knots of pale-coloured ribbon. She was bare-headed; but she balanced in her hand a large parasol, with a deep border of embroidery; and she was strikingly, admirably pretty" (*Daisy Miller* 9).[23] Instead we see Mae as she sees herself: in the mirror, rather than through the eyes of a male admirer: "Life and color and youth, a-tremble and a-quiver in every quick movement of her face, in the sudden lifting of the eyelids, the swift turn of the lips, the litheness and carelessness of every motion; above and beyond all, the picture possessed that rare quality which some artist has declared to be the highest beauty, that picturesque charm which shines from within, that magnetic flash and quiver which comes and goes 'ere one can say it lightens'" (98). The peculiar power of Mae's beauty affects those around her in a fashion similar to that of Daisy Miller, with its "youth, and intense life, and endless variety," and these qualities, as Mason knowingly observes, "usually carry the day with a man's captious heart" (98).

As flighty and impressionable as Daisy Miller, Mae irresistibly falls under the spell of the magnificent Bero, whose attractions consist largely of his elegant uniform and impressive physique. Of a type different from the urbane Italian dandy who pursues Daisy, Bero, like Mr. Giovanelli (whom Daisy refers to as "the handsomest man in the world—except Mr. Winterbourne!" [25]), is exceptionally attractive; upon espying Bero for the first time, in company with another soldier, Mae gasps, "O, Eric, are they gods or men?" (32). (In *Shawl-Straps* Alcott sings the praises of these "dark-eyed heroes" (196), declaring, "The Officers from Turin are things of beauty and joys for ever to those who love to look on manly men" [183].) Although Mason, unlike James, expends little ink lingering over her heroine's outward appearance, she rhapsodizes about the officer's physical charms in a passage that mirrors James's delightful depiction of Daisy:

> The Piedmontese officer is godlike. He must be of a certain imposing height to obtain his position, and his luxurious yellow moustaches and blue black eyes, enriched and intensified by southern blood, give him a strange fascination. The cold, manly beauty and strength of a northern blonde meet with the heat and lithe grace of the more supple southerner to produce this paragon. There is a combination of half-indolent elegance and sensuous languor, with a fire, a verve, a nobility, that puts him at the very head of masculine beauty. Add to the charms of his physique, the jauntiest, most bewitching of uniforms, the clinking spurs, the shining buttons, the jacket following every line of his figure, and no wonder maidens' hearts seek him out always and young pulses beat quicker at his approach. (32–33)

Apparently more benign than the mercenary fortune hunter of *Daisy Miller*, Bero poses no immediate threat to Mae, other than as a distraction from Norman and rival for his affections. Nevertheless, this superlative specimen of male beauty causes Mae a great deal of discomfiture by catapulting her into a series of compromising situations.

Mae Madden shares with James's heroine the intriguing, "maddening," and "inscrutable combination of audacity and innocence" (*Daisy Miller* 27) that struck such a chord with James's audience that "Daisy Miller" and "Daisy Millerism" entered the popular vocabulary for a time as common nouns. On the occasion of their first conversation, after Bero "rescues" Mae from what he erroneously believes to be a bothersome beggar, Mae—who is slightly more conscientious than Daisy—is suddenly seized with embarrassment. In a scene strikingly similar to that in which Mrs. Walker passes Daisy and Giovanelli in her carriage, Mae realizes, in a way that Daisy never does, that her conversing with the handsome officer is an unsuitable pastime for an unescorted, unattached young lady:

> Mae saw the sunlight strike his hair; she half heard his deep breath; and, like a flood, there suddenly swept over her the knowledge that this new friend, this sympathizing soul, was an unknown man, and that she was a girl.

145

What had she done? What could she do? Confusion and embarrassment suddenly overtook her. She bent her eyes away from those other eyes, that were growing bolder and more tender in their gaze. "I—I—" she began, and just at this very inauspicious moment, while she sat there, flushed, by the stranger's side, the clatter of swiftly-approaching wheels sounded, and a carriage turned the corner, containing Mrs. Jerrold, Edith, Albert, and Norman Mann. They all saw her. (47–48)

As in *Daisy Miller*, Mae's "recklessness" arouses the suspicions of those around her, prompting some to question the heroine's innocence and all to question her judgment. As an unsympathetic reviewer for the *Literary World* wrote: "The heroine, 'Mae Madden,' is a volatile, willful, hair-brained [*sic*] young creature, who finds delight in the gravest social improprieties, and, in utter selfishness, gratifies her own longings at any cost. She talks slang, 'goes wild,' frequently makes a horse of herself, and sometimes a 'black-and-tan dog'" ("Minor Book Notices" 117). Even her faithful American admirer is at a loss to understand her. Just as Winterbourne asks himself, "Would a nice girl—even allowing for her being a little American flirt—make a rendezvous with a presumably low-lived foreigner?" (*Daisy Miller* 27), Norman Mann wonders whether enchanting young Mae is as naive and virtuous as she appears.

Mrs. Jerrold's response to Mae's "wayward" behavior is to issue "commands never to go out alone in Rome, because it wasn't proper" (51)—a response echoed in *Daisy Miller* by the punctilious Mrs. Walker, who remonstrates, "Should you prefer being thought a very reckless girl?" (*Daisy Miller* 28). Norman, however, realizes that "Albert and Edith and Aunt Martha [Mrs. Jerrold] are too vexed and shocked to do the little rebel any good" and therefore takes it upon himself "to keep her from something terribly wild." Norman faces the same predicament as Winterbourne, however, since he has "no possible authority over her, or power, for that matter" (50). Moreover, just as the gallant Mr. Mann resolves to save Mae from further folly, he observes Bero outside her window during the evening hours, after she has retired to her chamber (53).

The situation looks worse and worse for poor Mae, who only bridles at her companions' judgments and stubbornly refuses to mend her ways. To Norman, she retorts, "You had better content yourself with the fact that you have four proper traveling companions, and bear the disgrace of being shocked as best you may by one wild scrap of femininity who will have her own way in spite of you all" (59). That evening, at the theater, Mae proceeds to prove her point, acknowledging her Piedmontese officer with "a free, glad, welcoming smile on her lips" (68). Naturally,

> Norman Mann saw it and followed it, and caught the officer receiving it, and thought "She's a wild coquette."
> And Mae knew what he saw and what he thought. (68)

Further confusion occurs when Norman spots Mae and Bero together at a little church near Capo le Case. (On a grander scale, James, who, coincidentally, rented an apartment in Via Capo le Case in 1877, has Winterbourne "[perceive] Daisy strolling about" St. Peter's "in company with the inevitable Giovanelli" [*Daisy Miller* 33].) Later, Norman discovers that Bero has made a habit of flinging bouquets onto Mae's balcony during the festivities of Carnival. Just as in *Daisy Miller*, circumstances conspire to sway the young man's opinion of the girl until he finally begins to despair of her heart along with her virtue. In the penultimate chapter, when he discovers Mae and Bero together, alone, in a boat on the Bay of Naples, Norman clings desperately to the one scenario that could possibly justify such shocking behavior. When the boat lands, he demands of Mae, "Are you married?" to which Mae replies "I! married! What do you—what can he mean?" (168). Similarly, both Winterbourne and Mrs. Miller grasp at a similar explanation for Daisy's inexplicable conduct: Winterbourne remarks, "Ah! . . . if you are in love with each other it is another affair" (32), and Daisy's mother chimes in, "I keep telling Daisy she's engaged!" (*Daisy Miller* 34). Daisy meets both suggestions with the same mixture of protest and confusion with which Mae responds to Norman's inquisition.

In *Mae Madden*, Mason's heroine continually wavers between repentance and defiance: after Albert admonishes his sister by chiding, "We shall have to buy a chain for you soon," she retorts, "If you do . . . I'll slip it" (80). Unlike James, who creates a sense of drama and suspense by restricting the point of view to Winterbourne, Mason presents both sides of the relationship. In defense of Mae, she writes: "Bless us! who is to blame a young woman for forgetting everything but the 'other man' when he is a godlike Piedmontese officer, with strong soft cheek and throat, and Italian eyes, and yellow moustaches, and spurs and buttons that click and shine in a maddening sort of way?" (68–69). While Mason captures precisely the kind of physical, purely visual response to an attractive member of the opposite sex that James attributes to Winterbourne, she also acknowledges that for Mae "there was a malicious sort of teasing pleasure in running away from Norman, mingled with a shrinking modesty" (136). This coy, coquettish quality is, of course, the very hallmark of the pretty American "flirt" immortalized in *Daisy Miller*.

Throughout Mason's novella, amid a volley of imprecations against Mae's "recklessness, her waywardness" (123), the narrator interjects numerous cautionary remarks about the social dangers of venturing out alone in the city of Rome and as many ominous reminders about the pestilential air of the sultry Roman nights. Mae writes to her mother, "I seriously think I shall die if I stay here much longer. There's a spirit-malaria that eats into my life" (25), a remark that anticipates Daisy's offhand "We are going to stay all winter—if we don't die of the fever" (*Daisy Miller* 87). Later, sulking over Mrs. Jerrold's condemnation of her friendship with Bero ("How dare they accuse me of flirting?" she asks herself [52]), Mae retires to her room, where she "opened her window wide, and held her head out in the night air—the poisonous Roman air" (51). Norman, who witnesses this scene, cautions Mae the next morning "that the Roman air at midnight [is] dangerous to your health" (60), just as Mrs. Miller warns Daisy, "You'll get the fever as sure as you live" (*Daisy Miller* 85). A few nights later, Norman repeats the warning, admonishing, "We had better go in now; this night air is bad for you" (124), perhaps saving Mae from the untimely death that awaits Daisy.

In addition to marshaling these conventional elements of American women's travel writing, from the superiority of American girls to the social and environmental hazards of foreign locales, Mason draws on an older tradition of "woman abroad" narratives, incorporating a theme already well established in both European and American novels about women travelers. From de Staël's *Corinne* to Hawthorne's *The Marble Faun*, literary artists had exploited the cultural richness of Italy, with its exotic scenes, stirring history, and gorgeous works of art, as a backdrop against which to explore the intellectual and artistic development of creative women.[24] *Mae Madden*, although ostensibly a lighthearted and superficial romance, contains the elements of the female *Bildungsroman* and *Künstlerroman* that distinguish this long tradition of novels about English and American women writers and artists in Italy—elements that James squarely rejects in *Daisy Miller*.

The founder of this feminine tradition of fictionalized travelogues was Madame de Staël, whose *Corinne; or, Italy* appeared in 1807. A love story involving an enigmatic young woman of mysterious origins, as brilliant as she is beautiful, and the Scottish nobleman (Oswald, Lord Nelvil) who ultimately betrays her, *Corinne* quickly became an international sensation.[25] Frequently cited in nineteenth-century American literature, both *Corinne* and its author came to symbolize, in the popular imagination, the struggle of the woman of genius for honor and love.[26] *Corinne* exerted a powerful influence on *The Marble Faun*: in one scene, Hawthorne explicitly evokes de Staël by having the artist Miriam reenact a scene from the novel. Miriam, whose dark beauty and mysterious sorrow are echoed in Mason's Lillia, just as Miriam recalls Corinne, instructs Donatello, "I have often intended to visit this fountain by moonlight ... because it was here that the interview took place between Corinne and Lord Nelvil, after their separation and temporary estrangement. Pray come behind me ... and let me try whether the face can be recognized in the water" (*Marble Faun* 146).[27] For Hawthorne, as for de Staël, Rome is a place where the female artist may enjoy freedom "to a degree unknown in the society of other cities" (*Marble Faun* 55). Of the ethereal copyist Hilda, he writes: "This young American girl was an example of the freedom of life which it is possible for a female artist to enjoy at Rome. She dwelt in her tower, as free to descend into the corrupted atmosphere of the city beneath, as one of her companion-doves to fly downwards into the street;—all alone, perfectly independent, under her own sole guardianship, unless watched over by the Virgin, whose shrine she tended;—doing what she liked, without a suspicion or a shadow upon the snowy whiteness of her fame" because, Hawthorne suggests, in Rome "the customs of artist-life bestow such liberty upon the sex, which is elsewhere restricted within so much narrower limits" (*Marble Faun* 54). Like Hawthorne's Miriam, Mae Madden even goes so far as to exercise this liberty by disguising herself as a *contadina* in order to sample firsthand the peasant life. In both Hawthorne's and Mason's narratives, as in *Corinne*, this contrast between the "shackles" and "insufferable restraint" (*Marble Faun* 55) of life at home and a free, unfettered existence in Rome acts as a leaven on the creative energies of the Anglo-Saxon woman abroad.[28]

Like de Staël and Hawthorne, Mary Murdoch Mason constructs a narrative in which the role of the imagination and the intellect is crucial to plot, setting, and character. For Mae enacts an interior journey as well as an exterior one, a journey that is only partly one of adventure and romance. Mae, whose "greatest idol" is Shakespeare (56), speaks Italian and sings snatches of *Il Trovatore* (30); debates the merits of translating *Othello* into Italian (55–57); defends pre-Raphaelite art from its detractors (101); "loves"

Wordsworth and, according to Eric, "holds the 'Daffodils' and 'Lucy' as her chief jewels, and quotes the 'Immortality' perpetually" (102). She also contemplates Hawthorne and Byron as she views the celebrated statues of the Faun and the Gladiator (137); and occupies her mind, during periods of nervous anticipation, by reciting poetry (25, 133). Her friend Edith says of her, "She craves beauty and poetry in everything" (74). In a letter to her mother, Mae writes, "I feel as if all the volumes of Roman history bound in heavy vellum, that papa has in his study, were laid right on top of my little heart, so that every time it beats, it thumps against them" (25). She recovers from this sense of oppression, however, upon experiencing an epiphany as she contemplates the exquisite marbles in the Capitol: the site of Corinne's splendid debut in de Staël's novel. (In contrast, Daisy tells Winterbourne that upon arriving in Rome, she was sure they "should be going round all the time with one of those dreadful old men that explain about the pictures and things," adding, "but we only had about a week of that, and now I'm enjoying myself" [*Daisy Miller* 26]). Moreover, in moments of homesickness and amid feelings of remorse, Mae, who complains that the tourists in Rome "take travel so solemnly . . . and treat Baedeker, like the Bible" (29), longs for the familiar articles of home, in particular "the dear old library" (42)—"and a book!" (163).

Journals and epistolary narratives were common modes for nineteenth-century travel writers, and *Mae Madden*, although primarily conducted by a limited third-person narrator, is something of a pastiche, incorporating the occasional Italian folktale, Mae's correspondence with her mother, and a sampling of Mae's own creative efforts (we are given the full text of a "pre-Raphaelite" poem she writes, titled "All on a Summer's Day"). When Mae makes her way to the Bay of Naples, Norman speculates that "Mrs. Jerrold [has] searched [her] trunks and read all [her] private papers" (174), an indication that Mae has been committing her thoughts and experiences to paper. In James's narrative, however, Daisy Miller is all exterior, or surface—all ruffles and flounces and fashion and mannerisms—so that readers have no access to Daisy's thoughts. Whereas Mary Murdoch Mason characterizes Mae as both reader and writer, James transfers these functions to Winterbourne, who becomes reader (of character) and writer (of plot).

In chapter 8, Mae's traveling companions discuss the merits and demerits of her poem, which has been published anonymously in Rome's English-language newspaper. Little suspecting the identity of the poet, Mae's brother Albert suggests that "work or study, and a general shutting up of the fancy is what this mind needs" (106), but Eric, who throughout the novel is more sympathetic to Mae, declares, "She needs . . . to be married. She is in love. That's what's the matter" (106). Mae responds with indignation, but of course Eric's diagnosis is near to the mark. And although Bero seems to offer some relief from bookishness (Mae tells him, "I am tired and sick of books, and people, and reasons" [45]), as does her flight to the Bay of Naples (to which, incidentally, Corinne and Oswald run off together in de Staël's novel), Norman reaffirms Mae's love of imagination, aesthetics, and art. He tells her: "The world is full of color and beauty, and poetry you love. All study is full of it—most of all it lives in humanity" (176).

The endings of *Daisy Miller* and *Mae Madden* align, to some extent, with the divergent endings of *Corinne* and *The Marble Faun*: Daisy, like Corinne, dies in Rome, albeit of Roman fever rather than a broken heart; Mae, like Miriam, dons the colorful raiment of a *contadina* and runs off to frolic with the "children of the sun." But the exotic Miriam easily slips into her new identity and, with Donatello by her side, melts into the Italian landscape, whereas Mae balks at her new surroundings. The romantic vision of the Bay of Naples, with its blue waters and picturesque *lazzarone*, dissipates, leaving in its stead a repellent display of poverty and squalor. Out on the bay, seated in a boat across from her Piedmontese idol, Mae awakens simultaneously to the magnitude of her indiscretion and the tenacity of her New England roots: "Could she take that villa for her home? That man for her husband? She had half thought till now in soft luxurious Italian, but 'my home' and 'my husband' said themselves to her in her own mother tongue. She gave a long shiver, and pulled her eyes from his. It was like waking from a dream. 'No—oh, no; take me home,' she gasped, and turned toward the shore, where, erect, with folded arms and head bared, stood Norman Mann" (167). After the boat has landed and its passengers have disembarked, Mae stands poised between the two men, torn with indecision. Half-convinced that Norman must despise her, she is momentarily tempted to cast her lot with the Piedmontese officer: "She held out weakly her right hand toward Bero; but the left stretched itself involuntarily to Norman. Then the two met in each other's pitiful clasp over her bent head, and with a low wailing cry she fell in a little heap on the sand" (169). When Mae comes to, her decision is clear. She implores Norman to take her home and gently dismisses the ever obliging Bero.

The resolutions of *Daisy* and *Mae, Corinne* and *The Marble Faun*, point to the various alternatives open to the Anglo-American woman abroad as her sojourn draws to a close: death, returning home, assimilation, or escape into the foreign unknown.[29] The path Mae chooses is the one typically taken by American women abroad in nineteenth-century narratives, and like other American women who left Italy for the United States, Mae must become reconciled to the loss of her recent freedom and the exchange of art and imagination for familiar "domestic" pleasures: those of her own country as well as those of hearth and home. Contemplating the future, she reflects: "I've said good-bye to my dreams of life—the floating and waving and singing and dancing life that was like iced champagne. I'd rather have cold water, thank you, sir, for a steady drink, morning, noon and night. I'm going to be good, to read and study and grow restful. . . . I am going to grow, if I can, unselfish and sympathetic, and perhaps, who knows, wise, and any way good" (175–76).

At the conclusion of the Bay of Naples episode, this negotiation plays out symbolically as Mae and Norman dally on the beach, whiling away the time before the arrival of the next train to Rome. When Mae idly writes her name in the sand, Norman traces pictures depicting Mae at progressive stages of her life, from the tender age of one to "Sweet Sixteen" (182). From this innocent pastime, the two proceed to narrate, by turns, the history of Mae's life, taking note of the authors and books she read at various stages of her childhood and adolescence—popular British poet Eliza Cooke, a very revised edition of the Arabian Nights, Charlotte Brontë's *Villette* (her first novel), some history.[30] As the waves lap the shore, Norman's artwork gradually dissolves, leaving Mae to observe that "all the Mae Maddens have faded away" (184). On the brink of engagement and on the verge of her journey home, her story draws to a conventional romantic conclusion as the image of the American girl abroad is inexorably effaced from the foreign landscape: no longer an immature scamp, the innocent abroad is ready to return.

The "end" of Mae Madden's young life, signaled by her engagement to Norman and symbolized by the evanescent storyboard on the sand, lacks the grim finality of Daisy's end. Even her erasure on the beach is only fleeting: after Mae remarks that "all the Mae Maddens have faded away," Norman appends his own surname to Mae's signature in the sand. His tacit proposal of marriage, represented by the inscription "Mae Madden Mann," brings her back, in a sense: she is revived, redeemed, and, ultimately, repatriated through marriage. She affirms to Norman: "'No, Italy is not my home, although I love it so well. There is a certain wide old doorway not many miles from New York, and the hills around it, and the great river before it, and the people in it, all belong together, too. That's where we belong, Norman, in America, our home,' and Mae struck a grand final pose with her hands clasped ecstatically, and her eyes flashing in the true Goddess of Liberty style" (188).

Mason leaves no doubt, however, that "Mae Madden Mann" will be a different person from the old Mae Madden. In the final chapter, as the newly engaged couple savor their last days in Italy before summering with the rest of their party in Switzerland (where *Daisy Miller* begins), Mason remarks that "this young woman was losing half her character for willfulness, and Norman was growing into a perfect tyrant, so far as his rights were concerned" (186). Mae, who throughout the novella has delighted in reading books, reciting poetry, composing verse, and listening to stories, announces her intention to turn her attention to domestic concerns. After Norman scoffs at the idea that Mae has "work" to do—he declares, "To think of your coming down to work, you young butterfly" (188)—a conversation unfolds between the two in which Mae anticipates the kind of work that is to occupy her in her new life:

"I don't expect to come to stone-cutting or cattle-driving, but I do expect to settle down into a tolerable housewifely little woman, and—"
"And look after me."
"Yes, I suppose so—and myself, and probably a sewing-class and the cook's lame son. Heigh-ho-hum! What a pity it is, that it is so uninteresting to be good. . . . No, there'll be nothing to say about me any more." (188–89)

Although he hastens to reassure his sweetheart, avowing, "If you and I were in a story-book, you would have ten pages to my one, to keep the reader awake," Norman hastily qualifies his assertion by demurring, "But then, story-books aren't the end of life" (189). He refrains from adding the tacit phrase "for a woman," but the message is nonetheless clear. For Mann (man), "story-books" might become the "end" of life—as they did for Henry James and, indeed, for Mason's own husband, who went on to write a series of adventure books for boys late in his life.[31] For a women, however—whether Mae Madden Mann or Mary Murdoch Mason, who never wrote another novel—the only acceptable "end" of life is approached through those same "narrow galleries, built about with customs and conventionalities more impervious than stone" from which Ella Thompson so gladly retreated before she embarked on those *Beaten Paths*.[32]

✣ ✣ ✣

Clearly, the parallels between *Daisy Miller* and *Mae Madden* are both numerous and strongly suggestive of a line of influence between Mary Murdoch Mason and Henry James. Indeed, James's three major occupations at the time *Mae Madden* was published—book reviewing, travel writing, and fiction writing—very likely brought Mason's narrative into his purview. The differences between the two texts are at least as interesting as the similarities, however, offering an opportunity both to assess the distinctive Jamesian stamp and to analyze his response to the genre of women's travel writing and the popular motif of the American woman abroad. Ironically, as recent criticism has shown, James exhibited a great deal of interest in popular writing, much of which emanated from women writers, and he aspired to popular success even as he scorned the literary tastes of "the multitude" and condemned the work of women writers in both his private and his public writings.[33] In *Daisy Miller*, James transforms the story of *Mae Madden*, revising and masculinizing the narrative of the American woman abroad in order to reclaim this type of fiction as a gentlemanly pursuit.

The final page of *Mae Madden* finds Mae and Norman comfortably ensconced in their new lodgings in Florence. As the couple gaze out the window together, contemplating a letter they have just received from Bero and Lillia, Mae dreamily imagines the wedding of the Piedmontese officer and his magnificent Italian bride. As she awakens from her reverie, Mae's eyes gravitate to another window on the opposite side of the street, where a stranger surreptitiously observes them from afar:

> Her gaze wanders back to the coral and mosaic shops below in the street, and up across to the opposite window, where a long-haired, brown-moustached, brown-eyed man leans, puffing smoke from his curved lips, and holding his cigarette in his slender fingers. She meets his gaze now, as she has met it before. "He is wondering what life will bring to these two young people, I fancy," says Mae.
>
> "Our own wedding-day, Mae," Norman replies; and they both forget all about Lillia, and Bero, and the stranger, and suddenly leave the window. The long-haired man puffs his cigar in a little loneliness, and wishes that wedding bells might ring for his empty heart too. (192)

The scene is full of intrigue: a mystery to be unraveled in an otherwise unenigmatic text. Who is this "long-haired, brown-moustached, brown-eyed man"? What significance lies in the statement, "She meets his gaze now, as she has met it before"? The text records no prior interaction between Mae and this unidentified stranger, nor does Mason make any allusion elsewhere in the narrative to such a person. The identity of this lonely bachelor, whether friendly spectator or detached voyeur, will most likely remain an impenetrable secret, if, indeed, a real-life model existed. Nevertheless, his presence in the text offers a tantalizing clue as to how male storytellers appropriated the stories and experiences of women writers and women travelers. For in this scene, it becomes clear that Mae and her story are subject to the male gaze in much the way that the American woman abroad is the object of Winterbourne's scrutiny and James's analysis in *Daisy Miller: A Study*.

Shortly before Mae and her sweetheart retire to the window where Mae observes the mysterious stranger, Norman jokes that he has "half preached a sermon" to her. Offhandedly, Mae replies, "So long as you take me for a text, you may preach as you want to" (190). Her response incorporates the traditional language of Puritan liturgy, but the notion of taking the girl as a "text" raises a relevant question: Whom did James "take for a text" in writing *Daisy Miller*? Leon Edel speculates:

> It may have been while they were galloping over the daisies of the Campagna, or one evening while they were together at [their mutual friends] the Bootts. At some point, Alice Bartlett [companion of both Henry James and Louisa May Alcott] had occasion to mention an episode which had occurred in Rome during the previous winter [1876]. . . . Her anecdote concerned a simple and uninformed American woman who had been trailing through the hotels of Europe with a young daughter, "a child of nature and freedom." The girl picked up with the best conscience in the world, a good-looking Roman "of a rather vague identity." The Italian seemed astonished at his luck. He was serenely exhibited, and introduced, in the Victorian-Roman-American society, where "dating" was much less relaxed than it is today. Miss Bartlett seems to have furnished few details. There had been some social setback, some snub administered to the innocent girl. Henry's pencil made a brief record of this seemingly inconsequential anecdote. (298)[34]

According to Edel, "The evidence points to its having been Miss Bartlett [who told James this anecdote], for James was to write later that he had the story from a friend then living in the Eternal City, 'since settled in a South less weighted with appeals and memories'—and of his Roman period it was Alice Bartlett who lived ultimately in South Carolina" (298).

Although the historical record leaves no trace that James ever met Mary Murdoch Mason, he did spend much of 1873 in Rome—the year after Mason married (1872), which was very likely soon after the events that suggested the plot of her novella. And although it seems odd that shortly after the Civil War, James should refer to the ravaged state of South Carolina as "a South less weighted with appeals and memories," it may be significant that during the period in question Mason resided in Florida, in Mexico, and in Colombia, South America, all three of which might be more plausibly described in those terms, at least from a northern or North American perspective. Moreover, the resemblance between the vernal nicknames "Daisy" and "Mae" reinforces that of the alliterative occupational surnames "Miller" and "Mason," a similarity underscored by Mrs. Costello's allusion to Daisy's friendship with Giovanelli as "that young lady's—Miss Baker's, Miss Chandler's—what's her name? Miss Miller's intrigue with that little barber's block" (*Daisy Miller* 103).[35] And notwithstanding James's complaint that "everyone seems to be in Rome" and that "these shoals of American fellow residents with their endless requisitions and unremunerative contact, are the dark side of life in Rome,"[36] this "colony" of Americans abroad was evidently compact and close-knit; in a letter to, Grace Norton, James lamented that "entanglements with the American colony" in Rome were "inevitable (or almost so)."[37]

Even if he (or Bartlett) never encountered Mason in Rome, he almost certainly read, or read of, her novella. Indeed, one of James's principal occupations at the time of *Mae Madden*'s publication was writing and reviewing for the *Nation*[38]—it was this task, along with finishing *Roderick Hudson*, that "kept me alive," James confided (*Complete Notebooks* 215); and in the *Nation*'s 3 February 1876 issue appeared the following review, unsigned but penned by James's childhood friend and lifelong correspondent, Thomas Sargent Perry.[39]

> Mae is to be seen travelling with a party of friends and relatives, but their hold upon her is very slight, and she makes the acquaintance of the godlike officer, who finally proposes to her to share his villa on the shore of the Bay of Naples. She refuses him, however, and marries Norman Mann, her American lover, after she has disported herself in a way that French novelists and dramatists consider to be customary with all of our fellow countrywomen. M. Alexandre Dumas may read this story, and disarm any hostile criticism of his new play by pointing to "Mae Madden" as a novel written by an American woman about an American woman, and as probably true.[40]

Even he would find it hard to invent a bolder disregard of conventional decorum than fills this little book, of which the main characteristic is its innocent silliness. ("Recent Novels" 83)

Moreover, a notice of Philip Gilbert Hamerton's *Round My House: Notes of Rural Life in France in Peace and War*, a notice known to have been written by James, appears in precisely the same installment of "Recent Novels," increasing the already high likelihood that James read Perry's review. [41] Then, too, James very often singled out Italian-themed books for reading and criticism, "confess[ing] to a sneaking kindness for the well-worn theme," which he pronounced "one of the most charming possible" (*Literary Criticism* 1: 1011, 1049). The *Nation*—though specifically recommending itself as "of value and interest" to Americans "traveling or residing in foreign parts"[42]— was not available on newsstands in Paris even fifteen months earlier,[43] but James's correspondence indicates that he received copies through the post on a regular basis, sometimes from his parents and sometimes directly from the magazine's offices, and when delivery was interrupted, he wrote home to rectify the situation.[44] His correspondence with Perry also comments on Perry's work for the *Nation* (Harlow 291), and his letters to his brother William regularly mention Perry and his critical contributors (see *Correspondence of William James*). Therefore, the foregoing notice of *Mae Madden*, which appeared in such close proximity to James's own review of *Round My House*, almost certainly caught his attention.

A decade after the appearance, nearly in tandem, of *Daisy Miller* and *Mae Madden*, in an essay on Constance Fenimore Woolson (1887), James wrote about the dominance of women writers in the American literary marketplace:

> Flooded as we have been in these latter days with copious discussion as to the admission of women to various offices, colleges, functions, and privileges, singularly little attention has been paid, by themselves at least, to the fact that in one highly important department of human affairs their cause is already gained. . . . In America, in England, to-day, it is no longer a question of their admission into the world of literature: they are in force, they have been admitted, with all honors, on perfectly equal footing. In America, at least, one feels tempted at moments to exclaim that they are in themselves the world of literature. (*Literary Criticism* 1: 639)

A decade later, James affirmed "the extraordinary dimensions" of the American reading public, of which women constituted "some of the largest masses": "The public taste . . . has become so largely *their* taste, their tone, their experiment, that nothing is at least more apparent than that the public cares little for anything that they cannot do" (*Literary Criticism* 1: 656). James's ambivalence toward the women writers who had become tantamount, in his estimation, to "the world of literature" has been a subject of lively debate. In *Henry James and the "Woman Business*," Alfred Habegger argues that James habitually wrote against "the enormous culture of nineteenth-century literary women" (4), revising and reshaping the women's fiction that was so popular at the time.[45] He explains:

> [James's] early fiction, like his reviews, . . . *answered* the women, showing them how they should have told their story. His first novel, *Watch and Ward*, took one of the women's favorite stories—the orphan heroine who grows up to marry her guardian—but tried to get it right by transforming the guardian from a tyrant into a tolerant encourager and by making the girl grow up to be a proper lady. Indeed, in this novel James lifted a scene from one of the agonists' [Habegger's term for a specific class of woman writer] novels (the same scene his review had singled out) and laundered it of its flaw (the same flaw the review had ridiculed). James's early reviews establish an unbroken line between the agonists' novels and his own corrective narratives. Once he started retelling the ladies' fictions, however, their original logic began to assert itself and work against his own gentlemanly impulses. (24–25)

That James was "correcting" *Mae Madden*—"laundering" it of its "innocent silliness"—when he wrote *Daisy Miller* and that *Mae Madden* was yet another point on the "unbroken line between the agonists' novels and his own corrective narratives" seem highly plausible developments.

Regardless of James's specific knowledge of *Mae Madden* and its author, however, in writing *Daisy Miller* he was clearly fashioning his own response to the popular tradition of "women abroad" narratives. In *Daisy Miller*, he revises, or "answers," the conventional story of the American woman abroad. Instead of stressing greater freedom for women in Italy, as do Mason and other writers who found inspiration in *Corinne* and her sisters, James portrays the Anglo-American society in Rome as one of greater restrictions. He also strips the American girl of her intellectual and artistic aspirations and diminishes her mental accomplishments.[46] One reviewer, Richard Grant White, declared that Daisy, "without being exactly a fool, is ignorant and devoid of all mental tone or character" (qtd. in Gard 61). In addition, James Europeanizes the central male character—Winterbourne "had become dishabituated to the American tone" (12)—so that his failure to "read" Daisy's character and behavior is predicated on, and becomes a commentary about, his expatriate status. In *Mae Madden*, Norman Mann has not lived so long overseas as has Winterbourne; he is still American to the core, and thus the conflict is fundamentally different. More important, however, James shifts the interior conflict from the young woman to the young man. Although the American girl had to guard against dangers imposed by the foreign "wolf," Winterbourne might have sympathized with Count Otto Vogelstein in James's story "Pandora," for whom "there appeared now to be a constant danger of marrying the American girl; it was something one had to reckon with, like the railway, the telegraph, the discovery of dynamite, the chassepot rifle, the socialist spirit: it was one of the complications of modern life" (*Daisy Miller and Other Stories* 100). Most important, instead of having access to the girl's thoughts, as in *Mae Madden*, readers of *Daisy Miller* have insight only into the male protagonist's limited point of view.[47]

In effect, then, James skillfully builds on the popular genre of the American girl abroad, expanding its base, successfully capturing a wider audience (one that includes men as well as women), thereby reclaiming the international theme as a masculine pursuit and elevating the genre to the level of the "upper middle cultured" (qtd. in Hayes 60). In doing so, however, he recasts the time-honored figure of the American woman abroad as a superficial object of study for the idle male observer and reorients the conventional progression of women's travel writing: the narrative shifts from the intellectual development of the "international American girl" to her social and physical demise.[48]

⚜ ⚜ ⚜

SCENE. Deck of an ocean steamer
*Characters*. Mrs. Jerrold, matron and chaperon in general.
Edith Jerrold, her daughter.
Albert Madden, a young man on study intent.
Eric, his brother, on pleasure bent.
Norman Mann, cousin of the Jerrolds, old class-mate of the Maddens.
Mae Madden, sister of the brothers and leading lady. (Mason 11)

It is ironic that Mary Murdoch Mason should choose to begin her narrative of the American girl abroad in the form of a play, as James, writing in Boston in 1882, brought his more famous narrative to a new conclusion in the same genre. Yet *Daisy Miller: A Comedy*, the product of this retooling, is not merely a translation to dramatic form of *Daisy Miller: A Study*. Instead, James makes a number of crucial alterations to the plot—modifications that actually close the gap between the story lines of *Daisy Miller* and *Mae Madden*. First, he shifts the events of the final act to Rome during Carnival. (One of the five known reviews and notices of *Mae Madden* enthusiastically praised Mason's use of the Carnival setting as "clever" ["Books Received" 936].) More significantly, Daisy Miller does not die of Roman fever in James's play. Instead, the convalescent Daisy becomes overwhelmed by the crush and confusion of Carnival, as does Mae in the same situation, and collapses in a faint, as does Mae at the Bay of Naples. Finally, just as *Mae Madden* concludes with the reconciliation of Mae and Norman and their imminent return to America, so the stage version of *Daisy Miller* ends with the engagement of Daisy and Winterbourne, who eagerly contemplate their return to their native shores. Thus, in this unexpectedly lighthearted dramatization, James eliminates the most significant difference between the plots of *Daisy Miller* and *Mae Madden* and, at the same time, introduces new elements of setting and characterization that bring *Daisy* into striking, even startling conformity with *Mae*. Perhaps James believed that a more conventional approach to the story of the American girl abroad would be received with greater enthusiasm by theatergoers than a play that retained the unconventional and barely credible twist he gave to *Daisy Miller: A Study*.[49] Perhaps he felt compelled to deliver a happy ending to this hoped-for audience—as he evidently did when he similarly revised the ending of *The American* for the stage. Or perhaps, as Habegger suggests of other stories James modeled on women's writing, the narrative's "original logic began to assert itself and work against his own gentlemanly impulses" (25). In any event, the rejection of the play in 1882, followed by its conversion back into print the following year,[50] illustrates the extent to which James had found—or made[51]—and fulfilled a market of his own: a market defined by innovation rather than convention and shaped by the fixity of print rather than the plasticity of performance.

# Chapter Six

# A BLUE AND GOLD
# MYSTIQUE

These are the days when skies resume
The old – old sophistries of June –
A blue and gold mistake.
                           —Emily Dickinson (c. 1859)

IN HER LAST book, a collection of stories titled *A Garland for Girls* (1888); (see figure 9), Louisa May Alcott repeatedly emphasizes the importance of reading in the lives of her characters.[1] In "May Flowers," six blue-blooded Boston girls meet regularly to discuss books read in common; the thoughtful protagonist of "Poppies and Wheat" reads for self-improvement during her grand tour of Europe; "Mountain-Laurel and Maidenhair" contrasts a jaded rich girl who has no true appreciation for poetry with an unsophisticated farmer's daughter who reads it avidly. In "Pansies" a refined and learned elderly woman advises three young ladies which books to read and which to avoid (figure 10). Alice, the most serious of the girls and an admirer of George Eliot, is cautioned to "choose carefully" lest she become "greedy, and read too much," since "cramming and smattering is as bad as promiscuous novel-reading, or no reading at all" (78–79). Eva, the youngest of the three, is gently steered away from the girlhood favorites Charlotte Yonge and Susan Warner to "fine biographies of real men and women" (81). Carrie, however, poses the greatest challenge to the sage Mrs. Warburton, for she delights in "thrilling" novels and frivolous romances.[2] Nevertheless, Mrs. Warburton succeeds so well in reforming the girl's taste in literature that Carrie forsakes the "crumpled leaves of the Seaside Library copy" of *Wanda*, an "interminable and impossible tale" (71) by the popular novelist Ouida (Marie Louise de la Ramée).[3] She resolves instead "to take her blue and gold volume of Tennyson on her next trip to Nahant" (94).[4]

161

FIGURE 9. The cover of Alcott's *A Garland for Girls*. The distinctive letterforms and ornamental design suggest the influence of Sarah Whitman. Author's collection.

" Alice, with both elbows on the table, listened with wide-awake
eyes." — PAGE 80.

FIGURE 10. Frontispiece in *A Garland for Girls*, by Jessie McDermott,
illustrating "Pansies." Author's collection.

Alcott's allusion to the "blue and gold Tennyson" is not idiosyncratic; references to blue and gold volumes abound in the mid-nineteenth-century culture of books. In *A Mid-Century Child and Her Books* (1926), for example, Caroline M. Hewins recalls, "My grown-up library began with the first edition of Hawthorne's 'Marble Faun' and was soon increased by Longfellow's 'Golden Legend,' a blue and gold Tennyson and Jean Paul's 'Titan' in two thick volumes" (36).[5] Soon after Ticknor and Fields introduced the format in 1856, other publishers rushed to copy the design, and before long, "blue and gold" became a generic descriptor in book announcements and criticism. Roberts Brothers advertised its new edition of Jean Ingelow's *Poems* as "the prettiest Blue and Gold volume ever issued" (qtd. in Kilgour 35). And when Edmund Clarence Stedman received a new "blue and gold" edition of Thomas Bailey Aldrich's poems, published by Rudd & Carleton in New York, he complained, "I don't like Blue and Gold in so large a type; it looks too much like cheap gilt children's books" (Stedman and Gould 1: 308).[6]

Still, Ticknor and Fields retained the strongest association with the style it had successfully popularized, so that Henry Wadsworth Longfellow, upon receiving a barrel of cider from William D. Ticknor in January 1863, could quip, "If instead of this iron-bound cask you had sent me a copy of 'Cider, a Poem in two Books' by J. Philips, bound in Blue and Gold, I should not have been half so grateful" (4: 311).[7] Indeed, so closely was the design identified with Ticknor and Fields that the colors suggested their imprint even when they appeared beyond the covers of a book. Thus, in a parodic vignette published in the magazine *Vanity Fair* in 1860, a fictionalized Prince of Wales pays his respects to a "magnificent (*i.e.* for Boston) creature gotten up gorgeously in blue and gold, a la Ticknor & Fields" ("Stupendous Enterprise" 180).[8]

A remarkable feature of allusions such as these is that the phrase "blue and gold" appears without explanation. Whatever these colors signified was a given; it was cultural knowledge that evidently needed no contextualization for contemporary readers.[9] In the context of Alcott's story, the "blue and gold Tennyson" clearly symbolizes Carrie's intellectual progress, her development from a reader of the much-maligned Anglo-French novelist Ouida to a reader of Tennyson, poet laureate of England and exemplar of literary refinement. But divorced from the individual author, and considered within the broad context of nineteenth-century American literature and culture, the ubiquitous references to blue and gold editions raise a number of questions. Why are blue and gold volumes singled out and so often evoked?[10] What role does the physical format of a book play in market segmentation and the targeting of readers? Can the packaging of books tell us something about the texts themselves or the readers for whom they were intended? Can the design of a book be said to perform a kind of cultural work beyond, or different from, that performed by the text itself?

The physicality of the book does, indeed, convey messages. Gérard Genette has argued that the "paratext"—the verbal and nonverbal productions that surround a text—is a "threshold of interpretation," a "conveyor of a commentary" (1–2). With a similar emphasis on the physical book, Jerome McGann explains, "Every literary work that descends to us operates through the deployment of a double helix of perceptual codes: the linguistic codes [or 'conceptual message'], on one hand, and the bibliographical codes [or 'physical medium'] on the other" (77). The bibliographical codes are particularly conspicuous in series of books such as Ticknor and Fields's Blue and Gold editions, for no particular title or author stands entirely apart from the series as a whole. I read Alcott's short story "Pansies" in the context of the Blue and Gold series as a means of unraveling the interwoven relationship between text and paratext, linguistic codes and bibliographical codes, both in the series and in the story. Recovering the contemporary meaning of Alcott's juxtaposition of the "blue and gold Tennyson" and the Seaside Library edition of *Wanda* shows how the "history of the book," in the bibliographic as well as the disciplinary sense, illuminates the story even as the story illuminates the "history of the book." A fascinating commentary on the functions of books and reading in nineteenth-century America, "Pansies" thus offers a key to interpreting both the materiality of the text and the symbolic power of the book as it reveals the oft-evoked but seldom examined "blue and gold" mystique.

In the poem beginning "These are the days when Birds come back" (J. 130), Emily Dickinson describes the false spring that precedes the onset of fall. Deceptively displaying the outward appearance of June, the skies of an Indian summer are, in her analysis, "a blue and gold mistake." As is so often the case in Dickinson's verse, the image is sensuous, evocative, pleasingly cryptic, and vaguely eccentric. Yet for all her characteristic originality, she joins a number of her contemporaries of the late 1850s in painting the month of June in shades of blue and gold.

The occasion that helped fix this poetic association of month and hue was the appearance, in June 1856, of two volumes of Tennyson's poems in a pocket-sized (32mo) edition, bound in blue cloth having a wave grain and embellished on the front cover with an intricate, blind-stamped floral cartouche framed by a triple-ruled border (figure 11), an ornate frame of gold filigree on the spine, brilliant gilt-edged leaves, chocolate-brown or orange-yellow endpapers, and an engraved portrait of the poet as the frontispiece (figure 12). Initially, the volumes bore no official series designation. Thus, in November 1856, Ticknor and Fields advertised its new "Pocket Edition of Longfellow's Poems, (Uniform with Tennyson's,) Complete in Two Volumes," noting simply that this "miniature" edition will be "bound in 'blue and gold,' like Tennyson's" ("Educational Books" 737). Readers and reviewers immediately began to refer to the miniature edition of Tennyson as the "blue and gold edition," however, thereby effectively helping to establish the series as such. Eventually, after Ticknor and Fields issued further titles in the same format, the publisher began to advertise them as "Books in Blue and Gold" and to herald them collectively as the "Blue and Gold series" (see table). The line had probably been inspired by the 1853 pocket edition of John Greenleaf Whittier's poems published by the London firm of Routledge.[11] James T. Fields, who "wanted a small handy volume, printed in easy-to-read type on thin but good paper" (Tryon, *Parnassus Corner* 229), designed the Tennyson binding with his brother George, and Henry O. Houghton of the Riverside Press designed the interior typography and layout (Pye 26).[12] Ticknor and Fields "issued a good Edn" but "the demand ... exceeded ... expectations."[13] Despite high production costs, the large sales of the Blue and Gold Tennyson soon brought profits, and "the format caught on like wildfire" (Tryon, *Parnassus Corner* 229).[14]

Before long, poets whose work appeared in the series, as well as those who aspired to the new format, were singing its praises. Bayard Taylor inquired rhetorically of a Blue and Gold edition of his *Poems*:

> Shall this an emblem be of that blue sky
> Wherein are set the golden stars of song?

Oliver Wendell Holmes prefaced his own Blue and Gold with an epigraph ("To My Readers," *Poems* iii), which includes the following lines:

> Go, little book, whose pages hold
>     Those garnered years in living trust;
> How long before your blue and gold
>     Shall fade and whiten in the dust?

166

FIGURE 11. The cover of *The Poetical Works of Alfred Tennyson*, in Ticknor and Fields's Blue and Gold edition. Courtesy, University of Minnesota Libraries.

FIGURE 12. Frontispiece portrait of the poet in the Blue and Gold
Tennyson. Courtesy, University of Minnesota Libraries.

The best example of verse celebrating the elegant little volumes, however,
is George S. Hillard's thirty-two-line poem, "On Receiving a Copy of Tennyson's Poems," dated 6 June 1856 and inscribed "To J. T. F." (publisher
James T. Fields):

> When your new Tennyson I hold, dear friend,
> Where blue and gold, like sky and sunbeam, blend,—
> Not too large a grasp
> For queen Titania's dainty hand to clasp,—
> I feel fresh truth in the old saying wise,
> That greatest worth in smallest parcel lies.
> Will not the diamond, that fiery spark,
> Buy a whole quarry-full of granite stark?
> Does not the flaunting holly-hock give place
> To that pale flower, with downward-drooping face,

168

Which summer fashions of the moonbeams' sheen
And sets in tents of the purest emerald green?
Well suits your book with this sweet month of June,
When earth and sky are in their perfect tune.
For, when I read its golden words, I think
I hear the brown thrush and the bob-o-link;—
I hear the summer brook, the summer breeze,
I hear the whisper of the swaying trees.
Between the lines red roses seem to grow,
And lilies white around the margin blow.
Cloud-showers swift across the meadow pass
And fruit-trees drop their blossoms on the grass.
Thanks to the poet, who to dusty hearts
The balm and bloom of summer fields imparts;
Who gives the toil-worn mind a passage free
To the brown mountain and the sparkling sea;
Who lifts the thoughts from earth, and pours a ray
Of fairy-land around life's common way.
And thanks to you who put this precious wine,
Red from the poet's heart, in flasks so fine,
The hand may clasp them, and the pocket hold;—
A casket small, but filled with perfect gold.

With its conventional evocations of nature and imagination and its subtle intimations of luxury and leisure, Hillard's poem was an ideal epigraph to the volume and to the series. Showing characteristic marketing savvy, Ticknor and Fields promptly appropriated the lines for inclusion in subsequent printings of the Blue and Gold Tennyson.

Less blatant an encomium than Hillard's, Alcott's "Pansies" testifies to the degree to which the Blue and Gold format came to symbolize culture, taste, and gentility in nineteenth-century America. If, as Richard Bushman claims of this period, "books, more than any other possessions, came to identify cultivated people, rivaling parlors as symbols of refinement" (283), then the Blue and Gold marked the pinnacle of cultivation. "Pansies" achieves more than a tribute to the skillful design and impeccable content of the new series, however. In the context of a story for and about teenage girls, it probes the complex negotiations among gender, culture, and consumption in the marriage market as well as the literary market. Through a frame narrative in which Mrs. Warburton regales her three young listeners with the story of her own courtship and marriage, Alcott suggests that

## Chronological Listing of Books in Ticknor and Fields's Blue and Gold Series

| Author | | Title | Year |
|---|---|---|---|
| Tennyson | Alfred | *The Poetical Works of Alfred Tennyson* | 1856 |
| Longfellow | Henry Wadsworth | *Poems* | 1856 |
| Longfellow | Henry Wadsworth | *Prose Works of Henry Wadsworth Longfellow* | 1857 |
| Jameson | Mrs. (Anna) | *Characteristics of Women, Moral, Poetical, and Historical* | 1857 |
| Massey | Gerald | *The Poetical works of Gerald Massey* | 1857 |
| Jameson | Mrs. (Anna) | *The Diary of an Ennuyé* | 1857 |
| Jameson | Mrs. (Anna) | *Memoirs of the Loves of the Poets: Biographical Sketches of Women* | 1857 |
| Whittier | John Greenleaf | *The Poetical Works of John Greenleaf Whittier* | 1857 |
| Hunt | Leigh | *The Poetical Works of Leigh Hunt* | 1857 |
| Bowring | John, Sir | *Matins and Vespers: With Hymns and Occasional Devotional Pieces* | 1857 |
| Jameson | Mrs. (Anna) | *Sketches of Art, Literature, and Character* | 1857 |
| Lowell | James Russell | *The Poetical Works of James R. Lowell* | 1858 |
| Jameson | Mrs. (Anna) | *Studies, Stories, and Memoirs* | 1859 |
| Motherwell | William | *The Poetical Works of William Motherwell* | 1859 |
| Percival | James Gates | *Poems* | 1859 |
| Jameson | Mrs. (Anna) | *Memoirs of the Early Italian Painters* | 1859 |
| Meredith | Owen | *Poems* | 1859 |
| Dobell | Sydney | *Poems* | 1860 |
| Meredith | Owen | *Lucile* | 1860 |
| Allingham | William | *Poems* | 1860 |
| Horace | | *The Odes of Horace* | 1860 |
| Jameson | Mrs. (Anna) | *Legends of the Madonna as Represented in the Fine Arts* | 1860 |
| Saxe | John Godfrey | *Poems* | 1861 |
| Clough | Arthur Hugh | *The Poems of Arthur Hugh Clough. With a Memoir* | 1862 |
| Holmes | Oliver Wendell | *The Poems of Oliver Wendell Holmes* | 1862 |

| Author | | Title | Year |
|---|---|---|---|
| Procter | Adelaide Anne | *The Poems of Adelaide A. Procter* | 1862 |
| Taylor | Henry, Sir | *Philip van Artevelde: A Dramatic Romance* | 1863 |
| Irving | Washington | *The Sketch-book of Geoffrey Crayon, Gent.* | 1863 |
| Jameson | Mrs. (Anna) | *Sacred and Legendary Art* | 1864 |
| Jameson | Mrs. (Anna) | *Legends of the Monastic Orders, as Represented in the Fine Arts* | 1864 |
| Taylor | Bayard | *The Poems of Bayard Taylor* | 1864 |
| Hawthorne | Nathaniel | *Twice-told Tales* | 1864 |
| Tennyson | Alfred | *Enoch Arden, &c.* | 1864 |
| Emerson | Ralph Waldo | *Poems* | 1865 |
| Holmes | Oliver Wendell | *The Autocrat of the Breakfast-Table: Every Man His Own Boswell* | 1865 |
| Emerson | Ralph Waldo | *Essays. First and Second Series* | 1865 |
| Aldrich | Thomas Bailey | *The Poems of Thomas Bailey Aldrich* | 1865 |
| (Craik) | Dinah Maria Mulock | *Poems* | 1866 |
| Hervey | Thomas Kibble | *The Poems of Thomas Kibble Hervey* | 1866 |
| (Allen) | Elizabeth Akers | *Poems* | 1866 |
| Burns* | Robert | *Poems* | 1866 |
| Coleridge* | Samuel Taylor | *The Poems of S. T. Coleridge* | 1866 |
| Dibdin* | Charles | *Sea Songs and Ballads* | 1866 |
| Goldsmith* | Oliver | *The Vicar of Wakefield* | 1866 |
| Hall* | Basil | *The Lieutenant and Commander; Being Autobiographical Sketches* | 1866 |
| Hall* | Basil | *The Midshipman: Being Autobiographical Sketches* | 1866 |
| Herbert* | George | *The Works of George Herbert, in Prose and Verse* | 1866 |
| Lamb* | Charles and Mary | *Tales from Shakespeare* | 1866 |
| Milton* | John | *Poems* | 1866 |
| | | *Robin Hood's Ballads* | 1866 |
| Shakespeare* | William | *The Plays of William Shakespeare* | 1866 |
| Southey* | Robert | *The Life of Nelson* | 1866 |
| Walton* | Izaak | *The Compleat Angler* | |
| | | *The Lives of Dr. John Donne; Sir Henry Wotton; Mr. Richard Hooker; Mr. George Herbert; and Mr. Robert Sanderson* | 1866 |

| Author | | Title | Year |
|--------|--------|-------|------|
| White* | Gilbert | *The Natural History of Selborne* | 1866 |
| Meredith | Owen | *New Poems* | 1868 |
| (Longfellow | Henry Wadsworth | *Christus: A Mystery* | 1873) |

NOTE: The order of titles is that given in the Ticknor and Fields's cost books (MS Am 2030.2, Houghton Library), adjusted, when possible, according to precise publication dates given in published bibliographies. When the actual date of publication does not appear in the cost book and when the entry falls near the end of the year, the year given is that of the earliest known extant copy. Ticknor and Fields occasionally postdated books. The first Blue and Gold edition of *Twice-told Tales*, for example, is dated 1865 even though the volume was published in October 1864. In two instances (Bowring's *Matins and Vespers* and Meredith's *Poems*), the cost book entries significantly postdate the date given on the title page of extant copies, suggesting that the books were printed from plates made earlier. Longfellow's *Christus* was published by James R. Osgood, successor to Ticknor and Fields.

*Imported titles advertised as "fine English blue and gold editions." These titles do not appear in the cost books and are listed in alphabetical order by author.

the materiality of the text impinges on readers (literally and figuratively) in unexpected and problematic ways.

Although Alcott does not specify the publisher of the "blue and gold Tennyson" by name, she clearly has in mind the same firm that Hillard (a close friend of Hawthorne's) eulogizes. Boston-based Ticknor and Fields was one of the most prestigious publishing houses in nineteenth-century America, and Alcott knew it well, personally as well as professionally.[15] Moreover, although several other publishers appropriated the blue-and-gold style, Ticknor and Fields were Tennyson's first American publishers, and most of their competitors respected the well-established practice of trade courtesy that served to protect such prior claims.[16]

William D. Ticknor had begun his publishing business in the 1830s as a specialist in medical books. The firm became a leading literary publisher after 1843 when Fields, who had joined Ticknor's Old Corner Bookstore as a clerk in 1832, advanced to junior partner. The company published the most highly respected American authors of the day, including Emerson (after the collapse of Phillips, Sampson in 1859), Thoreau, Longfellow, Hawthorne, Whittier, Lowell, and Holmes. They also published Scott, DeQuincey, Tennyson, Dickens, Thackeray, Browning, and other highly regarded British authors. Their forte was poetry, a distinction that added further luster to their image.[17] Indeed, as a result of its literary prowess, Fields, who was a poet in his own right, earned a reputation as "an educator of the public," one who "never stooped to vitiate the popular taste" (*Boston Transcript*, qtd. in "Fields, James Thomas" 379).[18]

It was not only in the brilliance of its list, however, that Ticknor and Fields excelled. The firm also pioneered the nascent art of book promotion.[19] In addition to procuring favorable reviews and orchestrating advertising campaigns for new titles, Fields proved that the physical book could itself be used as a medium for advertising and marketing and effectively overcame the difficulty many contemporary publishers faced in establishing a recognizable "brand."[20] The uniform physical design adopted for key titles—in particular, the standard brown volumes and the Blue and Gold editions—minimized, for the consumer, the element of variability in quality and "essence." Consequently, Ticknor and Fields's books became "status statements on a bookshelf" (Groves 93); or, as Raymond L. Kilgour put it, "Their imprint on a book was the vogue" (*Mssrs. Roberts Brothers* 22).

Although Ticknor and Fields achieved wide recognition as a literary house, a leading publisher of poetry and belles lettres, its well-crafted books were neither uniformly "fancy" nor expensive. The partners understood from an early date the advantages of bringing out several editions of a single author, variously priced and in a range of formats, thus segmenting their market by price point and design. In 1863, for example, the firm published a standard edition of Jesse Benton Frémont's *The Story of the Guard: A Chronicle of the War* and, because the Civil War had created a demand for low-priced, portable editions, quickly followed it up with a rival "Knapsack Edition," a 16mo volume priced at 50 cents in paper or 75 cents in cloth, which they advertised as follows:

> CHEAP EDITION OF MRS FRÉMONT'S 'STORY OF THE GUARD.'—Ticknor & Fields announce as nearly ready what they happily call the 'Knapsack Edition' of this popular book, already in its sixth edition. It will be well printed, and handsomely prepared every way for army reading. A great call for this work among our soldiers suggested this cheap *'Knapsack Edition'* (*American Literary Gazette and Publishers' Circular* [May 15, 1863] 154)[21]

In addition to mainstream and military readers, Ticknor and Fields perceived yet another market for Frémont's text: the sizable audience of German speakers in the United States. Acting on this observation, they came out in the same year with *Die Liebgarde: Eine Geschichte aus dem Kriege*, with the goal of tapping into this lucrative secondary market.

With such varied target audiences, *The Story of the Guard* may have been an unusually timely and versatile text. Nevertheless, the practice of bringing out parallel editions of its titles became a highly effective strategy for Ticknor and Fields. Once a book (particularly a collection of poems) proved successful in the firm's standard brown-cover format, it might be issued as a reprint in the Blue and Gold series—provided it was sufficiently high-toned. As a critic for the *Christian Examiner* observed: "A thin, brown volume of one hundred and eleven pages from the press of Ticknor and Fields,—we know at a glance that it is poetry. Do Messrs. Ticknor and Fields give the muses a probation in these russet robes before they admit them to the honors of the blue and gold?" ("Poetry and Fiction" 302). Further, successful Blue and Gold titles that had been released in two-volume sets might later be repackaged as omnibus "Cabinet Editions," as was the case with the poetical works of Tennyson, Longfellow, Whittier, and Holmes.[22] Such a text might then make yet another appearance in the form of a "Diamond Edition,"[23] a "Red-Line Edition," or a "Little Classics Edition," and later, perhaps, as a "Merrimac Edition," "Household Edition," "Family Edition," "Illustrated Library Edition," or some other special edition. Finally, the most enduring of the "classic" titles might make their encore as elegant "Riverside Editions" from the press of Houghton Mifflin Company, the direct descendant of Ticknor and Fields.[24]

In *Satisfaction Guaranteed: The Making of the American Mass Market*, Susan Strasser explains that in the modern American economy, pricing ceased to be "the outcome of a series of bargains and negotiations," becoming instead "part of the marketing process. Manufacturers would set prices, and the most sophisticated ones would do so with respect to targeted market segments, creating lines of competing but differently priced products" (269). The publication agenda of Ticknor and Fields, whereby a single text was packaged in a variety of formats all priced for and marketed to specific segments of the reading public, exemplifies this sophisticated marketing strategy. Its handling of Tennyson's poems is a case in point, as Warren Tryon explains: "The publishers sought, by the creation of new formats, to arouse interest and, by establishing a price range from fifty cents for a pamphlet edition to ten dollars for a de luxe illustrated one, to stimulate sales. They succeeded. Between 1842 and 1870 no less than 130 separate issues of the collected poems totaling 206,044 copies (in 267,948 volumes) were published. Every taste and every pocketbook was reached, and by 1865 the publishers could count an annual sale of between 25,000 and 30,000 copies of their various Tennysons" ("Nationalism" 305).

Ticknor and Fields's decision to put particular texts into their Blue and Gold series reflects both their high estimation of those texts and their authors and the high status potentially accruing to them.[25] Because all texts brought out in this series had a common "look and feel" (in today's marketing jargon), each title took on some of the luster of the other titles in the series. Each new book that appeared in the decorative blue and gold binding was supported, in terms of cultural status, by the series' distinguished backlist.[26] The strategy worked exceptionally well: readers and reviewers were quick to notice the series identity of the distinctive miniature volumes and readily recognized them as "characteristic of poetic issues of Messrs. Ticknor & Fields" ("Editor's Repository" [1866] 758).[27] It was a format symbolic of high literary value and subject to imitation.[28]

With one of the strongest backlists in the country, Ticknor and Fields could count on its existing series to lend financial as well as cultural capital to new titles.[29] Backlist sales potentially yielded higher profits than did new titles because the one-time costs of composition and stereotyping (as well as copyright, when it was a single fee) had already been covered. In addition, older titles, if they were good sellers, had already established their markets. Nevertheless, even tried-and-true "standard" texts carried risks, as Donald Sheehan explains: "The publisher of a well-known 'classic' could never be secure from rival editions. There was also the disagreeable fact that a permanent demand did not necessarily imply a turnover quick enough to insure a profitable investment. Consequently publishers found themselves caught between a fear of competition and a dread of slowly moving inventory. The most common solution was to choose the best works, and hope that an attractive format and a minimum price would bring success" (135). For Ticknor and Fields, the solution of bringing out their best texts in a pleasing but affordable format was highly effective. The Blue and Gold series wedded the requisite attractive design and reasonable price to the satisfaction—even the delight—of many thousands of consumers. Ticknor and Fields, rivaling the famous printers and publishers of London, had become "the MOXONS and MURRAYS of America," and "the 'Blue and Gold' pocket edition of Tennyson was considered a sort of crowning achievement" (Eidson 99).

Nineteenth-century readers often were discriminating consumers of books as objects. Book announcements and reviews routinely noted the physical appearance of the volumes (how they were "gotten up") and frequently provided minutely detailed descriptions. Indeed, Herman Melville devoted an entire review of a revised edition of Cooper's *The Red Rover* to a discussion of the book's design ("Thought on Book-Binding," [1850]). Given the fact that many nineteenth-century readers were quite knowledgeable about book design and construction, it is not surprising that Ticknor and Fields's attention to the physical quality of the books was perhaps the most highly praised feature of the series.[30] Many readers focused on its "typographical beauty" ("Editor's Repository" [1865] 125) and "luxurious style" ("Notices of New Works" [1860] 320). Upon receiving a Blue and Gold Tennyson, Sophia Hawthorne effused in a letter to Fields, "You have surpassed yourself in the beauty of its execution. [It is] miraculous how you could crowd all those poems into such a tiny compass & yet present them in such clear, large type" (qtd. in Tryon, *Parnassus Corner* 229; see figure 13). The *Christian Examiner* remarked, "We should have said that Tennyson could not be compressed into so small a space without crowding, but we find everything, including that sweetest, saddest of modern poems, the *"In Memoriam"* ("Notices of Recent Publications" 151).[31]

The Scottish poet Gerald Massey, whose poems issued forth in the Blue and Gold format in 1857, was one of many who declared the volumes "exquisite" (qtd. in Tryon, *Parnassus Corner* 229). A reviewer for the *Knickerbocker* exclaimed, "How exquisite they are, in the 'first appeal, which is to the eye'" (qtd. in Groves 85); a reviewer for *Putnam's Monthly Magazine* concurred that the Blue and Gold Tennyson exemplified "the most exquisite taste, in every way." Juxtaposing the "classic" Blue and Gold and the tawdry popular novel, this reviewer also drew the comparison Alcott makes in "Pansies" and reckoned that in the "beautifully printed and bound" Blue and Gold Tennyson "the poems of one of the truest poets that ever illustrated our language may be had for the price of the last worthless novel" ("Editorial Notes" 98).[32] Several reviewers were so taken with the formal elegance of the binding that they were moved to contrive poetic metaphors of ancestral privilege and inherited wealth. To one critic, the blue and gold binding formed the poet's "court attire" ("Book Trade" [1863] 109); another reviewer declared that *"Or* upon *azure* is good heraldry for a poet whose verses reflect the light of summer skies, and whose pictures shine with the golden tinges of the autumnal forest" ("Notices of

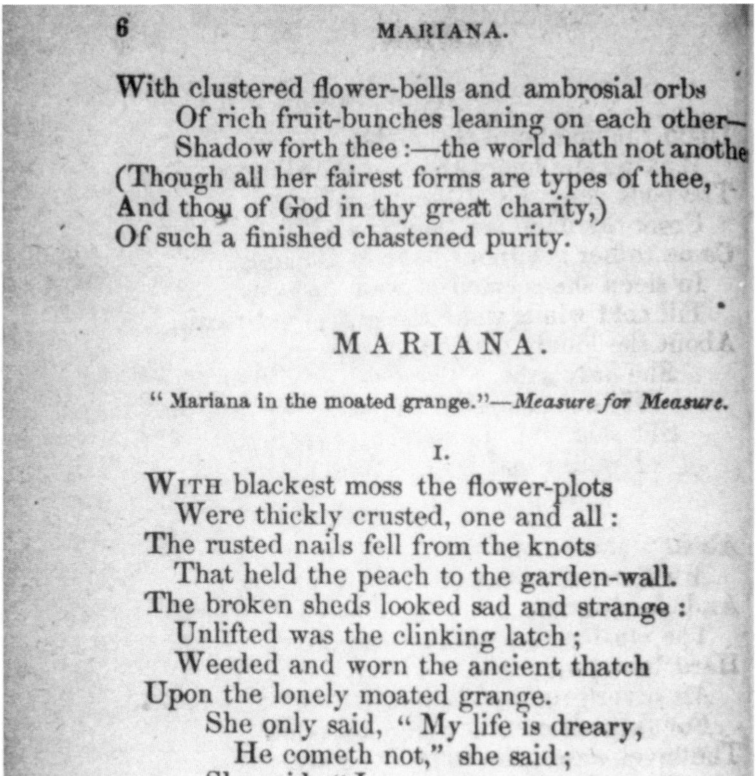

With clustered flower-bells and ambrosial orbs
   Of rich fruit-bunches leaning on each other—
   Shadow forth thee :—the world hath not anothe
(Though all her fairest forms are types of thee,
And thou of God in thy great charity,)
Of such a finished chastened purity.


# MARIANA.

*" Mariana in the moated grange."—Measure for Measure.*

## I.

WITH blackest moss the flower-plots
   Were thickly crusted, one and all :
The rusted nails fell from the knots
   That held the peach to the garden-wall.
The broken sheds looked sad and strange :
   Unlifted was the clinking latch ;
   Weeded and worn the ancient thatch
Upon the lonely moated grange.
      She only said, " My life is dreary,
        He cometh not," she said ;
      She said, " I am aweary, aweary,
        I would that I were dead ! "

## II.

Her tears fell with the dews at even ;
   Her tears fell ere the dews were dried ;
She could not look on the sweet heaven,
   Either at morn or eventide.
After the flitting of the bats,
   When thickest dark did trance the sky,
   She drew her casement-curtain by,
And glanced athwart the glooming flats.
      She only said, " The night is dreary,
        He cometh not," she said ;
      She said, " I am aweary, aweary,
       · I would that I were dead ! "

FIGURE 13. An example of the type used in *The Poetical Works of Alfred Tennyson*, Blue and Gold edition. Courtesy, University of Minnesota Libraries.

New Works" [1857] 315). A book notice in the *Merchants' Magazine and Commercial Review* referred to the two-volume *Poetical Works of Leigh Hunt* as "two more gems from the 'blue and gold' book mine of Ticknor & Fields, the peers of princely publishers" ("Book Trade" [1857] 652), and with reference to the New England poets Lowell, Longfellow, Whittier, and George Lunt (the latter not actually represented in the Ticknor and Fields series), a reviewer for the *Federal American Monthly* evoked "the 'blue and gold' editions which identify them as 'to the manor born' Bostonian" ("Author of 'Frontenac'" 328).

Readers also lavishly praised the small size of the 32mo volumes (approximately 14.5 cm × 9.5 cm).[33] In his poem "On Receiving a Copy of Tennyson's Poems" (quoted above), Hillard emphasizes the feminine aspect of the small format, referring to the Blue and Gold Tennyson as "A fairy tome—of not too large a grasp / For Queen Titania's dainty hand to clasp." The *Home Journal* echoed Hillard's fanciful diction and imagery when it mused, "'If books had been manufactured in those days when Oberon and Titania were mighty powers in the woodland, when every asphodel and every king's cup was the *chateau* of a fairy,' those books would have been just such beautiful little 'claspable tomes' as 'Ticknor's miniature Tennyson'" (qtd. in Eidson 99).

The portability of the volumes, another function of their miniature size, also received high praise. Hillard marvels, "The hand may clasp them, and the pocket hold;— / A casket small, but filled with perfect gold," and a reviewer for the *New York Daily Tribune*, for whom "immortality in miniature was never more excellently presented," remarked that the volume was small enough to "be taken without inconvenience on a journey or on a walk" (qtd. in Groves 84).[34] *Putnam's Monthly Magazine* declared that the "small, convenient pocket volume" was "the most perfect of summer books" ("Editorial Notes" 98)—a pronouncement which accords well with the fact that it was released in time for the summer holiday trade—and the *Christian Examiner* raved: "A real pocket edition of Tennyson, printed with good, plain type upon fair paper, and in very tasteful binding, must be admitted to be the very *vade mecum* of all others for our summer rambles, and our sojournings on the hill-sides and by the way of the sea. The publisher as well as the poet will be gratefully remembered under many a green tree and great rock, whilst Sirius has most things his own mad way" ("Notices of Recent Publications" 151). Alcott, too, points to the aptness of the small volumes for travel, not only when she writes of Carrie's intention to take the pocket-sized Blue and Gold Tennyson to Nahant but also in "Mountain-Laurels and Maidenhair" (the final story in *A Garland for Girls*), in which Emily, on a visit to the country, removes from her trunk "a pile of blue and gold volumes" (*Garland* 225), their spines emblazoned with the names of Whittier, Tennyson, and Emerson.

Aside from its convenience for the space-conscious traveler, another significant feature of the pocket format was that it was well adapted to the presentation of poetry. The volumes of the Blue and Gold series were too small to accommodate long novels, which it would have been uneconomical to publish in more than two volumes. Indeed, very little fiction and relatively few nonfiction prose titles exist in the series.[35] Conversely, the typical dimensions of novels were too large for most collections of verse; the pocket-sized Blue and Gold provided a more appropriate trim size.

It is not surprising, then, that the series was particularly dear to the hearts of poets. Two years after Ticknor and Fields brought out the Blue and Gold editions of his *Poems* and *Prose Works* (1857), Longfellow approvingly observed, "That little edition is having an extraordinary run." It was, he pronounced with more pragmatism than poetry, "a handsome little heifer, with a good deal of milk" (4: 108). Thomas Bailey Aldrich, who had been trying to persuade Fields to bring out a small volume of his poems since September 1856 (a few months after the appearance of the Tennyson), finally saw his poetry ensconced in the series—"the one reserved for the most important writers of the day" (Wolf 44)—but only after Rudd & Carleton had published a knock-off blue and gold edition. In September 1856, Aldrich had written to Fields, "I should like to get a volume out by next Spring, but am willing to wait four summers" (qtd. in Greenslet 34). Four years later, he again conveyed to Fields his desire to "bind himself" (note pun) with Ticknor and Fields: "Rudd & Carleton have brought out two volumes of mine . . . and are willing to try me again, but I would rather have your imprint if possible. It would be of such service to me. I write to you before binding myself with Rudd & Carleton. What cheer?" (qtd. in Greenslet 52). The new Rudd & Carleton edition, a "compact little volume, bound in blue and gold, in genial imitation of the Blue and Gold Series of immortals published by Ticknor & Fields" (Greenslet 63), appeared in 1863, followed by the authentic Ticknor and Fields two years later.

Whittier, too, expressly pursued publication in the series. After Fields sent him a copy of Longfellow's *Poems* in Blue and Gold, Whittier replied, "I like your new edition exceedingly, and wish some means can be devised to get my verses into a similar shape" (qtd. in Pickard 1: 392). Fields was glad to oblige, assuring the poet that the sale of his poems in an earlier edition "has been materially checked, and you have not had a fair chance in the poets [*sic*] market," and adding "now we hope you will have a wider hearing."[36] After the death of Whittier's original publisher, Benjamin B. Bussey, Fields managed to obtain the copyright on his early poems, and the Blue and Gold edition of *The Poetical Works of John Greenleaf Whittier* materialized in 1857. This volume, in turn, caught the attention of the British poet laureate, in company with yet another prominent American poet, Bayard Taylor. Caroline Ticknor, the daughter of William Ticknor, records, "In 1867 a letter written by Bayard Taylor described an evening spent with the English poet [Tennyson], when he had listened to the reading of 'Guinevere,' at which time a volume of Whittier, in 'blue-and-gold,' lay on Tennyson's table" (322).[37]

Upon receipt of his own *Poems* in the Blue and Gold format in 1864, Taylor had written to Fields: "The books are here, and they are charming. . . . I think I never had so much pleasure in looking at a book of mine as just this one. Each separate poem seems to read better than it ever did before" (*Life and Letters* 2: 426). Anticipating the publication of E. C. Stedman in the series, Taylor wrote him in 1867, "It will be like a poetic embrace to have you on the shelf beside me, in blue and gold" (319). And Gerald Massey informed Fields: "Of all pocket editions I think yours the choicest and am proud to find myself in its good company. The Blue and Gold are true colors also to sail under in crossing the Atlantic, and I desire to thank your firm for their fair and generous dealing with myself, and for their manner of getting up a bonny little book" (qtd. in Groves 88).[38]

Sometimes the little volumes served as gifts and as prizes for the literarily inclined. A reviewer for the *Merchants' Magazine and Commercial Review* confided, "If we were intending to bestow on some fair 'lady love' a presentation, on the approaching season of gifts, all that is pure and beautiful in literature, we should find no difficulty in deciding as to the propriety of such a gift as we find embraced in this series of elegant books" ("Book Trade" [1857] 652). A Blue and Gold Tennyson in the Harvard Libraries is inscribed to Sarah Orne Jewett by her "Grandpa Perry," and a volume of *The Poetical Works of James Russell Lowell* in the Library of Congress carries an inscription from the Public Latin School of Boston, recording that the book was "Awarded to George Santayana for a Poetical Translation from Horace."[39] The Blue and Gold was evidently the poet's series of choice, and poetry lovers were not far behind in their admiration. In a letter of 19 March 1863 a correspondent of Lowell's importuned, "Now I shall ask you, what I have wanted long ago to ask, to send me your poems in the little 'Blue & Gold' and write with love of J. R. L. just as you used to" (James Russell Lowell Papers).[40]

In his *Paratexts*, Gérard Genette emphasizes yet another important aspect of the pocket-sized format. With reference to the French *livre de poche*, Genette asserts that "the 'pocket edition' (that is, simply the republication at a low price of old or recent works that have first undergone the commercial test of the trade edition) has indeed become an instrument of 'culture,' an instrument, in other words, for constituting and, naturally, disseminating a relatively permanent collection of works *ipso facto* sanctioned as 'classics'" (20). Genette elaborates:

> Today, therefore, "pocket size" is basically no longer a format but a vast set or nebula of series—for "pocket" still means "series"—from the most popular to the most "distinguished," indeed, the most pretentious; and the series emblem, much more than size, conveys two basic meanings. One is purely economic: the assurance (variable, and sometimes illusory) of a better price. The other is indeed "cultural" and, to speak of what interests us, paratextual: the assurance of a selection based on *revivals*, that is, reissues. Occasionally someone speculates about the possibility of reversing the flow—publishing works first in pocket size, then producing in more expensive editions those titles that have triumphantly passed the first test—but this seems contrary to all the technical, media, and commercial givens, even if in particular situations certain books have taken this paradoxical journey and even if certain pocket series welcome, as experiments, some previously unpublished works that are thus immediately canonized. For undoubtedly the pocket edition will long be synonymous with canonization. (21)

The relevance of Genette's observation is suggested by a nineteenth-century critic who wrote, after enumerating the names of various Blue and Gold authors: "It would appear that Messrs. Ticknor & Fields are striving to make, in their series of blue and gold, a sort of test popularity for works of this kind, in aid of inspiration, and we heartily wish them good speed and a large sale" ("Book Trade" [1859] 775).

It is precisely in the capacity of "instruments of 'culture'"—a means of "constituting and . . . disseminating" a set of texts "sanctioned as 'classics'"—that the Blue and Gold series makes its appearance in Alcott's "Pansies." Indeed, the Blue and Gold Tennyson serves as an agent of Carrie's apparent acculturation into the system of values endorsed by Mrs. Warburton: a nineteenth-century culture of gentility in which the aim "was to enable a person to shine in the best society" (Bushman 310). Early in the story, Alcott characterizes Carrie as "one of the ambitious yet commonplace girls who wish to shine, without knowing the difference between the glitter of a candle which attracts moths, and the serene light of a star, or the cheery glow of a fire round which all love to gather" (*Garland* 76). In striking concurrence with Alcott, Yale luminary Noah Porter commented on just such a character defect in *Books and Reading; or, What Books Shall I Read and How Shall I Read Them?* (1870), an advice manual that went through several reprintings during the period between the heyday of the Blue and Gold series and the publication of *A Garland for Girls*. Porter cautions:

> Fashionable people, and people who aspire to give tone to society, may delight in low and vulgar novels. Even persons who are morally pure and right-hearted may want the capacity to discriminate between what is high and low toned in fiction. . . . [T]here are people whose aristocracy is unquestioned, and whose manners have the unmistakable confidence that bespeaks a well-established social position, who by the novels which they habitually read, betray the essential vulgarity of their intellectual tastes, and the low grade of the aesthetic culture. Few things are more properly offensive to the traveler than to see a second or third rate novel in the hands of a well-dressed and well-mannered lady. (222–23)

Carrie, who describes herself as "poor" (*Garland* 72), frequently feels "vulgar, ignorant, and mortified" in the society of Mrs. Warburton's friends, who "dressed simply, enjoyed conversation, kept up their accomplishments even when old" and are "genuine," well bred, "busy, lovable, and charming" (77). Alcott announces that the aims of Carrie's mother "were not high": Carrie and her sister "knew that she desired good matches for them, educated them for that end, and expected them to do their parts when the time came" (76–77). As a result, Carrie, like the "well-mannered lady" of Porter's diatribe, evinces an education woefully inadequate to the proper development of "aesthetic culture," or good taste.

Carrie's lack of discrimination—her inability to differentiate among candle, star, and fire—is precisely why she needs a series like Ticknor and Fields's Blue and Gold editions to guide her reading and shape her intellectual, aesthetic, and moral development. A deficiency of George Munro's

Seaside Library (the moth-tormented candle of Alcott's metaphor) was the utter lack of literary discrimination on the part of its publisher in selecting titles: any book sufficiently popular and sufficiently inexpensive to publish qualified for inclusion, with the result that Tennyson and Goldsmith rubbed shoulders with Ouida (see figures 14, 15, 16) and "The Duchess" (another author Carrie admits to reading).[41] The series comprised "classics" and potboilers alike, and many believed the Seaside's readers lacked the taste and education to discern the difference. In contrast, the imprint of Ticknor and Fields and, especially, the firm's Blue and Gold series, provided a guarantee of literary quality and the assurance of cultural approval. Indeed, as literary publishers deeply invested in the notion of cultural hierarchy, Ticknor and Fields engaged in a kind of editorial selection, exclusion, and classification (a process quite alien to the publisher of the Seaside Library) which ultimately resulted in the identification of their books as "literary." The *Knickerbocker* observed that "MESSRS. TICKNOR AND FIELDS, the popular publishers of Boston" had established a "reputation for the excellence of their selections, and the external beauty of their publications" ("Editor's Table" 307).[42]

In "Pansies," Alcott, as author, takes on the publisher's task of selecting, eliminating, and constructing a hierarchy of texts for the benefit of her readers. Through her characters, she classifies the productions of Ouida and "The Duchess" as "false and foolish" tales;[43] she characterizes the novels of Susan Warner and Charlotte Yonge as "dear homely books"; she elevates the novels of Walter Scott and Maria Edgeworth to an established tradition of standard works of fiction; and she dismisses Howells and James, whose "everlasting stories, full of people who talk a great deal and amount to nothing" exemplify "the modern realistic writers, with their elevators, and paint-pots, and every-day people" (*Garland* 80–83).[44] As for poetry, she designates Wordsworth "one of our truest poets" (90) and sets Tennyson at the pinnacle of the contemporary high culture to which Carrie, after her abashed rejection of *Wanda, Countess von Szalras*, aspires.[45]

The young ladies of Alcott's story have a shrewd literary adviser in the elderly Mrs. Warburton, whose motto is "Ask advice, and so cultivate a true and refined taste" (79). Nineteenth-century readers who lacked such a mentor could rely upon assembled sets of classics, such as Ticknor and Fields's Blue and Gold series, to separate the literary gold from the dross. In "Pansies," Alcott denounces Carrie's home life as "frivolous" and her public life showy (77). Her education, a primer in the art of courtship, has

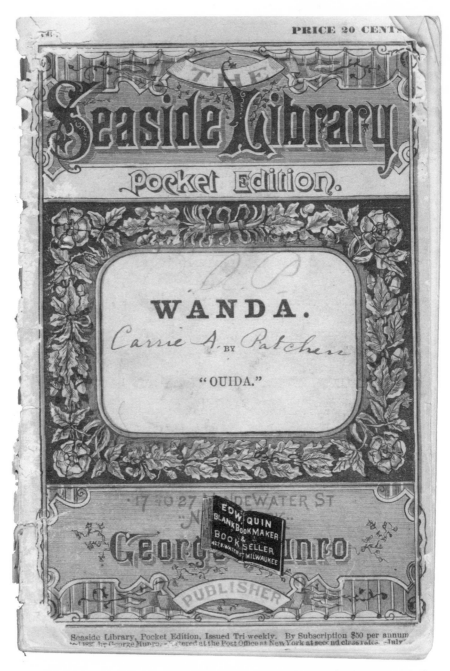

FIGURE 14. Cover of the Seaside Library Pocket Edition of Ouida's *Wanda, Countess von Szalras* (c. 1886). Courtesy, Albert Johannsen Dime Novel Collection, Rare Books and Special Collections, Northern Illinois University.

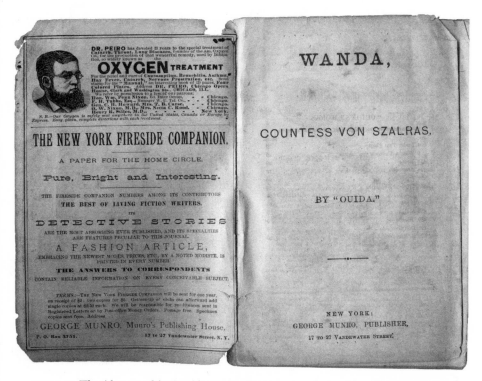

FIGURE 15. The title page of the Seaside *Wanda*, facing a page of advertising. Courtesy, Albert Johannsen Dime Novel Collection, Rare Books and Special Collections, Northern Illinois University.

failed to equip her with the reading habits appropriate to her station. As a remedy, the Blue and Gold Tennyson—and, by extension, the other books in the series—offer taste and culture "neatly packaged."[46]

Although not exclusively marketed for female readers, the Blue and Gold series boasted a list of titles ideally suited to the moral and aesthetic culture of the feminine mind.[47] In contrast, the Seaside Library carried precisely the kinds of novels that nineteenth-century critics held up as examples of books believed to be detrimental to female readers. In "What Girls Read" (1886), for example, Edward G. Salmon wrote: "Girls' literature performs one very useful function. It enables girls to read something above mere baby tales, and yet keeps them from the influence of novels of a sort which should be read only by persons capable of forming a discreet judgement. It is a long jump from Aesop to 'Ouida,' and to place [British

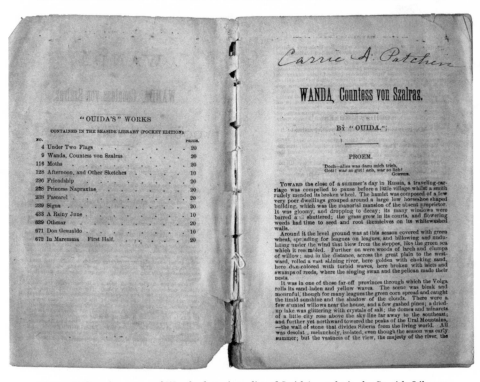

FIGURE 16. Opening pages of *Wanda*, featuring a list of Ouida's works in the Seaside Library. Courtesy, Albert Johannsen Dime Novel Collection, Rare Books and Special Collections, Northern Illinois University.

girls' novelist and hymn writer] Miss Sarah Doudney or [British religious novelist] Miss Anne Beale between Aesop and 'Ouida' may at least prevent a disastrous moral fall" (522). Similarly, in "Cheap Books and Good Books" (1887), Brander Matthews argued that "inferior foreign fiction . . . not only usurps the place of better literature, but spoils the appetite for it. . . . The cheap books to be bought in the United States are only too often the trivial trash of the ladies who call themselves 'Ouida' and 'The Duchess.' How much these may nerve a man or a woman for the realities of existence, how much the wisdom to be got from them may arm us for the stern battle of life, I cannot say" (584).

An article in *St. Nicholas* magazine went further (much further) in its condemnation of "illicit fiction." According to this publication (where "Pansies" initially appeared), sensational fiction "weakens the mental grasp, destroys the love of good reading, and the power of sober and rational thinking, takes away all relish from the realities of life, breeds discontent and indolence and selfishness, and makes the one who is addicted to it a weak, frivolous, petulant, miserable being" (qtd. in Hunter 61).

For Mrs. Warburton, too, reading the wrong kinds of books is not merely an aesthetic problem but a moral one. She confesses, "I always judge people's characters a good deal by the books they like, as well as by the company they keep" (79).[48] She cautions her young friends: "Many young girls ignorantly or curiously take up books quite worthless, and really harmful, because under the fine writing and brilliant color lurks immorality or the false sentiment which gives wrong ideas of life and things which should be sacred. They think, perhaps, that no one knows this taste of theirs; but they are mistaken, for it shows itself in many ways, and betrays them. Attitudes, looks, careless words, and a morbid or foolishly romantic view of certain things, show plainly that the maidenly instincts are blunted, and harm done that perhaps can never be repaired" (79). Once again, Alcott's view (or at least Mrs. Warburton's) is closely allied to that of Noah Porter, who wrote:

> The man or the woman who systematically dawdles away his or her time over a succession of third or fourth rate novels, weak in imagination and doubtful in morality, deserves a very low place in the estimate of people whose good opinion is worth regarding. There is no description of filth that is so filthy or so tenacious as that which comes from handling an equivocal or obscene novel. A white-gloved hand is for ever soiled by a smutch that cannot be drawn off with a glove, if seen to hold a low-lived and trashy tale, such as many a fashionable miss and pretentious coxcomb are known to handle. (226)

Conversely, Mrs. Warburton and Porter would agree, "they are never alone that are accompanied with noble thoughts,"[49] for the right kind of books allow us to "fortify ourselves with 'noble thoughts'" (Alcott, *Garland* 71, 95). Indeed, as a writer for *Harper's New Monthly Magazine* put it, authors and their works are "not only tests of taste but even of character" (qtd. in Levine 223). For better or for worse, as these statements imply, books combine to *create* one's character, inculcating or undermining culture and virtue in accordance with the moral and aesthetic properties of the texts they carry. "Reading," as Jane Hunter argues (and as Alcott illustrates), "once was a strategy for imprinting wisdom; the Victorian age transformed reading to a strategy for defining a self grounded in taste" (87).

Although Alcott has Carrie, initially a resistant reader, asseverate, "I don't *wish* to improve my mind, thank you: I read for amusement in vacation time" (*Garland* 71), she relents after Mrs. Warburton relates the story of her own courtship and betrothal. In this frame narrative, a young Mrs. Warburton (then Miss Harper) carelessly lets slip a small volume of Wordsworth that she has been reading on the upper balcony of a steamer while touring in Canada. The book strikes the head of Mr. Warburton, a distinguished man of science who happens to be standing on the lower deck, thereby knocking his hat into the St. Lawrence River. The misadventure precipitates a meeting, with the result that Miss Harper and Mr. Warburton become acquainted through their mutual esteem for the great English poet, fall in love, and by and by become husband and wife, united by common cultural and intellectual pursuits. In narrating her story, Mrs. Warburton paints a picture of a literary elite formed through selective reading, remarking that "cultivated persons have a free-masonry of their own, and are recognized at once" (86).[50] At the outset of "Pansies," Alcott encourages her readers to judge Carrie according to her penchant for "trashy" romances in sleazy bindings. At the end of the story, the change in Carrie's literary preferences signals her ostensible transformation, and, again, Alcott indicates that her choice of books reflects and, to some extent, "constructs" her character.[51]

Reviewing the revised edition of Cooper's *The Red Rover*, Melville suggested that books form the society of their (male) readers: "Books, gentlemen, are a species of men, and introduced to them you circulate in the 'very best society' that this world can furnish, without the intolerable infliction of 'dressing' to go into it. In your shabbiest coat and cosiest slippers you may socially chat even with the fastidious Earl of Chesterfield, and lounging under a tree enjoy the divinest intimacy with my late lord of Verulam" (238). Alcott's story establishes a similar relationship between books and female readers. Her personification of the Seaside Library edition of *Wanda*, for example, equates the novel with the heroine:

> Carrie tucked Wanda under the sofa pillow, as if a trifle ashamed of her society....
> "We were only talking about books," began Carrie, deeply grateful that Wanda was safely out of sight. (74, 78)[52]

Having established that people keep company with books, Melville took the argument a step further by advocating a kind of decorum between the outward appearance of books and their interior content. In his view, the appearance of books should aid readers in ascertaining the nature of their contents.[53] Melville explained, "Men, then, that they are—books should be appropriately apparelled. Their bindings should indicate and distinguish their various characters" (238).[54] Alcott's story complicates Melville's observation by effacing the boundaries between reader and text. In "Pansies," the bindings of books reflect and distinguish the characters of the *readers* who possess them as well as the nature of the *texts* that inhabit them.

In Alcott's formulation, Carrie, the naive reader (or consumer of texts) whose admiration for the novels of Ouida arises from their lavish descriptions of extravagant clothing, is ironically destined to become a product in the marriage market.[55] Meanwhile, her Blue and Gold Tennyson serves as the packaging that is to mark her as a cultured, well-bred young lady: an advertisement set out to attract a certain kind of buyer (i.e., an "eligible learned or literary man").[56] Just as the book becomes personlike through the trope of personification, the (female) person becomes booklike—a text to be decoded—through her objectification in the ritual of courtship. Displayed against the body of Alcott's female reader, the book operates as an outward sign of the woman's inward qualities. Like Mrs. Warburton's jewel-encrusted, pansy-shaped pin—a symbol of thought ("pansy" derives from *pensée*) and a memento as well of her beloved blue-stockinged sister—it is doubly symbolic.[57] As a lady's accessory, the physical book thus embodies two "texts": that of the writer and that of the reader.[58]

In *Paratexts*, Genette explains that extratextual bibliographic productions such as the cover of a book, the table of contents, typography, and correspondence "surround it [the text] and extend it, precisely in order to *present* it, in the usual sense of this verb but also in the strongest sense: to *make present*, to ensure the text's presence in the world, its 'reception' and consumption in the form . . . of a book" (1). In Alcott's story, the physical book becomes a kind of paratext for the reader: the book "presents" *her* to the world and gives *her* a presence in the world. No less conspicuously than the spectacular gown of *Vanity Fair*'s "magnificent . . . creature gotten up gorgeously in blue and gold, a la Ticknor & Fields," the material text surrounds the reader, ensuring her presence, influencing her reception, and ultimately affecting (if not effecting) her consumption in society.[59]

Near the end of "Pansies," Carrie, whose mother desired that she should make a good match and "educated [her] . . . for that end" (*Garland* 76), seems to have learned more from her mother than from Mrs. Warburton as she reflects that "a good marriage [is] the end of life" (94). Perhaps Alcott intended no irony in this juvenile narrative, although in light of her reluctance to marry off her "little women . . . in a very stupid style" [*Selected Letters* 121–22] and her linking of death and marriage elsewhere (M. Elbert 15), it is tempting to consider the possibility.[60] Certainly, the double entendre in the phrase "end of life" underscores the problematic nature of the story's denouement.[61] When the future Mrs. Warburton drops her book and startles her future husband with "a smart blow" (89) on the head, the purely physical reception of the book becomes a device that ultimately "resolves" the conventional marriage plot. Carrie, whose love of fine clothing is reflected in her admiration of Wanda's opulent gowns, develops from a reader metaphorically garbed in a tawdry Seaside Library romance to one figuratively arrayed, like the breathtaking belle of *Vanity Fair*, in the brilliant blue and gold trappings of the most distinguished literary publishers in the country; nevertheless, her transformation, like Mr. Warburton's reception of the volume of Wordsworth, occurs on a purely physical level. For the younger generation, outward display apparently trumps inward cultivation as a social signifier. It is fitting, therefore, that Alcott concludes her story by destroying the materiality of the cheap and disposable text while reinforcing the physical value of the literary text as a woman's means of announcing her cultural credentials for procuring a refined and intelligent mate: "Carrie sent Wanda and her finery up the chimney in a lively blaze, and, as she watched the book burn, decided to take her blue and gold volume of Tennyson with her on her next trip to Nahant, in case any eligible learned or literary man's head should offer itself as a shining mark. Since a good marriage was the end of life, why not . . . make a really excellent one?" (105).

※ ※ ※

Reflecting on his "early time" as a writer, Henry James reminisced in 1915 that "publishers' names had a color and character beyond even those of authors, even those of books themselves" (qtd. in Pye 3). For nineteenth-century readers, the Blue and Gold series, with all its celebrated Brahmin mystique, became a widely recognized emblem of the "color and character" of Ticknor and Fields, the quintessential literary publishers of New England. Consequently, when the firm moved into its new Tremont Street quarters in 1865, after the series' popularity had crested, the partners were eager to provide a physical setting that would fittingly showcase their flagship design. Tryon describes the new facility:

> The main showroom . . . was eighty feet long and thirty feet wide. The walls, the supporting columns, the counters, and all the woodwork were of highly polished, oiled western fir and exuded a grave and impressive air. Around the walls were shelves to exhibit the firm's regular offerings; at the end of the room was an elaborate arch, within which were glass cases to exhibit the colorful Blue and Gold series and other fine bindings. . . . Everywhere were rich carvings, ornate chandeliers for gaslights, and heavy moldings. (*Parnassus Corner* 281)

Recognizing the essential relationship between product and packaging, presentation and display, exploited with such elegance in Ticknor and Fields's Tremont Street offices, Jeffrey D. Groves has argued that distinctive designs such as the Blue and Gold format "demonstrate how literary books could in fact be judged by their covers" (77). In Alcott's estimation, readers could likewise be judged by their covers. Thus, in "Pansies," a story that identifies the embodiment of the text with the body of the female reader and conflates the personification of books with the objectification of women, Alcott effectively illustrates the tacit claim of so many publishers' ads, past and present: You are what you read.

# EPILOGUE

## The Margins of the Marketplace

My tales and essays were letters that I wrote, in my solitary chamber, and threw them forth, without direction, into the infinite; and by some miracle, they have found their way to the very friends for whom they were intended.

—Nathaniel Hawthorne (1843)

"Literature's like a big railway-station now, you know: there's a train starting every minute. People are not going to hang around the waiting-room. If they can't get to a place when they want to they go somewhere else."

—Edith Wharton, "The Angel at the Grave" (1901)

I N *THE ANATOMY of American Popular Culture, 1840–1861* (1959), a classic of cultural studies criticism, Carl Bode remarks upon the fortuitous concurrence of two revolutionary events in the nation's history: "the advent of the industrial revolution in the publishing business" and "the advent of popular literacy." The result of this simultaneity, Bode asserts, is that "the people and the printed word came together" (x). Certainly, the fact that the explosion of printed matter in the middle of the nineteenth century coincided with historically high and escalating literacy rates lends substance to this image of an easy coalescence of reader and text. At long last, there were enough books available—and affordable—for those who wished to read them, and enough readers with sufficient money to create a steady demand for the new supply of books.

Contrary to the implicit logic of Bode's formulation, however, the authors, readers, and publishers represented in this study paint a rather different picture of nineteenth-century print culture in the narratives they wrote, the records they left, and the products they produced. Far from reflecting an effortless union of readers and texts, the evidence reveals that in a very real sense the people and the printed word did not come together—at least not immediately and not automatically. Indeed, the difficulty of connecting authors, readers, texts, and publishers preoccupied both producers and consumers of literature throughout the nineteenth century. Readers could easily be baffled by the abundance and diversity of books and periodicals available. At the same time, for many authors the identity—sometimes even the existence—of a recognizable audience for their work remained an inscrutable mystery.[1] Positioned between the authors and the readers, publishers struggled meanwhile to respond to the pressures of a diverse, demanding, crowded, and competitive market by devising more effective and precise methods with which to locate readers, attract their attention, and persuade them to buy. Hawthorne's observation in a letter to Goodrich (6 May 1830) that "an unpublished book is not more obscure than many that creep into the world" (*Letters* 15: 205) is understandable in this context.

The six case studies presented in this book highlight, from various perspectives, the nineteenth-century literary community's efforts to connect the people and the printed word. By the close of the century, the often scattershot means through which Hawthorne and many of his contemporaries sought readers had become obsolete. In the teeming literary marketplace of the late nineteenth century, the participants became organized into specialized "classes" of readers, writers, and publishers. Authors evinced a greater awareness of their readerships and of the need to make their own markets. As William Dean Howells wrote of James, "I suspect that he must in a great degree create his audience" (letter to Charles Eliot Norton, August 1867; qtd. in Gard 21). At the same time, readers clustered into an array of clearly identifiable (but flexible and overlapping) literary subcultures, each with unique interests and patterns of consumption. Meanwhile, publishers, also intent on making markets, became ever more adept at manipulating text, book, author, and reader in order to bring the various components of their trade into a profitable alignment. Writing to Louisa May Alcott in 1870, Thomas Niles commiserated, "You have had publishers who have failed to make a market for your books—You might find them still."[2] By the turn of the century the literary enterprise, so recently envisioned as "one vast grab game" (Didier 21), could be reimagined as a "big railway-station": modern, efficient, and commercially viable, with "a train starting every minute" (Wharton 122). The literary field had been restructured, and the new relationships that emerged among authors, publishers, books, and readers influenced patterns of production and consumption and shaped both books and readerships.

Ironically, the purest example of market segmentation in nineteenth-century America may have been those literary artists who self-published their works and distributed them to a precisely targeted audience consisting of close friends and colleagues. Emily Dickinson—who wrote to Thomas Wentworth Higginson (7 June 1862) that "to publish" was as "foreign" to her thought "as Firmament to Fin" (*Selected Letters* 174)—painstakingly organized her poems into handmade books and circulated them among a highly select group of acquaintances. In a similar gesture of self-publication, Walt Whitman designed the first edition of *Leaves of Grass*, helped set the type, and dispatched a portion of the first printing to a handful of carefully selected recipients (most famously, Ralph Waldo Emerson). Although motivated by very different ideals of poetry, authorship, and audience, both Dickinson and Whitman—like numerous other literary artists of the period—used specialized forms of publication as a means of getting their works into just the right hands.

In the twenty-first century, one does not have to look far to find analogues in contemporary media to the diverse yet fragmented print culture of nineteenth-century America. The staggering array of magazines at a well-stocked bookstore provides a snapshot of the myriad niche markets that have emerged in the publishing field. In addition, the explosion of television broadcasting from three major networks to seven networks and hundreds of cable and satellite channels has been accompanied by tireless efforts on the part of media planners to segment the viewing public in order to maximize advertising revenue.[3] Media analyst John Rash views "the three network universe of previous generations, which lumped men and women together," as "an artificial construct," because "audience fragmentation has always existed in all media forms to the extent that it has been technologically feasible. . . . Specifically, there have been unlimited [production] abilities in terms of books, magazines, music or movies, so there has been and always will be fragmentation among age, income, education, interest level and, of course, along gender lines" (qtd. in Lambert, "She-TV" 2E).[4]

According to Brian Lambert, television professionals recognize that women have probably always made up the majority of the viewing audience, but as one insider reported, not until "cable began fragmenting the viewing audience" did the television industry begin "taking an interest in who was watching." In response to a viewing public that is consistently skewed toward the female (typically, around 60 percent women between the ages of eighteen and forty-nine), almost across the board, "the networks program toward female viewers" [Lambert, "She-TV" 1E]).[5] The scenario seems a close parallel to the conflation of novel readers and women in the nineteenth century, a phenomenon that James observed in his 1892 review article on Mrs. Humphrey Ward: "An observer of manners, called upon to name to-day the two things that make it most completely different from yesterday . . . might easily be conceived to mention in the first place the immensely greater conspicuity of the novel, and in the second the immensely greater conspicuity of the attitude of women. He might perhaps be supposed even to go on to add that the attitude of women *is* the novel, in England and America, and that these signs of the times have therefore a practical unity" (1: *Literary Criticism* 1371). As a result of the "calculated formating [*sic*] of television to the tastes of women" (Lambert, "Relationship-Driven News" 4E), media watchers have begun to echo literary critics in their talk of "the feminization of television," a trend that has reportedly given rise to "strong, self-directed [female] characters" (qtd. in Lambert, "She-TV" 3E) but also to news broadcasts that are increasingly skewed toward so-called discretionary news features and "stories TV decision-makers think appeal to women: health, family, childcare and safety issues" at the expense of politics, international affairs, and economics (Lambert, "Relationship-Driven News" 5E).

"Gender disparity" among the viewing public and the consequent feminization of television are not the only recent media developments that have clear parallels in the nineteenth-century literary marketplace. Media analysts and critics have also pointed out that "there aren't enough network-television hours to satisfy the demand for programming aimed at teen-agers—laugh-track sitcoms, vampire slayers, pouty dramas and 'Total Request Live'" (Peiken 1F). In response to this increased demand, we can expect media planners to respond with more shows directed toward the youth market, just as nineteenth-century publishers responded to the demands of adolescent readers with entertaining series designed especially for them. Moreover, the Internet offers additional parallels to the nineteenth-century book industry. In March 2000, when Stephen King's latest thriller, *Riding the Bullet*, became available online in a format that readers could download for little or no cost, the publisher received a staggering 400,000 orders within the first twenty-four hours (Carvajal 1A).[6] With the minimal cost to consumers reflected in a format hardly fit for preservation or display (customers could read the text on a computer monitor or print it out for themselves), this "extraordinary surge of interest" (Carvajal 1A) in the electronic book recalls the great enthusiasm of consumers for the cheap reprint libraries of the 1870s and 1880s. Finally, even as publishers have targeted this mass-market audience in cyberspace, an extensive year-long study by the Washington-based Children's Partnership revealed in 2000 that "information geared toward Americans with low incomes or poor reading skills is scarce and difficult to find on the Internet"; as a result, "nearly 50 million Americans . . . are 'on the other side of the content gap because the Internet does not have the information and services they could use'" (Turay 17a). In addition, although Internet use among minority and low-income children reportedly "surged" between 2001 and 2003, gaps persist in the kind of access available to them ("Study: 'Digital Divide' Shrinks").

Of course, if there is commercial gain to be had, one can expect this "digital divide" to narrow as entrepreneurs devote resources to attracting members of underrepresented groups—just as nineteenth-century publishers discovered ways to extend their markets to include people outside the traditional book-buying public. As I showed in Part One, children, who had once accounted for only a small proportion of the market for books, came to occupy a position of tremendous economic importance in the literary economy, and girls, long overlooked by authors and publishers alike, gradually emerged to become a vital segment of the juvenile fiction market. In addition, both the subscription books that Samuel Clemens and others marketed and cheap reprint series such as the Seaside Library reportedly garnered large sales among people presumed to be "utterly unknown to bookstores." Even elite publisher James T. Fields actively pursued buyers outside the traditional book-buying public by making Ticknor and Fields's Diamond Editions "*cheap, cheap, cheap*, so as to open a market far away among the unbuying crowd hidden away in the dust holes of our country" (qtd. in Currier 107). From lowbrow readers like the Laphams to the "middling masses" of Mark Twain, the "upper middle cultured" of Henry James, and beyond to the highbrow audience for Ticknor and Fields's Blue and Gold editions, the maturing literary marketplace reflected a degree of social and cultural stratification that brought literature of various forms and formats to a wide spectrum of readers.

In *Highbrow/Lowbrow: The Emergence of Cultural Hierarchy in America*, Lawrence W. Levine charts the transformation of the United States from a "general culture . . . experienced . . . by a catholic audience that cut through class and social lines" (149) to a culture that was not "a unity but a multiple" (171) and that "everywhere . . . was undergoing a process of fragmentation" (207), a process borne of modernization and emblematic of modernism.[7] As Levine persuasively argues, "The United States in the first half of the nineteenth century did experience greater cultural sharing in the sense that cultural lines were more fluid, cultural spaces less rigidly subdivided, than they were to become" (233). In the latter half of the century, however, "theaters, opera houses, museums, auditoriums that had once housed mixed crowds of people experiencing an eclectic blend of expressive culture were increasingly filtering their clientele and their programs so that less and less could one find audiences that cut across the social and economic spectrum enjoying an expressive culture which blended together mixed elements of what we would today call high, low, and folk culture" (208). And "inevitably," Levine emphasizes, "in a heterogeneous nation in which the working classes were more and more composed of recent immigrant groups and migrant blacks, the ideology of culture assumed ethnic and racial dimensions" (219).

Inevitably, too, the literary field responded to race and ethnicity as it had to other categories of difference. In the eighteenth century, Elizabeth Carroll Reilly and David D. Hall have demonstrated, "the fissures in American culture and therefore in reading preferences ran along doctrinal or denominational lines" (399), but in the nineteenth century, as American society became increasingly secular and culturally heterogeneous, so did the potential audience for books. What we would now consider ethnic reading communities had existed in North America from the beginning of the colonial period. By the eighteenth century, German-language publishing was a thriving concern; Swedish and French settlers in the East could find American-made books published in their native tongues; and in colonial California printers in Sonoma and Monterey published books in Spanish (Tebbel 1: 163, 501–2). During the nineteenth and early twentieth centuries, some of these communities became assimilated into the mainstream of Anglo-American culture to the point where they no longer patronized specialized foreign-language publishers. Others, however, continued to function as discrete, dynamic segments of the literary marketplace throughout the twentieth century (see Danky and Wiegand).

In some cases, the arrivals of new immigrants reinforced the separateness of particular reading communities, leading to the formation of new literary submarkets. Occasionally, publishing houses arose within immigrant populations (for example, Jewish immigrants who published books in Yiddish).[8] In other cases, mainstream publishers targeted specific ethnic reading communities. John P. Jewett, for example, produced a German-language edition of *Uncle Tom's Cabin* for the domestic market, and the

American News Company included in its trade catalogues an extensive listing of German-American publications. The German-American segment truly entered the mainstream in the 1880s when George Munro, of Seaside Library fame, launched his Deutsche Library, a series of German-language books consisting mainly of German novels and German translations of English and French novels. At the same time, Ernst Steiger courted the domestic German-language market with his Deutsche-Amerikanische Bibliothek, a series boasting such titles as *Alte Bekannte aus dem New Yorker Deutschen Viertel* (Old acquaintances from New York's German quarter), *Mein Onkel Fischer in Baltimore* (My Uncle Fischer in Baltimore), and *Anton in Amerika: Novelle aus dem Deutsch-amerikanischen Leben* (Anton in America: A novella of German-American life). So popular in American cities did Munro's Deutsche Library become that the series had grown to more than 200 titles by 1890 (Dzwonkoski, "Norman L. Munro" 316).[9]

The African American community—long an invisible population from the perspective of mainstream commercial publishers—represents another case in which publishers both inside and outside the community sought to consolidate its members as a distinct segment of the literary marketplace. During the antebellum period, evangelical groups such as the American Bible Association, the American Sunday School Union, and the American Tract Society targeted African Americans (Cornelius 105–41), usually with free Bibles and religious tracts, while abolitionist organizations such as the American and Foreign Antislavery Society sought to reach free blacks in the North, as well as antislavery whites, with their special-interest publications. Some subscription publishers also issued titles specifically designed to appeal to an African American readership (Arbour xii). By the turn of the century, however, a number of specialized publishers had emerged from within the black communities, offering a forum in which to link African American readers and writers (see Joyce). The *Christian Recorder*, the official publication of the A.M.E. Church, sought "to establish itself as a black counterpart to white publications like the *Atlantic*" (Robbins 179), and the Colored Cooperative Publishing Company, chiefly remembered as the publisher of the *Colored American Magazine*, made a brief foray into the book market during this period with the publication of Pauline Hopkins's novel *Contending Forces: A Romance Illustrative of Negro Life North and South* (1900).

Of course, publishers multiplied their risks when they targeted relatively small market segments. Moreover, many members of the black literary community felt the need to reconcile their desire to cultivate literacy and literariness within their own race and their desire to bring about change in the majority population through their own literature. Ultimately, however, distribution remained limited, the target audience not yet large enough, affluent enough, or leisured enough to support such specialized concerns. As a result, publications such as the *Colored American Magazine* have sometimes been held responsible for relegating their contributors to obscurity.[10] Yet as I have suggested, the success of such endeavors should be assessed not in terms of circulation statistics or revenue but rather in terms of their role in forming and shaping distinct reading communities and bodies of literature.

Clearly, as the example of German-language publishing illustrates, the tension between assimilation and the preservation of difference influenced whether an ethnic readership would be targeted by a mainstream publisher or a specialized publisher. Susan Strasser explores this "particularly American marketing problem":

> In the United States, marketers confronted a genuinely multicultural population. About a third were foreign-born or of foreign parentage in 1900; even higher proportions of immigrants lived in the industrial cities of the Northeast. These people brought tastes and traditions with them from the old countries. In all of the large cities, ethnic and class differences challenged the manufacturers and their advertising agents. Variations in lifestyles and tastes between city and country, between North and South, and between East and West further complicated matters. . . . Marketers had a choice between, on the one hand, attempting to create standardized products that might be sold in all regions and to all classes and nationalities, and on the other, exploiting differences in tastes—in modern jargon, positioning products for segmented markets. They did both. (139–42)

In the 1920s, Street & Smith, well known as a publisher of dime novels, launched its Alger series, which republished books by Oliver Optic, Horatio Alger, Edward Stratemeyer, and others. The series, which gathered multiple immigrant communities into a single market segment, advertised itself as an instrument of acculturation into the American way of life: "There are legions of boys of foreign parents who are being helped along the road to true Americanism by reading these books which are so peculiarly American in tone that the reader cannot fail to absorb some of the spirit of fair play and clean living which is so characteristically American" (qtd. in D. Jones 111). Although the corresponding "legions" of girls received no special attention from Street & Smith, William Dean Howells took note of them in his introduction to *Different Girls* (1895), a volume of *Harper's Novelettes* that he co-edited with Henry Mills Alden. Observing that one of the stories, "Cordelia's Night of Romance" by Julian Ralph, "contributes a fresh East Side flower, hollyhock-like in its gaudiness, to the garden of American girls, Irish-American in this case," Howells goes on to predict that this newcomer among fictive American girls is "destined to be companioned hereafter by blossoms of our Italian-American, Yiddish-American, and Russian-American civilization, as soon as our nascent novelists shall have the eye to see and the art to show them" (vi-vii).

Of course, categories of books and readers are not monolithic, and the boundaries between them are permeable and fluid. Inevitably, some books find their way into the hands of readers who fall outside the target audience, whether through a change of venue (as when Hawthorne's "Little Annie" graduated from *Youth's Keepsake* to *Twice-told Tales*), or because the audience was not clearly defined to begin with (as in the case of Mark Twain's Tom Sawyer and Huck Finn narratives), or because readers resist easy classification (like the adolescent and preadolescent girls who enjoy reading boys' books). These kinds of slippages may lead to new genres (for example, the "boy-book"), new audience definitions (teenagers or young adults, as opposed to juvenile readers), and innovative approaches to subject matter or style (such as tomboy heroines and James's twisting of the American-girl-abroad motif). Yet another kind of slippage occurs when publishers combine the features of different kinds of books or series to create a hybrid. In the 1890s, for example, many traditional publishers did a large business in "Handy Volume Editions," a hybrid format (Barth): cheap and "handy" (like the Seaside Library, although hardbound), but emphasizing the excellent editorial taste underlying the selection of titles (like the Blue and Gold series).

The segmentation of the literary marketplace had both benefits and drawbacks. Many authors discovered that tailoring their work to a specific market segment helped them find a secure foothold in the literary field. At the same time, however, overspecialization might thwart an author's creativity. Some critics argue, for example, that becoming too closely identified with the girls' market stifled Alcott's considerable potential as a "serious" literary artist—that is, as a writer of novels for adults. Certainly, Thomas Niles recognized in Alcott enormous potential as a writer of fiction for adults, urging, "I wish you were immortalizing yourself on a *grown up* novel." With reference to her adult novel *Moods*, he explained, "It is for *this* class of people that I want a book." And later he insisted: "I see no reason why you should not command just such an audience as Geo. Eliot has for her novels, or if you will Mrs Southworth and Mrs Holmes. I know you have the 'vein,' which only wants to be worked to prove a bonanza."[11] Late in her life, Alcott acknowledged this tension in her career, admitting, "I yet hope to write a few of the novels which have been simmering in my brain while necessity and unexpected success have confined me to juvenile literature" (Stern, "Louisa May Alcott's Self-Criticism" 357).

Similarly, an 1879 review of James's *Transatlantic Sketches* asserted: "Mr. Henry James is certainly a very remarkable illustration of the tendency of our age to subdivide in the finest way the already rather extreme division of labour, till a very high perfection is attained in producing articles of the most curiously specialised kind, though apparently without the power of producing anything outside that kind. For a long time we have had novelists who are wonderfully skilful in a particular form of novels, but who seem almost unable to master more than one form for themselves" (qtd. in Hayes 71). Readers, too, could become overspecialized and, consequently, self-limiting in their literary interests. With a dose of irony, an 1887 article in the *Book Buyer* declared:

> After a hundred years of experiment America has succeeded in producing three well-marked types of educated people: the first is thoroughly provincial, absorbing its ideas from the community and State in which it lives or adapting all foreign knowledge to those conditions; the second *was* provincial, had aspirations and went to Boston where it found their complete fulfillment; the third might have been for a time the first or second, but it went "abroad" and became entirely cosmopolitan, claiming the world for its country.
>
> These three types have found their expression, respectively, in the novels of "Craddock," Howells and Crawford. (Droch 22)[12]

In the long run, however, the benefits of market segmentation far outweighed the costs. To some extent, it did tend to reinforce, or codify, certain social distinctions. As Wendell R. Smith has noted, segmentation, which is "based upon the demand side of the market" and "tends to bring about recognition of several demand schedules where only one was recognized before," is ultimately "disaggregative in its effects" (qtd. in Frank, Massy, and Wind 5). Yet at the same time the segmentation of the literary marketplace did a real service to marginalized readers—young people, females, the poor, the geographically isolated, the less educated, and, to an extent, ethnic minorities—by bringing literature within their cultural purview and economic reach and by creating among individual communities of readers a positive sense of participation and collective identity in the cultural field.[13] In recognizing male and female readers, adults and children, and people of different social, economic, and ethnic backgrounds as distinct submarkets, authors and publishers acknowledged that members of these groups might have different interests and concerns and different reading habits and ways of using books. Literature that addressed those needs and interests—whether by providing new ways of thinking about childhood (*A Wonder Book, Little Women, Tom Sawyer*), adolescence (*Little Women, Huckleberry Finn, Mae Madden, Daisy Miller*), social divisions (*Silas Lapham, Daisy Miller*, "Pansies"), or gender relationships (*Little Women, Mae Madden, Daisy Miller*, "Pansies")—carried out a kind of cultural work uniquely tailored to meet the demands of the specialized classes of readers it served.

And while the text performed one type of cultural work, the book performed others. Whether conveying literature to the masses or safeguarding culturally sanctioned texts, whether functioning as ladies' accessories or as gentlemen's furnishings, books actually *formed* culture in nineteenth-century America by gathering readers together into distinct readerships, shaping their collective identities, and establishing their presence in the cultural field. By initiating the large-scale market segmentation that has come to characterize culture industries in the United States, the various constituents of the nineteenth-century literary marketplace thus gave rise to an enduringly diverse—and diversified—culture of the book.

# Notes

## PROLOGUE

1. Frederick Law Olmsted to Charles Eliot Norton, 20 Dec. 1865, bMS Am 1083.1(59), *The Nation* Papers.

2. Prospectus for the New York Nation, bMS Am 1083.2 (70), Godkin Family Correspondence.

3. These Whitman essays were "Democracy" (*Galaxy*, December 1867) and "Personalism" (May 1868).

4. In the eighteenth century, fiction accounted for only 9 percent of the titles appearing in a sample of booksellers' catalogues (Reilly and Hall 399). Joseph Rosenblum estimates that "by 1850 new and old fiction comprised the majority of titles published" (n.p.).

5. Earlier studies that help lay the groundwork for examining the segmentation of the American literary marketplace include Richard Brodhead's *Cultures of Letters*, Louise Lehuu's *Carnival on the Page*, and Lawrence Levine's *Highbrow/Lowbrow*.

6. The segmentation of the market for books was preceded by the segmentation of the periodical market in the late eighteenth and early nineteenth centuries. See Frank Luther Mott, *A History of American Magazines*. In his compelling study of periodicals in England during the Romantic period, Jon P. Klancher argues that its "contradictory role—cementing the small audience while subdividing the larger public—made the periodical a singular but socially unstable institution for defining, individualizing, and expanding the audiences who inhabited the greater cultural landscape" (20). See also William Charvat, *The Profession of Authorship in America*, 185, for a discussion of the corresponding segmentation of the literary reviews in mid-nineteenth-century America; and R. Gordon Kelly, *Children's Periodicals in the United States*, for an overview of the segmentation of the juvenile market.

7. I am indebted to Ken Carpenter for encouraging me to experiment with this idea in an early version of Chapter 6.

8. In adopting the phrase "cultural work," I benefit from Jane Tompkins's influential study, *Sensational Designs: The Cultural Work of American Fiction, 1790–1860*. Rather than confining my analysis to the cultural work of particular titles, however, I am interested in uncovering the cultural work performed by physical books, as well as intangible texts, and, more broadly, in the cultural work performed by "the book" in nineteenth-century America.

9. Pierre Bourdieu's phrase "symbolic power" refers to "diverse forms of capital which are not reducible to economic capital" (*Field of Cultural Production* 7).

10. See Richard D. Brown, *Knowledge Is Power: The Diffusion of Information in Early America, 1700–1865*, for an account of the role of print in stratifying American society along these divisions.

PART ONE

1. Most critics of children's literature agree with Kimberley Reynolds, who asserts, "Children's literature resists change at all levels" (98). Only recently, for example, has children's literature acknowledged homosexuality, and books such as *Daddy's Roommate* (1990) by Michael Willhoite and *Heather Has Two Mommies* (1991) by Leslea Newman are still frequently banned from public schools and libraries. In *Don't Tell the Grown-Ups: Subversive Children's Literature* (1990), Alison Lurie offers a dissenting view.

2. This is true of contemporary children's literature, but it is also true historically. Examples include evangelical Protestantism and abolitionism in nineteenth-century juvenile literature; the "problem literature" of the 1960s and 1970s, which addressed issues such as divorce, poverty, and substance abuse; and multiculturalism and environmentalism in recent children's books.

3. The *Oxford English Dictionary* traces the use of "juvenile" as a noun meaning "a book written for children" to 1849.

4. Like Scudder, many recent critics of juvenile literature, including MacLeod, Gillian Avery, and Mary Lynn Stevens Heininger, regard the nineteenth century as pivotal in the transformation of the social construction of childhood. Ellen Butler Donovan relates "a new narrative strategy," exemplified by Alcott's *Little Women* and Thomas Bailey Aldrich's *The Story of a Bad Boy*, to "a new awareness or understanding of children's experience and a trust in the child reader's abilities to interpret and judge" (143); Richard Butsch explains that "from the 1880s onward children assumed a new prominence in the middle-class family, which was restructured around child rearing" (7). For brief surveys of changing nineteenth-century attitudes toward children, see Heininger's "Children, Childhood, and Change in America, 1820–1920"; Bernard Wishy, *The Child and the Republic*; and Gail Schmunk Murray, *American Children's Literature and the Construction of Childhood*. On the changing conceptions of adolescence, see Bakan; Demos; and Hunter.

5. Scudder repeatedly returns to this correspondence between the "discovery" of childhood and the development of literature written expressly for children. For example, "There was a time, just beyond the memory of men now living, when the Child was born in literature. At the same period books for children began to be written" (3), and "From the time when childhood was newly discovered, that is to say, roughly, in the closing years of the last century, there has been a literature in process of formation which has for its audience children themselves" (17).

6. Reilly and Hall trace the "recognition of children as readers who deserved or should be addressed through a distinct set of publications" to the mid-eighteenth century in England but note that "this movement would not take hold in America until after 1800" (398).

7. The same applies to young adult literature in the twentieth century. Officially recognized by the American Library Association in 1958 as literature addressing readers between the ages of twelve and eighteen (Kismaric and Heiferman 96), the genre was promoted and exploited energetically by twentieth-century publishers.

8. In these chapters, my primary interest is in books that teens and preteens read on their own, without adult supervision. As MacLeod notes, "Adolescence was the fork in the road where boys' and girls' paths diverged" ("*Caddie Woodlawn Syndrome*" 109).

9. This was probably *The Balloon Travels of Robert Merry, and His Young Friends, Over Various Countries of Europe*, Edited by Peter Parley (New York: J. C. Derby, 1856).

## 1. WONDER BOOKS

1. The 1835 edition of *Youth's Keepsake*, the longest-running American gift book for children, was published in Boston by E. R. Broaders. For further publication information, see Ralph Thompson 162–63; and Kirkham and Fink 407–8. For a reproduction of the frontispiece by Joseph Andrews and a discussion of Hawthorne's relationship with Park Benjamin (1809–64), see Gilkes.

2. Andrew Preston Peabody, writing for the *Christian Examiner*, wrote, "There is hardly anything in the volume, which pleases us more than 'Little Annie's Ramble,' which is a mere sketch, simple, natural, full of child-like feeling, of a child's stroll with her friend through the gay streets of the town, by the print-shops and the toy-shops, through all the little worlds of gorgeous sights, which arrest infancy's lingering steps on its earliest walks." In his précis in the *North American Review*, Henry Wadsworth Longfellow exclaimed, "What minute delicacy of touch, and womanly knowledge of a child's mind and character, are perceptible in 'Little Annie's Ramble.'" Evert A. Duyckinck reproduced the tale in full in an essay in the *Democratic Review*, explaining, "It is so cheerful a sketch and so full of pleasant imagery that we give it entire to the reader without apology." (Qtd. in J. D. Crowley, *Hawthorne* 65, 82, 99). In general, early reviewers who encountered the tale for the first time in *Twice-told Tales* did not identify "Little Annie's Ramble" as a children's story. Twentieth-century critic Roy Harvey Pearce refers to the sketch as "yet another example of the lovingly sentimental hackwork that from the outset he was willing to undertake in order to make his way as a writer" (288).

3. In the version of the sketch that appeared in *Youth's Keepsake*, Annie was versed in "Robin Carver's tomes." Just prior to the publication of "Little Annie's Ramble," Robin Carver had published several volumes of juvenile nonfiction, including *Stories about Boston, and Its Neighborhood* (1833), *Stories of Poland* (1833), *Anecdotes of Natural History* (1833), *History of Boston* (1834), and *The Book of Sports* (1834). Hawthorne inserted the allusion to the more widely known Peter Parley books when he was revising the text for *Twice-told Tales*; see J. D. Crowley, "Editorial Emendations" 586. The *Juvenile Miscellany: For the Instruction and Amusement of Youth*, edited first by Lydia Maria Child and then by Sarah J. Hale, was published in Boston from September 1826 to March 1836. The magazine featured historical sketches and dramas, biographical sketches, moral tales, pedagogical dialogues or "conversations," poems, conundrums, riddles, puzzles, and woodcuts. Its target audience ranged from the very young of around three years to children ten or twelve years of age; see MacDonald 258–62.

4. As Daniel Roselle explains, "When there came to America the two interlocking lines of historical development in children's books—the morally didactic and the romantically fanciful—there was a tendency in the beginning to stress the former at the expense of the latter" (59).

5. *True Stories from History and Biography* "represents Hawthorne's attempts to write for an established juvenile market in an established juvenile genre," according to

Pearce, whereas "*A Wonder-Book* and *Tanglewood Tales* are products of his flourishing self-confidence after the success of *The Scarlet Letter* in 1850" (287).

6. This period also coincides with Hawthorne's marriage to Sophia Peabody in July 1842 and his growing concerns with "how I am to earn my bread"; see E. Miller 238. His notebooks from the 1830s and 1840s include numerous ideas for juvenile sketches and tales, most of which were never realized; see his *American Notebooks*, 25–29; 239–44.

7. The project of publishing only works by American authors became a mission for Goodrich as early as 1819. See Raymond, "S. G. Goodrich"; and Roselle 103–4. In the preface to the *Token and Atlantic Souvenir* for 1833, Goodrich disclosed his nativist bias in an apology for the volume's nonoriginal engravings, pleading that "the great beauty of many of them will compensate for the fact that they are from designs of European origin" (xix). For a useful discussion of Goodrich in the context of early American print culture, see Hall. For more on the *Token*, see R. Thompson, *American Literary Annuals and Gift Books*; and Faxon, *Literary Annuals and Gift-Books*.

8. Hawthorne drew the erroneous conclusion that Goodrich had financed the publication of *Twice-told Tales*. Horatio Bridge, the true (and anonymous) financier of the volume, ultimately dissuaded his friend from dedicating the collection to Goodrich; see W. Jones, "Sometimes Things Just Don't Work Out" 128.

9. See also Gilkes 105; and Goodrich, *Recollections* 2: 281. This strategy of commissioning freelance authors to write books from outlines was later implemented by publishers of dime novels and series books (including, most famously, the Stratemeyer Syndicate).

10. Hawthorne served Goodrich in the capacity of editor of the *American Magazine of Useful and Entertaining Knowledge* from January through June 1836, editing the March–August issues. The arrangement soured when the promised salary failed to materialize and the Bewick Company, which published the magazine (and of which Goodrich was a member), went bankrupt. In the words of Wayne Allen Jones, "Goodrich lured Hawthorne aboard a sinking ship and persuaded him to become its pilot" ("Hawthorne-Goodrich Relationship" 118). On 15 February 1836, Hawthorne wrote to his sister Louisa of his obviously strained relationship with his employer: "My mind is pretty much made up about this Goodrich. He is a good-natured sort of man enough; but rather an unscrupulous one in money matters, and not particularly trustworthy in anything. . . . He made the best bargain with me he could, and a hard bargain too. This world is as full of rogues as Beelzebub [the family cat] is of fleas" (*Letters* 15: 236). More than twenty years later, Hawthorne's feelings toward Goodrich had softened somewhat, although he retained the sense that Goodrich had manipulated and exploited him. On 13 August 1857 he wrote to his sister-in-law Elizabeth Peabody, "As for Goodrich, I have rather a kindly feeling towards him, and he himself is a not unkindly man, in spite of his propensity to feed and fatten himself on better brains than his own. . . . His quarrel with me was, that I broke away from him before he had quite finished his meal, and while a portion of my brain was left. . . . He was born to do what he did, as maggots to feed on rich cheese" (*Letters* 18: 89–90). See also Turner, *Hawthorne as Editor*.

11. Roselle estimates total (lifetime) sales of Peter Parley books to be near twelve million (54), and Parley was translated into "nearly every foreign language, including modern Greek and Persian" (Derby 122).

12. Writing of this volume in the early twentieth century, historian Edward S. Ellis remarked that "more read than all his other books combined was his country's story for young people" (1: 9).

13. Mary M. Van Tassel sees Hawthorne's "troubled association with Goodrich" as "symptomatic of his problem with readership and publication in general." In her view, Goodrich "typifies the conditions of marketplace publication that not only frustrated Hawthorne's aims but also created the Hawthorne image and the Hawthorne readership" (172).

14. Hawthorne also expressed concern with making money from children's books in his letter to Longfellow of 21 March 1838, in which he writes of a proposed collaboration, "What is of more importance to me, though of none to a Cambridge Professor, we may perchance put money in our purses" (*Letters* 15: 267).

15. Child's contributions to this genre include *Biographical Sketches of Great and Good Men* (1828)—which contains sketches of several of the figures Hawthorne profiles in *Grandfather's Chair* and *Biographical Stories*—and *Good Wives* (1833), later published as *Biographies of Good Wives*. Francis Lister Hawks (1798–1866) wrote, under the pseudonym "Uncle Philip," a series of "conversations with children" about geography, natural history, and religion that Harper & Brothers published in their highly didactic Boy's and Girl's Library.

16. Mellow traces the origin of the chair device to Hawthorne's second cousin, Suzy Ingersoll (175).

17. Half a century later, Edward S. Ellis recalled Hawthorne's allusions to Goodrich when he bestowed on his own ten-volume history of the United States for children the title *A Grandfather's Historic Stories of Our Country from Its Discovery to the Present Time; After the Style of "Peter Parley," as Suggested by Nathaniel Hawthorne*.

18. Hawthorne uses a third-person narrator to frame Grandfather's narration, which is punctuated by frequent exchanges with his four grandchildren. Goodrich generally uses Peter Parley as a first-person narrator directly addressing his young readers (as in the original volume, *The Tales of Peter Parley about America* [1827]). Sometimes he has Parley paraphrase the stories of other characters, and occasionally he presents his material in the form of a dialogue, as in *Peter Parley's Farewell* (1839).

19. Pearce observes, "That reissue, and also the two that followed in 1851 and 1854, at long last brought Hawthorne at least a small measure of financial return. (A total of nine printings—9,000 copies—brought him $667.50 in royalties by 1863")" (296–97).

20. Like Goodrich, Samuel Colman made a mission of publishing American authors; he was also the New York agent for Goodrich's "Peter Parley" series (see Hutchinson).

21. This quotation leads me to disagree with Laura Laffrado's assertion that, for Hawthorne, children's literature was "a genre where the competition seems less fierce and the rewards just as great" (44).

22. In this letter, Hawthorne suggested that this work would be "far more creditable" than writing children's histories "and perhaps quite as profitable." He clearly envisioned his role in the collaboration as secondary to Longfellow's: "I wish you would shape out your plan distinctly, and write to me about it. Ought there not to be a slender thread of story running through the book, as a connecting medium for the other stories? If so, you must

prepare it. . . . You shall be the Editor, and I will figure merely as a contributor; for, as the conception and system of the work will be yours, I really should not think it honest to take an equal share of the fame which is to accrue" (*Letters* 15: 266).

23. The publication of Goodrich's *Fairy Land, and Other Sketches for Youth* (1844) reveals that Goodrich became reconciled to fairy tales to some degree. "Fairy Land: Or Titania's Trial," the first sketch in this collection of fairy stories, poems, and fables, presents an allegory in which Truth ("the King") approves their influence, declaring, "though they are fictions, they subserve the cause of truth; they convey important lessons of life, in a pleasing guise; and are calculated to plant the seeds of virtue in the mind" (32–33). As for Peter Parley, "Truth" assents that "he seems to be no great favorite of the [Fairy] Queen, and not very deeply touched with her inspiration. There is not enough of fancy in him to make him dangerous!" (34).

24. *Des Knabens Wunderhorn*, an anthology of German folk ballads collected by Ludwig Achim von Arnim and Clemens Brentano, had caught Longfellow's attention in Heidelberg (Hawthorne, *Letters* 15: 267 n); he professed to know the collection "almost by heart" (see L. Thompson 309). Although it appears that Longfellow may have decided to pursue "The Boys' Wonder-Horn" independently, Hawthorne seems not to have borne Longfellow any ill feelings, writing him on 12 January 1839: "You see I have abundance of literary labor in prospect; and this makes it more tolerable that you refuse to let me blow a blast upon the 'Wonder-Horn.' Assuredly, you have a right to make all the music on your own instrument; but I should serve you right were I to set up an opposition—for instance, with a corn-stalk fiddle, or a pumpkin vine trumpet" (*Letters* 15: 288). See also Turner, "Hawthorne and Longfellow" 3–11; and Mellow 154.

25. See, for example, Attebery 60–63. In addition, Pearce identifies Hawthorne as "the first writer in English to recast stories out of classical myth for children" (311). (This claim is complicated by the existence of *Tales about the Mythology of Greece and Rome*, a spurious Peter Parley book published in London by Thomas Tegg in 1839; see Goodrich, *Recollections* 2: 551, 554.) Jane Hunter points out that myths and legends were recommended reading for young readers not yet ready for history (60).

26. Goodrich would later echo these words in *Parley's Book of Fables* (1850). Noticeably uneasy with this genre, he announces in a note "To the Young Reader" that "these *stories* . . . are not *histories*; and I do not pretend that these things actually did happen; I only *imagine* them to have happened; and my object in telling them, is not to make you believe what is false, but to impress upon your mind what is true" (7–8). Characteristically, Goodrich proceeds to illustrate his method with a story about a mouse who disobeyed his mother and "got his leg torn off in a trap." The object of the tale is "that disobedience and deception are very wicked and very dangerous" (8).

27. Although coeducation was by this time the norm outside the South (Tyack, Hansot, and Tyack), Hawthorne opposed it in his own family (see Mellow).

28. The lack of emphasis on the gender of the children is reflected in the narrator's remarking, "I can hardly tell how many of these small people there were; not less than nine or ten, however, nor more than a dozen, of all sorts, sizes, and ages, whether girls or boys" (*WB and TT* 6).

29. The unfitness of his historical material is felt most forcibly in *Liberty Tree* when, after listening to the story of the Boston Massacre, little Alice begins to sob violently: Grandfather, "in his earnestness, . . . had neglected to soften down the narrative, so that it might not terrify the heart of this unworldly infant" (*True Stories* 170).

30. Clearly, the myths permitted a license in their retelling which the history of New England did not. While he balked at sanitizing one of the bloodiest episodes of early American history for his young readers (resulting in Alice's torrent of tears), Hawthorne blithely informed Fields of his intention, in *A Wonder Book*, to "purge out all the old heathen wickedness, and put in a moral wherever practicable" (*Letters* 16: 437).

31. Longfellow wrote to Hawthorne, "Fields also gives me rapturous accounts of the forth-coming 'Wonder-Book'" (3: 306).

32. Writing in September 1853, this reviewer may have been picking up on an increasing tendency in publishing to differentiate textbooks from other kinds of books for children, as pedagogical works came to be "rigidly distinguished" from juvenile literature designed primarily to amuse rather than to instruct.

33. Richard Henry Stoddard (1825–1903) was a poet, critic, and editor. A protégé of Hawthorne's, he patterned his *Adventures in Fairy-Land* (1853) after *A Wonder Book* (West 3, 109–10).

34. The firm of C. S. Francis (1826–60) published Charles and Mary Lamb's *Tales from Shakespeare* (1849), some collections of Hans Christian Andersen's fairy tales, and several of Lydia Maria Child's juvenile works. Charles Stephen Francis (1805–87) opened his bookstore at 189 Broadway in 1826. By 1835 it had become one of New York's largest bookstores and thereafter moved to the 252 Broadway location that Goodrich described in 1856 (see Walker). According to Harry B. Weiss, Francis's store "for many years, was the headquarters for various men of letters" (*Printers and Publishers* 8; see also Derby 580–84).

35. Although C. S. Francis did not publish juvenile books exclusively, children's literature, both European and American, was his forte. In addition to publishing *Parley's Magazine*, which Goodrich founded, from 1833 to 1844, he was the first American publisher of *Mother Goose Melodies* (1833) (Derby 581), and his series for children included *Juvenile Classicks* (one of the earliest of the large, numbered publisher's series for children in the United States) and *Library of Instructive Amusement*. Two earlier American booksellers who operated specialized children's bookstores were Samuel Wood (1760–1844), whose Juvenile Bookstore at 357 Pearl Street, New York, had opened by 1815, and Mahlon Day (1790–1854), whose New Juvenile Bookstore, also on Pearl Street, was open from 1820 to 1845 (see Weiss, *Samuel Wood & Sons* and *Mahlon Day*). I am indebted to Cornelia King and Laura Wasowicz for providing this information.

36. Cundall published some forty to fifty children's books between 1845 and the beginning of 1849, including two early English editions of Hans Christian Andersen. Conceived as an effort to "reform" children's books with its avowed "anti-Peter Parleyism," his *Home Treasury* series, comprising some two dozen titles, was pronounced "the most finely designed children's booklets ever produced." The firm was acquired by Chapman & Hall in 1846. See McLean, "Joseph Cundall," (*DLB* 120; McLean, *Joseph Cundall* 4, 18; and McLean, "Joseph Cundall" (*Penrose*).

37. Sir Henry Cole (1808–82), an accomplished engraver, etcher, and designer, served on the executive committee for the Great Exhibition of 1851 in London. He also proposed and raised funds for the building of the Royal Albert Hall, which opened in 1871, and helped found the National Training School for Music, which opened in 1876.

38. Van Tassel has argued that "hidden behind his reference to Peter Parley . . . is his [Hawthorne's] disillusioned knowledge that Annie's reading taste, shaped by men like Goodrich, rejected his serious work and demanded fiction that women and children could safely enjoy, innocuous pieces such as this very sketch, published in household magazines and children's annuals" (172). Although Van Tassel's reading is consistent with the nature of the literary apprenticeship Hawthorne served under Goodrich, Elizabeth Freeman's inference that Little Annie "is a veritable maven of the emerging nineteenth-century juvenile reading culture" (878) is, I think, closer to the mark. As I have suggested, the growing interest in fairy tales and other imaginative stories on the part of Little Annie and her contemporaries ultimately helped establish the market for the juvenile "classics" Hawthorne went on to produce in the 1850s. This trajectory of his career (in distinct counterpoint to that of his adult fiction) thus auspiciously accorded with the broader development of American literature. (With respect to his writing for adults, in contrast, Nina Baym observes that Hawthorne did not "foresee the evolution of both popular and critical taste away from the gothic, romantic, and historical toward the domestic, realistic, and contemporary" [*Shape of Hawthorne's Career* 17]).

## 2. STORIES OF THEIR LIVES

1. John Newbery, the first dedicated publisher of children's literature in England, experimented with gender-based marketing gimmicks by packaging *A Little Pretty Pocket Book* (1744) with a ball for boys and a pincushion for girls, but this strategy was designed to make a *single* book equally attractive to both male and female children. Samuel F. Pickering Jr. traces the first "significant differentiation made between books for little girls and for little boys" to Mary Ann Kilner's *The Adventures of a Pin Cushion* (1783?) and *Memoirs of a Peg-Top* (1783); see Segel, "As the Twig Is Bent" 168. Gender-specific periodicals appeared earlier in the nineteenth century, and Britain preceded the United States in the trend toward gender-specific juvenile literature.

2. Jacob Abbott's Rollo and Lucy books (dating from 1835 and 1841, respectively) were the first American juvenile series of note to be clearly differentiated by gender; for more on Abbott, see D. Johnson. The series I discuss in this chapter targeted a slightly older group than Abbott's. For a bibliographical overview, see *Girls' Series Books: A Checklist of Titles Published, 1840–1991* (Minneapolis: U of Minnesota P, 1992). Deidre Johnson's "19th-Century Girls' Series" (online at http://readseries.com/index.html) is also a valuable resource. For helpful discussions of gender differentiation in the British market, see Reynolds; J. S. Bratton; and Stoneley 9–10.

3. A reviewer for *Arthur's Illustrated Home Magazine* identified the audience for *Little Women* as girls from ten to sixteen years of age (Norton Critical Edition 548). Peter Stoneley notes that the adolescent girl "was discussed in a growing number of [social-sexological]

treatises from the 1870s onward" (a period corresponding to the emergence of girls' fiction) which focus on girls at the "awkward age" (6).

4. Clark also regards *Little Women* as genre-defining: "It can be seen as inaugurating a new genre for children, as it melded some aspects of the sentimental novel popular in the 1860s . . . with the domestic fiction long a staple of literature for children" (*Kiddie Lit* 105).

5. Stoneley affirms that Alcott was "the leading exemplar of this first generation of girls' fiction" (21).

6. This was the kind of juvenile literature Alcott read, or listened to, in her own childhood. Her childhood diary records her reading, or being read, stories by Edgeworth and Fredrika Bremer. This reading is reflected, in turn, in that of Marmee and the March girls in *Little Women* (see Alcott, *Louisa May Alcott*; Alcott, "Recollections"; and Crisler).

7. *Flower Fables* (dated 1855) was published by George W. Briggs & Company for the Christmas trade in December 1854, with a first edition of 1,600 copies. The book, dedicated to Ellen Emerson and sponsored by Sophia Hawthorne (Payne xi), was based on stories a sixteen-year-old Alcott had made up to amuse the nine-year-old daughter of Ralph Waldo Emerson (Shealy, *Louisa May Alcott's Fairy Tales* xxi–xxii). *The Rose Family. A Fairy Tale* was published by James Redpath in 1864, and Horace B. Fuller brought out *Morning Glories, and Other Stories* in 1868. As Shealy points out, Alcott returned to fantasy stories from time to time in her magazine fiction (republished in *Aunt Jo's Scrap-Bag*) and in *Lulu's Library* (see introduction to *Louisa May Alcott's Fairy Tales and Fantasy Stories*). All of Alcott's fantasy stories can be found in Shealy, ed., *Louisa May Alcott's Fairy Tales and Fantasy Stories*.

8. "Robert Merry" (like "Peter Parley") was a pseudonym of Goodrich, who had launched *Merry's Museum* in 1841. Horace B. Fuller acquired the magazine in 1867 and hired Alcott to edit it at an annual salary of $500.

9. Its title as well as its structure clearly influenced by Hawthorne, *Will's Wonder Book* is a collection of dialogues between two children and their grandmother about animals and insects; it appeared in *Merry's Museum* from April to November 1868 and was published in book form by Horace B. Fuller in 1870. Alcott also recorded writing "Jamie's Wonder Book" (*Journals* 131), which Madeleine Stern speculates was an earlier title of *Will's Wonder Book*; see the introduction to Louisa May Alcott, *Louisa's Wonder Book: An Unknown Alcott Juvenile*.

10. Thomas Niles to Louisa May Alcott, 16 June 1868, Roberts Brothers Papers (hereafter RB Papers), bMS Am 1130. 8(1–44).

11. Even toward the end of her life, after her success with girls' fiction had become nearly legendary, Alcott expressed distaste for the genre of girls' books, remarking in a letter to a reader, "'Little Women' was written when I was ill, & to prove that I could *not* write books for girls. The publisher thought it *flat*, so did I, & neither hoped much for or from it. We found out our mistake, & since then, though I do not enjoy writing 'moral tales' for the young, I do it because it pays well" (*Selected Letters* 232). Alcott's resistance to the genre shows up in feisty, unconventional female characters like Jo March and (later) Nan Harding.

12. The first part of *Little Women* was published in early October 1868, with a first printing of 2,000 copies. See Joel Myerson and Daniel Shealy, "The Sales of Louisa May Alcott's Books."

13. George Haven Putnam explained: "The firm of Roberts Bros. began in the later sixties a publishing business which, largely through the efforts of its literary manager, Mr. Niles, won prompt reputation for its recognition and effective management of good literature, English and American" (62).

14. In his history of Lee & Shepard, Raymond L. Kilgour speculates further about this connection between Adams and Alcott on the eve of *Little Women*, suggesting that Niles "must have mentioned the tremendous success of the Optic books as an inducement" for Alcott to attempt a book for girls (*Lee and Shepard* 73). Sarah Elbert concurs, stating that "Niles wanted to tap the market for girls created by popular writers of boy's fiction like 'Oliver Optic'" (141) and further suggesting that "Louisa's incentive to write *Little Women* had been the Oliver Optic series" (181). Despite these tantalizing hints of a channel of influence between Adams and Alcott, the connection has remained largely unexplored.

15. *The New York Sunday Times* declared that "'Oliver Optic' is a *nom de plume* that is known and loved by almost every boy of intelligence in the land" (qtd. in Lee & Shepard catalog, rpt. Dzwonkoski, *DLB*). Hurst & Co., which republished the Oliver Optic Books for Boys in the early twentieth century, boasted that "few boys are alive to-day who have not read some of the writings of this famous author, whose books are scattered broadcast and eagerly sought for" (qtd. in Adams, *Try Again*, n.p.; see also Derby 525).

16. An article in the *American Literary Gazette* (15 July 1871) declared, "It is, no doubt, safe to state this firm [Lee & Shepard] publishes a larger number of juvenile books than any other house in the country" (qtd. in Kilgour, *Lee and Shepard* 114).

17. Sometimes the connections among these books were rather forced. Kilgour explains: "A novel selling device, perhaps original with L&S and, in any case, more efficiently employed by them at an earlier date than by any other firm, was the grouping of titles only faintly related in high-sounding sets" (*Lee and Shepard* 95). As examples, Kilgour cites the Frontier Series and the Wonderland Series, each containing books by more than one author. The technique became quite common. Horace B. Fuller included Alcott's *Morning-Glories, and Other Stories* in his multiauthor Morning Glory Series, and *Will's Wonder Book* was part of his Dirigo Series.

18. Also called the Oliver Optic Series and later retitled The Famous "Boat Club" Series: A Library for Young People, Oliver Optic's Library for Young People consisted of *The Boat Club; or, The Bunkers of Rippleton* (1854); *All Aboard; or, Life on the Lake* (1856); *Now or Never; or, The Adventures of Bobby Bright* (1856); *Try Again; or, the Trials and Triumphs of Harry West* (1857); *Poor and Proud; or, The Fortunes of Katy Redburn* (1858); and *Little by Little; or, The Cruise of the Flyaway* (1860). The Riverdale Story Books consisted of twelve books aimed at readers aged six to ten.

19. Adams did eventually produce a story about a girls' boat club, *The Dorcas Club; or, Our Girls Afloat*, but not until 1874, twenty years after *The Boat Club*. More important, as Adams points out in his preface, the real hero of that book is a boy, Prince Willingood. In fact, the girls of the Dorcas Club are little more than props, providing the hero with a convenient damsel in distress and the opportunity to flex his muscles and exercise his chivalry as "Professor" of rowing.

20. These include *The Young Man's Guide* by William Alcott (1833), Lydia Sigourney's *The Boy's Reading-Book* (1839), Horace Mann's *A Few Thoughts for a Young Man* (1850),

and Henry Ward Beecher's *Lectures to Young Men, on Various Important Subjects* (1846), to name just a few.

21. According to Mary Noel, a similar phenomenon characterized story papers in the 1870s (217–18).

22. Lovett's sense of embarrassment was shared by a later generation of boys whose admiration of the movie version of *Little Women* led them to read Alcott's novel—but with the cover concealed by plain brown wrappers (Payne 56). For a contrasting report of men and boys openly reading *Little Women* when it was all the "rage," see Clark, *Kiddie Lit* 105. As recently as 1986, Elizabeth Segel observed that "people who work with children can testify to the sad fact that reading a book about a girl is still cause for embarrassment for many young male readers" ("As the Twig Is Bent" 182). On the ironies of girls being permitted greater range in their reading than boys, despite greater social restrictions in other areas, see also Reynolds. See Segel also for a provocative assessment of the "denigration of the female" implicit in these attitudes toward boys' and girls' reading and the controversial ramifications for curriculum development.

23. Mary Cadogan and Patricia Craig elaborate: "A separate, comprehensive body of girls' fiction did not come into being until the end of the [nineteenth] century: it was then a progressive sign, since it marked a recognition of the particular nature and interests of young girls. There is an intricate relation between a society and the kinds of expression it gives rise to, however, and girls' books quickly became a medium for the reinforcement of social prohibitions and expectations" (9).

24. Not all reviewers agreed with the assertion of the *Lady's Friend* that the novel was "sure to influence them [girls] for good" ("New Publications" 857). For a survey of contemporary reviews of Alcott's fiction, see Zehr.

25. Alcott further developed this theme in *Work: A Story of Experience* (1873), a novel for adults.

26. Dolores Blythe Jones's *An "Oliver Optic" Checklist: An Annotated Catalog-Index to the Series, Nonseries Stories, and Magazine Publications of William Taylor Adams* includes no listing for "Katy Redmond"; presumably, Elbert means "Redburn."

27. In *A Hunger for Home: Louisa May Alcott and "Little Women,"* Sarah Elbert writes: "In addition to boys' 'Great Western Series,' 'Lake Shore Series,' and 'Yacht Club Series,' he [Adams] had also produced a promising girls' story about 'Katy Redmond' [sic]. His heroine was a self-reliant twelve-year-old whose exploits signalled a change in girls' fiction that struck a responsive note in Louisa" (142). *Poor and Proud* is arguably a girls' novel, although it was generally marketed as "a story for young people." The ambiguity over the audience came to the fore in 1886 when Lee & Shepard reissued the book as part of its American Boys' Series—with the subtitle changed to "A Story for Girls"!

28. In a retrospective article titled "Books That Girls Have Loved" (1897), Erin Graham wrote of the March sisters: "We liked them all, but with one voice Jo was declared our favorite. Every girl whom I have known regards the boyish Jo with feelings of tenderness. Meg was more domestic, Amy more graceful, and Beth more gentle; but Jo, dear old blundering Jo, romped into our hearts at once" (430–31). Cary Ryan, editor of *Louisa May Alcott: Her Girlhood Diary*, describes Jo as "the first liberated girl in American literature" (xi).

29. Jo was not the first tomboy heroine in American literature, although she was very close to it. According to Elizabeth Segel, the tomboy heroine "arrived on the scene with a splash in the decade following the Civil War" ("*Gypsy Breynton* Series" 67) with Elizabeth Stuart Phelps's *Gypsy Breynton* (1866). Gypsy was soon followed by Jo March and Susan Coolidge's Katy Carr, the protagonist of *What Katy Did* (1872) and its sequels. As Segel notes, all three heroines were extremely popular and all inspired multiple sequels. Even some male authors picked up on the appeal of the tomboy heroine (see Kilgour, *Lee and Shepard* 156), including Henry James in his first novel, *Watch and Ward* (1871). According to Christian McEwen, however, "It was not until 1876 that the word ['tomboy'] began to take on . . . positive connotations (xii)."

30. Anna Quindlen, in her introduction to *Little Women*, calls it "the first great American coming-of-age book for girls, the companion piece to Huck Finn's raft trips down the Mississippi" (n.p.).

31. The last paragraph of the first part of *Little Women* informs readers that the appearance of a second part "depends upon the reception given to the first act of the domestic drama called 'Little Women'" (239). Several reviewers picked up on this hint and voiced their desire for additional installments (see *Little Women*, Norton Critical Edition 549–50). In Britain, the second volume was titled *Good Wives*. Starting in 1870, both parts were published together as a two-volume set; from 1880, they were combined in a single volume.

32. *Eight Cousins* first appeared as a serial in *Good Things: A Picturesque Magazine for the Young of All Ages* in 1874. To a reader in Holland, Alcott wrote on 7 August 1875, "My next book comes out in October, and is called Eight Cousins. . . . There is to be a sequel in which the cousins are adults" (*Selected Letters* 194). The two remaining volumes of the Little Women series, *Under the Lilacs* (1878) and *Jack and Jill* (1880), depart from the pattern by adhering to a continuous time line. In *Jack and Jill*, however, Alcott obliges us with a proleptic "peep into futurity" ten years hence, when Merry is living in Italy, the wife of a sculptor; Molly (like Maud in *An Old-Fashioned Girl*) is "a merry spinster"; and Jill marries Jack at the age of twenty-five (281). Both these novels were serialized in *St. Nicholas* before being issued in book form.

33. As T. Walter Herbert notes, "Alexis de Tocqueville observed that the transition from girlhood to womanhood in democratic America was a drastic change, and while he tried to put an attractive face on it, his description makes clear it was a change for the worse" (39).

34. Alcott's emphasis on becoming rather than being is reflected in Ryan's observation that "Louisa's writing has shown generations of readers who they are gently alongside what they could become, reassuring them that the distance in between is only a human step" (1), and in Barbara Sicherman's statement that "reading *Little Women* has been a rite of passage for generations of adolescent and preadolescent females of the comfortable classes" ("Reading *Little Women*" 247).

35. In her journal, Alcott recorded, "Girls write to ask me who the little women marry. . . . I *wont* marry Jo to Laurie to please any one" (*Journals* 167). A few months later, she wrote to Alfred Whitman, "All my little girl-friends are madly in love with Laurie & insist on a sequel," adding, "I wanted to disappoint the [little dears] young gossips who vowed that Laurie and Jo *should* marry" (*Selected Letters* 120). In a letter to Elizabeth Powell dated

20 March 1869, Alcott elaborated, "'Jo' should have remained a literary spinster but so many enthusiastic young ladies wrote to me clamorously demanding that she should marry Laurie, *or somebody*, that I didn't dare to refuse & out of perversity went & made a funny match for her" (*Selected Letters* 124–25). Given the unpopularity of the author's decision to marry Jo to Mr. Bhaer, it is significant that in the final chapter of *An Old-Fashioned Girl*, Alcott writes: "Intimidated by threats, denunciations, and complaints showered upon me in consequence of taking the liberty to end a certain story as I liked, I now yield to the amiable desire of giving satisfaction, and, at the risk of outraging all the unities, intend to pair off everybody I can lay my hands on" (314). Given her reluctance to "pair off" Jo, it is significant that she allows Maud, a relatively minor character, to remain "a busy, lively spinster all her days" (325).

36. Gillian Avery identifies this practice of the "marketing of books in named series" as "a particularly American phenomenon," one that "presumably saved bulk buyers the trouble of reading any more than the title" (190). Although neither Kilgour, the writer for the *Independent*, nor Avery takes into account the age of the typical buyer (adult or child?) and the relationship between buyer and reader (a parent buying *for* a child?), one can conclude that the practice of issuing books in named series might have been especially beneficial when the buyer was someone other than the primary reader, as is frequently the case with juvenile literature.

37. Thomas Niles to Louisa May Alcott, 30 December 1882, 16 June 1868, and 25 July 1868, RB Papers. bMS Am 1130.8.

38. A month later, Alcott wrote to Elizabeth Powell that "[a] sequel will be out early in April, & like all sequels will probably disappoint or disgust most readers, for publishers wont let authors finish up as they like but insist on having people married off in a wholesale manner which much afflicts me" (*Selected Letters* 124–25). Alcott reiterated her dislike in 1876: "Get an idea and start 'Rose in Bloom,' though I hate sequels" (*Journals* 201).

39. Niles to Alcott, 14 April 1869, 29 April 1869, and 26 May 1869, RB Papers, bMS Am 1130.8.

40. Niles to Alcott, 13 April 1870, RB Papers, bMS Am 1130.8.

41. Niles to Alcott, 17 January 1871, RB Papers, bMS Am 1130.8.

42. Niles to Alcott, 17 March 1871, RB Papers, bMS Am 1130.8.

43. Niles to Alcott, 5 January 1883, 25 August 1883, and 26 July 1881, RB Papers, bMS Am 1130.8. Earlier, Niles had suggested to Alcott the idea of publishing some of her letters from Europe as "Jo's Letters from Abroad to the March's [*sic*] at home" or "Little Women and Little Men Letters or Letters to 'Jo' by 'Little Women' and 'Little Men,' the latter to serve "as an advertising medium" that would be bound to "have a marked effect on the sale of [her] books" (letters of 30 August 1870 and 14 August 1871, RB Papers, bMS Am 1130.8).

44. Adams aired his rebuttal and launched a counterattack in *Oliver Optic's Magazine* for 1875. Adams was not the first to turn the table on Alcott and charge that her novels employed slang. As Janet S. Zehr comments, "Several reviews [of *Little Women*] complained that children might learn bad grammar and diction from her book" (330).

45. Ironically, Alcott appears to have made an effort to move away from the female focus of *Little Women* by following it with *Little Men*, *Eight Cousins*, and *Jo's Boys*, all of which

feature many more male characters than female. Later in her career, Alcott even projected a new story tentatively called "An Old-Fashioned Boy," noting that she "had meant that for the title of a book, but another woman [Martha Finley] stole it" (*Selected Letters* 248). The tale was to have for its protagonist a boy of the American Revolution. In addition, Alcott addressed boys as well as girls in her prefaces: "the little men and women, for whom it is an honor and pleasure to write" (*Old-Fashioned Girl* vi). Nevertheless, the market was determined that she be a girls' author, and so she remains. For a discussion of *Little Men* as a "story of boys" that "is not necessarily a boys' story," see Clark, "Domesticating the School Story" 323–42.

46. As Barbara Sicherman comments, "Reading has long been recognized as a topic of absorbing interest to adolescents, especially adolescent girls. For girls books have represented an important arena for shared friendship as well as means of creating a world more satisfying than the one ordinarily inhabited, a world in which to formulate aspirations and try out different identities" ("Sense and Sensibility" 208). Jane Hunter also comments on juvenile readers' sense of gratification at participating in a shared youth culture in which magazine readers were linked to their peers (68–69).

47. The line of influence emanating from Alcott's girls' books is equally noteworthy. In an interesting reversal of the Optic-Alcott scenario, L. Frank Baum was commissioned by his publisher to provide "the manuscript of a book for young girls on the style of the Louisa M. Alcott stories, but not so good, the authorship to be ascribed to . . . some . . . mythological female" (qtd. in Rogers 135). The result was "Edith Van Dyne's" Aunt Jane's Nieces series. (I am indebted to Alan Pickerell for this detail about Baum.)

48. In the opinion of Mary Thwaite, "The careful separation of stories into series, which publishers and librarians could complacently label 'Boys' or 'Girls', had . . . become a minor oppression of young readers in the later nineteenth century" (qtd. in Segel, "As the Twig Is Bent" 175).

49. Before his death, Oliver Optic passed his torch to a young Horatio Alger, whose first novel, *Ragged Dick; or, Street Life in New York* (1867), had been serialized in Adams's magazine, *Student and Schoolmate*. In turn, Edward Stratemeyer, creator of the Stratemeyer Syndicate, completed unfinished manuscripts by Alger as well as Adams after their deaths. See Carol Billman, *The Secret of the Stratemeyer Syndicate: Nancy Drew, the Hardy Boys, and the Million Dollar Fiction Factory* (New York: Ungar, 1986), 19.

50. Not only has *Little Women* never been out of print, but in 1997 Delacorte Press launched its Portraits of Little Women series, a testament to the enduring popularity of Alcott's characters. With over a dozen titles (written by Susan Beth Pfeffer), the books, which include "crafts, recipes, and other activities that bring the stories to life," are designed to "capture each of the March sisters at age 10" (from the publisher's promotional materials). For a discussion of recent adaptations, see Margaret Mackey, "*Little Women* Go to Market: Shifting Texts and Changing Readers," *Children's Literature in Education* 29.3 (1998): 153–73.

51. The authors of an early twentieth-century study of the reading interests and habits of adults reported that "up to eight or nine years of age there seems [*sic*] to be few differences in the reading interests of boys and girls. Between the ages of ten and thirteen notable differences appear" (Gray and Munroe 106).

52. This argument resurfaces from time to time. In 1976, for example, Mary Cadogan and Patricia Craig declared, "At the present time girls' fiction appears almost redundant as a genre. . . . Classification along rigid sexually-determined lines is, or should be, no longer valid" (9). Similarly, Segel notes that in the United States "the boundaries [between writing for boys and writing for girls] began to loosen a bit" in the 1960s ("As the Twig is Bent" 165). Recently, series such as J. K. Rowling's Harry Potter books and Eoin Colfer's Artemis Fowl series have shown a remarkable ability both to cross gender lines and to span generations, winning fans among adults and teenagers as well as younger boys and girls.

53. Interestingly, in the popular girls' series of the twentieth century, the emphasis shifted away from the growth of the protagonist from girl to woman. Instead of focusing on the development of the girl's character, the books place a stable (some would say "static") protagonist in a seemingly endless sequence of novel settings and surprising situations. How to grow up is no longer the predominant concern; rather, like the boys' series books, these narratives explore the limitless possibilities for adventure and discovery in the world beyond the home.

54. Of Britain in the 1930s, Geoffrey Trease remarked, "Books were labelled, as strictly as school lavatories, 'Books for Boys' or 'Books for Girls'" (qtd in Segel, "As the Twig Is Bent" 165). The best examples of gender-differentiated children's books in the United States during the same period are the myriad productions of the Stratemeyer Syndicate, creators of Nancy Drew, the Hardy Boys, and numerous other series heroes.

55. A case in point is the Nancy Drew line, which currently includes the Nancy Drew Mystery Stories, marketed to girls eight to eleven years old, the Nancy Drew Files, written for girls in grades 6–11, the Nancy Drew Notebooks, aimed at five- to eight-year-olds, and the Nancy Drew on Campus series, targeting teenage girls (Kismaric and Heiferman 125–26), as well as the recently launched Nancy Drew Girl Detective series, for nine- to twelve-year-olds.

### 3. BOY'S LIFE

1. The phrase is Leslie Fiedler's, although subsequent critics have adopted it.

2. Hereafter cited as *MTLP*.

3. For a useful discussion of subscription publishing, together with primary materials and a discussion of Mark Twain, see Cook, "Reshaping Publishing."

4. Catalogue of Books.

5. As the national demographics shifted toward a more urban population, the market for subscription books declined. According to Francis Halsey's 1902 account, "Our Literary Deluge and Some of Its Deeper Waters": "Costly folios no longer succeed. People do not want them. In large cities people commonly live in flats, hotels, and apartments, where it is impossible to house them. And therefore the publishers are adapting their manufactures to changed conditions. They make books that will go into small book-cases. They no longer count on centre-tables as repositories" (78). Of course, town- and city-dwellers also had access to bookstores and did not need to rely on door-to-door canvassers.

6. *Mark Twain's Letters*, ed. Albert Bigelow Paine. The more recent University of California edition of the letters is cited simply as *Letters* to avoid confusion.

7. Thomas Niles, to Louisa May Alcott, 26 July 1881, RB Papers, bMS Am 1130.8.

8. "It was not until 1873 that a subscription house, the American Publishing Company, ventured to publish a novel, *The Gilded Age*"; Bliss also experimented with poetry—another departure for subscription publishers (Hill 13, 17).

9. Although originally printed on a good quality of paper, *Tom Sawyer* was reprinted on thicker paper during the first year of publication after agents reported customers' complaints that the book didn't measure up, in thickness, to earlier books such as *The Innocents Abroad* (Johnson 29).

10. Catalogue of Books.

11. *Mark Twain's Letters*, ed. Edgar Marquess Branch et al. Hereafter cited as *Letters* to avoid confusion with the 1917 Bigelow edition cited as *Mark Twain's Letters*.

12. Hereafter cited as *MTHL*.

13. Clemens's reluctance to consider his novel a children's book should be read in light of his professed dislike of children's literature. In a letter to his brother Orion, 15 March 1871, he declared that children's writing is "wholly worthless, for I never saw [any] that I thought was worth the ink it was written with . . . . I have no love for children's literature" (qtd. in Lowry 80). To Beverly Lyon Clark, Clemens's contradictory remarks about the audience of *Tom Sawyer* "reflect the extent to which the two audiences [adults and children] were not yet fully discrete" (*Kiddie Lit* 81).

14. Although Clemens includes girls and women, the book, as Lowry argues, "delimit[s] a world of essential boyhood" (81), and its "assumed audience was the male reader" (87). Perhaps he recognized, with Alcott and others, that boys' books attracted a mixed audience, and perhaps like Oliver Optic he wished to avoid excluding a portion of his potential audience. It is possible, too, that Clemens was cognizant of a tip to book canvassers that advised, "Do not slight the women[;] thousands of them subscribe" ("How to Canvass," fig. 5.1 in Arbour).

15. Thacker and Webb also trace a blurring of "the boundaries between adult and children's fiction in the American canon" to the "powerful trope" of "America-as-child" (51).

16. Recognizing that an important function of these texts was the nostalgic portrait of childhood it offered to adult readers, Clemens fixed the ages of Tom and Huck in an eternal but indeterminate youth that is denied the March sisters. Tom has recently lost his baby teeth in *Tom Sawyer*, but Huck is fourteen in *Huckleberry Finn*, which takes place a few months after *Tom Sawyer* ends.

17. For a discussion of "bad boy literature," see Charles A. Norton. Lowry also views Tom Sawyer as a reaction against such "model boy" literature as Jacob Abbott's Rollo stories, a view borne out by contemporary criticism. John Macy's *The Spirit of American Literature* (1913), for example, suggests, "It may be that Tom Sawyer and Huckleberry Finn, Aldrich's *Story of a Bad Boy*, Howells' *Flight of Pony Baker*, and Warner's *Being a Boy Again* are the reaction of humor and naturalism against the era of St. Rollo" (qtd. in Anderson 319). See also Clemens's parodic sketches "Story of the Bad Little Boy" (1865) and "Story of the Good Little Boy" (1870), rpt. in *Sketches, New and Old* (1875).

18. In 1880, J. S. Ogilvie published anonymously Metta Fuller Victor's *Bad Boy's Diary*, which was soon attributed to Clemens. Against this "piece of trash" (Charles Webster's

description), Clemens protested, "I would not be the author of that witless stuff . . . for a million dollars" (*Mark Twain, Business Man* 197).

19. As Wolf notes, *The Story of a Bad Boy* "precipitate[d] a long line of bad boys in children's literature and a tradition of the boy in American literature" (47).

20. When Aldrich's *Story of a Bad Boy* appeared, Howells remarked that "no one else seems to have thought of telling the story of a boy's life, with so great desire to show what a boy's life is, and so little purpose of teaching what it should be" (qtd. in Donovan 149–50). Similarly, Brander Matthews claimed of Huck Finn: "He is almost as much a delight to any one who has been a boy as Tom Sawyer. But only he or she [*sic*] who has been a boy can truly enjoy this record of his adventures, and of his sentiments and of his sayings" (qtd. in Anderson 123).

21. It took six years to sell 40,000, the number that James D. Hart estimates as Clemens's "steady and immediate market" of purchasers (148).

22. The *Century Magazine*, a literary magazine for adults, printed advance excerpts from *Huckleberry Finn* in December 1884, January 1885, and February 1885, concurrently (or nearly so) with Howells's *The Rise of Silas Lapham* and James's *The Bostonians*. The *Century*, a literary and journalistic magazine for adults, was particularly noted for the high quality of its illustrations and for its role in encouraging the reconciliation of the North and the South during Reconstruction and cultivating southern writers (see *The House of Appleton-Century* 32–33).

23. Ned Buntline, *The Black Avenger of the Spanish Main; or, The Fiend of Blood. A Thrilling Story of the Buccaneer Times* (Boston: F. Gleason, 1847).

24. In an article for the *Saturday Review* (31 January 1885), Brander Matthews wrote: "The boy of to-day is fortunate indeed, and, of a truth, he is to be congratulated. While the boy of yesterday had to stay his stomach with the unconscious humour of *Sandford and Merton*, the boy of to-day may get his fill of fun and of romance and of adventure in *Treasure Island* and in *Tom Brown* and in *Tom Sawyer,* and now in a sequel to *Tom Sawyer,* wherein Tom himself appears in the very nick of time, like a young god from the machine" (qtd. in Anderson 121).

25. For an overview of the critical debate, see "The Controversy over the Ending: Did Mark Twain Sell Jim Down the River?" in *Adventures of Huckleberry Finn: A Case Study in Critical Controversy*, ed. Gerald Graff and James Phelan (Boston: Bedford–St. Martin's, 1995), 279–84. Most of the controversy centers on the question of whether Clemens took Jim and the problem of racism seriously. Notably, Shelley Fisher Fishkin has suggested that the last third of the novel is a "satire on the reenslavement of freed blacks in the post-Reconstruction South" (190).

26. Fiedler remarks, "If *Tom Sawyer* was always a boy's book, even when Twain thought he was writing for adults, *Huckleberry Finn* is from the start, on one of its levels at least, not merely an adult but a subversive novel" (278).

27. Crossed out, at the bottom of the letter, was a note from Clemens: "Send me Washington Irving's." Eleven days later, on 17 July 1884, Clemens wrote to Webster, "Don't need any more Injun books" (*Mark Twain, Business Man* 270). In their annotations to *Huck Finn and Tom Sawyer among the Indians* (271–72), Dahlia Armon and Walter Blair

note that Clemens's principal source about Indians was Richard Irving Dodge, *Our Wild Indians* (1883). Other sources he consulted included Dodge, *The Plains of the Great West and Their Inhabitants* (1877); De Benneville Randolph Keim, *Sheridan's Troopers on the Borders* (1870); Francis Parkman, *The Oregon Trail* (1849); George Armstrong Custer, *My Life on the Plains* (1874); and the autobiography *The Life of the Hon. William F. Cody, Known as Buffalo Bill, the Famous Hunter, Scout and Guide* (1879).

28. In 1869 Clemens had begun a story about a man who travels from India across Asia and the Pacific Ocean to Illinois but abandoned it after a few pages, noting, "While this was being written, Jules Verne's 'Five Weeks in a Balloon' came out and consequently this sketch wasn't finished" (qtd. in Inge 3).

29. "In *Tom Sawyer, Detective*, Twain tries to get aboard the Sherlock Holmes bandwagon by substituting the tried and true characters of Tom and Huck for Doyle's Holmes and Watson" (Robinson 15).

30. These fragments are published in *Mark Twain's Hannibal, Huck and Tom*: the title given for this unnamed fragment is Blair's. Tom Sawyer also figures in "Schoolhouse Hill" (1898), an early version of the posthumously published (1916) *Mysterious Stranger*.

## PART TWO

1. On the feminization of culture, see Fred Lewis Pattee, *The Feminine Fifties* (New York: D. Appleton, 1940); and Ann Douglass, *The Feminization of American Culture* (New York: Knopf, 1977).

2. As Helen Papashvily notes, "The new reading public [of the late nineteenth century], although immeasurably larger, lacked the homogeneity of the old" (37).

3. On the stratification of American culture in the late nineteenth century, see Levine. The terms "highbrow" and "lowbrow," which derived from theories of phrenology, first appeared in the 1880s and early 1900s, respectively (Levine 221–22; see also Rubin).

4. Although twentieth-century critics often speak about the early American novel in terms of subgenres, for the most part the terms they apply are anachronistic labels. In *Revolution and the Word*, for example, Cathy Davidson analyzes several different types of novels in early America: the seduction tale, sentimental fiction, the picaresque and female picaresque, early American gothic, and so forth. Nineteenth-century authors and critics did use adjectives such as sentimental, picaresque, and gothic, but these terms had less currency among publishers and general readers.

5. In *Cultures of Letters*, Richard Brodhead describes the process whereby publishers divided the literary field into distinct cultural "zones" and helped to organize a "mass audience" in America alongside a "self-consciously high culture" (68). Bourdieu provides additional insight into the correlation between hierarchies of audience and hierarchies of genre in *The Field of Cultural Production*.

6. Writing of the British market, Richard Altick observes, "This diversification of binding styles, either under a single series heading or under a new name for each style, was common Victorian practice. Many, if not most series were offered in both paper and cloth, and some also were available in at least one kind of leather" ("From Aldine to Everyman" 15). Leslie Howsam speculates further that "the myriad series of standard works, with

minute variations in their advertising, pricing, format and especially binding design, were, presumably, meant for rather specific segments of the middle-class and working-class markets" (23).

7. Thomas Niles wanted to issue both "a cheap 50 cent" paperback of *Little Women, Little Men*, and *An Old-Fashioned Girl* for "railroad sales" and a deluxe, illustrated *Little Women* "done in the style of the new English Edition of Dickens now publishing" (Shealy, "Author-Publisher" [1985] 177).

8. Howsam comments, "There can be no question that the series was a publishing form whose numbers grew dramatically through the second half of the century, a conclusion that invites speculation about how the idea of books in series was experienced, in turn by publishers, by authors, and by readers. The series, like the children's book, was a form invented and refined by publishers, in whose minds the marketing of books as commodities ranked equally with or above literary considerations" (22).

9. For an overview of criticism that treats "the intertwining of text and social structure in terms of genre," see Dorothy Winsor, "Ordering Work," according to which, C. R. Miller (1984) "was the first to define genre as a form of social action, a typified textual response to a typified social situation" (155).

10. A recent example of new subgenres arising in response to the concerns, needs, and desires of targeted groups is the spate of novels about well-educated middle-class women in their twenties and thirties who bemoan their fate as "singletons" while pursuing empty, meaningless careers. Dubbed by one critic the "Bridget Boom" (after British writer Helen Fielding's "supersuccessful" novel *Bridget Jones's Diary*), this species of "chick-lit" received an aggressive push from "Stateside publishers [who] have realized that a lot of female readers out there will spring for hardcovers—even the ones Oprah doesn't endorse" (Weiner n.p.).

11. William Charvat suggests that it wasn't until well after midcentury that the market permitted authors to specialize by focusing on particular genres, styles, subjects, or audiences: "The stratification which gives writers a degree of freedom in our time did not begin in America until well after 1850. In 1846 . . . books were offered to an undifferentiated audience of men, women, and adolescents, and were therefore subject to fantastically wide ranges of response" (*Profession of Authorship* 211–12). Anne Scott MacLeod concurs: "While it was relatively easy for a writer to get his work published in the antebellum period, few authors were well paid, or could afford to be specialists. They therefore wrote whatever they could—prose and poetry, books and periodical articles, fiction and nonfiction—and they were frequently editors as well as writers" (*Moral Tale* 32).

## 4. SEASIDE AND FIRESIDE

1. The link between Howells's principal characters and the world of literary publishing is reinforced by the claim that Silas was modeled partly on Henry Houghton and James R. Osgood and Tom Corey on a young George Mifflin (see Ballou 273–75). *Tears, Idle Tears* may allude to Clement Scott's one-act drama *Tears! Idle Tears!!* (1883).

2. In his study of the way nineteenth-century readers used literature, Richard Bushman suggests that "one way to conceive of the influence of fiction is to recognize that people

thought of their own lives as stories, following narrative lines like the ones they so frequently read" (288).

3. According to Robert S. Freeman, who defines "library" as a series of uniformly bound, uniformly priced books, the first library was Constable's Miscellany (1825); it was soon followed by Charles Knight's Library of Useful Knowledge and, two years later, Library of Entertaining Knowledge, published under the auspices of the Society for the Diffusion of Useful Knowledge. In the United States the practice of issuing books in libraries began with the Harper Brothers in the late 1820s.

4. Donald Sheehan explains, "In 1842, Park Benjamin began issuing the most popular of the English novels in paper covers at prices ranging from seven to twenty-five cents. The sales of these literary 'extras,' which were marketed like newspapers rather than books, reached such proportions that they upset the book market and led the regular publishers to retaliatory measures. Book prices lowered, and the first wide-scale effort of the trade to reach a mass buying public ensued" (62).

5. Those who originally framed the U.S. postal laws assumed that "the government had a responsibility to underwrite the dissemination of public information" and further recognized that the post office could play a role in sustaining national unity. Consequently, the newly created postal laws "facilitated the widespread circulation of news" through subsidies and other policies, the most important of which was a nearly flat rate structure for periodicals, established in 1792 and maintained almost continuously until 1917 (Kielbowicz, "Post Office" 524).

6. Carey's *Library of Choice Literature* (1835) was an early experiment in cheap book publishing which failed when the postal rates increased so that postage for these 10-cent volumes was nearly as much as the retail cost of the books (Tebbel 1: 242). A special "book rate" came into effect in 1940 by presidential order of Franklin D. Roosevelt; Congress added the book rate to the postal laws in 1942 (Kielbowicz, "Post Office" 525; see also Kielbowicz, "Mere Merchandise").

7. The American News Company was formed in New York City through the conglomeration of H. Dexter, Hamilton & Company and Tousey & Company. Sinclair Tousey became president of the new company; Henry Dexter, vice president; Solomon W. Johnson, treasurer; and John Hamilton and Patrick Farrelly, superintendents.

8. See *American Booksellers Guide* 2 (1870): 439. This trade journal, which was published by the ANC and supplied free of charge "to every Publisher, Bookseller, Newsdealer, Music-Dealer, and Stationer in the United States and Canada," stated, "The American News Company supply booksellers, music-dealers and stationers at publishers' rates. . . . Orders for any thing in the market, new or old, whether for one copy or one hundred, are filled by the Company at the publishers' lowest rates" (2 [1870]: 11). The American News Company grew to encompass several subsidiaries, including the Union News Company, the International News Company, and the New York Publishing Company (a mail-order business). During the twentieth century, it also provided a library service known as Readmore Lending Libraries. It was renamed Ancorp National Services in 1962; and a short time later it "phased out its book wholesaling business," concentrating instead on food service and newsstand operations. It merged with Sodexho in 1979, following "several years of financial and legal difficulties (including an investigation into organized

crime activities)" (Laura Miller 120 n). See the *Dictionary of Literary Biography*, volume 49, for the 1873 catalogue of the ANC.

9. The pattern of expansion of the American News Company roughly followed the extension of the railroads: Chicago (1866), St. Louis (1867), Philadelphia (1868), Boston (1868), Newark (1870), Albany (1870), Cincinnati, (1872), Pittsburgh (1872), Providence (1872), two more branches in New York City (1874), San Francisco (1875), Detroit (1876), Montreal (1880), Denver (1881), Kansas City (1881), Omaha (1881), St. Paul (1881), New Orleans (1882), Cleveland (1883), and Buffalo (1888).

10. E. C. Swayne of E. P. Dutton & Co. was reportedly "the first man to persuade drygoods houses to handle books as part of their stock" (*Seventy-five Years* 39). Writing in the early twentieth century, Francis Halsey declared that "no more remarkable influence has entered the trade than the influence of the dry-goods stores, where departments devoted to the sale of the day's popular books have grown to large proportions" (17). Robert Hertel notes that "by the 1880s, the large department stores had begun to form separate book departments which could cater to the bargain instincts of customers, because of quantity of purchase of books" (90).

11. In 1890 P. Farrelly of the American News Company estimated that about 20 percent of the printed matter supplied by the ANC was conveyed through the post (Wanamaker 132); the volume may have been higher in the previous two decades. It is important to note, too, that Farrelly's claim was made in defense of the vaguely defined periodical rates and may therefore have been an underestimation.

12. The *Tribune* published twenty-six such novels in ten years (Mott 151) under the editorship of Whitelaw Reid, who succeeded founding editor Horace Greeley in 1872.

13. According to Shove, "The Lakeside Library was the real pioneer among cheap quarto libraries in this country," since it "marked the first successful attempt to publish dime novels of good literature at regular intervals, in quarto form, and under the name 'library'" (5, 71).

14. The rivalry between these two brothers was fierce. Twice, Norman sued George for copying the name "Munro Publishing House" and allegedly sabotaging his brother's sales leads (Noel 125).

15. Howells's allusion to the Seaside Library (like his allusion to Daisy Miller in chapter 1) is thus an anachronism in a novel set in 1875.

16. Munro, a native of Nova Scotia, arrived in New York in 1856. In 1867 he launched the *New York Fireside Companion*, a popular family newspaper. George Munro & Company also published dime novels, including Harlan P. Halsey's popular Old Sleuth series.

17. The volume of novels published necessitated a highly mechanized book factory in Munro's new (1882) Manhattan quarters; see Comparato 125–26.

18. Regarding the firm Pollard & Moss, *Publishers' Weekly* complained in 1889, "They have been so far outside the lines of the 'regular' trade that we have found it almost impossible to get bibliographical record of their books each year, despite every effort on our part to do so" (qtd. in Shove 42). *PW* began to include the more popular of the cheap libraries in its annual summaries of new titles in 1881 (Shove 12). The ANC's *American Bookseller*, which "devote[d] particular attention to cheap 'libraries' and popular literature" (Growoll 22), regularly announced additions to the cheap series.

19. The absorption of other series helped Munro achieve national distribution by building on the regional strengths of individual series. Before 1879, for example, circulation of the Seaside had been confined almost exclusively to the East, whereas the Chicago-based Lakeside Library, which Munro acquired in 1879, had wide distribution in the West as well (*PW* 15 [1879]: 308; Shove 74).

20. The ANC was the prime distributor for the Seaside Library and, in later years, even established several reprint series of its own (Hertel 250): Superb Library (1899–1901), National Series (1906), and People's Library (1899–1904).

21. In a letter of 1879, Harper Brothers declared, "The Lakeside enterprise was followed by the Seaside, and both affairs were nourished by the American News Company, without whose encouragement they would have been short-lived" (qtd. in Harper 446).

22. The magnitude of these numbers is evident when one considers that at this time few hardbound novels sold more than a few thousand copies ("Cheap Books" [*Hour*], 498).

23. In 1885 the Seaside Library issued 465 new titles. Harper's Franklin Square Library, which was conceived as a means of mitigating the effects of other publishers' appropriating novels from *Harper's Weekly* and *Harper's Monthly* (Hertel 22), peaked in 1884 with 82 new titles.

24. When George Munro died in 1896, the trade journal *Publisher and Retailer* estimated that a thousand titles had been sold in Seaside editions, and speculated that their total sales over two decades "were not far short of being as many as of all the dollar and dollar-fifty novels ever published in this country" (qtd. in Tebbel 2: 490). Shove, however, calculates that "if the supposed minimum printing of ten thousand copies is taken as an average sale for each volume, the Seaside must have sold somewhere in the neighborhood of thirty million volumes by . . . 1890" and suggests that "there is reason to believe that the sale may have been even larger" (61).

25. Brander Matthews noted that "the Seaside Library, . . . the Franklin Square Library, and their fellows" were "devoted almost wholly to fiction; by actual count of their catalogues, nine volumes out of ten are novels" (2: 580).

26. Trade courtesy was a kind of "gentleman's agreement" whereby publishers granted exclusive rights of publication to the first one to announce plans to publish a particular title. Commenting on this "principle, or lack of principle, of *first grab*," I. K. Funk & Co. charged that "for three years it has been utterly broken in upon on the side of literature of doubtful value, so that the practical effect of this 'law' has been to handicap good books and to force bad books into millions of homes." Funk went on to plead that the principle of trade courtesy be restored: "In the absence of an international copyright law, it is urged that the house which introduces an author to the American public and makes a market for his books should be allowed to reap the full harvest" (499).

27. Copyrights, which were of forty-two years' duration, expired on works by Nathaniel Hawthorne, Oliver Wendell Holmes, Harriet Beecher Stowe, William Hicklin Prescott, and other "standard" American authors in the early 1890s (Hertel 107).

28. The point these correspondents made was a valid one. Four years earlier a writer for *Publishers' Weekly* had implored, "The cut-throat policy of both publishers and booksellers is largely the cause of the enormous quantity of cheap literature now flooding the market; and since the publisher persists in the effort to reduce the profits of the bookseller by underselling

him with his own customers, *is it surprising that the bookseller in turn should push this cheap stuff, even if it does pay only a small percentage of profit?*" (*PW* 18 [1880]: 187).

29. Shove points out that the practice of assigning an artificially high list price to allow the bookseller a substantial discount was customary at this time (89).

30. According to Comparato, Harper & Brothers' Franklin Square Library "almost unintentionally lent the whole cheap movement considerable respectability (despite some titles at 10¢, Harper still paid royalties on English works)" (128).

31. Shove explains, "At first they [the libraries] were sold almost exclusively by news dealers, the profit of three cents a copy not being sufficient to induce most booksellers to offer them in possible competition with more profitable editions on their shelves, but before long they came to be more and more handled by the latter" (8).

32. In 1870 the *American Bookseller's Guide* had cautioned, "Cheap substitutes abound for almost every thing of value. The newspaper is the cheap substitute for the book, and it will supply the place of the book unless publishers push books upon the public" ("The Men Who Advertise" 259).

33. In 1890, Postmaster General John Wanamaker summarized the conditions under which an item could be admitted to the second-class rate, according to an act of 3 March 1879: (1) "it must regularly be issued at stated intervals as frequently as four times a year, and bear a date of issue, and be numbered consecutively"; (2) "it must be issued from a known office of publication"; (3) "It must be formed of printed paper sheets, without board, cloth, leather, other substantial binding, such as distinguish printed books for preservation from periodical publications"; (4) "it must be originated and published for the dissemination of information of a public character, or devoted to literature, the sciences, arts, or some special industry, and having a legitimate list of subscribers" (129). It was within the power of local postmasters to grant or deny publications the special periodical rate, as evidenced by the temporary denial of the second-class rate to the Lakeside Library by the postal authorities in New York after three years of circulation at the periodical rate (Shove 73).

34. Some of the cheap publishers achieved this quick rate of publication (an entire novel could be produced in ten hours) by carrying on manufacturing as well as editorial functions "in house." Such houses, which often relied on poorly paid women typesetters, were derisively termed "sawmills" by the trade (see Shove 25, 29, 37).

35. The Seaside began to appear in a pocket (duodecimo) format at the end of 1883, and by 1887 these "handy" editions had supplanted the quarto version. Most of the other cheap libraries had switched to the pocket format earlier in response to the popularity of the cheap 12mos issued by John W. Lovell, by Belford, Clarke & Company, by Pollard, Moss & Company, and others. The Seaside's change in format was precipitated by the return of 1,200,000 Seaside Library books by the American News Company after other publishers had popularized the pocket editions (an indication of the tremendous influence of the ANC on the business of cheap book publishing). According to Shove, the new format "gave an impression of permanency more than did the old quartos, and offered a good field for experimentation" (21).

36. Some critics of the cheap libraries suspected that the subscription rates were merely a ruse to help support the pretense that these books were indeed periodicals. Postmaster General Wanamaker conjectured, "The probability always is that there are

either no subscribers at all, or none to speak of. In some cases, indeed, the advertised cost of single issues is much less than the purchaser would pay if he really subscribed for the books by the month or year—affording almost absolute proof that no subscriptions exist" (131). Annual subscription to the Seaside Library, however, was $36 in 1883 and had risen to $50 by 1886.

37. Hertel identifies an additional reason for the new emphasis on the marketing possibilities of book covers: "Since advertising in book trade journals became more expensive, paperback publishers had to restrict their advertising to the book itself, and depend upon an attractive paper cover to sell their paperbound series to the casual customer of the newsstand" (76).

38. Catalogue notice for the Seaside Library edition of *Miss Harrington's Husband* by Florence Marryat Lean (New York: George Munro 1886).

39. For a discussion of these effects, see Strasser, chap. 2.

40. This rate was reduced from three cents per pound in 1874 to two cents in 1879 and from two cents to one cent per pound in 1885.

41. In 1899, Postmaster General Charles E. Smith echoed these sentiments: "They do not possess a single one of the attributes which Congress meant to require in publications that should be entitled to the second-class rate. Their 'consecutive numbering' is a travesty; their issuance at 'stated intervals' a parody; their 'subscription list' a fiction; their claim of being published 'for the dissemination of information of a public character' a burlesque" (qtd. in Kielbowicz, "Mere Merchandise" 185).

42. In 1895, *PW* took it to be a "fact that paper-covered novels are in demand by the loungers on the sea-shore" ("Decadence of Cheap Books" 681).

43. Writing in 1879, Eugene Lemoine Didier similarly confounded form and content, declaring, "those 'cheap and nasty' 'libraries' which have flooded the country during the last two or three years . . . are the most villainous *things* in the shape of books that ever offended the eyes of man or woman. The devil combined with the lowest class of book pirates to produce this atrocious trash, which can only be called literature as the immortal daubs of Whistler ['made immortal by the terrible criticism of Ruskin'] are called art" (8).

44. Traditionally, the book industry had eschewed third-party advertising. The ANC's *American Bookseller's Guide* urged a more aggressive approach, asserting, "We believe books might have a much larger market than they enjoy, if book publishers had pursued a bolder course in advertising" ("The Men Who Advertise" 259). In 1890, "Craige Lippincott complained that his firm had sold for twenty cents books that cost nineteen cents to publish and that, for some publishers, the only profit was derived from the advertisements which were printed in the last pages of the book" (Hertel 51).

45. Hertel has a different version: "George Munro sold three million copies of his outmoded and unsalable quarto edition of the Seaside Library to a soap manufacturer for $30,000" (28).

46. Brodhead draws the following conclusions about readers of story-papers such as the *Ledger*: "At a nickel or dime an installment, story-papers also formed—and advertised that they formed—a cheaper entertainment than the magazine or hard-bound book of more genteel reading cultures. Their print formats geared them to readers poor in cultural as well as economic capital: in their materials and layout, story-papers produced literary writing

into a likeness with the most everyday reading matter of the most rudimentary literacy levels, the newspaper—a likeness reiterated by their emphasis on the series, the weekly renewal of standard formats, rather than the individual work of writing. . . . Mid-nineteenth century domestic fiction had its audience centered among people (often women) already possessing, or newly aspiring to, or at least mentally identifying with, the leisured, child-centered home of middle-class life. Story-paper fiction, while no doubt overlapping with domestic fiction's readership in part, is known to have incorporated many groups situated outside such feminized ease: farmboys, soldiers, German and Irish immigrants, and men and women of a newly solidifying working class" (78–79).

47. In my own unpublished sample of nearly two thousand titles (a work in progress), approximately 70 percent of the texts in the Seaside Library were British, 22 percent French, and 5 percent American.

48. In 1889, George Munro, detecting that the market for foreign reprints was becoming saturated, launched his Library of American Authors (not to be confused with Wiley and Putnam's canon-building Library of American Books), issued monthly, priced at 25 cents per volume, and including novels by Lucy Randall Comfort, Mary E. Bryan, Mrs. Alexander McVeigh Miller, Laura Jean Libbey, and others.

49. The *Critic* reported, "Encouraged by the success of 'The House on the Marsh,' Messrs. Appleton have followed it up with 'At the World's Mercy,' by the same author, which has also been published in the Seaside Library" ("Lounger" 198).

50. Tebbel explains: "Competition did not really catch up to Munro until 1887, when he was compelled to cut 'Seaside'"s wholesale price to ten cents for twenty- and twenty-five-cent numbers, and five cents for the ten-cent items. But the hoped for consequent sales' increase did not materialize; instead, drygoods stores sold out the books at less than half-price" (2: 489).

51. The pirating of the Seaside Library name prompted Munro to obtain a patent for the series on June 7, 1887.

52. Publishers of the cheap libraries opposed international copyright as long as there was money to be made in reprinting European works. Sheehan explains, "The distributors of cheap books, including some of the large jobbers, did not want to see their main source of supply dammed up [by an international copyright agreement]; after the Harpers shifted their views in 1878, the principal opponent was the American News Company" (214).

53. Some of the libraries (including the Seaside) continued to thrive for a few more years, weathering both the Chace Act of 1891 and the Panic of 1893.

54. The company exerted such power over the periodical business that Mary Noel attributes the failure of the *New York Mercury* in the early 1870s to the proprietors' tendency to "pick quarrels" with the American News Company and its precursors (107).

55. The impact of the cheap libraries on the book trade has been understated by critics who view the changes they brought about as temporary. Hertel, for example, stresses that they "upset traditional publishing practices, reduced opportunities for American authorship, prolonged the dependence of American culture upon English literature, and promoted price-slashing tactics which threatened the profits of publishers and booksellers. All parties which had suffered from the effects of widespread competition on uncopyrighted fiction . . . joined forces to restore the prosperity of the book trade through the enactment

of international copyright legislation" (190). See Schurman, "The Effect of Nineteenth-Century 'Libraries' on the American Book Trade."

## 5. INNOCENCE ABROAD

1. The subtitle "A Story" appeared in the book's initial announcement in *Publishers' Weekly*. It does not appear in the published volume.

2. "Daisy Miller: A Study" first appeared in the *Cornhill Magazine* in June and July 1878. Two American periodicals quickly pirated it: *Littell's Living Age* in July 1878 and *Home Journal* in July and August (using the subtitle "Americans Abroad"). The first authorized American edition, a 32mo paper-covered pamphlet, priced at 20 cents, issued from Harper's on 1 November 1878 as part of *Harper's Half-Hour Series* (Ohi 46–47). The same year, Harper & Brothers released another edition as *Daisy Miller: An International Episode*. James had first submitted the story to *Lippincott's Magazine*, which returned the manuscript without comment; it has generally been assumed that the editor found the story offensive to American womanhood. This is sheer speculation, however, and it is certainly possible that the topic seemed too familiar, or overdone. A. K. Loring (who published Alcott's *Moods* and other "Books for Young Ladies") published James's story "A Bundle of Letters" in an unauthorized edition that was pirated again by George Munro, who put it in the Seaside Library in the same volume as Sir Walter Besant's *Sweet Nelly, My Heart's Delight*. James was not a fan of Besant; what he thought of the Seaside Library can only be imagined.

3. According to Reilly and Hall, by the mid-eighteenth century "American booksellers and writers [had begun] to issue books and periodicals linked to gender" (397).

4. Nina Baym applies the label "woman's fiction" to a specific subset of writing for women and by women that shares certain recurring motifs and plot elements: "This fiction was by far the most popular literature of its time [1820–70], and on the strength of that popularity, authorship in America was established as a woman's profession, and reading as a woman's avocation" (*Woman's Fiction* 11).

5. On the feminization of travel writing, see Dolan, *Ladies of the Grand Tour*.

6. Katherine Swett makes a similarly relevant point: "The post-bellum feminization of travel, like the antebellum feminization of literature, was both attractive and threatening to male writers such as Howells and James," who faced a "decision in relation to their female audiences. They wanted to please them even as they questioned the women's right to be there in the first place" (21–22).

7. Habegger offers encouragement in this endeavor, urging, "It is necessary to take a longer, closer look at the many women's narratives that helped compose the literary cosmos James grew up in" (15).

8. Twenty-five years earlier, a review of *Daisy Miller* in the *Pall Mall Gazette* had asserted, "Indeed, he [James] has revealed to many of us a new distinct variety of womankind in these sketches of American girls" (qtd. in Hayes 74).

9. The author of a 1995 dissertation on the theme of the American girl abroad, for example, writes, "Between 1874 and 1881, one may argue that the American Girl Abroad was willed into literary existence by Henry James and William Dean Howells" (Matsukawa 34).

10. Writing in 1936, Ralph Thompson observed, "The now-familiar theme of a rich American girl's seeking to marry a titled foreigner—or vice-versa—is at least a century old, as is shown in *The Gift* 1837 by Mrs. E. C. Embury's 'The Count and the Cousin'" (35). Several contemporary reviews of James's fiction also indicated that the theme of the American (girl) abroad was a familiar one. A review of *Daisy Miller* in the *Pall Mall Gazette* (March 1879) remarked that "Travelling Americans are a tempting subject, and many people have attempted to describe them" (qtd. in Hayes 74); and a review of *The Europeans* in the *Atlantic Monthly* (February 1879) admitted that "one cannot help wishing that our native authors would have done with this incessant drawing of comparisons between ourselves and the folk in Europe, and our respective ways of living, thinking, and talking" (qtd. in Hayes 63). James complained in an 1865 review of Alcott's *Moods* that "we are utterly weary of stories about precocious little girls" (qtd. in Anthony 179).

11. As Carl Bode explains, "Works on travel dot the pages of Orville Roorbach's antebellum bibliographies; lectures on travel became one of the staples of the lyceum system; and novels and short stories with a faraway setting grew in number" (222). Ronald Zboray's research into reading patterns in antebellum America suggests that next to novels, travel writing was the most popular genre (163); Mary Suzanne Schriber notes that "of more than 1,800 books (in addition to innumerable articles in periodicals) of foreign travel by Americans published in America before 1900, some 195 . . . were the work of women" (*Telling Travels* xxi), and the number was escalating toward the close of the century.

12. Already, by the 1870s, publishers were actively promoting books for summer reading at the start of the season. These typically included tour guides, travel narratives, and novels.

13. Barbara Sicherman suggests that reading was a way for Victorian women to "overcome some of the confines of gender and class," for "reading provided space—physical, temporal, and psychological—that permitted women to exempt themselves from traditional gender expectations, whether imposed by formal society or by family obligation" ("Sense and Sensibility" 202).

14. Thompson alludes to Whittier's poem "Maude Muller's Spring."

15. *Shawl-Straps* originally appeared as a serial in Henry Ward Beecher's paper, *The Christian Union*, March 13, 20, 27, and April 3, 1872 (5. 12–15) and was republished the same year as volume 2 of *Aunt Jo's Scrap-Bag*.

16. As far back as 1724, Mary Astell wrote in her preface to Lady Mary Wortley Montagu's "Embassy Letters" that "whilst it [the World] is surfeited with Male Travels, all in the same Tone, and stuft with the same Trifles, a *Lady* has the skill to strike out a New Path and to embellish a worn-out Subject with a variety of fresh and elegant Entertainment" (qtd. in Dolan 272). See also Foster 52.

17. In *Shawl-Straps*, Alcott casts herself as "Lavinia," her younger sister May as "Matilda," and May's friend Alice Bartlett (also a friend of Henry James) as "Amanda." Alcott drew on her earlier journey to Europe as a paid companion in the second part of *Little Women*, which records Amy's career as companion to Aunt March. A review in *Harper's New Monthly Magazine* questioned "whether to class *Shawl-Straps* . . . with fiction or with books of travel. It is the latter under the guise of the former" ("Editor's Literary

Record" 616). For a discussion of the Alcott-Bartlett-James connection, see Wadsworth, "What Daisy Knew."

18. The similarity between the maiden and married names of author and protagonist (Mary [Elizabeth] Murdoch [Mason] and Mae Madden [Mann]) strongly suggests a close identification between the two. In 1872, Mary Murdoch married Alfred Bishop Mason, an editorial writer for the *Chicago Tribune*. Mason, who had graduated from Yale in 1871, was admitted to the bar in 1875 and published a *Primer of Political Economy* the same year. He held the positions of president of the Jacksonville, Tampa & Key West Railroad (1883–89) and of American Cotton Oil Co. (1892), president of Vera Cruz & Pacific Railroad in Mexico (1898–1902), and president of Cauca Railroad in Colombia, South America (1905–7). In the early twentieth century he wrote boys' books (the *Tom Strong* series) as well as several works of nonfiction. Apart from *Mae Madden*, the only published works of Mary Murdoch Mason's that I have been able to discover are four sketches ("Unknown Persons," "Three Christmases," "Joke of the Gemini," and "The Flying Man"); a history of New York coauthored with her husband ("The Fourteen Miles Round"); three poems ("Once, When a Child," "O Brothers Blind!" and "The Surgeon's Hand"); two children's stories ("Bob and Joshua, and Balaam" and "The Admiral and the Midshipmite"); and a review titled "The Fourth Art." She died in 1912. I am indebted to James Keeline for supplying biographical leads on Alfred Bishop Mason.

19. A slightly longer version of this poem, "A Dream of Italy; An Allegory Introducing 'Mae Madden,'" appears in Miller's *Songs of Italy* (1878) under the title "The Ideal and the Real"; a sequel, "The Ideal and the Real, Part II," is dated "Venice, 1874." Two concluding stanzas appended to the version in *Mae Madden* carry the date "Chicago, Nov. 1875." The connection between Mary Murdoch Mason and Joaquin Miller is somewhat vague, though both authors were published by Jansen, McClurg, and Miller was in Italy the year prior to the publication of *Mae Madden* (1874–75). Miller's novel *The One Fair Woman* (published in 1876, a few months after *Mae Madden*) features an "unabashed American abroad, young Mollie Wopsus" (*American National Biography*), based on Mrs. Frank Leslie (Miriam Follin Squier) of *Leslie's Magazine*, and Miller dedicated his 1884 autobiography, *Memorie and Rime*, "To Miriam." In 1892 Miller alleged that *Daisy Miller* was based on *The One Fair Woman*. See Frost, 75–79.

20. Jansen, McClurg was "one of the largest and most successful houses of the West"; General McClurg, one of the partners, had been chief of staff to Jefferson Davis during the Civil War ("Personal Mention" 958).

21. Matsukawa notes, "In Europe, the American Girl Abroad that we encounter in fiction rarely traveled with a full set of parents—she was either with a chaperon or her mother or with siblings—and therefore she was allowed the liberty of compensating for the lack of male authority by taking on some of the characteristics of the 'man of the house'" (26).

22. Mae hails from New England, somewhere near the Hudson River valley, and Mason singles out New York girls for admiration, writing, "Praise Parisian models all you will, but for genuine style, a New York girl, softened a trifle by commonsense or good taste, leads the world—certainly if she is abroad" (65–66).

23. Quotations from *Daisy Miller* are from the original printing (*Cornhill Magazine*), as reproduced in the Penguin Classics edition, edited by Geoffrey Moore.

24. On the experience of Americans in Italy during the nineteenth century, see Van Wyck Brooks, *The Dream of Arcadia: American Writers and Artists in Italy, 1760–1915* (New York: E. P. Dutton, 1958); Paul R. Baker, *The Fortunate Pilgrims: Americans in Italy, 1800–1860* (Cambridge: Harvard UP, 1964); Nathalia Wright, *American Novelists in Italy: The Discoverers: Allston to James* (Philadelphia: U of Pennsylvania P, 1965); and Erik Amfitheatrof, *The Enchanted Ground: Americans in Italy, 1760–1980* (Boston: Little, Brown, 1980). Shirley Foster's chapter on Italy in *Across New Worlds* is also helpful.

25. As Richard Brodhead notes, *Corinne* was "one of the works that most helped to romanticize Rome and expatriate women artists for nineteenth-century audiences" (qtd. in Staël 477 n). See Dolan for a discussion of eighteenth-century women writers who sought "to elevate themselves through travel" (5).

26. A fine example is Constance Fenimore Woolson's story "At the Chateau of Corinne," in which an American woman poet is forced to choose between her art and the man who loves her but scorns literary women as traitors to their sex, declaring of Madame de Staël, "'A woman of genius'! And what is the very term but a stigma! No woman is so proclaimed by the great brazen tongue of the Public unless she has thrown away her birthright of womanly seclusion for the miserable mess of pottage called 'fame'" (263).

27. Daisy's insistence on seeing the Coliseum at night is probably indirectly linked to a passage from *Corinne*: "You cannot know the feeling aroused by the Colosseum if you have seen it only by day. In the Italian sunshine there is a brilliance which gives everything a festive air, but the moon is the star of ruins. Sometimes, through the apertures in the amphitheatre which seems to rise up to the skies, a part of heaven's vault appears behind the building like a dark blue curtain. Plants, which cling to dilapidated walls and grow in lonely places, take on the colours of the night; the soul, finding itself alone with nature, shudders and is touched at the same time" (Staël 276).

28. See Dolan for further discussions of the contrast between restrictions at home and freedom abroad for British women travelers.

29. The tragic figure of Margaret Fuller, who had become almost legendary as a "New England Corinne" (James, *William Wetmore Story* 1: 128), surely hovered over these narratives of American women in Italy. Fuller, who married the Marquis Angelo Ossoli in Italy, drowned in 1850 with her husband and child when the ship in which they were returning to America was wrecked off Fire Island.

30. Hunter's research into nineteenth-century girls' reading corroborates that "there were appropriate ages for the reading of different books" (65).

31. These were *Tom Strong, Washington's Scout* (1911), *Tom Strong, Boy Captain* (1913), *Tom Strong, Junior* (1915), *Tom Strong, Third* (1916), and *Tom Strong, Lincoln's Scout* (1919).

32. Woolson's story "The Front Yard" tells the other "what if" story suggested by *Mae Madden*: American heroine marries Italian "child of the sun" and becomes a hard-worn peasant woman.

33. In a letter of August 1872 to his brother William, James wrote that he "must give up the ambition of ever being a free-going and light-paced enough writer to please the multitude," adding, "The multitude, I am more and more convinced, has absolutely no taste—none at least that a thinking man is bound to defer to" (qtd. in Gard 27). Adeline R. Tintner notes that

in James's "first signed tale, 'The Story of the Year' (March 1865), . . . certain details indicate that he may have been reading [Alcott's] *Hospital Sketches*. . . . James's early tales contain many borrowings from literature and in his own words show 'an admirable commerce of borrowing and lending . . . not to say stealing and keeping'" (265).

34. Most critics follow Edel in tracing the germ of *Daisy Miller* to this real-life anecdote, but a few have sought textual models for the novella. Some have pointed to the novel *Paule Méré* by the French writer Cherbuliez (to which James alludes directly in *Daisy Miller* 22 by having Mrs. Costello request that her nephew bring her a copy of this novel when he comes to Rome) as a source for *Daisy Miller*, but others disagree. Katharine Anthony suggests that Louisa May Alcott's experiences abroad may have influenced James, writing of *Daisy Miller*: "This is all exceedingly reminiscent of Louisa's adventures with her Polish youth (Ladislas) in Vevey and Paris; they were to have met in Rome, but never did. Louisa Alcott had already used the Vevey episode for her Americanized Jo and Laurie, and Henry James used it all over again in his first successful novel of manners. Not often is a romance found to be so fruitful" (178–79). It is also significant that James sometimes rode on the Campagna with another Alice—Alice Mason (no known relation to Mary Murdoch Mason)—whom he had known as a child living in Paris (Novick 263). Alice Mason, a cousin of Clover Hooper Adams (wife of Henry Adams), shared a flat in Rome with Alice Bartlett and was awaiting a divorce from her husband, Massachusetts Senator Charles Sumner (this scandal, which had its own resemblance to Daisy's, would filter into Henry Adams's novel *Democracy*). James found Alice Mason "superior & very natural," "very charming," and "lovely"— though "limited by a kind of characteristic American want of culture" (W. James 198, 274). (See also note 19, above.)

35. I don't want to claim that James never thought of the kinds of characters, conflicts, and themes he presents in *Daisy Miller* before *Mae Madden* appeared. In *Watch and Ward* (serialized in the *Atlantic Monthly* in 1871, published separately in 1878), in *Roderick Hudson*, and in his early short fiction, James contrasts the social prohibitions of Europe with the relative freedom of America and presents male characters perplexed by the mingled audacity and innocence of the young American woman. Nevertheless, the similarity between *Daisy Miller* and *Mae Madden* and James's close connection to Perry and the *Nation* strongly suggest that the parallels between the two are more than coincidental.

36. Henry James Jr. to Henry James Sr., 4 March 1873, *Selected Letters* 100.

37. Henry James Jr. to Grace Norton, 5 March 1873, *Selected Letters* 103.

38. In the twelve-month period surrounding the *Nation*'s notice of *Mae Madden*, James contributed no fewer than sixteen reviews (unsigned) to this weekly periodical. Writing to his parents from Florence on 16 November 1873, he had affirmed: "The *Nation* as you say is appreciative & I shall cling to it devoutly. . . . I could easily review a book a week for it if I could only get the books" (Henry James Papers. bMS Am 1094[1817]); *Henry James Letters* 1: 411. The difficulty of getting eligible books to review he repeated in a letter to his brother William in March 1876: "I would do more for the *Nation* but I have no English books" (*Henry James Letters* 2: 34).

39. Perry contributed numerous reviews and articles to the *Nation* from 1871 until 1878. He also contributed newsletters to the London *Academy* from 1874 to 1876 and additional reviews to the *Atlantic* and *North American Review*.

40. Perry refers to *L'Etrangère*, which opened at the Theatre Français in the winter of 1876. James reviewed it in his letter to the *New York Tribune* dated February 28, 1876 (*Parisian Sketches* 84–91).

41. In addition to reviewing for the *Nation*, James published no fewer than three books around the time of *Mae Madden*, all of different genres: *A Passionate Pilgrim, and Other Tales*; *Transatlantic Sketches*; and *Roderick Hudson*. Thus, in a single year he was able to test the marketability of his travel sketches, short stories, and novel (specifically, a novel about an American who travels to Italy) and gain a sense of the relative demand for each. The fact that the travel sketches sold in significantly higher numbers than the fiction (White 207) must have provided a powerful incentive to the young James, who was striving to support himself through his writing. At the same time, through his reviewing for the *Nation*, James learned about what kinds of novels other people (primarily women) were writing and what kinds of books were selling.

42. Prospectus for the New York *Nation*, *The Nation* Papers. bMS Am 1083.2(70).

43. James Russell Lowell to Edwin L. Godkin, 11 July and 17 October 1874, Edwin L. Godkin Papers, bMS Am 1083(510, 512). In the October letter, Lowell urged, "Did I ever tell you that the *Nation* cannot be bought in Paris? There should be an agency there, for there would be a sale & the paper would do good. In Geneva I got it regularly for ten cents." It is possible that, following Lowell's suggestion, Godkin had arranged a Paris agent by 1876. In a letter to Howells dated 3 February 1876 (the precise date of the number of the *Nation* that carried the brief notice of *Mae Madden*), James mentioned that he had seen the latest issue of the *Atlantic Monthly* at Galignani's, the well-known English-language bookshop in Paris (Anesko 115; *Henry James Letters* 2: 23). A year later, after he had moved to London, James reported that he subscribed to Mudie's, the popular lending library, and borrowed six books at a time (*Henry James: A Life in Letters* 76).

44. Henry James Jr. to Mrs. Henry James, Sr., 13 July [1872]; Henry James Jr. to Henry James Sr., 15 September [1872]; Henry James Jr. Mrs. Henry James, Sr., 17 February [1873], Henry James Papers. bMS Am 1094(1781, 1790, 1802; *Henry James Letters* 1: 342). Writing from Switzerland on 11 August 1874, James notified his father of an interruption in his receipt of the *Nation*: "You say you send me the *Nation* regularly; but it doesn't come" (James Papers, bMS Am 1094[1784]). On 29 September 1876, James asked Arthur George Sedgwick, "Would you kindly add your efforts to [Wendell Phillips] Garrison's, by the way, to ensure the *Nation*'s being sent me" (*Henry James Letters* 2: 68).

45. Habegger describes his study as "not simply of one particular male writer but of the interaction between him and a whole insurgent culture of female writers, who, from his point of view, often looked like usurpers wrongly established from the first." He adds: "What I have to tell is to some extent the story of the collision and interaction of two different ways of dreaming the world, male and female. The opposing daydreams mesh, and do not mesh; but they meet in James's powerful imagination" (15).

46. With respect to May Marcy McClellan—another Mae/May (as well as another "MMM")—who lived in Florence and "had published a gossipy letter in the New York *World* (14 November 1886) about some members of Venetian nobility" (Gillen 75), James wrote: "Good heavens, what a superfluous product is the smart, forward, over-encouraged,

thinking-she-can-write-and-that-her-writing-has-any-business-to-exist American girl! Basta!"
(*Henry James Letters* 3: 155).

47. As a review for the *Graphic* (5 April 1879) shrewdly observed, "Daisy Miller, . . . and her strange freaks and caprices, are altogether an episode in the life of Winterbourne, the man through whose eyes we are made to see her" (qtd. in Hayes 75).

48. Habegger observes: "With few exceptions James's heroines would either connive at their own defeat, or their creator would weaken their powers of resistance at the critical moment. Why is Daisy Miller the one who dies of malaria, even though Giovanelli and Winterbourne are also exposed? Behind James's narratives there is found the ancient theory that women are weaker than men. Daisy, Isabel, and Verena, like Joyce's Gerty, have been lamed in secret by their author" (26).

49. In an early review of James's fiction, Thomas Powell had written: "None of his books end in a conventional way, probably because he is not a conventional writer, and those who look for 'and they lived together happily ever after' at the end of the last chapter of any of his novelettes will be disappointed" (qtd. in Hayes 9).

50. New York's Madison Square Theatre rejected the play in 1882 (the year of its composition), and the following year it appeared in the *Atlantic Monthly*, having failed to make the desired transition from page to stage. Later in 1883, James R. Osgood of Boston published *Daisy Miller: A Comedy* in book form, and at least one twentieth-century critic (William T. Stafford) has speculated that the play has never been produced (*James's Daisy Miller* 43).

51. In the *Atlantic Monthly* (April 1879), Howells wrote, "He [James] has already made his public" (qtd. in Gard 31).

## 6. A BLUE AND GOLD MYSTIQUE

1. I am grateful to Stuart T. Walker of the Boston Public Library for offering valuable insights into the ways the cover design of *A Garland for Girls* mimics, but doesn't strictly conform to, the designs of the highly regarded Boston designer Sarah Wyman Whitman. I am also extremely grateful to Jeffrey Groves, Libby Chenault, and Doris O'Keefe for supplying bibliographical data, clarifications, and additional insights into the production and growth of the Blue and Gold series.

2. Ironically, the kinds of tales Carrie enjoys are just the sort Alcott produced for the *Saturday Evening Gazette* and *The Flag of Our Union*.

3. Ouida (1840–1908) is best known today as the author of *A Dog of Flanders*. In a slightly earlier periodical version of "Pansies" (*St. Nicholas* 15 [November 1887]: 12–19), the references to the "Seaside Library" and *Wanda* are veiled, with Carrie "turning the crumpled leaves of a cheap copy of a sentimental and impossible tale" (12). It is likely that Mary Mapes Dodge, the editor of *St. Nicholas*, was responsible for the omission of the specifics.

4. Nahant, a peninsula adjacent to Lynn, Massachusetts, was a popular seaside resort in the nineteenth century. Between 1850, when the Longfellow family spent the first of many summers there, and the early 1880s, it became a kind of "Harvard Summer Annex," hosting

many New England luminaries, including Emerson, Hawthorne, Holmes, Lowell, and Whittier, in addition to Longfellow and James T. Fields (Paterson and Seaburg 85).

5. Hewins (20, 113–14) also mentions reading several books by Anna Jameson, "a widely known art critic and nineteenth-century taste maker" (Thomas, "Anna Jameson" 54), who, with nine volumes, had more titles in Ticknor and Fields's Blue and Gold series than any other author.

6. Before Lee & Shepard acquired and revamped Oliver Optic's early books, the firm of Phillips, Sampson published them in blind-stamped blue cloth identical, or nearly identical, in shade to that of Ticknor and Fields's Blue and Gold editions. Larger than the compact Blue and Gold volumes and embellished with gilt lettering and illustrations on the spine, these may have been the "cheap gilt children's books" that Stedman had in mind.

7. Longfellow alludes to *Cyder, a Poem* (London, 1708) by John Philips (1676–1709).

8. That the Blue and Gold editions continued to influence the popular imagination beyond 1868, the year Ticknor and Fields stopped adding new titles to the series, is indicated by the fact that Alcott wrote "Pansies" in 1887. The significance the publisher ascribed to the books' physical design is suggested by the fact that the series title reflects the binding, in contrast to designations such as "Standard Authors" (person-focused) or "Little Classics" (text-focused).

9. A twentieth-century analogue for this phenomenon is the Modern Library, an inexpensive, nicely bound publisher's series featuring classic (or would-be classic) writers.

10. These allusions take on additional significance in light of the fact that a number of different color-coded series developed by other publishers did not receive such attention. James Miller published a series of "Green and Gold" editions, for example, and near the end of the century Harper produced its "Black and White Series." In addition, many publishers advertised "Red Line Editions" in which the text was framed by a red border, and the firm of Thomas Y. Crowell was noted for its "Red Line Poets" (Lehmann-Haupt 228).

11. Thomas Currier notes, "It seems to have been the plan, not destined to be fulfilled, to include Whittier's prose writings in the series of Blue and Gold editions, for the Atlantic Monthly for June and July, 1864, advertises such a volume as 'in preparation'" (81). According to Currier, "The similarity between Ticknor's Blue and Gold binding and that of Routledge's London edition of Whittier's poems, 1853, indicates whence the idea of the former may have originated" (81). Jeffrey D. Groves elaborates: "In the early 1850s . . . Routledge published pocket editions of several American poets, including Holmes, Longfellow, and Lowell. These books were bound in blue cloth with gold ornamentation and edges. They probably served as direct models for Ticknor and Fields's blue and gold design" (98).

12. An article in the *Round Table* in 1864 related, "It was in 1856 that Mr. James T. Fields, having in mind Leigh Hunt's pleasant praise of pocket volumes, went to the Riverside Press with a little English book, and said to the printer that he wished to get up a small handy volume, something like the one he held, to contain all of Tennyson, and with type sufficiently large to be easily read" ("Literary Notes" 140).

13. William D. Ticknor to G. P. Putnam, 14 June 1856, Ticknor and Fields Papers, bMS Am 2030.2.

14. Michael Winship explains: "The 'blue and gold' style was an immediate success. A total of 11,204 copies in five printings of Tennyson's *The Poetical Works* . . . were produced by the end of 1856. In December a second title was issued in the same 'blue and gold' binding: two printings of 5,000 copies each of Longfellow's *Poems* . . . in two volumes were produced that month" (*American Literary Publishing* 124).

15. Around 1862, Alcott had submitted to Fields the manuscript of "Success" (later, "Work"). After reviewing it, Fields reportedly replied, "Stick to your teaching; you can't write" (Alcott, *Journals* 109). He later regretted his dismissal of Alcott's talent and engaged her to write several stories for the *Atlantic Monthly*, which he edited from 1861 to 1870.

16. According to Caroline Ticknor, Tennyson "recalled the fact that the first check (wholly unsolicited) ever paid by an American firm to an English author was received by him in 1842 from the Boston house" (76). As a result, Tennyson granted exclusive American rights to Ticknor and Fields; the firm printed his statement, "It is my wish that with Messrs. TICKNOR AND FIELDS alone the right of publishing my books in America should rest," in the front of their Blue and Gold edition of his poems (see also Eidson's *Tennyson in America*). His wish seems to have been well respected but did not prevent Harper Bros. from bringing out an edition of Tennyson poetry in the 1860s.

17. As Kilgour notes, "When Ticknor and Fields acquired from Little, Brown and Co. a famous series of English poets, it was asserted that this addition of the older writers made Ticknor and Fields the greatest publishers of poetry in the English-speaking world" (*Mssrs. Roberts Brothers* 22).

18. Fields's *Poems* (Boston: W. D. Ticknor) appeared in 1849, followed in 1881 by his *Ballads and Other Verses* (Boston: Houghton Mifflin).

19. See William Charvat, "James T. Fields and the Beginnings of Book Promotion" (*Profession of Authorship*).

20. As Groves explains, Ticknor and Fields achieved a recognizable imprint by marshaling a set of disparate texts into a series of "visually similar books" that allowed the buyer to "identify a Ticknor and Fields book at a glance" (78). The compelling appearance of these volumes enabled them to function as "visual signs crafted and repeated to encourage consumers to associate good literature with specific binding designs" (92).

21. James Redpath likewise brought out Alcott's *Hospital Sketches* in a 25-cent paper edition for a military readership.

22. The Cabinet Editions, which commenced as a series in 1864, used the same plates but each one combined the two Blue and Gold volumes into a single volume printed on larger paper. Apparently, Fields felt that the Blue and Gold margins were too narrow (Tryon and Charvat, *Cost Books* 363). A writer for the *Round Table* concurred that "the narrowness of the margin in this series has been an objection to some who wish to place them upon the shelf" ("Literary Notes" 140). Printing from the same plates on larger paper mitigated this defect. Roberts Brothers followed Ticknor and Fields, issuing books in their own imitative Blue and Gold and Cabinet Editions. Some British publishers also featured Cabinet Editions.

23. The audience Ticknor and Fields hoped to appeal to with the Diamond Editions (named for the small "diamond" font it used) is evident in a letter from Fields to Whittier (dated 27 September 1866): "The price pr vol. (each poet is to be in *one*) is to be *cheap*,

*cheap, cheap,* so as to open a market far away among the unbuying crowd hidden away in the dust holes of our country" (qtd. in Currier 107). Well suited to prose works, Diamond Editions were used extensively for Dickens's works.

24. The cost books of Ticknor and Fields list concurrent, or nearly concurrent, editions of Longfellow that included their "Farringford Edition" in addition to Cabinet, Blue and Gold, Diamond, Popular, and Red Line editions. Entries for Tennyson's poems included all of these plus "People's Edition," "Pocket Edition," "Half Dollar Edition," and "Globe Edition" (Cost Book, 1867–70, Ticknor and Fields Papers, bMS Am 2030.2).

25. It is important to recognize that, although the Blue and Gold volumes were relatively inexpensive, they were not minimally priced. Ticknor and Fields did sell pamphlets for as little as 25 cents between 1843 and 1860 but "published little in the way of cheap books" and "were famous throughout the nation for good taste, quality paper, printing, and binding" (Tryon, "Ticknor and Fields" 594). The Blue and Gold editions were typically priced between 75 cents for a single volume and $1.75 for a two-volume set, reflecting the high quality (and costs) of the paper, printing, and binding. (The average daily wage for a semiskilled worker was about $1.00.)

26. Commenting on Victorian book series, Leslie Howsam explains, "When publishers constructed systems like the Cornhill Library of Fiction, the Aldine Edition of the British Poets, or Redway's Shilling Series they were commissioning or resurrecting texts, then transmitting them to readers in such a way that the sum of the collected books was greater than their individual parts" (5). Also writing of the British market, Margaret Ezell observes that "once an author, for whatever reason was included in a series, he was likely to remain there throughout the nineteenth century. This practice, of course, had the effect of solidifying his or her reputation as a classic writer because of the continuing presence of the texts in these series; these texts, by virtue of their slot in a series, acquired 'timelessness,' the hallmark of a 'classic'" (14). With specific reference to Ticknor and Fields, Richard Brodhead has argued that once Fields had "gained monopolistic hold on the writings of Hawthorne, Emerson, Longfellow," he next "contrived the means to identify them as classics" and "then transferred this cachet to the new authors his publishing instruments brought to public life" (153).

27. A reviewer for the *Ladies' Repository* declared of *The Poetical Works of James Gates Percival* (1859), "As to the style in which these two volumes are gotten up, it is enough to say that they appear in the 'blue and gold' series of Messrs. Ticknor & Fields. This is our favorite edition of the British and American poets" ("Literary Notices" 442).

28. A reviewer for the *Southern Literary Messenger* was among many who pointed to "the luxurious style of blue and gold first employed by Ticknor and Fields, and made by them so popular" ("Notices of New Works" [1860] 320). The author of a "historical sketch of commercial bookbindings" (1894) affirmed that "the 'blue-and-gold' editions of various poets were hailed rapturously as novelties of the most 'elegant and refined' character, and the fashion died hard" (*Commercial Bookbindings* 7). The series inspired many imitators who hoped to associate their own titles with the Ticknor and Fields imprimatur. The *Round Table* explained, "Several publishers in New York and Philadelphia have issued some very cheap imitations of this 'blue and gold' style, which has hardly, however, affected the character of the originals with buyers of any discrimination. They have rather damaged

their own reputation by attempts to foist upon the unsuspecting the spurious for the genuine" ("Literary Notes" 140).

29. Conscious of the value placed on the series by the literati, Ticknor and Fields reportedly lowered the authors' royalty rate on the series from the standard 10 percent. Bayard Taylor complained in a letter of 14 February 1865, "They [T&F] actually insist on reducing the copyright [royalty] on their blue-and-gold editions to 7 *per cent.* on the retail price. This *I* have not submitted to, altho' they assure me that Longfellow, Holmes and Whittier have accepted" (*Selected Letters* 237). The large sales of the series may, of course, have compensated for the smaller royalty. According to the *Round Table* (1864), "The aggregate sales of the 'blue and gold' are now largely ahead of the same work in its less portable form. It is fair to say that the circulation of our popular poets in this shape is from three to five times larger than in the other styles, and in particular instances the difference is still greater" ("Literary Notes" 140). Winship lists the Blue and Gold Longfellow and the Blue and Gold Tennyson among the firm's most popular works from 1840 to 1859, giving numbers of copies produced as 24,308 for the Tennyson and 19,417 for the Longfellow (*American Literary Publishing* 55). The *Round Table* reported in 1864 that "Longfellow leads the rest [of the familiar poets of this series]. He circulates one-fourth to one-third more than Tennyson, who comes next, and about double the number of . . . Whittier, Holmes, Saxe, and Lowell, which four as a group occupy the third position of prominence. After these come at about the same grade, Adelaide Proctor, Owen Meredith, and Gerald Massey" ("Literary Notes" 140).

30. Even those who faulted the poets praised the volumes. Commenting on the Blue and Gold Whittier, a reviewer for the *New Orleans Picayune* declared, "The name of the most charming poet of New England is the synonym of abolitionist, and disfiguring the pages of one of the most beautiful collections of poems in the language. . . . Even the author of 'Hiawatha' and 'Evangeline' [Longfellow] has made his published works a distasteful addition to a Southern library, by mingling with the pure gold the basest alloy" (qtd. in Currier 83).

31. Many series in 32mo were not so easy on the eyes. As Richard Altick observes, "A magnifying glass may not always have been needed to read them . . . but it often would have helped" (*English Common Reader* 16n). Difficulty of reading was, in fact, a complaint frequently lodged against Ticknor and Fields's Diamond Editions.

32. The emphasis on taste that frequently appears in reference to Ticknor and Fields's Blue and Gold editions is nowhere more evident than in reviews of Mrs. Jameson's books, which epitomized, for nineteenth-century readers, exquisite taste both in content and in form. A reviewer for the *Southern Literary Messenger* announced, for example, that "Mrs. Jameson's 'Sketches of Art' is another one of those aurea-cerulean duodecimos which these tasteful publishers were the first to issue and which has [*sic*] become so popular. Mrs. Jameson is a genial and sympathetic writer and her art-criticisms are worthy of being read by all who would form correct opinions upon the aesthetic" ("Notices of New Works" [1858] 160).

33. Winship notes, "The cost books record the firm's attempts to achieve the desired volume size. On 29 April the firm ordered twenty reams measuring 22 in. × 29 in. from Tileston & Hollingsworth, but this paper was not used. It was replaced on 6 and 7 May

with a slightly larger paper of 22½ in. × 29 in., which was used in the first and second printings of *The Poetical Works of Alfred Tennyson*, the first volume in the series. For the third printing in July an even larger sheet measuring 22 ¾ in. x 29 in. was ordered, and this became the standard size of paper for volumes in what was soon to be one of the firm's most successful series" (*American Literary Publishing* 101).

34. In a similar vein, the *Round Table* pronounced it "convenient for the pocket and easy to the hand under circumstances when a more cumbrous volume would be unhandy" ("Literary Notes" 140), and the *Ladies' Repository* described the Blue and Gold edition of *The Poetical Works of William Motherwell* as "one of the most convenient and beautiful editions extant" ("Literary Notices" 377). Note the contrast between these portable volumes (implicitly suited to the pleasure journey or the leisurely ramble) and those of the Seaside Library (also portable, but associated, in spite of their name, with railway stations and street corners).

35. Irving's *Sketch-Book* and Hawthorne's *Twice-told Tales* are notable exceptions to the pattern. Most of the nonfiction prose titles are serious prose (philosophical essays, art criticism, etc.) rather than light prose, such as travel narratives, memoirs, and sketches—again, excepting Irving and Hawthorne.

36. James T. Fields to John Greenleaf Whittier, 21 February 1857. Ticknor and Fields Papers, bMS Am 2030.2.

37. Although the letter C. Ticknor cites is apparently unpublished, *The Selected Letters of Bayard Taylor* contains a contemporaneous letter (dated 11 March 1867) to Edmund C. Stedman in which Taylor describes his visit to Tennyson and Tennyson's reading of the idyll of Guinevere. Taylor makes no mention of Whittier's *Poetical Works*, focusing instead on the "magnum of wonderful sherry, thirty years old," and bottle of "Waterloo-1815" that the two bards imbibed. The previous year, however, on 15 April 1866, Taylor had written to Stedman "in the jolliest mood," reporting that "Tennyson praises my blue-and-gold poems, and cordially invites me to revisit him in England" (*Life and Letters* 2: 456–57).

38. As Groves notes (88), Ticknor and Fields publicized Massey's remark by printing it at the front of the Blue and Gold edition of his *Poetical Works*.

39. The *National Union Catalog, Pre-1956 Imprints* (London: Mansell, 1968–81) contains an entry for this volume (343: 388).

40. Sarah Blake Shaw to James Russell Lowell, 19 March 1863, James Russell Lowell Papers, Massachusetts Historical Society. Lowell's correspondent hints at another attribute of pocket editions: their suitability as collectibles. "The reader, whose reason for purchasing more than one title in a series was often, presumably, the hope that the first could guarantee the quality of the others" (Howsam 23), may also have been enticed by the prospect of a row of matching volumes attractively displayed in the parlor. (I am indebted to Emily B. Todd for the reference to Lowell.)

41. "The Duchess" was the nom de plume of Mrs. Margaret Wolfe Hungerford (1855?–97), after her novel *The Duchess*.

42. As Brodhead emphasizes, "The designation 'literature' . . . involves a prior act of hierarchization and elimination. This term is produced through a stratification in which most writing, including virtually all popular writing, gets marked as nonliterary and unworthy of attention . . . while some other writing gets identified as rare or select: in short,

as 'literature'" (157). Brodhead draws a distinction between the *Atlantic* and the popular story-papers (78–79) that is analogous to the distinction Alcott makes between the Blue and Gold series and the Seaside Library. In *Highbrow/Lowbrow*, Lawrence W. Levine sees this kind of cultural hierarchy as becoming entrenched late in the nineteenth century.

43. In 1934, Malcolm Elwin characterized Ouida as "an apostle of insidious immorality" to the Victorians, explaining that "she was smutty and 'not nice'; therefore everybody read her" (298). James wrote of her that "[a] certain garish and lascivious imagination was . . . this lady's stock-in-trade" (*Literary Criticism* 1: 1194). See also Thomas Sargeant Perry, "Ouida's Novels," *Lippincott's Magazine* 20 (1877): 732–37.

44. Alcott's dig at James's realism may be in retaliation for his early reviews of her novels: he had pronounced *Moods* "unnatural" (Tintner 266), and in *Eight Cousins* he found her "smart, satirical tone" disagreeable (267). He also complained of *Eight Cousins*, "There is no glow and no fairies; it is all prose, and to our sense rather vulgar prose" (qtd. in Zehr 338).

45. In equating Tennyson with high culture, Alcott echoed the *American Booksellers Guide* (2 [January 1870]: 9): "There is no mistake in the disposition of the laurel crown which graces the brow of Alfred Tennyson. He is pre-eminently the poetic voice of the refined and cultivated Englishmen of this generation; and if of Englishmen, it is still more true of Americans." For more on the reading typically prescribed for mental refinement, see Bushman 287; and Hunter 60–62.

46. Regarding nineteenth-century series, Peter Dzwonkoski notes, "It is clear from the evidence . . . that the American reading public had a strong appetite for sets of books. The popularity of ready-made libraries, which offered knowledge and culture neatly packaged, takes on added significance when one considers that only about one percent of the eligible population attended high school at the time [1873]. Education, or what there was of it, took place at home, and the American publisher provided the texts" (*DLB* 2: 590). And Bushman points out that "no single item was more essential to a respectable household than a collection of books, and no activity more effectual for refinement and personal improvement than reading" (282).

47. It is significant that more Blue and Gold titles may be attributed to Anna Jameson than to any other single author, for Mrs. Jameson was unquestionably a "ladies' author." As Clara Thomas explains, she "was one of many who began to write for a great and growing reading public of women whose predilections increasingly dominated popular letters as their influence dominated popular taste" ("Anna Jameson" 53).

48. Mrs. Warburton's statement is consistent with Bourdieu's argument in *Distinction* that "taste classifies, and it classifies the classifier." As Bourdieu explains, "Social subjects, classified by their classifications, distinguish themselves by the distinctions they make, between the beautiful and the ugly, the distinguished and the vulgar, in which their position in the objective classifications is expressed or betrayed" (6).

49. This quotation from Sir Philip Sidney appears as an epigraph to "Pansies."

50. Alcott's observation resembles one that Brodhead makes in *Cultures of Letters*: "The choices people make between now-separated writing worlds come to tell what 'kind' of people they are" (103). Brodhead's comment occurs in the context of a discussion of Alcott and *Little Women*; "people" here refers to writers, but it applies equally to readers.

51. See Hunter 86–90 for a discussion of the role of taste and reading in "constructing" Victorian girls' sense of identity.

52. The *St. Nicholas* version of the story lacks this personification, since *Wanda* is not named.

53. This idea is echoed in *Our Literary Deluge and Some of Its Deeper Waters* (1902), in which Francis W. Halsey speculates that "we are approaching a time when the binding of a book shall indicate something of its value inside,—when the Kiplings, as a matter of course, shall be well printed and the Hawthornes nobly bound" (81).

54. In his pertinent article "The Material Melville: Shaping Readers' Horizons," Michael Kearns usefully adopts Hans Robert Jauss's notion of a "horizon of expectations" to explain how the physical features of the book influence the reception of the text. See also Jauss, 23–34.

55. Carrie gushes, "Wanda's [clothes] were simply gorgeous; white velvet and a rope of pearls is one costume; gray velvet and a silver girdle another; and Idalia was all a 'shower of perfumed laces; and scarlet and gold satin mask dresses, or primrose silk with violets, so lovely! I do revel in 'em!" (*Garland* 72). Alcott seems to have taken pains to describe Wanda's wardrobe accurately.

56. Writing of current trends in wearable brand advertising, Susan Strasser remarks, "Now displayed even on our bodies, the brand has become a statement about consumers themselves" (286).

57. When the fiancé of Mrs. Warburton's sister left to practice his profession in the South, he presented her with the brooch, 'saying, "This *pensée* is a happy, faithful *thought* of me. Wear it, dearest girl, and don't pine while we are separated. Read and study, write much to me, and remember, 'They never are alone that are accompanied with noble thoughts'" (*Garland* 84). Alcott frequently uses flower symbolism in her fiction and was certainly familiar with flower books, so popular in nineteenth-century America, such as Sarah Josepha Hale's *Flora's Interpreter; or, The American Book of Flowers and Sentiments* (Boston: Marsh, Capen & Lyon, 1832), and Kate Greenaway's *Language of Flowers* (London: Warne, 1884). In *The Language of Flowers: A History*, Beverly Seaton gives several meanings for the pansy, based on a collation of multiple sources: "I share your sentiments"; "think of me"; and "thoughts / you occupy my thoughts" (186–87). See also Wadsworth, "Social Reading" 162–63.

58. Ezell, who points to the "growing connection between mass literary production and reading as a fashionable leisure activity" in Britain, remarks that the "ornamental presentation [of the 'classic' text] signalled the status of the text and of its owner simultaneously," reinforcing "the perception of the purchase and display of books as a type of socially accrediting activity" (13–14).

59. In light of this interpretation, it is important to consider what the materiality of Alcott's attractively bound *A Garland for Girls* (figure 8) signified to her own audience (young girls who, like the three young ladies in "Pansies," presumably liked to read). With its spare ornamentation, consisting of a simple wreath depicting the flowers named in the story titles, this elegant cover is in sharp counterpoint to what Sue Allen characterizes as the "crowded 'bulletin-board' layouts" that were "bursting the bounds" of book covers in the 1880s. Charles Gullans observes of Sarah Whitman, who likely influenced the design of

*A Garland for Girls*, "her covers are often feminine, sweet, and charming," adding, "After all, the audience for books was certainly feminine by a wide margin, and was attracted by the sweet and charming, and on occasion not averse to the bold" (Allen and Gullans 64). See Stoneley (21–36) for an explication of the relationship between femininity, class, and display in Alcott's fiction.

60. Indeed, when one considers Alcott's own contributions to the sensation literature of her day, it is tempting to read the entire story as ironic. Nevertheless, Alcott seems to have had a remarkable ability to compartmentalize her literary productions into distinct and separate categories aimed at discrete segments of the literary marketplace. See Brodhead's *Cultures of Letters* for a discussion of her ability to "write across generic boundaries" and "be an author of all kinds, at once 'blood and thunder' writer and high-literary aspirant and 'the Thackeray, the Trollope, of the nursery and the school-room'; and so . . . write toward the whole audience that was divided up in her time" (106). The sentence containing the phrase "a good marriage is the end of life" does not appear in the *St. Nicholas* version of "Pansies," suggesting the likelihood that Dodge, like James, detected an ironic tone unsuitable for a juvenile audience and expunged it.

61. After the publication of the first part of *Little Women* but before the appearance of the second part, Alcott wrote in her journal: "Girls write to ask who the little women marry, as if that was the only end and aim of a woman's life" (*Journals* 167).

## EPILOGUE

1. In the preface to *Literary Publishing in America, 1790–1850*, William Charvat comments that if he had included an additional chapter he might have devoted it to "the writer's struggle, in the immature publishing economy of that time, to discover who or what his audience was" (9).

2. Thomas Niles to Louisa May Alcott, 14 February 1870. RB Papers, bMS Am1130.8.

3. As media critic Brian Lambert explains, "Since the '80s, cable has steadily carved apart audiences the networks used to take for granted. Today, the entire industry strategizes to attract specific types of viewers" ("She-TV" 1E).

4. Although Rash omits ethnicity from this list, cable channels such as BET, Univision, and Telemundo have all found niches in the American cable TV market, while many local stations cater to minority groups in regional markets.

5. Lambert recognizes that "most programming decisions still are made (based on a lot of research) by male executives," and so "for the most part, those choices reflect what men believe women will watch" (1E).

6. NetLibrary reported sales at a rate of 400 per hour, and Amazon.com, which offered the book free for two weeks, received download requests every 1.5 seconds on the first day (Carvajal 17A).

7. Levine acknowledges that this sense of unity attributed to the past "was largely an ideal" as "from early in American history multiplicity had been the reality" (175).

8. The National Yiddish Book Center in Amherst, Massachusetts, is a major resource center for books in Yiddish, both American and foreign.

9. German-American scholarship is a burgeoning area of study. Peter Lang publishes an extensive series of monographs in its New German-American Studies series, and the Longfellow Institute at Harvard University sponsors a wide-ranging research program called "The German American Tradition." Important books on German-American print culture include Robert E. Cazden, *A Social History of the German Book Trade in America to the Civil War* (Columbia, SC: Camden House, 1984); Christopher L. Dolmetsch, *The German Press of the Shenandoah Valley* (Columbia, SC: Camden House, 1984); and the collection *German? American? Literature?* (New York: Peter Lang, 2002).

10. In his introduction to Pauline Hopkins's *Contending Forces*, for example, Richard Yarborough states that "Hopkins's novel was released with little fanfare and apparently no comment from the white mainstream literary community. That the rest of her considerable corpus was published primarily in Afro-American magazines with small circulations contributed further to Hopkins's relative anonymity" (xliv).

11. Thomas Niles to Louisa May Alcott, 5 February 1879, 3 October 1876, 16 December 1878, RB Papers, bMS Am 1130.8.

12. "Charles Egbert Craddock" was the pseudonym of Mary Noailles Murfree (1850–1922), a writer of local-color fiction set in the Tennessee mountains. The novels of F(rancis) Marion Crawford (1854–1909) were admired for their vivid portrayals of foreign settings and characters. His best-known novels treated Italy: *Saracinesca* (1887), *Sant' Ilario* (1889), and *Don Orsino* (1892).

13. In his recent study *The Making of American Audiences: From Stage to Television, 1750 to 1990*, Richard Butsch makes a similar case for the solidification of new audiences for stage entertainment in nineteenth-century America, viewing their assertiveness as "expressions of collective identity and action" (49) which grew out of traditional notions of audience sovereignty.

# Works Cited

## ARCHIVAL SOURCES

Houghton Library, Harvard University
  Edwin L. Godkin Papers
  Godkin Family Correspondence
  Henry James Papers
  *The Nation* Papers
  Roberts Brothers Papers
  Ticknor and Fields Papers
Massachusetts Historical Society, Boston
  James Russell Lowell Papers
New York Public Library, Special Collections
  *Nation* Records

## PRIMARY TEXTS

Adams, William T. *The Boat Club; or, The Bunkers of Rippleton. A Tale for Boys.* 1854. Rpt. New York: Hurst & Co., n.d.

———. *The Dorcas Club; or, Our Girls Afloat.* Boston: Lee & Shepard, 1874.

———. *Little by Little; or, The Cruise of the Flyaway.* Boston: Lee & Shepard, 1860.

———. *Poor and Proud; or, The Fortunes of Katy Redburn. A Story for Young Folks.* 1858. Rpt. New York: A. L. Burt, n.d.

———. *Rich and Humble; or, The Mission of Bertha Grant.* Boston: Lee & Shepard, 1864.

———. *Try Again; or, The Trials and Triumphs of Harry West.* 1857. Rpt. New York: Hurst & Co., n.d.

Alcott, Louisa May. *Eight Cousins; or, The Aunt-Hill.* 1874. Boston: Little, Brown, 1996.

———. *A Garland for Girls.* Boston: Roberts Bros., 1888.

———. *Jack and Jill.* 1880. Boston: Little, Brown, 1999.

———. *The Journals of Louisa May Alcott.* Ed. Joel Myerson and Daniel Shealy. Boston: Little, Brown, 1989.

———. *Little Women; or, Meg, Jo, Beth, and Amy.* 1868. Intro. Anna Quindlen. Boston: Little, Brown, 1994.

———. *Little Women.* [Pts. 1 and 2.] Norton Critical Edition. Ed. Anne K. Phillips and Gregory Eiselein. New York: W. W. Norton, 2004.

———. *Louisa May Alcott: Her Girlhood Diary.* Ed. Cary Ryan. BridgeWater Books, 1993.

———. *An Old-Fashioned Girl.* 1870. Boston: Little, Brown, 1997.

———. "Recollections of My Childhood." In *Little Women.* Norton Critical Edition. Ed. Anne K. Phillips and Gregory Eiselein. New York: W. W. Norton, 2004. 428–33

———. *Rose in Bloom: A Sequel to Eight Cousins.* Boston: Little, Brown, 1995.

———. *The Selected Letters of Louisa May Alcott.* Ed. Joel Myerson, Daniel Shealy, and Madeleine B. Stern. Athens: U of Georgia P, 1995.

———. *Shawl-Straps. Aunt Jo's Scrap-Bag. Vol. 2*. Boston: Roberts Bros., 1872.

Alger, Horatio, Jr. *Ragged Dick and Struggling Upward*. 1868. New York: Penguin, 1985.

Clemens, Samuel. *Adventures of Huckleberry Finn*. 1883. The Oxford Mark Twain. Ed. Shelley Fisher Fishkin. New York: Oxford UP, 1996.

———. *The Adventures of Tom Sawyer*. 1876. The Oxford Mark Twain. Ed. Shelley Fisher Fishkin. New York: Oxford UP, 1996.

———. *The Autobiography of Mark Twain*. Ed. Charles Neider. New York: Harper & Row, 1959.

———. *Chapters from My Autobiography*. The Oxford Mark Twain. Ed. Shelley Fisher Fishkin. New York: Oxford UP, 1996.

———. *Huck Finn and Tom Sawyer among the Indians and Other Unfinished Stories*. Ed. Dahlia Armon and Walter Blair. Berkeley: U of California P, 1989.

———. *Mark Twain, Business Man*. Ed. Samuel Charles Webster. Boston: Little, Brown, 1946.

———. *Mark Twain—Howells Letters: The Correspondence of Samuel L. Clemens and William D. Howells, 1872–1910*. Ed. Henry Nash Smith and William M. Gibson. 2 vols. Cambridge: Belknap, Harvard UP, 1960.

———. *Mark Twain's Hannibal, Huck and Tom*. Ed. Walter Blair. Berkeley: U of California P, 1969.

———. *Mark Twain's Letters*. Ed. Albert Bigelow Paine. 2 vols. New York: Harper & Bros., 1917.

———. *Mark Twain's Letters*. Ed. Edgar Marquess Branch, Michael B. Frank, Kenneth M. Sanderson, Harriet Elinor Smith, Lin Salamo, and Richard Bucci. 6 vols. Berkeley: U of California P, 1988–2002.

———. *Mark Twain's Letters to His Publishers, 1867–1894*. Ed. Hamlin Hill. Berkeley: U of California P, 1967.

———. *Sketches, New and Old*. The Oxford Mark Twain. Ed. Shelley Fisher Fishkin. New York: Oxford UP, 1996.

———. *Tom Sawyer Abroad*. The Oxford Mark Twain. Ed. Shelley Fisher Fishkin. New York: Oxford UP, 1996.

———. *Tom Sawyer, Detective, The Stolen White Elephant, and Other Detective Stories*. The Oxford Mark Twain. Ed. Shelley Fisher Fishkin. New York: Oxford UP, 1996. 107–90.

Clemens, Samuel, and Charles Dudley Warner. *The Gilded Age: A Tale of To-day*. Hartford, CT: American Publishing Co., 1873.

Dickinson, Emily. *The Complete Poems of Emily Dickinson*. Ed. Thomas H. Johnson. 3 vols. Boston: Little, Brown, 1951.

———. *Selected Letters*. Ed. Thomas H. Johnson. Cambridge: Belknap, Harvard UP, 1971.

Ellis, Edward S. *A Grandfather's Historic Stories of Our Country from Its Discovery to the Present Time; After the Style of "Peter Parley," as Suggested by Nathaniel Hawthorne*. New York: Hartley-Thomas, 1911.

Goodrich, Samuel Griswold. *Fairy Land, and Other Sketches for Youth*. Boston: J. Munroe, 1844.

———. *Parley's Book of Fables*. Hartford, CT: Silus Andrus and Son, 1850.

———. *Peter Parley's Farewell.* 1839. Philadelphia: R. S. H. George, 1841.

———. Preface. *The Token and Atlantic Souvenir.* Ed. S. G. Goodrich. Boston: Gray & Bowen, 1833.

———. *Recollections of a Lifetime; or, Men and Things I Have Seen.* 2 vols. New York: Miller, Orton, 1857.

———. *The Tales of Peter Parley about America.* Boston: S. G. Goodrich, 1827.

Harlow, Virginia. *Thomas Sergeant Perry: A Biography and Letters to Perry from William, Henry, and Garth Wilkinson James.* Durham, NC: Duke UP, 1950.

Hawthorne, Nathaniel. *The American Notebooks.* Ed. Claude M. Simpson. Columbus: Ohio State UP, 1972.

———. *The House of the Seven Gables.* Centenary Edition of the Works of Nathaniel Hawthorne. Vol. 2. Ed. William Charvat, Roy Harvey Pearce, and Claude M. Simpson. Columbus: Ohio State UP, 1965.

———. *The Letters, 1813–1843.* Centenary Edition of the Works of Nathaniel Hawthorne. Vol. 15. Ed. Thomas Woodson, L. Neal Smith, and Norman Holmes Pearson. Columbus: Ohio State UP, 1984.

———. *The Letters, 1843–1853.* Centenary Edition of the Works of Nathaniel Hawthorne. Vol. 16. Ed. Thomas Woodson, L. Neal Smith, and Norman Holmes Pearson. Columbus: Ohio State UP, 1985.

———. *The Letters, 1853–1856.* Centenary Edition of the Works of Nathaniel Hawthorne. Vol. 17. Ed. Thomas Woodson, James A. Rubino, L. Neal Smith, and Norman Holmes Pearson. Columbus: Ohio State UP, 1987.

———. *The Letters, 1857–1864.* Centenary Edition of the Works of Nathaniel Hawthorne. Vol. 18. Ed. Thomas Woodson, James A. Rubino, L. Neal Smith, and Norman Holmes Pearson. Columbus: Ohio State UP, 1987.

———. *The Marble Faun; or, The Romance of Monte Beni.* Centenary Edition of the Works of Nathaniel Hawthorne. Vol. 4. Ed. William Charvat, Roy Harvey Pearce, and Claude M. Simpson. Columbus: Ohio State UP, 1968.

———. *True Stories from History and Biography.* Centenary Edition of the Works of Nathaniel Hawthorne. Vol. 6. Ed. William Charvat, Roy Harvey Pearce, and Claude M. Simpson. Columbus: Ohio State UP, 1972.

———. *Twice-told Tales.* Centenary Edition of the Works of Nathaniel Hawthorne. Vol. 9. Ed. William Charvat, Roy Harvey Pearce, and Claude M. Simpson. Columbus: Ohio State UP, 1974.

———. *A Wonder Book and Tanglewood Tales.* Centenary Edition of the Works of Nathaniel Hawthorne. Vol. 7. Ed. William Charvat, Roy Harvey Pearcel, and Claude M. Simpson. Columbus: Ohio State UP, 1972.

Holmes, Oliver Wendell. *The Poems of Oliver Wendell Holmes.* Blue and Gold Series. Boston: Ticknor & Fields, 1863.

Howells, William Dean. *Heroines of Fiction.* Vol. 2. New York: Harper & Bros., 1903.

———. Introduction. *Different Girls. Harper's Novelettes.* New York: Harper & Bros., 1895. v–vii.

———. "A Possible Difference in English and American Fiction." *North American Review* 173 (July 1901): 134–44. APS Online.

———. *The Rise of Silas Lapham*. 1885. New York: New American Library, Signet Classic, 2002.

James, Henry. *The Bostonians*. Oxford World's Classics. Oxford: Oxford UP, 1984.

———. *The Complete Notebooks of Henry James*. Ed. Leon Edel and Lyall H. Powers. New York: Oxford UP, 1987.

———. *Daisy Miller*. Ed. Geoffrey Moore. Penguin Classics. New York: Penguin, 1986.

———. *Henry James Letters*. Ed. Leon Edel. 4 vols. Cambridge: Belknap, Harvard UP, 1975.

———. *Henry James: A Life in Letters*. Ed. Philip Horne. London: Penguin, 1999.

———. *James's Daisy Miller: The Story, the Play, the Critics*. Ed. William T. Stafford. New York: Charles Scribner's Sons, 1963.

———. *Literary Criticism*. Vol. 1: *Essays on Literature, American Writers, English Writers*. Ed. Leon Edel. New York: Library of America, 1984.

———. *Parisian Sketches: Letters to the New York* Tribune, *1875–1876*. Ed. Leon Edel and Ilse Dusoir Lind. New York: New York UP, 1957.

———. *Selected Letters*. Ed. Leon Edel. Cambridge: Belknap, Harvard UP, 1987

———. *Watch and Ward*. 1871. Phoenix Mill, Stroud, Gloucestershire, UK: Sutton Publishing, 1997.

———. *William Wetmore Story and His Friends; from Letters, Diaries, and Recollections*. 2 vols. Boston: Houghton Mifflin, 1903.

James, William. *The Correspondence of William James*. Vol. 1: *William and Henry: 1861–1884*. Ed. Ignas K. Skrupskelis and Elizabeth M. Berkeley. Charlottesville: UP of Virginia, 1992.

Longfellow, Henry Wadsworth. *The Letters of Henry Wadsworth Longfellow*. Ed. Andrew Hilen. 6 vols. Cambridge, MA: Belknap, Harvard UP, 1972.

Mason, Mary Murdoch. *Mae Madden*. Introductory Poem by Joaquin Miller. Chicago: Jansen, McClurg, & Co., 1876.

Miller, Joaquin. *The One Fair Woman*. 3 vols. London: Chapman & Hall, 1876.

Ouida (Marie Louise de la Ramée). *Wanda, Countess von Szalras*. New York: George Munro, 1893.

Peabody, Elizabeth. *Letters of Elizabeth Palmer Peabody, American Renaissance Woman*. Ed. Bruce A. Ronda. Middleton, CT: Wesleyan UP, 1984.

Pickard, Samuel T. *Life and Letters of John Greenleaf Whittier*. 2 vols. Boston: Houghton Mifflin, 1894.

Staël, Madame de. *Corinne; or, Italy*. 1807. Trans. Sylvia Raphael. Intro. and notes John Claiborne Isbell. New York: Oxford UP, 1998.

Stedman, Laura, and George H. Gould. *Life and Letters of Edmund Clarence Stedman*. 2 vols. New York: Moffat, Yard & Co., 1910.

Taylor, Bayard. *Life and Letters of Bayard Taylor*. Ed. Marie Hansen-Taylor and Horace E. Scudder. 2 vols. Boston: Houghton Mifflin, 1885.

———. *The Poems of Bayard Taylor*. Blue and Gold Series. Boston: Ticknor & Fields, 1865.

———. *Selected Letters of Bayard Taylor*. Ed. Paul C. Wermuth. Lewisburg, PA: Bucknell UP, 1997.

Thompson, Ella W. *Beaten Paths; or, A Woman's Vacation*. Boston: Lee & Shepard, 1874.

Tryon, Warren S., and William Charvat, eds. *The Cost Books of Ticknor and Fields and Their Predecessors, 1832–1858*. New York: Bibliographical Society of America, 1949.

Turner, Arlin. *Hawthorne as Editor: Selections from His Writings in* The American Magazine of Useful and Entertaining Knowledge. Baton Rouge: Louisiana State UP, 1941.

Urbino, Mrs. S. R. *An American Woman in Europe: The Journal of Two Years and a Half Sojourn in Germany, Switzerland, France, and Italy.* Boston: Lee & Shepard, 1869.

Wharton, Edith. *Roman Fever and Other Stories.* London: Virago, Little, Brown, 1983.

Whitman, Alfred. "A Foreword. Miss Alcott's Letters to her 'Laurie.'" *Ladies' Home Journal* 18 (1901): 5–6.

Whitman, Walt. *Walt Whitman: Representative Selections with Introduction, Bibliography, and Notes.* Ed. Floyd Stovall. New York: American Book Company, 1939.

Willard, Frances E. *Glimpses of Fifty Years: The Autobiography of an American Woman.* Chicago: Woman's Temperance Publication Association, 1889.

Woolson, Constance Fenimore. *Dorothy and Other Italian Stories.* New York: Harper & Bros., 1896.

———. *The Front Yard and Other Italian Stories.* 1895. Freeport, NY: Books for Libraries P, 1969.

## NINETEENTH-CENTURY NOTICES

Advertisement, Lee & Shepard. *American Bookseller* 1 (1876): 327.

Advertisement, Ticknor & Fields. *American Literary Gazette and Publishers' Circular* 1 (1863): 154.

"The American Novel—with Samples." *Catholic World* 28 (1878): 325–36.

Arbour, Keith. *Canvassing Books, Sample Books, and Subscription Publishers' Ephemera, 1833–1951, in the Collection of Michael Zinman.* Ardsley, NY: Hayden Foundation for the Cultural Arts, 1996.

"The Author of 'Frontenac.'" *Federal American Monthly* 66 (1865): 325–34.

"Books and Authors." Revision of *Mae Madden* by Mary Murdoch Mason. *Appleton's Journal: A Magazine of General Literature* 15 (1876): 87–90.

"Books and Girls." *Ladies' Repository* 1 (1868): 211–12.

"Books for Children." "Notices of New Works." *Southern Literary Messenger* 7 (January 1841): 80.

"Books for Our Children." *Atlantic Monthly* 16 (1865): 724–35.

"Books Received." Notice of *Mae Madden* by Mary Murdoch Mason. *Publishers' Weekly* 8 (1875): 936.

"Books in Summer Suits." *American Bookmaker: A Journal of Technical Art and Information* 5 (1887): 6.

"The Book Trade." *The Merchants' Magazine and Commercial Review* 37 (1857): 652; 40 (1859): 775; 48 (1863): 109.

Catalogue of Books Published by the American Publishing Company. *The Adventures of Tom Sawyer* by Mark Twain. Ed. Shelley Fisher Fishkin. New York: Oxford UP, 1996.

"Cheap Books." *Boston Globe*: 22 April 1883. Rpt. *Publishers' Weekly* 23 (1883): 522–23.

"Cheap Books." *Hour*: 21 April 1883. Rpt. *Publishers' Weekly* 23 (1883): 498–99.

"Cheap Books and Authors' Rights." *Publishers' Weekly* 27 (1885): 333.

"The Cheap Libraries." *Publishers' Weekly* 12 (1877): 396–97.

"Cheap Libraries." *Publishers' Weekly* 35 (1889): 428.

"The 'Cheap Libraries' Question." *Publishers' Weekly* 33 (1888): 634–35.

"Classified Index." *Publishers Trade List Annual* (1876): viii–xiii.

"Confidential Terms to Agents." Publishing Circular. *Adventures of Huckleberry Finn* by Mark Twain. Norton Critical Edition. Ed. Thomas Cooley. New York: W. W. Norton, 1999. 307.

"Contemporary Literature." Review of *Little Women* by Louisa May Alcott. *Ladies' Repository* [Cincinnati] (1868): 471–73.

"The Decadence of Cheap Books." *Publishers' Weekly* 48 (1895): 681.

Droch, Robert. "Types of American Fiction." *Book Buyer* (1887): 22.

"Editorial Notes." *Putnam's Monthly Magazine* 8 (1856): 95–107.

"Editor's Drawer." *Harper's New Monthly Magazine* 73 (1886): 807.

"Editor's Literary Record." Review of *Shawl-Straps* by Louisa May Alcott. *Harper's New Monthly Magazine* 46 (1873): 612–16.

"The Editor's Repository." *Ladies' Repository: A Monthly Periodical, Devoted to Literature, Arts, and Religion* 19 (1859): 442; 20 (1866): 758; 25 (1865): 125.

"Editor's Table." *Knickerbocker; or, New-York Monthly Magazine* 48 (1856): 304–30.

"Educational Books." *American Publishers' Circular and Literary Gazette* 2 (1856): 317.

Funk, Isaac K. "Foreign Authors and 'The Standard Series.'" *Publishers' Weekly* 17 (1880): 499.

Graham, Erin. "Books That Girls Have Loved." *Lippincott's Magazine* 60 (1897): 428–32.

"Have Magazines Hurt the Book Trade?" *Publishers' Weekly* 30 (1886): 16.

"How To Make Publishing 'Pay.'" *Publishers' Weekly* 36 (1889): 930–31.

"A Lesson from the 'Revolution.'" *Publishers' Weekly* 18 (1880): 185–86.

"The 'Library' Publishers' 'Combine.'" *Publishers' Weekly* 37 (1890): 274–75.

"Literary Notes." *Round Table: A Weekly Record of the Notable, the Useful and the Tasteful* 1 (1864): 140–41.

"Literary Notices." *Ladies' Repository: A Monthly Periodical, Devoted to Literature, Arts, and Religion* 19 (1859): 377–80, 442.

"The Literary Revolution." *Bookseller and Stationer.* Rpt. *Publishers' Weekly* 19 (1881): 390–91.

"The Lounger." *Critic*, n.s. 2 (1884): 198.

Matthews, Brander. "Cheap Books and Good Books." 1887. Rpt. *Dictionary of Literary Biography 49: American Literary Publishing Houses, 1638–1899.* Ed. Peter Dzwonkoski. 2 vols. Detroit: Gale Research, 1986. 2: 580–86.

Melville, Herman. "A Thought on Book-Binding." Review of *The Red Rover* by James Fenimore Cooper. Rev. ed. 16 March 1850. Rpt. *The Piazza Tales and Other Prose Pieces, 1839–1860.* Ed. Harrison Hayford et al. Evanston, IL: Northwestern UP, Newberry Library, 1987.

"The Men Who Advertise." *American Bookseller's Guide* 2 (1870): 259.

"Minor Book Notices." *Literary World* 6 (1876): 115–19.

Munro, George. "Cheap Literature in the Mails." *New York Sun.* 4 December 1878. Rpt. *Publishers' Weekly* 14 (1878): 805.

"New Books." Notice of *Mae Madden* by Mary Murdoch Mason. *American Bookseller* 1 (1876): 52.

"New Publications." Review of *Little Women* by Louisa May Alcott. *Lady's Friend* 5 (1868): 857.

"New Subscription Books for 1870." *American Bookseller's Guide* 2 (March 1870): 113.

Notice of *The Poetical Works of Alfred Tennyson*, Blue and Gold Edition. *American Publishers' Circular* 2 (1856): 361.

"Notices of New Works." *Southern Literary Messenger, Devoted to Every Department of Literature and the Fine Arts* 25 (1857): 315–20; 26 (1858): 159–60; 30 (1860): 319–20.

"Notices of Recent Publications." *Christian Examiner* 61 (1856): 142–54.

"Old and New Pirates." *New York Evening Post* 26 January 1883. Rpt. *Publishers' Weekly* 23 (1883): 175.

"Our Book Table." Review of *Little Women* by Louisa May Alcott. *Ladies' Repository* [Boston] (1868): 468–72.

Peabody, Andrew Preston. "Nathaniel Hawthorne." *North American Review* 76 (1853): 227–48.

"Periodicals vs. Books." *Boston Daily Advertiser.* 27 May 1885. Rpt. *Publishers' Weekly* 27 (1885): 711.

"Personal Mention." *Publishers' Weekly* 8 (1875): 958.

Peterson, T. B. "The Postal Rate on Books." *Publishers' Weekly* 33 (1888): 422.

"Poetry and Fiction." *Christian Examiner* 65 (1858): 302–6.

"Postage on Books." *New York Times.* April 10, 1888. Rpt. in *Publishers' Weekly* 33 (1888): 635.

"The Question of Cheap Novels." *Publishers' Weekly* 26 (1884): 667–68.

"Recent Novels." Review of *Mae Madden* by Mary Murdoch Mason. *Nation* 22 (1876): 83.

Rideing, W. H. "Boston Letter." *Critic* 11 (1887): 56–57.

Salmon, Edward G. "What Girls Read." *Nineteenth Century* 20 (1886): 515–29.

"Second-Class Postage on Books." *Publishers' Weekly* 38 (1890): 126–27.

"Starving the Book Trade." *Publishers' Weekly* 26 (1884): 643.

"Stupendous Enterprise." *Vanity Fair* 20 (1860): 180.

Sumner, William G. "What Our Boys Are Reading." *Scribner's Monthly* 15 (1878): 681–85.

"T. Niles—In Memoriam." *Publishers' Weekly* 45 (1894): 859–60.

Tomlinson, Everett T. "Reading for Boys and Girls." *Atlantic Monthly* 86 (1900): 693–99.

"United States Book Company. The American Publishers' Corporation Fails to Recover 'The *Seaside Library*.'" *Publishers' Weekly* 52 (1897): 16.

Wanamaker, Jno. "Postage on Periodical Publications Containing the Print or Reprint of Books." *Publishers' Weekly* 38 (1890): 127–32.

Warner, Charles Dudley. "The Editor's Drawer." *Harper's New Monthly Magazine* 73 (1886): 807.

"Who Breaks? Who Pays?" *Publishers' Weekly* 20 (1881): 797.

## SECONDARY BOOKS AND ARTICLES

Allen, Marjorie N. *One Hundred Years of Children's Books in America, Decade by Decade.* New York: Facts on File, 1996.

Allen, Sue. *American Book Covers, 1830–1900: A Pictorial Guide*. Washington, DC: Library of Congress, Binding & Collections Care Division, 1998.

Allen, Sue, and Charles Gullans. *Decorated Cloth in America: Publishers' Bindings, 1840–1910*. Los Angeles: UCLA Center for 17th- and 18th-Century Studies, William Andrews Clark Memorial Library, 1994.

Altick, Richard D. *The English Common Reader: A Social History of the Mass Reading Public, 1800–1900*. Chicago: U of Chicago P, 1957.

———. "From Aldine to Everyman: Cheap Reprint Series of the English Classics, 1830–1906." *Studies in Bibliography* 11 (1958): 3–24.

Alton, Anne Hiebert. "The Composition and Publication of *Little Women*." Appendix A in *Little Women* by Louisa May Alcott, ed. Anne Hiebert Alton. Peterborough, ON: Broadview P, 2001.

Amory, Hugh. "The New England Book Trade, 1713–1790." *A History of the Book in America*, Vol. 1, *The Colonial Book in the Atlantic World*. Ed. Hugh Amory and David D. Hall. Cambridge: Cambridge UP; Worcester, MA: American Antiquarian Society, 2000.

Anderson, Benedict. *Imagined Communities: Reflections on the Origin and Spread of Nationalism*. Rev. ed. London: Verso, 1991.

Anderson, Frederick, ed. *Mark Twain: The Critical Heritage*. London: Routledge & Kegan Paul, 1971.

Anesko, Michael. *Letters, Fictions, Lives: Henry James and William Dean Howells*. Oxford: Oxford UP, 1997.

Anthony, Katharine. *Louisa May Alcott*. New York: Alfred A. Knopf, 1938.

Attebery, Brian. *The Fantasy Tradition in American Literature: From Irving to Le Guin*. Bloomington: Indiana UP, 1980.

Augst, Thomas. *The Clerk's Tale: Young Men and Moral Life in Nineteenth-Century America*. Chicago: U of Chicago P, 2003.

Avery, Gillian. *Behold the Child: American Children and Their Books, 1621–1922*. London: Bodley Head, 1994.

Bakan, David. "Adolescence in America: From Idea to Social Fact." *Daedulus* 100 (1971): 979–95.

Baker, Thomas N. *Sentiment and Celebrity: Nathaniel Parker Willis and the Trials of Literary Fame*. Oxford: Oxford UP, 1999.

Ballou, Ellen. *The Building of the House: Houghton Mifflin's Formative Years*. Boston: Houghton Mifflin, 1970.

Baron, Xavier. "William Dean Howells." *Dictionary of Literary Biography 189: American Travel Writers, 1850–1915*. Ed. Donald Ross and James J. Schramer. Detroit: Bruccoli Clark Layman, Gale Research, 1998.

Barth, Marilyn. "Can't Judge These Books by Their Covers: 'Handy Volume Editions' at the Turn of the Last Century." Popular Culture Association and American Culture Association joint convention. New Orleans. 19 April 2000.

Baym, Nina. *Novels, Readers, and Reviewers: Responses to Fiction in Antebellum America*. Ithaca: Cornell UP, 1984.

———. *The Shape of Hawthorne's Career*. Ithaca: Cornell UP, 1976.

———. *Woman's Fiction: A Guide to Novels by and about Women in America, 1820–1870*. Ithaca: Cornell UP, 1978.

Bode, Carl. *The Anatomy of American Popular Culture, 1840–1861*. Berkeley: U of California P, 1960.

Bourdieu, Pierre. *Distinction: A Social Critique of the Judgement of Taste*. Trans. Richard Nice. Cambridge: Harvard UP, 1984.

———. *The Field of Cultural Production*. New York: Columbia UP, 1993.

Boylan, Anne. M. *The Origins of Women's Activism: New York and Boston, 1797–1840*. Chapel Hill: U of North Carolina P, 2002.

Boynton, Henry Walcott. *Annals of American Bookselling, 1638–1850*. 1932. New Castle, DE: Oak Knoll, 1991.

Bratton, J. S. *The Impact of Victorian Children's Fiction*. London: Croom Helm, 1981.

Brodhead, Richard H. *Cultures of Letters: Scenes of Reading and Writing in Nineteenth-Century America*. Chicago: U of Chicago P, 1993.

Brown, Richard D. *Knowledge Is Power: The Diffusion of Information in Early America, 1700–1865*. Oxford: Oxford UP, 1989.

Bushman, Richard L. *The Refinement of America: Persons, Houses, Cities*. New York: Alfred A. Knopf, 1992.

Butsch, Richard. *The Making of American Audiences from Stage to Television, 1750–1990*. Cambridge: Cambridge UP, 2000.

Cadogan, Mary, and Patricia Craig. *You're a Brick, Angela! A New Look at Girls' Fiction from 1839 to 1975*. London: Victor Gollancz, 1976.

Carvajal, Doreen. "King's Online Book a Best-Seller, But Some Publishers Are Skeptical." *New York Times*. Rpt. *St. Paul Pioneer Press* 16 March 2000: 1A, 17A.

Charvat, William. *Literary Publishing in America, 1790–1850*. 1959. Rpt. Amherst: U of Massachusetts P, 1993.

———. *The Profession of Authorship in America, 1800–1870*. Ed. Matthew J. Bruccoli. New York: Columbia UP, 1969; rpt. 1992.

Cheney, Ednah, ed. *Louisa May Alcott: Her Life, Letters, and Journals*. Boston: Little, Brown, 1928.

Clark, Beverly Lyon. "Domesticating the School Story, Regendering a Genre: Alcott's *Little Men*." *New Literary History* 26 (1995): 323–42.

———. Introduction. *Girls, Boys, Books, Toys: Gender in Children's Literature and Culture*. Ed. Beverly Lyon Clark and Margaret R. Higonnet. Baltimore: Johns Hopkins UP, 1999.

———. *Kiddie Lit: The Cultural Construction of Children's Literature in America*. Baltimore: Johns Hopkins UP, 2003.

*Commercial Bookbindings: An Historical Sketch, with Some Mention of an Exhibition of Drawings, Covers, and Books at the Grolier Club, April 5 to April 28, 1894*. New York: Grolier Club, 1894.

Comparato, Frank E. *Books for the Millions: A History of the Men Whose Methods and Machines Packaged the Printed Word*. Harrisburg: Stackpole, 1971.

Cook, Nancy. "Finding His Mark: Twain's *The Innocents Abroad* as a Subscription Book." *Reading Books: Essays on the Material Text and Literature in America*. Ed. Michele Moylan and Lane Stiles. Amherst: U of Massachusetts P, 1996. 151–78.

———. "Reshaping Publishing and Authorship in the Gilded Age." *Perspectives on American Book History: Artifacts and Commentary*. Ed. Scott E. Casper, Joanne D. Chaison, and Jeffrey D. Groves. Amherst: U of Massachusetts P, 2002.

Cornelius, Janet Duitsman. *"When I Can Read My Title Clear": Literacy, Slavery, and Religion in the Antebellum South*. Columbia: U of South Carolina P, 1991.

Cott, Nancy F. *The Bonds of Womanhood: "Woman's Sphere" in New England, 1780–1835*. New Haven: Yale UP, 1997.

Coultrap-McQuin, Susan. *Doing Literary Business: American Women Writers in the Nineteenth Century*. Chapel Hill: U of North Carolina P, 1990.

*Covering a Continent: A Story of Newsstand Distribution and Sales*. New York: American News Company, 1930.

Crisler, Jesse S. "Alcott's Reading in *Little Women*: Shaping the Autobiographical Self." *Resources for American Literary Study* 20 (1994): 27–36.

Crook, Mark. "The OCLC Online Union Catalog: An Incomparable Library Resource." *Electronic Databases and Publishing*. Ed. Albert Henderson. New Brunswick, NJ: Transaction Publishers, 1998.

Crowley, J. Donald. "Editorial Emendations in the Copy-Text." *Twice-told Tales*. Centenary Edition of the Works of Nathaniel Hawthorne. Ed. William Charvat, Roy Harvey Pearce, Claude M. Simpson. Columbus: Ohio State UP, 1974. 580–603.

———. *Hawthorne: The Critical Heritage*. New York: Barnes & Noble, 1970.

———. "Historical Commentary." *Twice-told Tales*. Centenary Edition of the Works of Nathaniel Hawthorne. Ed. William Charvat, Roy Harvey Pearce, and Claude M. Simpson. Columbus: Ohio State UP, 1974.

Crowley, John W. "*Little Women* and the Boy-Book." *New England Quarterly* 58 (1985): 384–99.

Currier, Thomas Franklin. *Bibliography of John Greenleaf Whittier*. Cambridge: Harvard UP, 1937.

Danky, James P. and Wayne A. Wiegand. *Print Culture in a Diverse America*. Urbana: U of Illinois P, 1998.

Davidson, Cathy N. "The Life and Times of *Charlotte Temple*: The Biography of a Book." *Reading in America: Literature and Social History*. Ed. Cathy N. Davidson. Baltimore: Johns Hopkins UP, 1989. 157–79.

———. *Revolution and the Word: The Rise of the Novel in America*. New York: Oxford UP, 1986.

Demos, John. *Past, Present, and Personal: The Family and Life Course in American History*. New York: Oxford UP, 1986.

Denning, Michael. *Mechanic Accents: Dime Novels and Working Class Culture in America*. Rev. ed. London: Verso, 1998.

Derby, J. C. *Fifty Years among Authors, Books and Publishers*. New York: G. W. Carleton, 1884.

Didier, Eugene Lemoine. *American Publishers and English Authors*. Baltimore: E. L. Didier, 1879.

Dolan, Brian. *Ladies of the Grand Tour: British Women in Pursuit of Enlightenment and Adventure in Eighteenth-Century Europe*. New York: HarperCollins, 2001.

Donovan, Ellen Butler. "Reading for Profit *and* Pleasure: *Little Women* and *The Story of a Bad Boy*." *The Lion and the Unicorn* 18 (1994): 143–53.

Dzwonkoski, Peter, ed. *Dictionary of Literary Biography 49: American Literary Publishing Houses, 1638–1899*. 2 vols. Detroit: Gale Research, 1986.

256

———. "George Munro." *Dictionary of Literary Biography 49: American Literary Publishing Houses, 1638–1899*. Ed. Peter Dzwonkoski. Detroit: Gale Research, 1986.

———. "Norman L. Munro." *Dictionary of Literary Biography 49: American Literary Publishing Houses, 1638–1899*. Ed. Peter Dzwonkoski. Detroit: Gale Research, 1986.

Edel, Leon. *The Life of Henry James: The Conquest of London (1870–1881)*. Philadelphia: J. B. Lippincott, 1962.

Edel, Leon, and Dan H. Laurence. *A Bibliography of Henry James*. 3rd ed. Oxford: Clarendon P, 1982.

Eidson, John Olin. *Tennyson in America: His Reputation and Influence from 1827 to 1858*. Athens: U of Georgia P, 1943.

Elbert, Monika. Introduction. *The Early Stories of Louisa May Alcott, 1852–1860*. New York: Ironweed P, 2000.

Elbert, Sarah. *A Hunger for Home: Louisa May Alcott and* Little Women. Philadelphia: Temple UP, 1984.

Eliot, T. S. Introduction. *Adventures of Huckleberry Finn* by Mark Twain. Norton Critical Edition. Ed. Thomas Cooley. New York: W. W. Norton, 1999. 348–54.

Elwin, Malcolm. *Victorian Wallflowers*. London: Jonathan Cape, 1934.

Emery, Michael and Edwin Emery. *The Press and America: An Interpretive History of the Mass Media*. 8th ed. Boston: Allyn & Bacon, 1996.

Englund, Sheryl A. "Reading the Author in *Little Women*: A Biography of a Book." *ATQ* 12 (1998): 199–219.

Evans, Ernestine. "Trends in Children's Books." *New Republic* 48 (1926): 338–39.

Ezell, Margaret. "Making a Classic: The Advent of the Literary Series." *South Central Review* 11 (1994): 2–16.

Faxon, Frederick Winthrop. *Literary Annuals and Gift-Books: A Bibliography with a Descriptive Introduction*. Boston: Boston Book, 1912.

Fiedler, Leslie. *Love and Death in the American Novel*. 1960. New York: Anchor Books, Doubleday, 1992.

Fields, James T. *Yesterdays with Authors*. Boston: Houghton Mifflin, 1899.

"Fields, James Thomas." *Dictionary of American Biography* 3. New York: Charles Scribner's Sons, 1946–58.

Finlay, Nancy. *Artists of the Book in Boston, 1890–1910*. Cambridge, MA: Dept. of Printing and Graphic Arts, Houghton Library, Harvard College Library, 1985.

Finley, Ruth E. *The Lady of Godey's: Sarah Josepha Hale*. Philadelphia: J. B. Lippincott, 1931.

Fishkin, Shelley Fisher. "The Challenge of Teaching Huckleberry Finn." *Making Mark Twain Work in the Classroom*. Ed. James S. Leonard. Durham, NC: Duke UP, 1999.

Foster, Shirley. *Across New Worlds: Nineteenth-Century Women Travellers and Their Writings*. Hemel Hempstead, UK: Harvester Wheatsheaf, 1990.

Frank, Donald E., William F. Massy, and Yoram Wind. *Market Segmentation*. Englewood Cliffs, NJ: Prentice-Hall, 1972.

Freeman, Elizabeth. "Honeymoon with a Stranger: Pedophiliac Picaresques from Poe to Nabokov." *American Literature* 70 (1998): 863–98.

Freeman, Robert S. "Harper's Family Library: A Commercially Produced Reading Program for Early Nineteenth-Century America." Popular Culture Association and American Culture Association joint convention. New Orleans. 19 April 2000.

Frost, O. W. *Joaquin Miller.* New York: Twayne, 1967.

Gard, Roger, ed. *Henry James: The Critical Heritage.* London: Routledge & Kegan Paul; New York: Barnes & Noble, 1968.

Gay, Carol. "Jacob Abbott." *Dictionary of Literary Biography 42: American Writers for Children before 1900.* Ed. Glenn E. Estes. Detroit: Bruccoli Clark, Gale Research, 1985.

——. "William Taylor Adams." *Dictionary of Literary Biography 42: American Writers for Children before 1900.* Ed. Glenn E. Estes. Detroit: Bruccoli Clark, Gale Research, 1985.

Genette, Gérard. *Paratexts: Thresholds of Interpretation.* Paris: Seuil, 1987. Trans. Jane E. Lewin. Cambridge: Cambridge UP, 1997.

Gere, Ann Ruggles. *Intimate Practices: Literacy and Cultural Work in U.S. Women's Clubs, 1880–1920.* Urbana: U of Illinois P, 1997.

Gilkes, Lillian B. "Hawthorne, Park Benjamin, and S. G. Goodrich: A Three-Cornered Imbroglio." *Nathaniel Hawthorne Journal.* (1971): 83–112.

Gillen, Shawn Patrick. "Ambivalent Realism: Women Writers and Readers in Selected Fiction by Henry James." Diss. U of Minnesota, 1994.

Gleason, Gene. "What Ever Happened to Oliver Optic?" *Wilson Library Bulletin* 49 (1975): 647–50.

Gray, William S., and Ruth Munroe. *The Reading Interests and Habits of Adults: A Preliminary Report.* New York: Macmillan, 1929.

Greenslet, Ferris. *The Life of Thomas Bailey Aldrich.* Boston: Houghton Mifflin, 1908.

Gribben, Alan. "I Did Wish Tom Sawyer Was There": Boy-Book Elements in *Tom Sawyer* and *Huckleberry Finn.*" *One Hundred Years of Huckleberry Finn: The Boy, His Book, and American Culture.* Ed. Robert Sattelmeyer and J. Donald Crowley. Columbia: U of Missouri P, 1985. 159–70.

——. *Mark Twain's Library: A Reconstruction.* 2 vols. Boston: G. K. Hall, 1980.

Gross, Seymour L. "Hawthorne's Income from *The Token.*" *Studies in Bibliography* 8 (1956): 236–38.

Groves, Jeffrey D. "Judging Books by Their Covers: House Styles, Ticknor and Fields, and Literary Promotion." *Reading Books: Essays on the Material Text and Literature in America.* Ed. Michele Moylan and Lane Stiles. Amherst: U of Massachusetts P, 1996. 75–100.

Growoll, Adolf. *The Profession of Bookselling: A Handbook of Practical Hints for the Apprentice and Bookseller.* New York: Publishers' Weekly, 1893.

Habegger, Alfred. *Henry James and the "Woman Business."* Cambridge: Cambridge UP, 1989.

Hall, David D. "The Uses of Literacy in New England, 1600–1850." *Printing and Society in Early America.* Ed. William L. Joyce, David D. Hall, Richard D. Brown, and John B. Hench. Worcester, MA: American Antiquarian Society, 1983. 1–47.

Halsey, Francis W. *Our Literary Deluge and Some of Its Deeper Waters.* New York: Doubleday, Page, 1902.

Harper, J. Henry. *The House of Harper: A Century of Publishing in Franklin Square.* New York: Harper & Bros., 1912.

Hart, James D. *The Popular Book: A History of America's Literary Taste.* Berkeley: U of California P, 1950.

Hayes, Kevin J. *Henry James: The Contemporary Reviews*. Cambridge: Cambridge UP, 1996.

Heininger, Mary Lynn Stevens. "Children, Childhood, and Change in America, 1820–1920." *A Century of Childhood: 1820–1920*. Ed. Mary Lynn Stevens Heininger, Karin Calvert et al. Rochester, NY: Margaret Woodbury Strong Museum, 1984. 1–32.

Herbert, T. Walter. *Dearest Beloved: The Hawthornes and the Making of the Middle-Class Family*. Berkeley: U of California P, 1993.

Hertel, Robert Russell. "The Decline of the Paperbound Novel in America, 1890–1910." Diss. U of Illinois, 1958.

Hewins, Caroline M. *A Mid-Century Child and Her Books*. New York: Macmillan, 1926.

Hill, Hamlin. *Mark Twain and Elisha Bliss*. Columbia: U of Missouri P, 1964.

Holt, Henry. "Competition." *Atlantic Monthly* 102 (1908): 516–26.

*The House of Appleton-Century*. New York: D. Appleton-Century, 1936.

Howsam, Leslie. "Sustained Literary Ventures: The Series in Victorian Book Publishing." *Publishing History* 31 (1992): 5–26.

Hunt, Linda C. *A Woman's Portion: Ideology, Culture, and the British Female Novel Tradition*. New York: Garland, 1988.

Hunt, Peter. *Children's Literature*. Blackwell Guides to Literature. Oxford: Blackwell, 2001.

——. ed. *Children's Literature: An Illustrated History*. Oxford: Oxford UP, 1995.

Hunter, Jane H. *How Young Ladies Became Girls: The Victorian Origins of American Girlhood*. New Haven: Yale UP, 2002.

Hutchinson, George. "S. Colman." *Dictionary of Literary Biography 49: American Literary Publishing Houses, 1638–1899*. Ed. Peter Dzwonkoski. 2 vols. Detroit: Gale Research, 1986.

Inge, M. Thomas. Afterword. *Tom Sawyer Abroad*. Oxford Mark Twain. Ed. Shelley Fisher Fishkin. New York: Oxford UP, 1996.

Inness, Sherrie A., ed. *Nancy Drew and Company: Culture, Gender, and Girls' Series*. Bowling Green, OH: Bowling Green State U Popular P, 1997.

Jacobson, Marcia. *Being a Boy Again: Autobiography and the American Boy Book*. Tuscaloosa: U of Alabama P, 1994.

Jauss, Hans Robert. *Toward an Aesthetic of Reception*. Trans. Timothy Bahti. Minneapolis: U of Minnesota P, 1982.

Johanningsmeier, Charles. *Fiction and the American Literary Marketplace: The Role of Newspaper Syndicates, 1860–1900*. Cambridge: Cambridge UP, 1997.

Johannsen, Albert. *The House of Beadle and Adams and Its Dime and Nickel Novels: The Story of a Vanished Literature*. Vol. 1. Norman: U of Oklahoma P, 1950.

Johnson, Deidre. "From Abbott to Animorphs, from Godly Books to Goosebumps: The Nineteenth-Century Origins of Modern Series." *Scorned Literature: Essays on the History and Criticism of Popular Mass-Produced Fiction in America*. Ed. Lydia Cushman Schurman and Deidre Johnson. Westport, CT: Greenwood P, 2002. 147–66.

Johnson, Merle. *A Bibliography of the Works of Mark Twain*. New York: Harper & Bros., 1935.

Jones, Dolores Blythe. *An "Oliver Optic" Checklist: An Annotated Catalog-Index to the Series, Nonseries Stories, and Magazine Publications of William Taylor Adams*. Westport, CT: Greenwood P, 1985.

259

Jones, Wayne Allen. "The Hawthorne-Goodrich Relationship and a New Estimate of Hawthorne's Income from *The Token*." *Nathaniel Hawthorne Journal* (1975): 91–140.

———. "Sometimes Things Just Don't Work Out: Hawthorne's Income from *Twice-Told Tales* (1837), and Another 'Good Thing' for Hawthorne." *Nathaniel Hawthorne Journal* (1975): 11–26.

Joyce, Donald Franklin. *Gatekeepers of Black Culture: Black-Owned Book Publishing in the United States, 1817–1981*. Westport, CT: Greenwood P, 1983.

Kaplan, Justin. *Mr. Clemens and Mark Twain: A Biography*. New York: Simon & Schuster, 1966.

Kearns, Michael. "The Material Melville: Shaping Readers' Horizons." *Reading Books: Essays on the Material Text and Literature in America*. Ed. Michele Moylan and Lane Stiles. Amherst: U of Massachusetts P, 1996. 52–74.

Kelly, R. Gordon. *Children's Periodicals in the United States*. Westport, CT: Greenwood P, 1984.

———. "Social Factors Shaping Some Late Nineteenth-Century Children's Periodical Fiction." *Society and Children's Literature*. Ed. James H. Fraser. Boston: David R. Godine, 1978.

Kielbowicz, Richard B. "Mere Merchandise or Vessels of Culture? Books in the Mail, 1792–1942." *Papers of the Bibliographical Society of America* 82 (1988): 169–200.

———. "Post Office and the Media." *History of the Mass Media in the United States: An Encyclopedia*. Ed. Margaret Blanchard. Chicago: Fitzroy Dearborn, 1998.

Kilgour, Raymond L. *Lee and Shepard: Publishers for the People*. Hamden, CT: Shoe String P, 1965.

———. *Mssrs. Roberts Brothers, Publishers*. Ann Arbor: U of Michigan P, 1952.

King, Kimball. "Local Color and the Rise of the American Magazine." *Essays Mostly on Periodical Publishing: A Collection in Honor of Clarence Gohdes*. Durham, NC: Duke UP, 1973.

Kirkham, E. Bruce, and John W. Fink, eds. *Indices to American Literary Annuals and Gift Books, 1825–1865*. New Haven: Research Publications, 1975.

Kismaric, Carole, and Marvin Heiferman. *The Mysterious Case of Nancy Drew and the Hardy Boys*. New York: Simon & Schuster, 1998.

Klancher, Jon P. *The Making of English Reading Audiences, 1790–1832*. Madison: U of Wisconsin P, 1987.

Klaus, Meredith M. "*The Child's Friend and Family Magazine*." *Children's Periodicals of the United States*. Ed. R. Gordon Kelly. Westport, CT: Greenwood P, 1984.

Laffrado, Laura. *Hawthorne's Literature for Children*. Athens: U of Georgia P, 1992.

Lambert, Brian. "She-TV: The Feminization of Television." *St. Paul Pioneer Press* 24 Jan. 1999: 1E–3E.

———. "Relationship-Driven News Keeps Monica at the Fore." *St. Paul Pioneer Press* 24 Jan. 1999: 4E–5E.

Lawes, Carolyn J. *Women and Reform in a New England Community, 1815–1860*. Lexington: U of Kentucky P, 2000.

Lehmann-Haupt, Helmutt, Lawrence C. Wroth, and Rollo G. Silver. *The Book in America: A History of the Making and Selling of Books in the United States*. New York: R. R. Bowker, 1952.

Lehuu, Isabelle. *Carnival on the Page: Popular Print Media in Antebellum America*. Chapel Hill: U of North Carolina P, 2000.

Levine, Lawrence W. *Highbrow/Lowbrow: The Emergence of Cultural Hierarchy in America*. Cambridge: Harvard UP, 1988.

Lovett, Robert M. "A Boy's Reading Fifty Years Ago." *New Republic* 48 (1926): 336–38.

Lowry, Richard S. *"Littery Man": Mark Twain and Modern Authorship*. New York: Oxford UP, 1996.

Lurie, Alison. *Don't Tell the Grown-Ups: Subversive Children's Literature*. Boston: Little, Brown, 1990.

MacDonald, Ruth K. "Samuel Griswold Goodrich." *Dictionary of Literary Biography 42: American Writers for Children before 1900*. Ed. Glenn E. Estes. Detroit: Bruccoli Clark, Gale Research, 1985.

MacLeod, Anne Scott. *American Childhood: Essays on Children's Literature of the Nineteenth and Twentieth Centuries*. Athens: U of Georgia P, 1994.

———. "The *Caddie Woodlawn* Syndrome: American Girlhood in the Nineteenth Century." *A Century of Childhood: 1820–1920*. Ed. Mary Lynn Stevens Heininger, Karin Calvert et al. Rochester, NY: Margaret Woodbury Strong Museum, 1984. 97–119.

———. *A Moral Tale: Children's Fiction and American Culture*. Hamden, CT: Archon Books, 1975.

Matsukawa, Yuko. "The Cartography of Expatriation: Mapping the American Girl Abroad in Fiction, 1874–1915." Diss. Brown U, 1995.

McEwen, Christian. *Jo's Girls: Tomboy Tales of High Adventure, True Grit, and Real Life*. Boston: Beacon P, 1997.

McGann, Jerome. *The Textual Condition*. Princeton: Princeton UP, 1991.

McHenry, Elizabeth. *Forgotten Readers: Recovering the Lost History of African-American Literary Societies*. Durham, NC: Duke UP, 2002.

McLean, Ruari. "Joseph Cundall." *Dictionary of Literary Biography 106: British Literary Publishing Houses, 1820–1880*. Ed. Patricia J. Anderson and Jonathan Rose. Detroit: Gale Research, 1991.

———. "Joseph Cundall: A Victorian Editor, Designer, Publisher." *Penrose Annual* 56 (1962): 82–89.

———. *Joseph Cundall: A Victorian Publisher*. Pinner: Private Libraries Association, 1976.

Mellow, James R. *Nathaniel Hawthorne in His Times*. Baltimore: Johns Hopkins UP, 1998.

Miller, Edwin Haviland. *Salem Is My Dwelling Place: A Life of Nathaniel Hawthorne*. Iowa City: U of Iowa P, 1991.

Miller, Laura J. "The Rise and Not-Quite Fall of the American Book Wholesaler." *Journal of Media Economics* 16 (2003): 97–120.

Miller, Perry. *The Raven and the Whale: Poe, Melville, and the New York Literary Scene*. Baltimore: Johns Hopkins UP, 1956.

Moses, Montrose J. *Children's Books and Reading*. New York: Mitchell Kennerley, 1907.

Mott, Frank Luther. *Golden Multitudes: The Story of Best Sellers in the United States*. New York: R. R. Bowker, 1947.

———. *A History of American Magazines*. 5 vols. Cambridge, MA: Belknap P, Harvard UP, 1957–1968.

Murray, Gail Schmunk. *American Children's Literature and the Construction of Childhood.* New York: Twayne, 1998.

Myerson, Joel, and Daniel Shealy. "The Sales of Louisa May Alcott's Books." *Harvard Library Bulletin* n.s. 1 (Spring 1990): 47–86.

Nance, Donna. "American News Company." *Dictionary of Literary Biography 49: American Literary Publishing Houses, 1638–1899.* 2 vols. Ed. Peter Dzwonkoski. Detroit: Gale Research, 1986.

Noel, Mary. *Villains Galore: The Heyday of the Popular Story Weekly.* New York: Macmillan, 1954.

Norton, Charles A. *Writing* Tom Sawyer: *The Adventures of a Classic.* Jefferson, NC: McFarland, 1983.

Novick, Sheldon J. *Henry James: The Young Master.* New York: Random House, 1996.

Ong, Walter J. *An Ong Reader: Challenges for Further Inquiry.* Ed. Thomas J. Farrell and Paul A. Soukup. Cresskill, NJ: Hampton, 2002.

Papashvily, Helen. *All the Happy Endings.* New York: Harper, 1956.

Paterson, Stanley C., and Carl G. Seaburg. *Nahant on the Rocks.* Nahant, MA: Nahant Historical Society, 1991.

Pawley, Christine. *Reading on the Middle Border: The Culture of Print in Late-Nineteenth-Century Osage, Iowa.* Amherst: U of Massachusetts P, 2001.

Payne, Alma J. *Louisa May Alcott: A Reference Guide.* Boston: G. K. Hall, 1980.

Pearce, Roy Harvey. "Historical Introduction: *True Stories, A Wonder Book, Tanglewood Tales.*" *Centenary Edition of the Works of Nathaniel Hawthorne.* Vol. 6. Columbus: Ohio State UP, 1972. 287–311.

Peiken, Matt. "Jerry-Rigged: A Young Man with a Plan Markets His TV Talk Show as the 'Springer' for Teens." *St. Paul Pioneer Press* 12 March 2000: 1F, 3F.

Porter, Noah. *Books and Reading; or, What Books Shall I Read and How Shall I Read Them?* 1870; rpt. New York: Charles Scribner, 1882.

Putnam, George Haven. "Fifty Years of Books: A Sketch of Book Publishing in the United States in the Half-Century Succeeding 1860." *Nation* 101 (1915): 62–66.

Pye, John William. *James T. Fields: Literary Publisher.* Portland, ME: Baxter Society, 1987.

Radway, Janice. *Reading the Romance: Women, Patriarchy, and Popular Literature.* Chapel Hill: U of North Carolina P, 1991.

Raymond, David W. "S. G. Goodrich." *Dictionary of Literary Biography 49: American Literary Publishing Houses, 1638–1899.* 2 vols. Ed. Peter Dzwonkoski. Detroit: Gale Research, 1986.

Reilly, Elizabeth Carroll, and David D. Hall. "Customers and the Market for Books." *A History of the Book in America.* Vol. 1. *The Colonial Book in the Atlantic World.* Ed. Hugh Amory and David D. Hall. Worcester, MA: American Antiquarian Society, Cambridge UP, 2000. 387–98.

Reynolds, Kimberley. *Girls Only? Gender and Popular Children's Fiction in Britain, 1880–1910.* New York: Harvester Wheatsheaf, 1990.

Riley, Glenda. *Inventing the American Woman: A Perspective on Women's History.* Arlington Heights, IL: H. Davidson, 1987.

Robbins, Sarah. *Managing Literacy, Mothering America: Women's Narratives on Reading and Writing in the Nineteenth Century*: Pittsburgh: U of Pittsburgh P, 2004.

Robinson, Lillian S. Afterword. *The Stolen White Elephant and Other Detective Stories*. The Oxford Mark Twain. Ed. Shelley Fisher Fishkin. New York: Oxford UP, 1996.

Rogers, Katharine M. *L. Frank Baum: Creator of Oz*. New York: St. Martin's P, 2002.

Roselle, Daniel. *Samuel Griswold Goodrich, Creator of Peter Parley: A Study of His Life and Work*. Albany: State U of New York P, 1968.

Rosenblum, Joseph. Introduction. *Annals of American Bookselling, 1638–1850*. By Henry Walcott Boynton. 1932. New Castle, DE: Oak Knoll, 1991.

Rubin, Joan Shelley. *The Making of Middlebrow Culture*. Chapel Hill: U of North Carolina P, 1986.

Sandhusen, Richard L. *Marketing*. New York: Barron's, 1987.

Saunders, David. *Authorship and Copyright*. London: Routledge, 1992.

Scharnhorst, Gary. *Critical Essays on* The Adventures of Tom Sawyer. New York: G. K. Hall, 1993.

Schorer, Calvin Earl. *The Juvenile Literature of Nathaniel Hawthorne*. Diss. U of Chicago, 1948.

Schriber, Mary Suzanne. *Telling Travels: Selected Writings by Nineteenth-Century American Women Abroad*. Dekalb: Northern Illinois UP, 1995.

———. *Writing Home: American Women Abroad, 1830–1920*. Charlottesville: UP of Virginia, 1997.

Schurman, Lydia Cushman. "The Effect of Nineteenth-Century 'Libraries' on the American Book Trade." *Scorned Literature: Essays on the History and Criticism of Popular Mass-Produced Fiction in America*. Ed. Lydia Cushman Schurman and Deidre Johnson. Westport, CT: Greenwood P, 2002. 97–122

———. "Those Famous American Periodicals—The Bible, *The Odyssey*, and *Paradise Lost*—or, The Great Second-Class Mail Swindle." *Publishing History* 40 (1996): 33–52.

Scudder, Horace E. *Childhood in Literature and Art, with Some Observations on Literature for Children*. Boston: Houghton Mifflin, 1894.

Seaton, Beverly. *The Language of Flowers: A History*. Charlottesville: UP of Virginia, 1995.

Segel, Elizabeth. "'As the Twig Is Bent . . .': Gender and Childhood Reading." *Gender and Reading: Essays on Readers, Texts, and Contexts*. Ed. Elizabeth A. Flynn and Patrocinio P. Schweickart. Baltimore: Johns Hopkins UP, 1986. 165–86.

———. "The *Gypsy Breynton* Series: Setting the Pattern for American Tomboy Heroines." *Children's Literature Association Quarterly* 14 (1989): 67–71.

*Seventy-Five Years; or, The Joys and Sorrows of Publishing and Selling Books at Duttons from 1852 to 1927*. New York: Dutton, 1927.

Shealy, Daniel. "The Author-Publisher Relationships of Louisa May Alcott." Diss. U of South Carolina, 1985.

———. "The Author-Publisher Relationships of Louisa May Alcott." *Book Research Quarterly* (Spring 1987): 63–74.

———. ed. *Louisa May Alcott's Fairy Tales and Fantasy Stories*. Knoxville: U of Tennessee P, 1992.

Sheehan, Donald. *This Was Publishing: A Chronicle of the Book Trade in the Gilded Age.* Bloomington: Indiana UP, 1952.

Shove, Raymond Howard. *Cheap Book Production in the United States, 1870–1891.* Urbana: U of Illinois Library, 1937.

Sicherman, Barbara. "Reading *Little Women*: The Many Lives of a Text." *U.S. History as Women's History: New Feminist Essays.* Ed. Linda K. Kerber, Alice Kessler-Harris, and Kathryn Kish Sklar. Chapel Hill: U of North Carolina P, 1995. 245–66.

———. "Sense and Sensibility: A Case Study of Women's Reading in Late-Victorian America." *Reading in America: Literature and Social History.* Ed. Cathy N. Davidson. Baltimore: Johns Hopkins UP, 1989. 201–25.

Stern, Madeleine. *Louisa May Alcott: A Biography.* New York: Random House, 1996.

———. "Louisa May Alcott's Self-Criticism." *Studies in the American Renaissance* (1985): 333–82.

———, ed. *Louisa's Wonder Book: An Unknown Alcott Juvenile.* Mount Pleasant: Central Michigan UP, 1975.

Stoneley, Peter. *Consumerism and American Girls' Literature, 1860–1940.* Cambridge: Cambridge UP, 2003.

Strasser, Susan. *Satisfaction Guaranteed: The Making of the American Mass Market.* Washington, DC: Smithsonian Institution P, 1995.

"Study: 'Digital Divide' Shrinks among U.S. Kids." *Reuters.* 20 March 2003. http://www.cnn.com/2003/TECH/internet/03/20/digital.divide.reut/.

Swett, Katherine Barrett. "Improper Places: Scenery Fiction in the Works of Nathaniel Hawthorne, William Dean Howells, Constance Woolson, and Henry James." Diss. Columbia U, 1995.

Tebbel, John. *A History of Book Publishing in the United States.* 4 vols. New York: R. R. Bowker, 1972–75.

Thacker, Deborah Cogan, and Jean Webb. *Introducing Children's Literature: From Romanticism to Postmodernism.* London: Routledge, 2002.

Thomas, Clara. "Anna Jameson and Nineteenth-Century Taste." *Humanities Association Review* 17 (1966): 53–61.

———. *Love and Work Enough: The Life of Anna Jameson.* Toronto: U of Toronto P, 1967.

Thompson, Lawrance. *Young Longfellow (1807–1843).* New York: Octagon Books, 1969.

Thompson, Ralph. *American Literary Annuals and Gift Books, 1825–1865.* New York: H. W. Wilson, 1936.

Ticknor, Caroline. *Glimpses of Authors.* Boston: Houghton Mifflin, 1922.

Tintner, Adeline R. "A Literary Youth and a Little Woman: Henry James Reviews Louisa Alcott." *Critical Essays on Louisa May Alcott.* Ed. Madeleine B. Stern. Boston: G. K. Hall, 1984. 265–69.

Todd, Emily B. "Antebellum Libraries in Richmond and New Orleans and the Search for the Practices and Preferences of 'Real' Readers." In *Libraries as Agencies of Culture.* Ed. Thomas Augst and Wayne Wiegand. Madison: U of Wisconsin P, 2001.

Tompkins, Jane. *Sensational Designs: The Cultural Work of American Fiction, 1790–1860.* New York: Oxford UP, 1985.

Tryon, Warren S. "Nationalism and International Copyright: Tennyson and Longfellow in America." *American Literature* 24 (March 1953): 301–9.

————. *Parnassus Corner: A Life of James T. Fields, Publisher to the Victorians.* Boston: Houghton Mifflin, 1963.

————. "Ticknor and Fields' Publications in the Old Northwest, 1840–1860." *Mississippi Valley Historical Review* 34 (1947–48): 589–610.

Turay, Ismail. "Web Offers Little Help to Poor, Illiterate." Cox News Service. *St. Paul Pioneer Press* 16 March 2000: 17a.

Turner, Arlin. "Hawthorne and Longfellow: Abortive Plans for Collaboration." *Nathaniel Hawthorne Journal* (1971): 3–11.

Tyack, David B., Elisabeth Hansot, and David Tyack. *Learning Together: A History of Co-education in American Public Schools.* New York: Russell Sage Foundation Publications, 1992.

Vallone, Lynne. *Disciplines of Virtue: Girls' Culture in the Eighteenth and Nineteenth Centuries.* New Haven: Yale UP, 1995.

Van Tassel, Mary M. "Hawthorne, His Narrator, and His Readers in 'Little Annie's Ramble.'" *ESQ: A Journal of the American Renaissance* 33 (1987): 168–79.

Vogelback, Arthur Lawrence. "The Publication and Reception of *Huckleberry Finn* in America." *American Literature* 11 (1939): 260–72.

Wadsworth, Sarah. "Social Reading, Social Work, and the Social Function of Literacy in Louisa May Alcott's 'Mayflowers.'" *Reading Women: Literary Figures and Cultural Icons from the Victorian Age to the Present.* Ed. Jennifer Phegley and Janiet Badia. Toronto: U of Toronto P, 2005.

————. "What Daisy Knew: Reading against Type in *Daisy Miller: A Study.*" *Henry James: A Blackwell Companion to Literature and Culture.* Ed. Greg W. Zacharias. Malden, MA: Blackwell Publishing, forthcoming 2007.

Walker, Evelyn A. "C. S. Francis." *Dictionary of Literary Biography 49: American Literary Publishing Houses, 1638–1899.* Ed. Peter Dzwonkoski. 2 vols. Detroit: Gale Research, 1986.

Warner, Michael. *The Letters of the Republic: Publication and the Public Sphere in Eighteenth-Century America.* Cambridge: Harvard UP, 1990.

Weiner, Jennifer. "Readers Beware: Some Chick-Lit Just Isn't Enough to Chew On." Knight-Ridder News Service. Rpt. NewsBank, Inc., *St. Paul Pioneer Press* 13 Aug. 1999: n.p.

Weiss, Harry B. *Mahlon Day: Early New York Bookseller and Publisher of Children's Books.* New York: New York Public Library, 1941.

————. *The Printers and Publishers of Children's Books in New York City, 1698–1830.* New York: New York Public Library, 1948.

————. *Samuel Wood & Sons: Early New York Publishers of Children's Books.* New York: New York Public Library, 1942.

West, Mark I., ed. *Before Oz: Juvenile Fantasy Stories from Nineteenth-Century America.* Hamden, CT: Archon Books, 1989.

White, Craig. "Henry James." *Dictionary of Literary Biography 189: American Travel Writers, 1850–1915.* Ed. Donald Ross and James J. Schramer. Detroit: Gale Research, 1998.

Winship, Michael. *American Literary Publishing in the Mid-Nineteenth Century: The Business of Ticknor and Fields.* New York: Cambridge UP, 1995.

———. "The Transatlantic Book Trade and Anglo-American Literary Culture in the Nineteenth Century." *Reciprocal Influences: Literary Production, Distribution, and Consumption in America*. Ed. Steven Fink and Susan S. Williams. Columbus: Ohio State UP, 1999. 98–122.

Winsor, Dorothy A. "Ordering Work: Blue-Collar Literacy and the Political Nature of Genre." *Written Communication* 17 (2000): 155–84.

Wishy, Bernard. *The Child and the Republic: The Dawn of Modern American Child Nurture*. Philadelphia: U of Pennsylvania P, 1968.

Wolf, Virginia L. "Thomas Bailey Aldrich." *Dictionary of Literary Biography 42: American Writers for Children before 1900*. Ed. Glenn E. Estes. Detroit: Bruccoli Clark, Gale Research, 1985.

Worthington, Marjorie. *Miss Alcott of Concord: A Biography*. Garden City, NY: Doubleday, 1958.

Wright, Lyle H. "A Statistical Survey of American Fiction, 1774–1850." *Huntington Library Quarterly* 2 (1939): 309–18.

Yarborough, Richard. Introduction. *Contending Forces: A Romance Illustrative of Negro Life North and South*. By Pauline Hopkins. 1900. Schomburg Library of Nineteenth-Century Black Women Writers. New York: Oxford UP, 1988.

Yonge, Charlotte. *What Books to Give and What to Lend*. London: National Society's Depository, 1887.

Zboray, Ronald J. *A Fictive People: Antebellum Economic Development and the American Reading Public*. New York: Oxford UP, 1993.

Zboray, Ronald J., and Mary Saracino Zboray. *Literary Dollars and Social Sense: A People's History of the Mass Market Book*. New York: Routledge, 2005.

Zehr, Janet S. "The Response of Nineteenth-Century Audiences to Louisa May Alcott's Fiction." *ATQ* n.s. 1 (1987): 323–42.

# Index

*Page references to illustrations are in italics.*

Born and raised in the San Francisco Bay Area, Sarah Wadsworth was an editor in trade publishing for five years before embarking on her doctoral studies. She holds degrees from Reed College, the University of North Carolina at Chapel Hill, and the University of Minnesota. Her dissertation won the A. Garr Cranney Outstanding Dissertation Award from the International Reading Association in 2000, and in 2001 she received the Leon Edel Prize from *The Henry James Review*. For her work on *In the Company of Books* she was awarded the Houghton Mifflin Fellowship in Publishing History by Harvard University (2000–2001) and an AAUW American Fellowship (2002). Her essays have appeared in numerous scholarly journals, reference books, and edited collections. She recently guest-edited a special volume of the journal *Libraries and Culture* devoted to the Woman's Building Library of the 1893 World's Fair in Chicago and is currently working with Wayne A. Wiegand on a collaborative study of this library. Formerly a visiting assistant professor at Carleton College, Wadsworth is now assistant professor of English at Marquette University.